You have become special to
my experience of God's World!
Charles W. Bieber

Around God's World For Eighty Years

by Charles M. Bieber

Printed 2002 by
Masthof Press
219 Mill Road
Morgantown, PA 19543-9516

DEDICATION

With deep gratitude to God,

for I cannot take credit,

I dedicate this book

to

My FAVORITE wife,

Mary Beth,

and our *wonderful family*.

CONTENTS

Dedication iii

1. Poet In The Making? 1

2. Forebears 6

3. Elementary School Days 12

4. Seeds of Faith 18

5. High Times at High School 22

6. A Freshman at Juniata College 25

7. Socializing Sophomore 30

8. Enter Mary Beth 35

9. Training as a Nurse 41

10. Called to the Ministry 46

11. Mary Beth Again! And Marriage! 49

12. Bethany Seminary; Nursing in Chicago 59

13. Pastoral Service 65

14. Missionaries, But When? 73

15. Missionaries, Almost 82

16. Missionaries, At Last 88

17. What Does a Missionary Do? 96

18. How the Kingdom Grows 108

19. Furlough Time 118

20. New Assignments 125

21. Visitors—The Highs And Others 135

22. Change, Tension, and Relaxation 140

23. Inside Faith, Outside Help 147

24. Furlough Coming Up 152

25. Special Persons 164

26. Big Swatara 185

27. Beyond the Local 200

28. The Biafra Experience 204

29. Back at Big Swatara 213

30. The Move to Black Rock 221

31. Lay Witness Mission 227

32. More of the Black Rock Church 229

33. Golden Anniversary In Nigeria 235

34. Southern District Youth 239

35. Getting Personal 243

36. Moderator Elect! 247

37. Annual Conference Moderator 251

38. From Black Rock to Northern Indiana 258

39. The District Minister 261

40. Travel, Trauma, and Triumph 270

41. From District Minister to Local Pastor 274

42. Visits to Zambia 278

43. From Mingo to Ephrata 286

44. Golden Wedding Anniversary 291

45. From Ephrata to China 296

46. Still Trying to Serve 303

47. Australia at Last 308

48. Nigeria Church Diamond Jubilee 314

49. Family, Brethren Village, and Nigeria 319

50. Machu Picchu and the Amazon 327

51. Bendictions 332

INTRODUCTION

Dad wrote this book at our request. My older siblings, Larry, Dale, Bonnie, Marla, and I wanted a permanent record of our father's life. Dad would probably say we are his permanent record. For some reason not clear to us, he has always said we are his proudest accomplishment. In reading through the book that follows, you will see this is one rare time he was wrong.

It's difficult to get a humble man to write his life story. Dad may be the most intelligent man I have ever known. I never needed a dictionary when Dad was nearby. He would be a formidable player on Jeopardy and has conquered even the toughest crossword puzzles daily for years. He's a gifted leader and an able, organized administrator. He has a quick sense of humor and loves to tease, especially children. However, Dad has always been aware that his earthly father was a laundryman and his heavenly Father the Giver of his many talents and achievements.

A constant sense of God's goodness and grace led Dad to a lifetime of serving Him by serving others. As a nurse, he brought healing to patients' bodies. As a pastor and missionary, he brought Jesus Christ's healing to men's souls. Dad accepts, respects, and works with all types of people. He found many black sons in Nigeria, several of whom are still part of our family today. Dad has always enabled and encouraged the women around him. It was as natural for me to become a physician as it was for my two older brothers. One sister is a clinical psychologist and the other a pastor. We have all learned from our parents to use our time and talents in the service of others.

Dad is loving and tender, a good listener, and a good counselor. Years ago, I came to him with my adolescent confusion and hurts. I always left feeling understood, wiser because of his comments, and reassured by his prayers. Dad speaks from his own experience and knowledge, but is always aware that he is only God's instrument to bring understanding, healing, and hope. He almost named this autobiography Glimmers of a Lesser Light to reflect his own awareness of Christ's sovereignty and goodness as the Light of the World.

We children thank our father for sharing his light unselfishly with us and many others. We hope this book will encourage you to share your light also.

- Doreen (Bieber) Miller

Chapter One

A POET IN THE MAKING?

I walked down East Third Street in Williamsport, Pennsylvania, one brisk autumn day, en route to my birthplace at 590. I was eager to see the plaque that had been placed on the house to identify it as the place where my life began on September 11, 1919. When I arrived at 590, with some difficulty because the houses I remembered along that street were no longer there, I was dismayed to find there was no plaque. In fact, there was no house; it had given way to the edge of a broad new highway. (Well, what can a lesser light expect?) Then I reflected: I had no memory of lying before the fireplace to study, as had Lincoln. There was no remembered cherry tree in the backyard, as per Washington. After all, I had spent only about four babyhood months there.

The Red Oak Apartment just across the street, I remembered much better; I had lived there for nearly six years. I crossed the street to see that plaque. There was no plaque. The two-story, two-dwelling house of brick and siding was still there, but it was dilapidated and no longer in use. No plaque! Aulston's Laundry, which had been next door and where Dad, and sometimes Mom, had worked, was gone. I wondered what had happened to Dad's boss, Bill Aulston. Mr. Aulston had been a tall Negro (the polite term we used in those days) with a notable potbelly and a slender white wife. None of our family saw anything unusual in a mixed marriage, and we had only the smallest smattering of racial prejudice. The Aulstons owned a seven-passenger touring car with jump seats, and since Mrs. Aulston did not drive, we were often privileged to ride along when Dad or Uncle Myles chauffeured her.

Seeing the Red Oak brought back other memories. We lived, at first, in the upstairs apartment. It was there that I was awakened, at about thirty months of age, by a dream in which I had floated gently across the alley beside our house and landed on the tiny porch of the store beyond. I awakened to discover I had fallen out of bed.

When we had moved later to the first floor, I remember contracting scarlet fever. There was a purple quarantine sign at our front door. I was in a room, desperately ill at the age of four, until the stage of recovery where I could sit by the window to eat my lunch. My sister, Mae, recalls that it was while we lived at the Red Oak, when Dad was on a ladder painting a bedroom, that I pulled the paint bucket over my head. I don't remember the incident, but I do remember that, even years later, there were paint spots on one of our comforters.

There are other Red Oak memories. It was from there that I started at Jefferson School, about a ten minute walk. It was while we were there that the Boys Industrial Home, located about fifty yards down the street, burned in what was one of Williamsport's historic fires. While we lived there, I took two, long, lonely walks. One was up Third Street toward the business section of town. I had asked for a shovel and rake for my birthday so I could help Dad in the garden, and I was sure Mom would bring them. So I walked to meet her, all the time watching the trolley when it went by, just in case Mom was on it. Neither happened, so I turned around and walked back home to discover that everybody thought I was lost! What! Me lost? When any of us kids would cry without an injury to blame, Mom might call us a crybaby. So, of course, on one day that was filled with work and pain and boisterous kids, Mom was crying, and I called her, "Crybaby!" I was the next one who cried. The spanking didn't seem fair, so at age 41/2 I ran away, all the way across the 150-yard vacant lot behind our house to the railroad bank. Far enough. They would have learned by then not to treat me mean, so I went back.

Enough of Red Oak. Maybe the plaque had been reserved for two blocks east on the other side of that same street. But—you guessed it— neither plaque nor house was there, again the edge of the highway. It had been a double house, and our next door neighbors were the Silvermans, a Jewish family. Such good neighbors were they that none of our family had any prejudice toward Jews. 724—that was the house number—stirred some old memories. There was that tall, slender, child-loving Alice Cady, our first grade teacher. Miss Cady frequently lost her lap to a pupil whom she was comforting because of pain, sadness, or slight illness. There was the day I came home from school and announced that I had my first girlfriend; she was blonde, blue-eyed Shirley. When second grade started, I came home and reported, "I have the same girlfriend this year." I think I also fell in love with my second grade teacher, a young and very pretty Anne Miller.

It is the third grade, however, taught by Phyllis Briel, who liked the kids all right but didn't know how to control them, that brings back the most vivid pictures. The child who could best recite Clement Moore's "'Twas the Night Before Christmas" would have the honor of reciting it for the Christmas program. I studied hard and had the poem well in mind as I waited in the cloakroom for my turn. I waited—and waited—and waited. Then came the moment when my bladder would not wait any longer, and when Miss Briel came for me she found a puddle on the floor and a badly embarrassed boy. Fortunately, I do not recall any of the ensuing moments, except that I did win the contest. Mayhap the puddle did it for me.

Miss Briel's effort to keep the class in reasonable control led her, about biweekly, to march the class members past the recitation bench in front of the room. She gave each child one whack with the paddle, asking, "Were you talking?" One dared not lie, for who knew but that she had seen us talking? Those who admitted talking were seated for the nonce, and when the procession was over, they got several whacks. I don't know which Pennsylvania Normal School taught that method of discipline.

I was always somewhat on the cowardly side, perhaps an adjunct of my shyness. It was as a third-grader that I fled home, chased by an upper class bully whom I had somehow offended. I was sadly aware that my younger brother, George, would probably not have run; he would have fought with the no-matter-how-big guy.

At 724, Mom took in boarders and roomers. (My warmest memory is of Howard Sobers, who loved strawberry shortcake so much that he would discover the first berries available in the spring, and the last to be preserved in a restaurant ice box.) Those were depression years, but Dad had work except for a week involving nose surgery and two weeks when he left Aulston's and became foreman of the City Laundry. Two weeks without pay made it tough—for months we lived on the edge of poverty. I was sent on frequent trips to pay just fifty cents to the electric company to keep our lights on or to the coal man to ensure another delivery. We escaped welfare, but we exchanged food frequently with welfare recipients who had too much of—say—cornmeal.

Mom worked hard. She was not a healthy lady, but she sang and whistled a lot, and she loved her kids. At one period, she was very sick at home with colitis and a high fever. How startled I was when I entered the sick room one day, and she cried out, "Get that kid out of here! That's not Charles!" Mom had her own ways of getting compliance with her intentions. One morning I went to school after having offended her in some way and having heard her threaten to leave home if I wouldn't behave better. When we arrived home from school each day, we always expected to find her there. That day I could not find her and I was sure she had left. I was crying when I found her hiding behind the living room stove.

Sister Mae and Brother George and I argued and scrapped a lot, but we were a family. We played games indoor and out together; we sang around the piano; we gathered around our first radio, a small Atwater Kent, and we were regular at Sunday School, prayer meeting, and church services about four blocks down the street. One evidence of our togetherness: one Saturday morning Mom had a number of errands to run, so neighbor Willa, a high school girl, was to sit with us. Willa must have overslept; she didn't show up. Ten-year-old Mae was sick—a headache, I think—and was crying. What could I, with my eight years of wisdom, or George with his six years of experience, do? Nothing. So we cried with her. Suddenly, as we looked at all that crying, it seemed hilarious, and we all burst out laughing. Then the pain hit Mae; her crying resumed, and we rejoined her. It was a process several times repeated.

Let there be no misunderstanding. The houses that we rented, usually for about a five-year period, were not in the luxury section of Williamsport. Mom chose them for their accommodation of our family and boarders, for proximity to Jefferson School and Third Street Methodist Episcopal Church, and for price, not for luxury. Consider this: 150 yards back of our house at 724 ran part of the unofficial city dump. Our backyard was largely given to garden; behind it ran an unpaved alley of access to the dump beyond. All manner of trash and garbage was deposited there.

Rats ran rampant. A popular sport by some with guns was to shoot rats in the dump. I do not remember that any of the rats ever came to our house; with Mom's tender but effective housekeeping, they would hardly have dared!

The home at 724 took me through grade school. I loved school, but during the first three grades, I was frequently sick, usually with stomach upset or nausea, when I missed school or had to be taken home early. During the last nine years, I did not miss a single day! In the fourth grade, my teacher was black-haired Gertrude Richards. My grades were exceptional. I consistently got E (for excellent); G was for Good, M for Medium, D for Doubtful, and F for Failure. I also constantly got an M for deportment (that's what they called it!). Why only an M for this mama's boy? Maybe it was because of incidents like the situation in which Miss

Richards caught me—dipping into my inkwell the hair of the girl in front of me. I was properly spanked.

Fifth grade found me in the large, two-grade assembly hall of the school. Fifth graders sat on the left, a wide aisle was the great divide, and six graders sat on the right. We met there for opening exercises each morning with Principal Charles E. Spotts (we called him, "Chick," but not to his face) on a one-step platform at the head of the aisle. Opening exercises included the pledge of allegiance to the flag, the recitation of the Lord's Prayer (so there, ACLU!), and a poem recited by an assigned one of the fifth graders. I remember well my own poetry:

> *I had a little monkey; I put him in a tree.*
> *I turned to look at him and he threw a coconut at me.*
> *I saw a little snowflake falling out of the sky.*
> *I turned my face toward it and it hit me in the eye.*

Surprisingly, there were no repercussions to that unoriginal, anonymous (probably Longfellow?) gem of poetry, except Miss Hunter's expressed regret that I had not chosen better. Both fifth and sixth graders left the assembly hall to go to classes.

Helen Hunter for English and spelling; Clara McCollum for arithmetic and music; and Alice Hess for geography and history. Surely Chick taught something, but I can't for the life of me remember what it was. It was as a fifth grader that I began to wear glasses for the myopic eyes I inherited from Mom, and the whole world seemed brighter.

Chapter Two

FOREBEARS

Before I take off for junior high school and high school, leaving behind any idea of an identifying plaque, let me bring us up to date on other important matters. My dad was George Albert Bieber, born in 1894, the first son (second child) of Annie (Dieffenbacher) Bieber and Lloyd Wertman Bieber. My memories of Grandma's side of the family are sparse. Her sister, Lulu Confer, lived just up the road from the Biebers; Great-Grandma Dieffenbacher lived with them until I was about four, when her funeral took place from the Confer home. Another sister, Lizzie Burson, lived in Colorado; from time to time Dad would send her a box of pretzels. Grandma's father, I learned later, was Edmund Ellis Dieffenbacher, son of David and Elizabeth (Trockenmiller) Dieffenbacher, a family known to be in Pennsylvania about 1860.

The Biebers, I knew better. Grandpa was a roof painter; he specialized in covering old barn or house roofs with waterproof tar. He fell from the roof one time, as did two of my uncles and, many years later, my brother. Grandma loved having her family around her, which was not easy at reunion time in their small house. Two echoes of Grandma reverberate in my mind: First, she ALWAYS cooked dried lima beans for me to eat during the summer weeks I spent with her. Second, when the rest of the family would gather for games or chatter after the big dinner, Grandma would be in the pantry washing dishes.

Puzzled, because washing dishes was certainly not my favorite pastime, I asked her, "Grandma, do you LIKE washing dishes?"

With a smile on her well-wrinkled face, she said, "Oh, yes! Dirty dishes mean people had something to eat."

"But, Grandma," I wondered, "when there are so many dishes?"

"That just means a lot of people had something to eat."

Bieber reunion time was very special. For most of those early years it was at Grandma and Grandpa's house, where the only plumbing was a hand pump on the back porch. Even for dishwashing, the water had to be carried to the pantry. Toilet facilities were a two-holer down the garden path. I well remember the day when, as a thirteen-year-old boy, I was seated over one of those holes, anticipating use of the Sears catalog pages. My oldest aunt, Aunt Mary, came nonchalantly trucking in, raised her dress, most likely (though I didn't look) lowered her underwear, and squatted beside me. I loved those aunts and uncles, and those cousins. In usual summers, there were weeklong exchange visits with one or another of the cousins.

Along with the myriad misbehaviors that claimed us at reunion time, we spent a lot of time in Grandma's back parlour, poring over albums of old pictures and producing music (?) on the reed organ. There was, for a time, a player piano on which we did produce music, simply by pumping. It turned out that the piano was being purchased on a time payment plan. Alas, the payments ran out, and so did the piano.

While we waited for meals, we sat on the front porch and earned money. We were paid a penny for every ten flies we would swat. We counted large numbers, but I don't think the flies even noticed their colleagues were gone. There were always ball games to be played with an indoor baseball; all of the Bieber men of Dad's generation seemed to be good ball players. In the evening there were five hundred or poker games, the poker winners becoming the treaters to ice cream. As years passed, the number of Biebers and the fun of being together increased and reunion extended to two or three days. Grandma and Grandpa played endless games of Flinch, and I loved watching them cheat each other!

The Biebers sprang from the Huguenots. Their earliest history goes to the early sixteenth century and a French village known as Beauvoir, so they were the von Beauvoir family until they fled to Germany, the Lutheran Church, and Germanization of the name. Our branch of Biebers has been identified in Saarbrucken from about 1501. The earliest Biebers in America appear to have begun with Jacob, my great-great-great-grandfather, who was sixteen years old when he sailed with mother and sister in 1731. Great-great-grandparents were Samuel and Mary (Deysher) Bieber. Great-grandparents were Amos and Elisabeth (Wertman) Bieber, and then came my Grandpa, first born (1870) and only survivor from infancy in his generation.

Dad's older sister, Mary, went to business school in Washington and married William Pettis, a tile and marble contractor. Next in line were my Uncle Homer, a shoe cutter; Aunt Florence, who wed a grocer who later operated his own (Ted Plymette's) garage; Theodore, who became a tile mason; Eddie, the first of his generation to enter college and later seminary, a Lutheran minister; Sarah, who also had advanced education and married Lutheran minister Stuart Lengel; Richard, who died at age eight; and Harold, a tile setter.

Dad had only six years of education; as the oldest son he had to seek gainful employment early. He liked school, and told many stories of it. There was the story of walking to school on top of the snow, right over the fence tops. There was his teacher, who required boys to cut their own hickory switch for the impending spanking. Dad's story, probably apocryphal, told how he cut the switch, then cut notches in it so that when it was applied it fell apart. At about age twelve, he began dragging a small wagon about town to pick up laundry from the more affluent. By age eighteen, he had moved into the laundry and become foreman, and he managed laundries until age seventy-four.

Mom was Edith Fae Seriff, daughter of Harry and Lida (McKee) Seriff. Afflicted by severe myopia, it took her ten years to finish eight grades of school. Sadly, I know nothing of how Dad and Mom met or of their courtship, except one story. They were riding along in the buggy when they stopped and Dad dismounted to check one of the wheels. Something spooked the horse, and it took off down the road, Dad chasing after shouting, "Kidder! Kidder!" (his pet name for her). Obviously the horse finally stopped. I don't know how they behaved in the buggy, but years later, when I bragged to Dad about driving the car one-handed while I hugged my girlfriend, he commented, "When we had a horse and buggy, I didn't need either hand to drive."

When George and Edith married in 1916, they lived in Milton for a short time; then the country boy was transported to Williamsport and ran the laundry for Bill Aulston. He worked long hours. His summertime spare hours were spent in gardening, which he loved and on which he was expert. He retained many of the country-boy skills. He spent many evening hours making small models of structures he remembered from boyhood— houses, barns, machinery shed, garage, corncrib, train station, local feedstore, metal railroad bridge, stone road bridge. How well I remember: at age five, I dearly wanted an electric train, not at all aware of how well it fit into the Christmas "yard" of model structures and roadways. On Christmas Eve in 1924, I awoke from sleep in order to go to the bathroom (?). Dad and Uncle Myles were setting up the yard in the living room. I thought I saw a train, as well, but with the innate slyness of a five-year-old, I asked only, "Where is Santa Claus?"

"Had to go up town to get something he forgot," explained my uncle. Dad maintained the Christmas yard with artificial green grass, white sand roads, and the train tracks until our high school years. I was very proud to show it off to my friends. The only problem was that after working all night to set up the yard, Dad wasn't much on Christmas Day.

Dad loved to take us on short trips. The sixteen-mile trip to Watsontown to visit either grandparent was an all-day venture. Earlier we took it in the Aulston Cadillac, with its mica and leather curtains which were closeable during cold weather or rains. The used Dort sedan he bought in 1927 was quite a comedown from the Cadillac, but it served us well. Dad liked to go picnicking in public parks. He also liked to buy us small treats. Money was not plentiful and Mom was the treasurer, but Dad would manage to bring us ice cream cones from the store next door, or make home-made root beer for summer refreshment. Dad had started to smoke when he was eighteen and always, I suspect, regretted it. He promised— and fulfilled the promise—to buy gold watches for his sons if they refrained from smoking until they were eighteen. (No such promise for Mae, but then girls rarely smoked in those days.) Dad's smoke was a cigar or a pipe; many years later he boasted, "The easiest thing I ever did was to stop smoking; I've done it fourteen times."

It was only recently that I learned anything about Mom's family. Her two younger brothers, Myles and Bob, would regularly talk at the annual one-day Seriff reunion about the Russian Jews from whom we were descended. They were such wags that we never knew whether or not to believe them, but there does seem to be some truth in their story. I knew Grandma Seriff, of course, but not my grandpa who died when I was about age two. I do remember my Great-Grandma McKee and her sister, a deaf mute known as Auntie Hannah, whose funeral I attended when I was just old enough to know that she was somehow different. I also remember several McKee and McCormick uncles, notably Great-Uncle Bert McKee, who lived with us at intervals. He was fond of his cups and had an inter- esting vocabulary, possibly of Irish derivation.

Grandma McKee had been a Shannon. The Shannons were de- scended from James Brown, a Scotch Covenanter who was martyred by the Anglican Church in the early seventeenth century. The Browns were Scots, but they wandered back and forth between Ireland and Scotland in an effort to find religious freedom. Their lineage reflects a large number of teachers, ministers, and civic leaders. Mom's oldest living sibling was Aunt Laura, who married Harry Harlacher, a coal miner in Shamokin. Her next older sister was Aunt Anna, whose husband, Dick Strine, died before I met him: she reared four children by operating a small "tearoom." Uncle

Myles, a delivery truck driver, and Uncle Bob, a barber, then an engineer, lived with us at times. The Seriffs also had an annual family reunion, but it was usually just an afternoon at Watsontown Park. Seriff relatives were just as dear to me, but somehow the reunion wasn't as much fun, maybe because I wasn't the oldest boy.

Mom was an excellent cook, albeit an economical one. She would plan ahead the meals for the week, enabling her to shop carefully for needed groceries. She rarely used a recipe, though I do remember her admitting once, "This is Grandma McKee's cake," whereupon my two uncles chimed, "I thought it seemed awful old." Her pies, especially dried apricot and cherry, were fit for consumption at the heavenly feast. Mom was also a meticulous (spelled fussy) housekeeper. She taught us about wiping the tops of doors and windows, washing the surbases, and dusting the pictures on the wall. She insisted that my brother or I—we took turns—clean our room every Thursday. (It had to be Thursday, no matter what more exciting occupations may have been calling us.) She was somewhat of a perfectionist, and her deep love for us made her perfectionistic about our obedience. Even with less than perfect health, she was usually a happy person, and we would often hear her singing or whistling hymns. Her favorite was, "Life Is Like a Mountain Railroad," and I also remember her singing, "Hello, Central. Give me heaven, for my mamma's there. You will find her with the angels on the golden stair." Her voice was loud and on tune, but not a solo voice, and that strong voice could often be heard among other singers in church. As my brother has described it, "She led congregational singing from a rear pew."

Mom was also our teacher of many things—not only about cleaning, but also about such things as cooking. "Your wife might be sick sometime," she would explain. We were so good at girls' jobs that we accepted the neighborhood sobriquet, "The Bieber Sisters," without complaint. It was Mom who got us to Sunday School and church, and Mom who taught us that the angels kept track of our lives on a big book in heaven. If there was the least reason, by school record or church activity, for her to be proud of one of us, she let us know, and often there were only feeble reasons.

Neither Mom nor Dad ever taught us that babies were not delivered by storks. It was my cousin, Newman Strine, who enlightened me about the birds and bees with lurid details, but without demonstration. Kindly, he even offered to bring a neighbor girl for me to practice on, an invitation I quickly declined.

A few years after Grandpa Harry Seriff died, Grandma married David D. Long, the extremely Dutch owner of a country store at Hunter Station, near Herndon, Pennsylvania and, of course, became Grandma Long. My new grandpa's accent was so broad that I was hard put to understand him. I did enjoy playing with some of the Long stepcousins. who lived not far from Grandpa's store and going to Sunday School and church at the Lutheran Church just across the road. Grandma Long, VERY heavy by now, found it quite difficult to get around, but she did enjoy crocheting, and she did enjoy playing Rummy or Pinochle. What she did not enjoy was the smell of cantaloupe. A kind but not very well-informed wellwisher might bring her a nice, fresh cantaloupe, and she would quickly instruct: "Take that thing around to the other end of the porch if you want to eat it."

In those days, my favorite moments at Grandma's house at Hunter's Station were of two kinds: One was to snitch penny candy or gum after the store was closed at night. The other was to sit among the Dutchmen on one of the long benches near the stove, listen to them spout Dutch, and watch them spurt tobacco juice with amazing accuracy.

Chapter Three

ELEMENTARY SCHOOL DAYS

You've had enough rest now; it is time to get back to school. Our moving to 517 East Third coincided with my entry into Curtin Junior High School. My first girlfriend, Shirley, was also there—her elementary school also fed into Curtin—but boys and girls had separate classes, so I did not see her often. Our dwelling at 517 was half a double house. In the other half lived the Kline family, including a girl of my age. Alas, Janice was both plain and rather seclusive. On the other side, our parents unintentionally extended our non-prejudice upbringing. Near neighbors were a Catholic family who did not wear horns or forked tails and were just as friendly, helpful, and companionable as anyone else we knew.

At Curtin, we were alphabetically assigned to homerooms in which we would assemble before classes and to which we would return before afternoon dismissal. One pupil was appointed to lead us to our classes. Our homeroom teacher, a tall, slender, blonde woman named Dickert, also taught spelling and English, and I think it was she who first awakened my interest in writing. Grades at Curtin were based entirely on the results of the term final examinations. Taking exams has always been fun for me— I like puzzles of all kinds—so a grade average of 99.9 after three years did seem that great an accomplishment. First in the class, right? Nope; second. First went to Betty Laudenslager, who was perfect in every exam for three years. An average of 100%! WOW!

Surprisingly, I did miss the honor roll once, for which I have never forgiven my art teacher. In that term we were to come up with color designs such as might be used in the border around a room. I came up with a set of impressionistic tulips that I thought was pretty good; certainly I was convinced that it was the best I could do. Eva L. Keller gave me a C (by then we are graded A-B-C-D-E-F) which kept me off the honor roll. I met with her after school and asserted that one could not, after all, produce art beyond his or her talent and mine was an effort worth more than a C. She disagreed.

There were no other subjects that I disliked, from woodworking and auto mechanics to biology and algebra, though history and civics did not really interest me. Each of the thirty boys' gym classes had its own soccer team, and when the season ended, I was surprised to have been named to the all-star team. (In my more honest moments, I admit I am not an athlete.) Curtin did enter me in the all-city field day as a chinner. By that time I had successfully chinned (raised my chin over a horizontal bar about six feet off the ground) thirty-nine times. When my turn came, my hands slipped from the bar, made slippery by those preceding me, after I had chinned only four times. The winner that day reached thirty-two.

My two best-remembered teachers at Curtin come to mind for two completely different reasons. One was Timothy Ferguson, geography teacher and basketball coach. (I tried out for basketball, but he readily saw how inept I was.) In geography, I was perfect. That didn't help me when Mr. Ferguson observed me one day, taping a sign on the boy in front of me, saying, "Kick Me, Please."

"Let me see that," he demanded. When he did, he immediately dubbed me, "Kickapoo," and invited me to visit him before school next morning. I did. He asked whether I would rather be punished by paddle or kicking. I chose kicking, and he "booted" me just once. Maybe good grades did cut down the punishment. The other favorite teacher was John Scaife, our eighth grade homeroom and math teacher. For some reason, I became his favorite pupil that year and he appointed me to all the important jobs. I have a small hunch that he liked me because I sold him tickets to the dinners and plays which our church produced, and he enjoyed them. He would call occasionally, even after I had left Curtin, to see how things were going with me.

Good friends I made during those junior high years—notably George Barnes and Bob Andrews—have remained special to me, especially George. He was a short, red-haired lad with tons of energy and some real artistic skills. From a large family, he eked out their income by painting sales signs for a large supermarket. He also loved boxing, at which he danced about so effectively that we began calling him "Skip," after the fleas he brought to mind. The three of us were frequently together in games or in studies. Bob's dad was a guard at the Huntingdon Reformatory. Skip's dad was a laborer. When Skip and I would walk or bike to school, we would pass a tiny candy shop operated by a little old lady. Among her wares she included what were known as "chances," small, round, chocolate-covered discs like peppermint patties, which sold, as most of her wares, for a penny each. The right chance, broken open to uncover a green, blue, or pink center, merited a prize. Now I did not have much money—a quarter a week of which three cents went to the church, and a few pennies I could save from my lunch money. I discovered a way to identify the winners and almost always won prizes. On one occasion, we had all the prizes when most of the candies were still left, and the little lady was left with a real sales problem.

Our home at 517, as at 724, was also backed by a dump. It was smaller and dryer than the "official" one, with mostly dry trash. An alley separated our yard from the dump where sumac trees hid small "camps" for some of the many hoboes who were on the road in those days. One evening as several of us boys were playing cops and robbers or some such, I tripped and fell, one hand landing on a rusty tin can, the other on a broken bottle. Blood spurted from my right wrist; even at age twelve I knew that meant an artery. George ran for Dad, who was making root beer, and Dad rushed me to the emergency. I held my left hand tight around the left arm and held the arm up to reduce bleeding. I spent over an hour in the E.R., while the intern searched for the two ends of—what? tendon? nerve? both? Every time—frequently—he touched one end of nerve, my "crazy bone" would shriek. The wrist healed, but I never did regain lateral movement control of the two smaller fingers. That made it tough to learn typing, which class I entered that eighth grade, but I adapted to a hunt-and-peck by my right hand and a proper touch system with the left and my A came through.

All little boys in those days wore knickers. No, dear, I did not say bloomers, though they looked about the same. Mine seemed long continued. That had one advantage: for some boyish reason, I prized horse chestnuts, and my knicker legs would hold many of them. It was not until I came to the end of the ninth grade that I got my long trousers. Those long trousers are absolutely the only thing I remember about graduation from Curtin Junior High School (of course, there were not caps and gowns at that level).

By then, we had made the break—moved from East Third Street, to 913 Tucker Street—same church, same school district. My brother and I eked out our allowance in those days by selling salted peanuts, and eventually by caning chairs at two cents per square inch. Dad learned it from a man who was left over from Boys' Industrial Home when Gummo Laundry bought it out.

At school, I kept seeing Shirley, my first-grade sweetheart for whom I still had a great deal of admiration, and we did attend some parties together. When I had reached the ripe old age of fourteen and had saved a little money, I got permission from my parents to ask her for a date. I invited her to go to the movies with me. I would meet her at her home, and we would take the city bus to the movies; we would get an ice cream or something afterward (big spender, I!), and then we would prolong our date by walking home. She agreed. We—at least I—enjoyed the movie. We were walking home, not holding hands or anything, just walking and talking. My bladder—do you remember that it gave me some problems when I was in the third grade?—spoke up. I had to GO! I figured that I could hold my bladder in check until we reached her home, then I would leave, beat a hasty retreat into some bushes and go on home. My bladder disagreed. As we were walking—didn't stop, mind you—the urine ran down my legs, filled my shoes, ran over. From then on, it was a noisy walk. My feet kept saying. "Squeech! Squeech!'' as my leather shoes complained about their inundation. I don't think Shirley ever understood why I so adamantly declined her invitation to come in for a while. It was, after all, well in advance of my curfew—but not my bladder. As high school came on, I did go a few other places with Shirley, but I was aware that she seemed interested in Bill Winn, and I did not have the courage to overcome my broken heart.

Curtin Junior High received pupils from several elementary schools. Williamsport High School, the only high school in the city, received pupils from Curtin, Stevens, and Roosevelt. The high school was about seven miles from our home, and I went to school sometimes on foot, sometimes by bike, and occasionally in very bad weather, on commercial bus. (No, Junior, there weren't any school buses.) Some idea of the size of the high school can be gained from the fact that it was one of the major high schools across the state, and that my—eventual—graduating class had 467 members. My preference to playing Monopoly over doing homework dropped me to ninth in the class.

It seems strange as I look back, that although I looked at sciences as my forte and thought I might go into medicine, it is the languages that spring most quickly to mind. The yen toward medicine arose, I think, from the fact that Mom was sick so much. How much of it was real and how much hypochondria, I don't know, but some doctor—maybe I— ought to be able to help her. On the other hand, I love words. I like to know their source. I like to be able to recognize shades of meaning. Verna Noll, tyrannical Latin teacher, so entranced me with that "dead" language ("first it killed the Romans and now it's killing me") that I took a third, elective, year of it. Obviously, I was a rarity among high school students—a real freak. I also took two years of German.

The Tucker Street neighborhood was much more roomy than those on East Third Street. For the first time in more than ten years, we did not live in front of a dump. In fact, there were two apple trees in our backyard, ample space for a garden, and an unused building lot between our neighbors and us. And there were lots of kids in the neighborhood. There was "Junior" Fausey who lived next door. It would be silly to use the modernly appropriate term, "challenged," for Junior. He really didn't have enough to be challenged. He was hydrocephalic; his head was so huge that the only way he could walk was for his father to walk close behind, giving support to the head. Occasionally he would become very irritated for some reason invisible to us. He spent his out-of-doors time sitting in a wagon, which he pushed about with his feet. None of our family developed prejudices toward the handicapped!

Carl Neidig lived above the corner grocery operated by his parents. Often he would bring treats that he had cadged from the store to the gang. At the end of our backyard, there was an alley on which three homes fronted. One belonged to an elderly man who was not always clear on what was going on, so the kids mercilessly teased him. The next belonged to the Dunkles. Ivan and Betty usually played in our evening games, but Harold and Herbie had to go to bed earlier. Next to them were the Stutzmans; Joe was my age and we spent a lot of time together. Bettibel Wurster, who lived a half-block up the street, and Bill Yocum, who lived a half-block in the other direction, often joined us. The most common out-of-doors evening game was "hide-and-seek" and indoors we played Monopoly or other games.

The Stutzmans struggled financially. Joe helped by selling newspapers at a corner of Market Square, the most prominent spot in the city. A number of his customers were in nearby apartments, where he delivered the daily papers and collected on Saturday. Collecting took a lot of time from sales, so we developed a plan by which I would go with him on Saturday. I made the collections. When the papers were gone, we headed for Woolworth's and a ten-cent pound of peanut butter kisses. From there, we went to the Keystone Theater for our weekly ingestion of a cowboy movie (Tom Mix, Ken Maynard, Bill Boyd, Tim McCoy, etc.). Cost: one dime. On financially flush days, we would stop at the Busy Bee on the way home for a hot dog. Cost: one dime.

On free afternoons and on Saturday morning in the fall, Joe and I were part of a group that played football on a sandlot about four blocks east. Joe's dad was a laborer—a big, strong, gruff man who scared me sometimes with his demanding ways. One Saturday when we were playing football, Joe stopped all of a sudden. He said, "I have to go home. My dad needs me." None of us had watches to indicate it was time for Joe to leave. No messenger had come. He just knew it was time for him to leave. I went with him and, sure enough, when he got home he found his father had fallen out of his chair, having suffered a stroke. Ever since then, if not before, I have believed in extrasensory perception.

Chapter Four

SEEDS OF FAITH

I haven't bothered you much with religion up to this point, in spite of the fact that my relationship with Christ and the church is very important to me—so brace yourself. Here it comes. I can't honestly say I remember the event, surprisingly enough, but I was told that I was baptized as a baby boy in the favored Methodist rite of sprinkling. My first honest memories come from Sunday School. I remember none of my primary teachers, but I clearly remember short, plump, disciplinarian but caring Mrs. Carrie Mitman, who was the Primary Superintendent for many years. Not only did she do all the behind-the-scene kinds of things which were expected of the super, but she also guided two after-school organizations of which I was a part. One group was "The King's Heralds," boys and girls in primary grades whose interest in foreign missions was being stimulated. I was president of that group, and Bettibel was the secretary. The other was "The Home Guards," junior high youth whose interest in missions in the United States was being similarly stimulated. I was president of that group, and Bettibel was the secretary.

I also remember our junior high teacher, Mrs. Kiefer. The five or six boys in our class, wanting to demonstrate a very doubtful superiority in singing, would do our best to sing LOUDER than anyone. It never seemed to embarrass Mrs. Kiefer, though it certainly did not add to the value of the opening worship. The opening exercises over, she would take us into our lessons with a great deal of patience. One of the things I liked best about her was that she was such a good customer when I sold salted peanuts or tickets to church dinners or dramatic productions. My high school teacher, Bill Phillips, also deserves special mention, but be patient; he gets a few stories of his own.

We Biebers were always involved in church activities; Mom would have it no other way. When a new preacher moved in with a son our age and wondered who would be a good companion, my brother and I were highly recommended—by persons who didn't know any better. Speaking of preachers—we were, weren't we?—I vaguely remember my first pastor. He was short and rather plump, and his name was Ilgenfritz. After him came a tall, white-haired, goatee-bearded, dignified man, Joseph Adams. Then came two who just didn't have it; at least, they didn't fit our congregation. Bidlack and Schuchart were assigned to our congregation by the bishop on recommendation of the district superintendent.

After those sad fiascos, the D. S. warned that if the next one didn't work, we would get a student from Dickinson Seminary, a junior college/ Bible School that eventually became Lycoming College. This time he sent one of the best pastors a church could hope for—Nevin G. McCloskey. He was my pastor all through high school. A strong pacifist, he introduced me to one of my life-time faith positions. He taught our catechism class, impressing us not only with his knowledge of church and the Christian faith, but also with the open way in which he could talk about boy-girl relationships. He introduced us to persons like Edwin Markham, American poet (in person), and Toyohiko Kagawa, great Japanese evangelist (by description). And then as I left for college, there was Arthur Faus, who had his Ph.D. and was a bit over the heads of our congregation, but showed a pastor's love and care.

If there were services at our church, we were there: Sunday School, morning worship, evening worship, midweek prayer meeting, any special events. Mom didn't expect much of us; during the worship service, as long as we read "Target" and stayed quiet, we were acceptable. Acceptable behavior, however, was not guaranteed. Once when we had a week-long revival in our church, it was decided that "Every Day with Jesus" would be the theme song. A group of five of us teen-age boys somehow eluded our parents and were sitting together in the back pew. Of course, we were having boy fun, until the pastor realized where the noise was coming from. When he had identified us, he "permitted" us to stand and sing the theme song.

It was the Bieber, Yocum, Wurster, Guisewhite, Snavely, and Dunkle kids who took part in the various Children's Day or Christmas presentations. My boy soprano singing voice was clear, and I was once asked to sing a Christmas carol solo from an out-of-sight spot while actors were performing on the stage. I did so well that a recruiter from the Trinity Episcopal Church Boys' Choir who heard me invited MY BROTHER to join their choir. He was NOT the one they heard singing, but God moves in mysterious ways; it turned out all right, and he later became a much better singer than I.

We even went to all-city Methodist meetings and to some of the district conferences. I particularly remember going to youth meetings at

Clearfield and at Aldersgate M.E. Church in York. When my younger brother "went forward" in response to the invitation at an all-city Methodist revival, I also went forward, less from conviction than from being afraid my brother would outdo me. George must have been serious; from that time forward he wanted to be a minister and actually began pastoring a church when he was only seventeen.

Third Street Methodist also sent us to camp, a truly remarkable service, since it was at Camp Newton Hamilton, Mount Union, Pennsylvania, almost a hundred miles away. When I was there as a twelve-year-old, we were taught a class in the life of Jesus by the bishop of Washington. I do not remember his name, but I do remember his saying, "No one ever really knew what God was like until Jesus came and put a face on him." I had my first genuine religious experience at that camp. On the closing evening of camp, we had gathered in the tabernacle, a wooden structure with canvas drop curtains available for rain or cold. While we were there, a heavy rainstorm came up, the drapes came down, and we were literally confined to the tabernacle. The strange but powerful thought ran through my mind that God wanted to keep us there until we were fully His, and I surrendered.

My best girl all during high school was Bettibel. We never went steady, but each knew that the other was SPECIAL. It was Bettibel who went on family outings with us. It was Bettibel whom I took to a play at Eaglesmere. It was Bettibel who was with me on return from a church camp weekend when the brakes gave out as we were going down a crooked mountain road, and who neither screamed nor flinched as we wove back and forth before finally coming to a stop at the very edge of a precipice. It was Bettibel whom I wanted to impress with what a good Christian I was, so on the closing evening campfire of senior high at Newton Hamilton, I sat beside her on the hillside. I dared to pray aloud (for Bettibel, most likely), making use of the words of "Fairest Lord Jesus." I showed her the "secret" promise I was making to God to be a missionary—the promise to be made final as the paper burned in the campfire. It was Bettibel whom I was taking to the football game at Mount Carmel when our car broke down. Fortunately, we were picked up by another Billtown car en route. The driver was kind, but the immature youths in the back referred to us as "the drawbacks." (Dad got the car going in time to get us home. There were other boys for Bettibel and other girls for me, but we always seemed to come back to each other. (Until Mary Beth showed up, that is!)

My high school Sunday School teacher was Bill Phillips, a graduate from Juniata College with a degree in sociology. He worked hard with us boys—classes were gender divided. He was definitely not the athletic, football-hero type of man that boys would easily accept. In fact, he was so gentle as to be almost effeminate, but he still commanded our respect. He had no family of his own; we were his family. He took us to camps. He took us "skinny dipping" (what a daring activity in those days of stricter morality) off Goose Island on the other side of the Susquehanna. He showed real interest in our school and social activities, asking about our "dates." I had practically none, but as a senior in high school I had three dates with the same girl.

Bill asked, "Did you kiss her goodnight?"

"NOOOO!" I answered, truthfully.

"Don't you think she expected it?" he wondered. After that, I didn't date her any more. Scared? Maybe. Back to Bettibel.

When Mary Savine, a fellow Juniata graduate, moved from Altoona to take a position at the Muncy women's penitentiary, she came to our church. She and Bill spent a lot of time together. Both had been students of Dr. Fayette Mackenzie, who occasionaslly asserted in his sociology classes that there was no such thing as a platonic relationship between opposite sexes. Mary and Bill set out to prove him wrong. They were platonic, weren't they? Sure, until they fell in love and got married. They had three children. Their oldest, also named Bill, was a co-winner of the Nobel prize in Physics.

Now, lest we overdo the religious bit, let's talk about money. I have already indicated that it was largely because of Mom's managing and Dad's hard work that we always had enough to eat. Still, the laundry, even for the foreman, was not a lucrative occupation. Mom would sometimes work there when extra help was needed. All of us children did laundry stints as we grew older. Once I caddied for Nelson Gummo, then Dad's boss at Gummo Laundry. Later I drove for him on brief trips. For a while I sold "White Cloverine Salve." George and I sold peanuts that mother had fried and salted. When I was about twelve, George and I began to cane chairs at two cents per square inch. None of this made us rich, but gave George and me some funds to finance the family "Holiday Celebration Club." We planned and financed family parties for each birthday and special event.

Chapter Five

HIGH TIMES AT HIGH SCHOOL

High school went well. I continued my honor roll streak in spite of the fact that I was not fond of studying. Fortunately, classes were seventy-five minutes long, and the last half hour was to be given to study. I was an enthusiastic follower of the "Millionaires," as the high school teams were called as a relic of the days when Williamsport had been the lumber capital of the world. I remember J. E. Nancarrow's annual speech at pep rally: "Let's get momentum! You may not be the biggest or the strongest, but if you put your hearts in it you can get momentum!" After-school activities were difficult for me, living so far from the school, but I did join the MathEngineers, the Hi-Y (a high school adjunct of the YMCA), and the Chemistry Club. In my senior year I was vice president of the student council and advertising manager of *The Cherry and White*, our school magazine.

My favorite teacher was Miriam Wendle, who taught English. Her command of grammar and rhetoric was very well grounded, and she was particularly skilled in developing that same command in her students. So much did I enjoy her English class that I determined to take Journalism as a junior year elective. Alas, it was scheduled for the same period as American History, a required course. I studied an American History book during the summer, scored 95 on the exam, and took Journalism. It was then that the seed planted by Miss Dickert four years earlier came to fruit, and I came to love writing.

I do not believe there was a national honor society in those days. Our high school had its own honor society into which I was inducted. College scholarships were not easily obtained, and the most common basis for granting a scholarship was a competitive examination for high school seniors. The department heads at Billtown High were aware of the system, and went out of their way determined to help their students. Some two dozen or so of us met with a department head after school three afternoons each week. They would review what they considered most

important in their respective fields, and they would give us general knowledge examinations. By the time we were ready to meet competition, we
had taken perhaps as many as twenty-five different examinations, so we
were well prepared. It paid off; all but three or four of the group earned
scholarships.

Sunday School teacher Bill Phillips hoped it would be possible for
me to attend his alma mater, Juniata College, and he knew how short money
was in our home. When college president C.C. Ellis came to Williamsport
to speak at the Holy Week noonday services sponsored by the churches,
Bill took me to meet him. Meeting him, I was so impressed that I had to go
to his college. Bill took me to the college for the competitive exam. When
I came from having written mine, Bill asked, "How did it go?"

I responded, "I don't know what I won, but I know I won something." Sure enough, I was granted a full tuition scholarship, the highest
awarded, and I credit those department heads.

Meanwhile, two unfortunate things had taken place in our family.
My older sister, lacking any sex education or advice, had become pregnant; her hopes of eventually going into nurses training were dashed. Our
lack of sex education may be illustrated as follows: I was sitting at our
dining room table, reading a book. Looking over my shoulder, Mother
saw the word "pregnant" and pointed to it.

"What does that mean?" she asked.

"Gee, Mom, I don't know," I lied.

"Well I hope not," she said. After all, I was only seventeen, and
my sister wasn't pregnant yet. The second negative occurrence was
Mother's development of a lower bowel cancer which required at least a
temporary colostomy for its removal. She was in the clinic, slowly and
painfully recovering when the news of my scholarship reached her, and I
heard about it when I visited after school that day. My first response was
to walk to the window and give thanks to God. Full tuition! Somehow I
would get to college.

Common superstition claims that misfortunes come in threes.
I doubt that superstition; yet the third catastrophe had taken place just a
few months earlier. The west branch of the Susquehanna River produced a
record flood. Ability to predict flood levels had not progressed to the skills
of today, so the severity of the flood was underestimated and losses were
enormous. ALL of central city business was inundated. When fire broke
out at the *Grit* newspaper, there was absolutely no way that firefighters
could get to it. As the waters were rising, I was at the laundry helping to

move everything possible to the top bins on the first floor. When water flowed through the building, it was already rushing thigh deep on the street outside. Dad and I joined hands for support, waded across, and found our way home. Our house was spared—we were higher up—but the waters came within a block of us. (All four of our erstwhile homes on East Third Street were flooded.) We followed the news on radio, admiring the ham operators who were trying to keep people informed and as assured as they could be under the circumstances. When the waters had receded, Dad and George and I and several others cleaned out the mud-invaded home of Clyde Harding, an elder "pillar" of our church. About two weeks later, I was the speaker for youth Sunday at our church, and I likened the power of God to the power of the water—completely irresistible. At Gummo Laundry, the water had covered much of the second floor, but as soon as the water went down they set about cleaning and making repairs. They were tremendously busy for several weeks, washing the mudsoaked "new" clothes from many stores, so there could be reasonable sales.

The high school was flooded. Only the upper floors were spared, and the gym and lower floors were completely useless. Much of our class work never did get finished, but the school year came to a close, and there would be all summer to get ready for the fall opening.

Chapter Six

A FRESHMAN AT JUNIATA COLLEGE

When graduation was finally past, I found a job at a dye house several blocks from home. My job, for fifty cents an hour, was to operate the receiving end of a fifty-yard-long stretching machine. When they were dyed, the huge bolts of rayon cloth would shrink somewhat, and the stretching machine—metal fingers holding the edge of the cloth and growing farther and farther apart—would stretch the cloth to its intended width. All I had to do, really, was to be sure the metal fingers were not letting go and, from time to time, change the completed bolts of goods. I worked changing shifts, 7-3, 3-1, 11-7, and only once in the night shift did I fall asleep and awaken to the catastrophe of a long machine whose fingers had not taken hold.

During free evenings, it was my practice to go to the nearby Sheridan School playground to play indoor baseball. Preceding softball, indoor baseball was so named because it could be played on a much smaller field than regular baseball. The ball itself was about five inches in diameter. No one seemed to like catching, and I liked the feeling of being always in the game, so I became the catcher for our playground team. The playground supervisor that summer was attractive Jean Koch, who had just graduated from high school with me and had been in one of my classes, but whom I knew only by name. For that summer and until I went off to Juniata, Jean was the love of my life. Rare were the evenings I did not spend with her, though I did still spend some time with Bettibel and the church gang. Summer ended and I was off to college, with enough money in hand to pay for the first semester and part of the second.

Jean and I corresponded regularly until I broke it off because somehow, in the absence of the two women in my life, I came to realize Bettibel was still the one.

College, obviously, was a new experience. Juniata, in those days, had a number of requirements aimed at keeping one's Christian faith alive, or perhaps bringing it to life. Bible was a required course for the first two years. Ethics, based on Judeo-Christian principles, was required of seniors. Daily worship services, about a half hour in length and with attendance required, took place in the chapel. (One of our favorite dismissals would come when President Ellis would request, "Will the students please remain seated while the faculty passes out." I suspect some of them had already passed out during the service.) Church attendance, at least once a Sunday, was also a rule, and the churches in town cooperated by collecting attendance cards from the students and submitting them to the college. For the first two years, I regularly attended the Methodist Church downtown and participated in its youth group.

I lived on the fourth floor of Founders Hall. I was to room with Willard Sackett, a Maryland resident whom I met briefly. It turned out he could not come to college, so my roomie became Mirror Tezai, from Brooklyn. His name and his home brought to mind the *New York Mirror*, then a popular newspaper, so he quickly became "Daily"—the Daily mirror. Most of those on Fourth Founders, the dorm whose denizens had lower financial resources, were frosh. Four of them, Lou Sileo, Ed Grega, Al Leopold, and Rod Gallagher, were out for varsity football. Others in the gang, besides Daily and me, were Clyde Barone, a blonde Italian from the Bronx, and John Valerie, older than the rest of us, a Pennsylvania coal miner. John stayed only one year.

The opening semester brought not only classes to attend. There was carefully outlined orientation for the freshmen, ostensibly to divorce them from high school loyalties and wed them to their new alma mater. We wore green felt caps known as dinks, and sizable name tags around our necks. Lacking one or the other threatened a trip to the dreaded tribunal. I suspect it was as a scholarship student I was one of the visible freshmen—I certainly had not broken any rule—that I was called before the tribunal. They asked me to sing the Alma Mater. I had learned it, and sang it accurately and fairly well. They sat there laughing at me. Unspoken, I felt some resentful dismay at their lack of respect for the college song. Wearing high school emblems was forbidden. We were not allowed to use the front steps of Founders or the diagonal walk between the street and Students Hall. All students were assigned dining tables, and dress-up—that is, coats and ties for the men—was expected for the evening meal. My research had suggested to me that chemical engineering would be a high-income occupation, so I took chemistry and biology along with English and Bible. With the excellent training in English I had received from Miriam Wendle, I found my course from slight, treble-voiced Silas

Dubbel to be a breeze. As a scholarship student, I became a lab assistant in chemistry, a means of helping to pay other expenses.

Learning that writers were needed for the weekly *Juniatian*, I quickly began writing sports news. Thus, I was a sports reporter as the time neared for the traditional freshman-sophomore football game. Barone and I, among others of course, were playing on the freshman team, which had a brief schedule of five games. It occurred to us, as Homecoming Day and the big game approached, that everyone would know the sophomores, but we freshmen would be strangers. I determined to write an article identifying the members of our team by nickname. Barone quickly became "Flash," and helped me choose such other names as "Gabby," "Slugger," "Powerhouse," "Lightning," "Stonewall," "Stubby," and "Goliath." Almost finished, I asked Flash, "What will we call me?" He said, "Let's call you 'Butch.' You are less like 'Butch' than anyone I can imagine." The names took, and "Flash" and "Butch" were our names from then on. The names didn't help; we lost the game.

Along with classes, the lab assistantship, my minor involvement with the Methodist youth group downtown, football practice and games, the weekly worship by the Student Volunteers, and having little money, my social life did not thrive. Bettibel was practically a "steady" to me then, and I did not date at the college until I fell for Kay Weber toward the end of the year. (We corresponded that summer, but our "romance" did not last.)

Even though I was busy, there always seemed to be time for tomfoolery—isn't there always? As Christmas approached during our freshman year, we discovered that the men on Third Founders were having a Saturday night carol sing to which they had not invited us. They gathered at the end of their hall near the window which opened on the fire escape. As we nursed our resentment at being left out, we hit upon a plan. All of us had metal wastebaskets, which we filled with water. We placed some at the window by the fire escape, and some at the usual access stairway to our floor. Raiding the trunk room where our luggage was stored, we built a barricade at the top of the stairway. Then two of us carried water down the fire escape to the third floor, opened the window, baptized the carollers, and fled back up the fire escape. When the singers reacted, they found cascades of water awaiting them at both sets of stairs, and eventually gave up their counter-attack. Now that is real tomfoolery. We mopped up the water on our two floors, but overlooked the fact that much of it had gone done the steps and was visible next morning in the hall outside the chapel.

On Monday morning, Dean of Men Clyde Stayer just happened (?) to meet me in the hall and politely invited me into his office. Just as politely, I accepted his invitation. "Butch," he opened, "there was water in the hall outside the chapel yesterday morning." I agreed. There had been.

"I am inclined to believe, Butch, that you had something to do with that."

"Dean," I said, "I will not deny that I was a part of it."

"I heard you were the ringleader."

"No, Dean, I would not say that."

At his request, I reviewed what had happened, adding the comment that it was all in fun.

"Well, Butch," responded that understanding dean, "we are not going to take any action. We can see that you were just trying to have fun. We just want to caution you: in the future, find ways to have fun which are not potentially destructive." (Dean Stayer always seemed so reluctant to penalize that I suspect he rather enjoyed the men's "innocent" escapades.)

An important event each year was the All Class Night. Each of the four classes prepared a skit for presentation, in competition with the other classes. I was volunteered by other class members to lead in preparing the freshman skit, and I succeeded in writing a minstrel show. Looking back at the show, which was well received but no prizewinner, I am embarrassed by my not recognizing that minstrel shows really made fun of Negroes. In an era when little attention was being paid to race problems, and my own racial prejudice simply did not exist, it never occurred to me that a minstrel show was an unkind approach. I also planned and wrote our class skits for the next two years, but they were not prizewinners either.

Another event of my freshman year that deserves telling records the beginning of a life-long friendship with John Grimley. He was a pre-ministerial student. I did not actually avoid him, but although I was a regular churchgoer I did not want to be thought a "goodie-goodie;" I did not approach him either. One day as I was talking to a friend in our hall, I needed a pencil. I stepped inside the nearest open door—a common enough practice—to pick up a pencil from the desk. Above the desk, I was startled to note, was a small poster about 8 1/2 by 11, labeled, "S___ List." The first name on the list was John Grimley. The second was Butch Bieber. I did not query our place on the list; I just concluded that, being on the same list, we must be kindred souls.

About halfway through my second freshman semester, I ran completely out of funds. Dad and Mom were able to send me only a dollar now and then. A note came from Treasurer O. R. Myers. I would have to pay my remaining balance of thirty dollars by Friday or leave. I knew of no source of funds, so I planned to leave after classes on Friday afternoon. Hopefully, I might find a short-term job, earn quick money, and return to complete the year. When mail came that Friday, it included, amazingly, a letter from Grandpa Bieber. In it, believe it or not, was a check for thirty dollars. Grandpa explained that years ago he had broken his arm in a fall from the roof he was painting. The doctor who cared for him had never been fully satisfied with the care he was able to provide. When the doctor died, he left Grandpa a legacy of three hundred dollars. Grandpa tithed it to me, telling me never to return it, but to pass it on.

During the summer after my freshman year, work was almost impossible to find. The laundry had contracted for a small addition, however, and Dad got me a job with the construction gang. It was hard work, carrying cement blocks and wheeling barrowloads of cement up a ramp. We had constructed a wooden floor, supported by wooden posts underneath. On the "floor" would be poured the eventual concrete floor. I was in the throes of a migraine headache (migraines began for me at age fourteen) and had just gone aside to vomit. Finally, I just couldn't take it any more, so I quit and went home. My boss couldn't take that, so he fired me. I learned afterward that the wooden floor had insufficient bracing, and it collapsed under the weight of the concrete. No one was hurt, but the whole mess had to be cleaned up and the project restarted from scratch. For the rest of the summer I had only odd jobs, and I did not return to college well supplied with money.

Chapter Seven

SOCIALIZING SOPHOMORE

Back to Juniata for my sophomore year. Daily Tezai had moved to the Cloister dorm. Lou Sileo's roomie, Rod Gallagher, had not been able to return to school, and John Valerie also left. Lou, Flash, Jack Rodgers, and I were able to get two adjoining rooms with a door between, this time in Third Founders. Lou became the resident assistant. My excellent high school education had gotten me past my reluctance to study, and I was still a lab assistant in chemistry. I became a Big Brother, assigned to help a freshman adjust well to the college. My "little brother" was George Detar, a loyal member of the Church of the Brethren from western Pennsylvania, and we have remained friends ever since, meeting at college or denominational events.

By the time Parents Day had come, and my parents came visiting, I had become the announcer for the football games. I was, of course, in the broadcasting booth, when an intense pain developed without warning in my right abdomen, and I was unable to complete the game. I was helped back to Dad and Mom, and it was promptly decided that they should take me home. They did and then to the hospital, where I underwent an emergency appendectomy. Spinal anesthesia numbed my lower half, and I remember awakening and wondering whose leg was in bed with me. Surgery had not reached the short-term-stay efficiency of modern medicine, and I was not allowed out of bed for a week. I was kept in the hospital for three more days, and my doctor allowed me to return to college only by wearing a support on my abdomen.

A day or two after my return, there was a home football game. Someone saw me come in, and the cheerleaders led a cheer: "Yay, Butch! Yay, Bieber! Yay, Yay, Butch Bieber!" A cheer which was usually reserved for a player starring in the game was accorded to a lowly, non-athletic sophomore. As I look back, I wonder if that might have been the moment when a latent longing for popularity broke to the fore. After all, I was essentially a shy young man, holding aloof from others except when sense of humor, assignment, or a particular skill such as writing would push me forward. At any rate, as I look back, I sense that being popular became of higher value than getting good grades. After all, grades had been easy to come by; popularity hadn't.

As the fall semester moved toward Thanksgiving, our group of men began thinking we had a special relationship and a special set of skills. We began calling ourselves the Big Ten. The ten of us included Flash and Lou, well-accepted Italians; Ed Grega and Al Leopold, football and basketball stars; Jack Rodgers, musician; Perry Tyson, halfback and class president; and his roomie, Jim Hallman; day student Bob Barben, already a tennis star; Daily, who cheered us on; and me, writer. We decided to "announce" ourselves, though on an intimate campus like Juniata there was hardly a need for announcement, by a Christmas greeting to town and gown. We recruited a cooperative freshman to make us a T-shaped sign, about eight feet wide and six feet high, saying:

MERRY XMAS
BIG TEN

and suspending it in the most prominent spot on campus, just under the clock on the front of Founders Hall. It was, for the most part, well received as a friendly gesture; it definitely made us the big group on campus. Even the town of Huntingdon took notice; the newspaper, Huntingdon's *Daily News,* observed, "Look for the greeting which a group on the college campus has issued to town and gown."

There was, however, another reaction as well. When I went into the bookstore which Dean Stayer operated, the dean brought me a negative reaction. "Butch," he began, "President Ellis was not pleased with the sign you fellows put up on Founders."

"But, Dean," I remonstrated, "it is a Christmas greeting. Doesn't President Ellis send Christmas greetings?" After a moment of thought he was back at me.

"I think the real reason is that it seems like an advertisement because the Big Ten name was added."

"But, Dean," my protest continued, "when the president sends Christmas greetings, doesn't he sign his name?" Our tolerant dean did not take the discussion any farther. When we were off the campus for Christmas vacation, the sign was taken down.

To add to our visibility and also to our group consciousness, the Big Ten designed and had made red caps with their emblem on them and wore them about campus. The four who were not on Founders (Perry, Jim, Daily, and Bob) did not participate fully in our activities, but they were clearly a part of us. Among ourselves, even as sophomores, we envisioned our senior year when, we were sure, all the male offices of the Student Senate would be taken by Big Ten members. I'm not sure, but I think the car that became available on rare occasions (when students did not have cars) came from the Rodgers family. We were able to visit in the Sileo home in Chester, meet Lou's delightful family and his beautiful red-haired girlfriend, Kay, and enjoy proper Italian spaghetti. We spent a Saturday afternoon and evening at Saxton, among Barone relatives. We also visited a very few night spots where the guys would declare their freedom by taking a few alcoholic drinks, except for Flash, who didn't like the stuff, and me, a strict teetotaler.

My social life blossomed. I spent too much time in the Social Rooms, just chatting or playing games. Dottie Leiter taught me how to play chess, challenging and time-consuming. (When, fifty years later, roomie Jack saw me at an alumni reunion, he exclaimed, "There's Butch, the chess player.") I still had very little money, so dates were little more than, very rarely, a movie or a trip to Skip's, the popular college hangout, for a dish of ice cream. I think I was a little afraid of the more popular girls; they would already be busy, surely, by the time I entered the picture. And of course there was still Bettibel, in nurses training at Williamsport Hospital. I did spend some time with Miriam Shearer, Eunice Keim, Janet Shultz, and others, and by the time the sophomore year was moving to a close, Charlotte Snoberger and I were "an item."

Academically, I was still coasting on high school knowledge. I did study some, of course, and I did write the required papers and do the required lab work. I earned an A in biology, becoming especially interested in disease-causing parasites. My earlier interest in medicine solidified, and I changed to a pre-med major, but it did not make a good student of me. As I look back now, I wonder how I maintained good enough grades to keep my full tuition scholarship.

Even with the scholarship, I ran out of money. The summer had not been lucrative. Once again the day came when I received a note from Treasurer O.R. Myers: "Mr. Bieber, you are still owing fifty dollars. It must be paid by Friday, or you will have to leave." I had absolutely no hope of funds. No letter came from Grandpa—or anyone else. After lunch on Friday, I was packing my suitcase when Flash came walking in. "Where are you going?" he demanded.

I showed him my note from O.R. "I just don't have fifty dollars," I reported, "so I am going home to see if I can work it up somehow."

"Well, I have fifty dollars," he said, and he immediately pulled out his wallet, extracted fifty dollars, and handed it to me. I objected. I knew his dad owned a dress factory in the Bronx, and Flash always seemed to have money, but he was definitely not a rich boy.

"Take it!" he insisted. "If you leave you might never come back. You can call it a loan and pay it sometime down the road." So I accepted, and there continued the unwritten agreement that when I could I would pay it back at simple interest, then about 2 1/2 per cent.

Although it doesn't fit the time line, I must complete that story. There was something special about Flash that made people like him despite a self-confidence that bordered on arrogance. Both intellectually and as an athlete he was well above average. He "admitted" his superiority without hesitation, but without flamboyance. As a junior, he entered the General Information Contest, a pre-TV-period game show that was almost invariably won by seniors. Miss McCrimmon, his Spanish teacher, knew he had entered the contest and mentioned in class one Friday morning that the award would be made that day in chapel. He ran to our room, found me there, said they were going to give the prize that day, and asked, "Do you think I should dress up?" I did think so. He did dress up, and sure enough he won the prize—and next year as well.

After graduation, we went in different directions. We had a few contacts, but obviously I had not reached a financial level that would enable my repayment of the loan. Nothing at all was ever said about it. I invited him to our wedding, but he was unable to come. As the years passed, I tried on several occasions to contact him, writing to his old address or trying to find a telephone number. Finally, a few weeks before our fortieth alumni reunion, I saw his name in the alumni bulletin as a donor. I called the office, got his address, and wrote to him, urging him to come to the reunion when I would pay up. He didn't get to the reunion, but he traced me down with a person-to-person call while I was at the reunion dinner. We chatted, briefly reviewing the important events of our lives. He was married, but had no children. He who as a college student had rebelled against rules and regulations had become a lawyer. "I have done very well," he chuckled. "I think you are the only one who ever did me out of my money."

He was joking, but I determined to pay. Back home, I wrote the check for $150+ and sent it to him. He sent it back with a thank you note.

I never saw him again. He died a few months later of a heart attack—energetic, health conscious Flash Barone. Even though we spent all those years apart, his going left a gap in my life.

*　　*　　*

When summer came, I once again found it impossible to find anything but short-term jobs. Then I awakened to the fact that Aunt Mary really seemed to have enough money. I wrote to her and asked for help, and she readily responded. She lent me $800 as an interest-free loan. I was the first of my generation to go to college and that pleased her. Money would not be a problem for the rest of my college life except for the paying back of it, which did not take place until about six years later. When I was at home, Bettibel was near, though busy at the hospital, and Charlotte slid into obscurity.

My junior year would change my life. By now I was sports editor of the *Juniatian*. I —shy, reticent, definitely not a social butterfly, I—was my class representative on the college Social Committee. George Detar was still with us, though he never needed much help from me. I took on a new "little brother," Tom Cooney, a limping, but smiling Irishman from the wilds of New Jersey with a keen interest in sports and journalism. We fit. He began to write articles for me, the *Juniatian* sports editor.

— Chapter Eight —

ENTER MARY BETH

It seems strange how little I remember of my first junior semester. I had not run out of girls I liked, but Bettibel was back home, and I did not settle on any one special at J. C.

Gene Metzler, a sophomore from Pottstown, and I had both observed one pretty, dark-haired freshman girl, a Mary Beth High, and had gone down together to watch her play field hockey. We debated and wondered: which of us would be the one to ask her for a date, and would she accept? Somehow, the first semester passed with neither of us having the courage—or perhaps it was the wherewithal. I kept noticing her in Student Volunteers and around campus, and it seemed clear she was a Christian. Would she accept a date with a ne'er-do-well like me?

February 1940 came, as well as what looked like an opportunity. I had heard that Mary Beth played the accordion. An announcement appeared that an accordion-playing evangelist was having revival meetings in the not-too-far-downtown United Brethren Church. Heart in throat and, if I had owned a hat besides the Big Ten cap, hat in hand, I invited her to go to the services with me. To make clear the innocence of my intentions, I also invited friend Lou Sileo and another coed to go along. It was February 4, 1940, when the four of us walked to the little church on Mifflin Street. Would you believe, the only things I remember from that earthshaking event are that the "date" took place and that Lou and I kept teasing a pretty, little, blonde, curly-headed girl. I suppose Clem Hershey played his accordian, but I won't guarantee it.

Still, the evening had passed pleasantly, and on the next Saturday I decided to take another chance. Charles Laughton was playing at the Clifton theater in, "The Hunchback of Notre Dame," which would be one of the decade's outstanding films. Besides, it was a literary masterpiece, which would make it more attractive, wouldn't it? I called and invited Mary Beth to the social room, which of course was the acceptable spot for such a meeting. "Charles Laughton and The Hunchback of Notre Dame are on downtown," I nervously blurted. "Would you go and see it with me?" I just as nervously invited.

That pretty young brunette stood quiet for a moment, then responded, "No, but thank you."

NO??? It didn't seem possible that she would say no. Girls didn't! And last Sunday evening we had innocent fun. Her acceptance of a call to the social room at least implied acceptance. My nervousness, of course, makes it obvious that I feared she would decline. Now I was the one to stand silent. Then, collecting myself though hardly believing what I had heard, I stammered, "You mean you don't want to go to the movies with me?" Again, her turn for silence.

Then, "I guess I mean I don't want to go to the movies."

Oooh! Then I remembered the most common "date" for short-of-money couples. "Can we go for a walk?"

She accepted. It was such a beautiful, warm February evening. We decided to walk the Little Loop, a stretch of just over two miles. The temperature was mild as we started, but winter suddenly attacked. By the time we returned to the campus, it was bitter cold. My feet were swollen in my shoes. (Of course, dummy, where else?) I knew she must be terribly cold, so I took her to the basement door so she could get inside more quickly. I went back to the social room and signed her in, then I rode downtown in the bus to see "The Hunchback." My swollen feet hurt, so I took off my shoes. By the time the movie was over the swelling had gone down and I was comfortable again. Now you might consider that date a fiasco and suppose that our relationship cooled. Yet as we talked together, we found a number of things in common and, in spite of the cold, we were warmer. I felt more and more attracted.

1940 was a leap year; had you remembered? As the only male member of the Social Committee, I had slyly suggested that we have a "Sadie Hawkins Week," actually only Wednesday to Saturday. The distaff members of the committee accepted the idea enthusiastically and enlarged on it. The girls would do the inviting; they would pay the bills; they would help the men with their coats, open doors for them, seat them at the dining table—the whole ball of wax. I waited for Mary Beth to invite me for—at least—another walk, a shorter and warmer one. Wednesday. Nothing, so I accepted an invitation from another girl. Thursday. Nothing, so I accepted an invitation from another girl. Friday. Nothing, so I accepted an invitation from another girl.

On Saturday evening, a Sadie Hawkins party was scheduled. Surely, Mary Beth would invite me to that, wouldn't she? Hoping—almost expecting—that she would, I turned down three exciting invitations—to a tobogganing party, to a play at Altoona, to a local movie. By Saturday afternoon I had given up hope; it was clear I would be alone that evening. I went to the gym to use some of the energy I had been saving. As I swung by my feet from the trapeze rings, my feet slipped out, and I fell straight down, landing on the mat on my most impervious part, the top of my head. No headache, but a very painful back. Returning to my room, I found a note from Mary Beth, the party invitation which I had given up. Lame back or no. I accepted. We enjoyed the party together. We played Ping-Pong, and she won (of course it was because of my lame back, but I made no excuses). With those three dates, our relationship jelled. On many an evening, we went walking along the streets of Huntingdon together; we chatted at great length in the social rooms; we had an occasional treat at Skip's, and we went to church and Volunteers together. She knew me as Butch—as all the campus did—until summer came.

What happened to Bettibel? Wasn't she still in Williamsport? Yes, she was. And didn't I always come to the place where relationships with other girls would come to a close with the resumption of our relationship? Yes, it always had and we always had. This time? Now, be patient. Don't get ahead of the story.

As the junior year came to a close, there were both disaster and triumph waiting for me. My pursuit of popularity over grades caught up with me. I had failed in two subjects by this time, and it was clear that to graduate with my class I would have to take summer classes and try to catch up. On the other hand, when various student offices were filled for next year, the Big Ten held strong. Tyson and Hallman continued to lead the class, and Tyson was also named football captain and Senate Vice-President. Barone and Barben were co-editors of the yearbook, *The Alfarata*, and Barben was also Chairman of Athletics. Rodgers was named Chairman of Freshmen. Leopold was Senate Treasurer and *Alfarata* Business Manager. I was named editor of the *Juniatian* and Chairman of Publications.

Summer school went well. My pint-sized roommate was Clinton Burket, an energetic young fellow easy to like but hard to get close to, and my grades were good. Of course, summer school provided time to write to Mary Beth. Between sessions, I found opportunity to visit her at her home. My visit coincided, not intentionally, with one of several family reunions held at the High home. The Highs had no nieces or nephews and no living siblings, so they stayed close to their cousins. I stayed at the Tyson home in Spring City; it would not have been quite proper for just-a-friend, especially a male, to stay at Highs. During my visit, I was suffering from a huge carbuncle on my knee, but that did not spoil a most pleasant visit with Mary Beth.

Preparing for the senior year, I also edited and produced *The Scout*, the annual handbook for the freshman class and other newcomers. I attended Camp Myler, a kind of leadership retreat for those who were actual or potential leaders, and managed to get Mary Beth invited.

As classes began, the Senate held an orientation session for the incoming class. Each Senate chairperson presented his or her program and explained its importance to the college. As Chairman of Publications, I spoke for that program, using an opening which has long been remembered. Three or four sentences into my speech, I interrupted myself with a series of throat clearing exercises. My apology and ensuing comments—in a very strained and largely hushed voice—went like this: "Please pardon me. I have been having some trouble with my left lung (Harumph!) I would like to continue, though. If I talk like this, can you hear me all right?" The amplification system was functioning, and the audience kindly nodded their heads. Unpleasant to hear, but they could manage. My talk continued in a low and strained voice: "As I was saying, I have this trouble with my left lung." Pause. Then I continued in a shout: "OF COURSE, MY RIGHT LUNG IS ALL RIGHT!" When they had finished laughing at themselves, I continued in a more usual mode. (I borrowed the opening from a missionary who had spoken to a reluctant-to-listen student body in high school days, and whose opening convinced us all he was worth listening to.) I found time to assemble the *Juniatian*, writing editorials and occasionally feature articles, taking much advantage of my staff, and using Jimmy Hallman as "The Tomahawk," undercover gossip columnist.

Almost every evening, Mary Beth and I would go walking or, as earlier on, to church or Volunteers. I learned about her church, the Church of the Brethren. I sat in the rear of the Stone Church as the congregation participated in their Love Feast (a service of feetwashing, a light meal in fellowship, and then what I knew as the Communion). Non-Brethren in those days were not allowed to participate, but were welcomed to observe. When I rarely thought of Bettibel, I identified our relationship as that of a close brother and sister. Together with Jimmy Hallman, whose home was at Pottstown and who was borrowing the family car, and a few others, we planned to go to Bethlehem on an early November weekend for the Moravian football game. Then I would spend Saturday night through Sunday dinner with Mary Beth before heading back to college.

Then my world fell apart—well, not the whole world, but the world of Mary Beth. A brief letter from her was given to me, informing me in as kind terms as she could muster, that it had been revealed to her that we were not to be together. An occasional walk, perhaps, but not the frequent togetherness which made the campus community talk about us as a couple. What could I say in response to what she understood was God's purpose? I could, and did, say in a letter of response that though my own perceptions were different, I would abide by hers. I told her that whenever I had thought of life in the future, that life had included her, but I would adjust my thinking in line with hers. Frequency of our walks? Well, I would let her determine that.

There was a faint glimmer of hope, though I did not recognize it as such at the time. We did have those arrangements for the Moravian game, three or four weeks down the road. It was so rare that we could attend an away game that we decided to carry through with it. Of course, it would not be comfortable for my friend Flash and me to spend the night at Mary Beth's home. I remembered that Eunice Keim, with whom I had spent time (see above) lived at Pottstown, about seven miles from Mary Beth's home. I wrote to her. Cleverly, I reminded her that I had always called her, "Wun" a word play on the name Eunice and the beginning of "wonderful." Would she be willing to meet us at the game at Bethlehem and be a hostess to Flash and me over Saturday night? The reply was prompt; she would. Came the day of the game, rain came also. Wun came to the game; we sat together. By the time the game was over, Juniata losing by more than sixty points, it was pouring. Thoughtfully, Wun had brought an umbrella, and we walked from the game under her umbrella. Something about seeing that simple togetherness made Mary Beth aware that she really wanted more than an occasional walk with me. Wun and I, and part of the time Flash, had a nice evening together. Next day, after going to the Lutheran Church with Wun, we found our way to the High house and enjoyed a sumptuous dinner. I noticed the absence of pepper. Was there any, I asked, thinking only to correct an oversight? It took searching by Mrs. High to find a pepper shaker!

After dinner, we headed back to Juniata. The others did not know that the warmth between Mary Beth and me had cooled, so they seated her beside me as I drove. As we rode along, I placed my hand on hers; to my surprise, she seized mine, and I drove one-handed for miles! That faint glimmer of hope became a bright light, and we have never separated since. Bettibel Wurster, great and special person that she was, no longer occupied my thoughts. (She had promised a picture of her when she graduated from nursing school, but before she would give it to me she asked me, frankly, if she was still that special to me. She was also becoming interested in a Cornell student. I confessed that there was another. No picture, but good brother and sister.)

By the time the second semester rolled around, it was apparent that I wasn't making the grade academically. I lost the last semester of my scholarship. I was asked to resign my *Juniatian* editorship. (Managing editor and good friend Charlotte Snoberger, reluctantly took over.) I did take the Med Caps, medical college qualifying test, and did so well in them that Professor Homer Will still considered my prospects good. I visited Georgetown University,a few blocks from Aunt Mary Pettis' home for an interview that seemed positive. But as I put together all it would cost, even borrowing from Aunt Mary, plus a lingering doubt that my grades would let me qualify, I abandoned medical school. Some other doctor would have to heal my mother.

Still, there was good news which sprang from my renewed and growing Christian faith. At age fifteen, I had manifested a somewhat less than enthusiastic turn toward foreign missions. Now, Mary Beth and I were participating in a group of students who called themselves the Foreign Missions Fellowship. We met together, studied the Bible, prayed, sought to hear missionaries on furlough, and tried to ascertain God's will for each one of us as to foreign missionary service. Mary Beth and I were not engaged; we just knew that we belonged together and some day would marry. We didn't want to miss God's will, so we agreed: if God called one, the other would know the call was for both of us. One evening in the dorm prayer meeting, it struck me with great force that God did want me to be a missionary.

As soon as our prayers were over, I went to the phone to call Mary Beth, but it was past ten o'clock; no phone calls accepted. Next morning I sent her a note at breakfast. Would she meet me briefly after breakfast? She would, and did. I told her my story. With a very happy smile of acceptance, she asked, "About what time was that?"

"Very close to a quarter to ten," I answered.

With an even bigger smile, she said, "Last night about a quarter to ten I turned to my roommate and said, "Mishie, suddenly I know that God wants me to be a missionary." We rejoiced in God's clear, double-barreled call.

Chapter Nine

TRAINING AS A NURSE

We had no idea when or how it would take place. Mary Beth still had two more years of college. I lacked the credits to graduate with my class and was only beginning to consider the next steps. Former Sunday School teacher Bill Phillips, still a very good friend, came with a suggestion."You like medicine. Have you thought of going into training as a nurse?" I hadn't, but I did, and entered training at the Pennsylvania Hospital School of Nursing for Men, in Philadelphia.

And so would begin a new phase of my life, still directed to medicine, still directed to serving with Mary Beth in some foreign country.

This would seem an appropriate time to interrupt the sequence and reflect on what nurses training meant. It meant, of course, long absences from Mary Beth, often more than I wanted to endure. But it also meant learning skills and information that would stand me in good stead for the rest of my life. The men in my class, working and learning at Pennsylvania Hospital's Department for Mental and Nervous Disease, were serious men, devoted to their learning and their patients. The school staff included Leroy Craig and Kenneth Crummer, graduates of McLain Hospital School of Nursing in Boston, and Tony and Andrew Mannino, graduates of our own school. Craig was the superintendent, a large man with a religious bent and a very dignified bearing. I never saw him outside his white trousers-and-jacket uniform.

Crummer, on the other hand, was a memorable character. A wizened little man with what may have been a minor tic in his jaw, he was deeply committed to the teaching of nursing and had absolutely no doubt that men make the better nurses. He never earned a college degree, though he had passed far beyond the necessary number of credits for such a degree. Much of his study had been done at the University of Pennsylvania. Somehow, begging, accepting gifts, or perhaps even pilfering, he had accumulated a large variety of anatomical specimens for use in teaching. He was determined that the anatomy and physiology learning of his students would approach that of the doctors with whom they would be working. He loved vocabulary as well, and sometimes found strange opportunities to use his. His small apartment was in the same dormitory as us students, and next to the game room. Frequent noisy games of table tennis would disturb his studying, and he would occasionally post a sign, "Due to the exigencies of the situation, there will be no table tennis this evening."

I roomed for the first year with George Hoza; like most of the men, his home was in eastern Pennsylvania's coal regions. My classmates and I were not in any competition; there was no reason to be. Yet we could not help comparing scores and experiences. I was the only college man. Bill Seibert had the advantage of Hershey Junior College. The others were high school graduates. There is no question in my mind but that Ed Slebodnick was the best student in the class. Still, only because I earned a higher score than he in the final exam, I was granted the coveted Fuller Award "for proficiency in psychiatric nursing."

Proficiency? Maybe. Experiences? Plenty. There were, basically, six types of patients in the hospital where I began my training. There were the admission patients, still to be assigned to a ward; the mildly ill, who simply needed protection while they were being treated; the chronic but relatively stoic group, some senile some not treatable by any then-known therapy; the senile, requiring constant vigilance, assistance, and care; the active patients, potentially and sometimes actively dangerous to themselves and others; and the convalescent, a group of patients so near to having regained health that they were almost a social club. Patients in our hospital tended to be wealthy or at least to come from wealthy families. Let me share a few patients and events, changing names even though it happened so long ago that it could hardly hurt to use their real ones.

There was Mr. Harper, who spent most of his many hospital years in the active ward and often in the enervating tub room. He could explode into violence at any time, but the warm tubs usually calmed him. One thing he definitely did not like, for some reason, was red food—tomatoes, beets, plums, cherries. If anyone inadvertently fed him (he had to be fed in the tub room) any red food, he would not say anything. He had his own response, which the nurses knew. Occasionally one of the greenhorn nurses would be arrogant and unpleasant, and one teaching method for him was to let him feed red food to Mr. Harper, without warning. One such student successfully fed several mouths full of red beets to him. Without even a grunt and without revealing it, Mr. Harper stored the beets in his mouth. Then, when his supply was sufficient, he vigorously spouted the whole red mouthful over the clean white uniform of the nurse. He said nothing, but one caught his message: "Feed me red food, will you? No, you won't!"

You might be interested in Mr. Rowan, an important government official suffering from a depression, who was openly and proudly homosexual. He was a man of pleasant mien and mild manner, with a certain innate dignity. It was, however, extremely unpleasant to spend time with him, which was of course expected of nurses; an important aspect of psychiatric nursing is listening. He persisted in telling of his sexual experiences with other men in most graphic and descriptive terms, so that one felt almost ill at the pictures he produced. He liked me. Mostly he liked me because he discovered that I had very tiny, but legible, handwriting, a skill I developed for economical use of paper in my lengthy letters to Mary Beth. I think he interpreted the handwriting as being effeminate, and indeed it may have been, but I wasn't.

From time to time, for reasons probably not known even to themselves, a patient would become violent, attacking another patient or a nurse, throwing things at him, striking him, kicking him, spitting at him. It was tempting, but obviously inappropriate, to react in kind; these were actions of sick persons. I remember only twice that I was attacked. Once I was in his room with Mr. Jonson, a corporation executive from the south who seemed to be on the road to recovery. Our conversation was just chitchat, but suddenly he reached out with both hands and grabbed me by the throat. I was able to free myself, but a wrestling match ensued. My aim was to leave the room and lock the door, lest he become harmful to other patients. But how does one leave a wrestling opponent behind? I started for the door several times, but each time he grabbed me. Finally I was able to place him for a few seconds on his bed, with his feet up in the air, and I escaped. As he recovered from his illness in the days that followed, neither of us ever mentioned the incident, and we became good patient-nurse friends.

A little more scary, because of its possible effect both on his welfare and on my own reputation, was an episode with wizened, eighty-seven-year-old Mr. Welmont. A very slender little man weighing not over 110 pounds, he had been led to attack another patient and was now in the active ward. He was quite confused. I asked him one day how old he was, and he said, "I am 120 years old. I came over on the *Mayflower* with Columbus, you know."

"But Mr. Welmont," I remonstrated, "Columbus came almost four hundred years ago."

"Yes, I know," he began his explanation. "All those dates were all right until FDR changed Thanksgiving a few years ago."

The attack I remember took place one noon when I took his lunch tray to him.

"I don't want that," he shouted. Placing his tray on the small table, I began to coax him into eating.

"Oh, Mr. Welmont, the food looks so good. I am sure you'll enjoy it."

"I don't want it!" he yelled, louder and, hauling off, struck me on the chin with his fist. I felt only a slight jar, but I was aghast when I saw him fall over backward, having lost his balance with all that effort, strike his head on the floor, and knock himself out. I could hear in my mind the accusations which would come of having struck that little old man. What could I do? Nothing. In just a few seconds, he opened his eyes, got up, thanked me for his lunch, and sat down to eat.

During my second year of training, George Hoza, Harry Saunders, and I were assigned to Jefferson Hospital in center city Philadelphia for training in surgical and medical nursing. We were the only male nurses there. There were several male aides, all of whom seemed to be homosexual. Jefferson is a very good hospital, and I really liked it there. Caring for medical or surgical patients was far different from caring for mental patients. Being scrub nurse in the operating room, with the kind of involvement that meant I must anticipate the surgeon's need and have the proper instrument ready for his hand, was challenging and exciting. Our training often placed us a little ahead, in procedure, of new resident doctors on the floor, so we could be of real help to them. One of them became aware of my hope to learn some obstetrics (not included in the men's course), so he invited me several times to attend at a delivery. The men, not requiring chaperones, were also able to witness autopsies fairly often, an excellent teaching experience.

Our living quarters, on the other hand, gave us experience in living in a tenement house. We lived, if one could call it that, on the fourth floor of a very old building which would last only a few more years before being razed. It was roach infested with the biggest roaches I have ever seen, often three inches long. If you will allow me some small exaggeration, I will tell you that they lined up behind our door and it took two of us to push through and get in. We did have indoor plumbing, but beside the tub there was a hole in the bathroom wall large enough to walk through, and we were glad we were the only ones on the fourth floor.

We survived. I learned something of the needs and feelings of patients. It became almost second nature to start an intravenous infusion. We could insert catheters, and occasionally use urological sounds, with the best of them. We were experts at dumping and sterilizing bedpans. I learned to call even a bowel movement beautiful when it came from the body of a man desperately in need of bowel activity. I also discovered the possibility of professional blood donation. It was by selling my blood that I accumulated the money ($50) to buy Mary Beth's engagement ring.

Chapter Ten

CALLED TO THE MINISTRY

An interruption in the nursing saga is essential here to prepare for a later incident. While at Jefferson, I had begun attending a Church of the Brethren. After all, I was going to marry that Brethren girl, and it seemed to me that I would be more open to change than she might be. I went through the trine immersion which was required for membership in the Philadelphia First Church of the Brethren where Dr. Ross Murphy was pastor. I was asked to sit with the deacons on the morning of the baptism, presumably to learn more about the Brethren. I sat silent with the deacons; they also sat silent, a most puzzling situation.

Gathering my courage, I asked, "Is someone going to tell me the difference between the Church of the Brethren and the Methodists?" Again, silence.

Finally, Rosa Trumbauer, a deaconess when all deacons seemed to be male, spoke up. "Well, Charles," she explained, "I think you should know that Brethren don't swear."

That was the difference? It wasn't until much later that I came to realize she was referring to the Brethren antipathy to taking oaths.

I liked Ross Murphy. He was a very dignified sort of person, a pastor well-tuned to the needs of his flock. Two of his repeated sayings have stayed with me. From time to time he would observe to the congregation, "You are good people."

I found it somewhat difficult to believe we deserved that commendation. The other was much more useful and amazingly accurate: "Where two people agree all the time, one of them isn't necessary." That from a deeply committed pacifist!

I became as active in the young adult group at First Church as my training schedule would allow. It was only a few months into my new denomination that Pastor Murphy approached me. He knew of my commitment to foreign mission service, and I rather think that he thought missionary men should be ministers. Making a surprise proposal, he asked,

"Charles, if the congregation would call you to the ministry, would you accept?"

He explained the Brethren pattern; in that era, more persons were "called" to the ministry by a congregation than "volunteered" for it. There would be a period of learning, experience, and personal testing which was called licensing, and sometime in the future could come ordination. It had long since become, and has always been, a part of my faith that when the church calls, one should hear the voice of God. I accepted. The congregation "called" me by secret ballot, and I was licensed.

Having returned by now to the base hospital at the Department for Mental and Nervous Diseases, I was a senior and, in times of nurse shortage, often a ward supervisor. I mentioned my licensing to only a few very close friends. Somehow, however, word got to Dr. Wright, chief of staff. He met me in the nursing office one day.

"I hear that you are a minister now, Mr. Bieber," he observed.

"Well, I have just begun and have a lot to learn," I demurred.

"I want to congratulate you," he said, "but I need to remind you that we do not want the patients to be disturbed by religious activities, efforts at conversion, and that sort of thing."

"I understand, sir, and I will not be approaching the patients with that kind of spiritual activity."

He seemed satisfied.

News does have a way of spreading. Some days later, on Tuesday before Thanksgiving, an air force officer, Captain Kwester, who was making almost no progress toward recovery from his depression, approached me, asking for a few moments of my time. As we sat together in his room, he said, "I have heard that you are a minister. Would you tell me what you believe and why?"

I would, although I had never actually formulated a personal faith statement. Faith in Jesus Christ had been instilled in me as a boy and re-born since. I made the stumbling effort. Doesn't the Bible say that the Holy Spirit will give us what we need to say? For an hour or more, I tried to explain my understanding of God, tried to answer his questions, tried to be honest about what was still missing (isn't there always something missing?). When I came on duty next morning, I heard someone in the bathroom singing, "Oh, what a beautiful morning..." It was the once depressed captain.

A little later, Dr. Wright made his rounds. When he came from the captain's room, he commented, "That man is so much better today I can hardly believe it. I am going to furlough him home for Thanksgiving." He did, and Captain Kwester's "cure" was so obvious that he was permanently discharged from the hospital. I do not know whether or not Dr. Wright knew of our long conversation; neither the doctor nor I ever mentioned it.

I think my favorite patient, however, was Mr. Moses, also a victim of depression who was head of a large pharmaceutical firm. He had entered the hospital with a reputation for repeated suicide attempts. He had made excellent progress and would soon be discharged. One day I was working the 3 to 11 shift, but with the shortage of staff there was no one to relieve me. I would work all night and cheerfully let my patients know they would have to put up with me for another eight hours. I was concerned when, early in the evening, I discovered that Mr. Moses was not playing games with the rest of the men. I peeked in his room, which was just across from the nursing station and, sure enough, he was asleep. Had he gone into depression again? Early to bed by one who has neither worked all day nor followed a busy schedule, tends to be a mark of depression. I decided to leave a note on his chart. Then, about 11:30, he came out of his room and to the office door.

"I went to bed early tonight," he explained. "I knew you were working an extra shift and it might be hard for you to stay awake, so I decided to spend some time with you and help you." What a thoughtful man! For the next couple of hours, both to keep me awake and to inform me, he described eight different ways in which he had attempted suicide. It would be good for me, he thought, to know some of the possibilities to watch for. Thank you, Mr. Moses!

Chapter Eleven

MARY BETH AGAIN! AND MARRIAGE!

Now, impatiently, I return to Mary Beth. It's all right; you may come along. During the two years after I left Juniata, we were together not nearly often enough. Her college schedule and my nursing schedule did not easily mesh, and we watched for times when we could spend hours, even short days, together. When she was at home during college break times, I could usually find time to take the train to Royersford or Spring City (two different railroads).

During the summer time when she was at home, Mary Beth could occasionally find a gap in my schedule so she could come to visit me. We exchanged letters—oh, how much of my time was spent in writing to her; the letters after our together times being partial reviews and partial anticipations of the next. Meanwhile, having exchanged my blood for an engagement ring, I was watching for the right moment to "propose."

As the time drew near for Mary Beth's graduation (and that of my brother who had transferred to Juniata from Dickinson Seminary), my thoughts began to come together. A traditional down-on-your-knees proposal did not seem apropos; we already knew we belonged together. I began to set the stage by dropping hints that maybe about Christmas after graduation 1943—she could expect a ring. Considering her friends at college, I struck on Dotty Pecht, daughter of a conservative Presbyterian minister, also expecting to be a missionary. I wanted to give Mary Beth her ring during graduation weekend, even though those would be full days. Would Dotty be able to arrange a party in a convenient campus location, unbeknownst to Mary Beth but inviting friends, perhaps on the pretext of a last party together? By correspondence, we explored possibilities. I was sure that the Highs would want to be involved somehow, so I wrote to Mrs. High, detailing my plans, asking her interest in making an engagement announcement, and other suggestions. Dotty was an excited co-conspirator. It was she who slyly learned Mary Beth's ring size and let me know. Mrs. High was pleased to have advance information and let me know when they would be on campus.

The time came. I was able to get Saturday, Sunday, and Monday off and by entraining Friday evening could reach Huntingdon late that night. Every time Mary Beth had free moments from the busy schedule of near graduates, we were together. In the times when we were apart, I was able to visit with some of my friends who were back on campus. Finally, Sunday evening came.

It would be our last time together at Juniata, so we decided that our walk would take us to the low bench at the water tower at Taylor Highlands where God had restored the warm relationship which had been interrupted, Moravian game time. We talked at length; didn't we always? The moment came when we knew we would have to get back to the campus for that last party with her friends. As always, we concluded our conversation with prayer, hands entwined. Mary Beth prayed first, then it was my turn.

As I came to the close of my prayer, I asked God, "Please bless us in the new relationship we are entering into," while I slipped the ring on her finger. The diamond was tiny; how much diamond can blood buy? But the love was measureless as was our happiness. We walked down the hill to the campus, entered the party, heard all the "Surprise! Surprise!" from those with whom Dotty had shared the news even before Mary Beth had it. Go ahead—cement your engagement in a hot air balloon or on the beach by the ocean or at the top of a Ferris wheel; we did ours in prayer by a water tower.

Mary Beth easily found a position, teaching fourth grade at the Lower Salford Township Elementary School in Harleysville, Pennsylvania. There she boarded with some old friends, the Nace family. Since she was only about thirty miles away, we could see each other more often, but my living in a hospital did not make it easier. I came to the opinion, surely not original with me, that there can't be anything much more difficult than an engaged couple being apart. Still, when my time off at the hospital would coincide with her weekends, and even on occasion with her living in Harleysville, I would find my way to her.

In my small way, I tried to be of help to her teaching. It was the practice in that school to give the fourth grade pupils the Otis Self-Adminstering Intelligence Test. As I have already said elsewhere, I liked examinations, so I corrected all those I.Q. tests in both years of her teaching.

I got to recognize the names of the bright kids and would recognize them years later.

When Mary Beth visited in Philadelphia, lodging was a real problem; where could she stay? Once we both stayed at the home of one of her college friends, but we offended the hostess by staying up long after the rest of the family had retired, just to talk. As a senior nursing student, I had a nice room rather apart from the rest, and with a separate entrance, so Mary Beth stayed there with me a couple of times. It was in violation of the rules (hopefully the statute of limitations will have run out by now), but otherwise, I assure you, it was quite innocent. I slept on the floor. Of course, it was embarrassing to be met as we walked in the early morning to the elevated station by nursing colleagues. Still, what they thought didn't matter that much; what God knew did.

There was another advantage of the location of my room. Thanks to the kindness of the dear, aging, short, stumpy Irish cook in our ward kitchen, Katie Hobden, I was able to obtain the necessary ingredients for waffles and jam or syrup to add to them. Using two electric plates and an antique Griswold waffle iron, I frequently invited friends in and we supplemented our regular meals with fresh waffles.

During college, Mary Beth had spent a weekend in my home in Williamsport, then an apartment at 832 Meade Street, and we had been able to visit my sister. Mae had married Charles Eckman, and they lived on East Third Street with their beautiful little daughter. (My poor sister, eventually the mother of two girls and a boy, had husband trouble. One might suppose that, sticking to family names, things would go well, but such was not to be the case. With a father George and brothers Charles and George, she married a Charles, nearly worthless, then a George, who badly mistreated her, and finally George, the good one. Alas, the good one died of liver cancer.) During the summer of 1943, we were also able to spend time with family again, and to enjoy the fun of a cabin along the Loyalsock Creek.

Confidently, because we knew it would take place, but tentatively, because we had to fit the date into my nursing schedule, we made plans for our wedding. Her parents had been married in February, mine in December, but ours had to be in June. My graduation would be in April, but my training would not end until September. Finally, we hit on June 24 as the date, Royersford Church of the Brethren to be the place, and Caleb Bucher, whom we both loved, to be the preacher.

Meanwhile, we discovered that my brother was also moving toward marriage. A tall, healthy young man who during his years at Juniata

College served as pastor to a Methodist charge of six small churches, he was very popular with the ladies. He managed to keep relationships so warm that three different women expected to be his wife. There was also a fourth, an admirer from greater distance, a young woman in his pastorate at Clearville. It was Peggy Work who finally won out, and their wedding took place just four weeks before ours was scheduled. I was his best man. (Mary Beth, with tremendous insight and perhaps a small prejudice, insisted that I was THE best man.)

The day of our wedding approached. Announcements were made, invitations sent out, showers (hen parties, of course) were enjoyed, and gifts began to come in. With some difficulty, I worked out my schedule: with the weekend, I was able to get sixteen days off. Sister Martha would be Mary Beth's maid of honor and Brother George my best man. Nursing school classmates, Bill Seibert and Oscar Luther, would be ushers, and my pretty, seven-year-old niece, Elizabeth Eckman, our flower girl.

The day before the wedding, I was still on duty. I took the train to Royersford in time for the rehearsal and stayed until the last train back. With so many guests, there was no place for me to stay and besides I dared not see the bride until she appeared at the church, so I was back at Pennsylvania Hospital. As seems always to be the case, the women at the wedding were much better dressed. Mother High, widely known as a dressmaker, made the beautiful gown beautiful Mary Beth wore as well as that of sister Martha. As for me, I didn't even own a dark suit. George and I both had a classy pair of white flannel trousers, relics of one of the floods in Williamsport, so we wore dark coats and white trousers. After the rehearsal I left mine across the street in a bedroom of William and Verna Price, where I would be dressing.

Saturday morning, we three nurses rode the train to Royersford and walked up the hill toward the church. It occurred to me that my brother might not have an appropriate tie, so I stopped in a haberdashery and purchased him a plain, dark blue one. I went to the Price house to dress, and found that my trousers had been nicely pressed by Lucille Heckman, a visiting friend of Mrs. Price who would later be a missionary colleague. I met the men at the church, and George and I paced—or at least, I paced— the small Sunday School room from which we would enter. The church was full. The Highs were fondly respected members of the congregation, and there were many friends and relatives as well. There were, we were told later, 200 there, and some could not find seats but stood in the rear.

While we waited, Mrs. (Verna) Price played the organ. Dottie Leiter sang, "Because" and, together with Catherine Hagerman and Ruth Hopewell, "O Promise Me" and "Oh, Jesus, We Have Promised." At last, the wedding march sounded, and we entered, and I impatiently awaited my bride.

A true vision of loveliness and with a smile on her face, she came down the aisle on her father's arm. Almost under her breath, she said to Pastor Bucher, "Well, I made it!"

The actual spot of our wedding may have caused nervousness in one way. We were standing on the wide register through which, in colder times, heat flowed to the room; a dropped ring would have been lost. But gently led by Caleb Bucher and following a slightly-adapted Presbyterian ceremony, we exchanged our vows.

"Will you?"

"I will."

"Do you?"

"I do." I placed the ring on Mary Beth's finger.

"This ring I give you in token and pledge of our constant faith and abiding love."

She presented me with a New Testament. "This Testament I give you in token and pledge of our constant faith and abiding love."

We kissed (no, junior, that wasn't the very first time). Caleb pronounced us husband and wife, and 200 people knew what we had known for many months: WE ARE ONE! We appreciated Caleb's ministry so much that for the rest of his life, Mary Beth wrote to him or called him each year on our anniversary to thank him for our wedding.

The wedding was at three o'clock. With greetings and congratulations, pictures, and the reception which followed, it became quite late. We had anticipated the lateness, so we had reserved a room at Raybert's Inn in Phoenixville. It was there we spent our first night together, husband and wife in the sight of God and humanity. Next morning we drove to Lewisburg for a day of reunion with the Biebers, then motored our way to our honeymoon castle, a small cabin on the banks of the Loyalsock Creek, southeast of Williamsport.

There were six days of sheer happiness, cooking, eating, walking, swimming, boating, playing, loving. One day I wrote what would become one of the better known of the low-grade (doggerel) but filled-with-love poems I have written for Mary Beth:

We're here in the woods away from the pipples,
And old Loyalsock is full of small ripples,
While getting dinner is my wife,
Who is the great joy of my life.

The kingfisher swoops low into the stream
And I'm so happy; it's just a dream,
For in that kitchen is my mate!
Oboy, oboy, it sure is great!

The sky is pretty blue and white;
My spirits are so gay and light.
For Mary Beth is now my Mrs.
Oh, my dear, what happiness this is.

I hear her scraping at the pans
With skillful twists of those white hands.
Well, there's at least a roof above her!
Oh gee, oh gosh, how I do love her!

Around us now the gentle breezes
Make soft music through the treezes,
And in there is my better half,
While I write poems to make her laugh.

(In case you want to use it, it isn't copyrighted.)

Our woodland sojourn ended—and in spite of our happiness, with poems like that, maybe it is just as well it ended—we headed to Lewisburg again, where we could visit with my parents, who had finally left Williamsport. I could show off my bride to my relatives. From there we drove to Washington to visit Aunt Mary and some of our nation's shrines. Those two weeks were the beginning of our honeymoon; it hasn't ended yet.

Because I had three months of training left, and then a position awaiting me as a supervisor in our hospital, it was essential that we live in Philadelphia. We found a palatial apartment about two blocks from the hospital at 4412 Chestnut Street. Well, to be completely honest, it wasn't that palatial. There were two rooms, a living-dining room and a bedroom stretched end to end to the bathroom, a kitchen which had been built into a 4x8 closet, and the essential furniture. It was worth every bit of the $50 monthly rent. I wasn't earning anything beyond the $7.50 monthly allowance given to all male students, but we lived on Mary Beth's savings, and then on our combined earnings. Mary Beth had a ride by elevated to the end of the line, a ride on Norristown-Western to the end of that line, and a car ride to Harleysville with a fellow teacher.

We lived only thirty miles from Spring City so, from time to time, Mother and Dad High and Martha came calling. Invariably, Dad High would place two large paper bags of groceries on our kitchen table. I never told him how that annoyed me. To me, it felt as if he were thinking he had to take care of his daughter, who had married this bloke unable to provide properly for her. I pouted after they went home, until one day when Mary Beth challenged my pout. When I admitted my problem, she explained that her dad was always giving things to people like that.

But Mary Beth is definitely a country girl. She never complained, but it was clear that she did not like the city at all. The city became worse when her fertility came to light. Along about October she began experiencing morning sickness, though in our naiveté we did not know it to be such. We visited a doctor who was a member of the Philadelphia First Church, and he kindly advised us we would be needing an obstetrician.

Daily Mary Beth would awaken nauseated. I would walk her to the el station, where she spit up. She would take the el to the end of the line, go the ladies' room, and spit up. She would ride to Norristown and visit the ladies' room before her auto ride, but by then the nausea was pretty well under control and she could manage her class. I think it was about March that her pregnancy (sorry, Mom, I do know what that word means, after all) reached the place where she was asked to resign. In those days, pregnant women and elementary school children did not go together. I left my job at Pennsylvania Hospital and we moved to Spring City, hoping that the rented side of the High house would soon become available. Meanwhile, they took us in.

I quickly found a job at the Valley Forge General Hospital, a military hospital specializing in care of the blinded, crippled, and neuropsychiatric patients, so we were still solvent. A year or so later they dismissed all civilian employees, and I found employment in the hospital of Pennhurst State School. Without the verbal cover-up of modern euphemism, it was simply a school for the feebleminded. Our patients included living beings in cribs, whose ages were known to be twenty-five or more, but who were completely unable to care for themselves and completely unaware, I am sure, of anything. They were alive, but they were not human—not in the sense of life which Jesus used. Seeds of perception planted in me then are probably partly to blame for my conviction that abortion is sometimes right.

We also had patients whose brain deficiencies affected certain of their body functions, such as the lad whose regular temperature was 103.4. We finally determined that was normal for him. And many of the "kids," aged ten to fifty, were really likable.

June came. It was a hot June. Our bedroom was sometimes stifling. On the night of June 23, it was so warm that we moved our mattress to the floor near the window to get all the air we could. Around one o'clock, Mary Beth awakened me. She was having severe pains, mostly in her back, and I blamed it for a moment on the not-so-comfortable sleeping arrangement. Then, remembering that she was a couple of weeks overdue, we recognized labor pains. I bundled her in the car and took her to Phoenixville Hospital. Now watch this:

While the night superintendent was going through admission procedures at the front desk, I told her, "I'll sit over here while you admit her. Then let me know so I can come with her." Remember, this was in 1945, when fathers were unwelcome in delivery rooms.

"You are not coming with her," firmly pronounced the superintendent.

"Yes, I am," I asserted, boldly. "I am a nurse and I expect to assist in the delivery,"

"Oh, no, you're not," she averred, again firmly.

"Ma'am," I politely reminded her, "I am just as much a nurse as you are. There is no reason I should not be there."

"We simply can't allow that," she asserted.

I aimed the big gun. "Look, if the doctor doesn't object, why should you?" (although I had not thought to discuss it with Dr. Gotwals, who had delivered Mary Beth twenty-two years earlier).

"Doesn't the doctor care?" the super reluctantly asked.

"Call him and ask," I proposed.

That beset lady wasn't about to call the doctor until labor pains were more frequent, and she yielded, gracefully. "Oh, all right."

When we arrived in the delivery waiting room and Mary Beth was in bed, the nurses asked me to go ahead and catheterize her. I had catheterized many a male and she was the first and only female, but it was a successful procedure. Eventually, we wheeled her into the delivery room. Dr. Gotwals strode in, saw that strange man, recognized who it was, and said not a word. He delivered a six-pound thirteen-ounce BOY. Delivery over, umbilical cord gone, and mother lying at rest, the doctor completed his examination of the boy, and said, "You have a fine baby boy!"

"Well, that's the first one," blurted the new mother.

"Now that's a new one," said the doctor. "Usually the mother says, 'Well, that's the last one!'"

Mary Beth resting now, I started home with the news of the arrival of Larien George. I had not left Phoenixville before tears of joy, relief, and thanksgiving poured out and I could not see to drive. I stopped at a phone booth and made the announcement to Highs and Biebers. There was an interesting personal sequel to my involvement in the delivery. Early that evening I received a phone call.

"I'm calling from the Phoenixville Hospital," said a lady's voice. "We desperately need an obstetrical nurse. Can you come in?" I regretted that I was already employed elsewhere and could not oblige. I have never known whether it was a bona fide call.

Now, with our new son, we were able to move into the rental part of the High residence. It was just the right size for our family. And, too, now came to life a love for gardening that I inherited from my dad. (Remember—way back then, I wanted garden tools so I could work with him.) I hand-dug—no, actually, I spade-dug—the plot in our backyard. Before gardening season, I had cleaned out the no longer used chick pens at Highs, bringing over several wheelbarrow loads of chicken manure and spreading it over our garden. What I remember best that season are the radishes. They grew to the size of a softball, but still stayed crisp and mild. I remembered how fond my brother was of radishes, so I packed a small box full and sent them to him in New York State.

While we were in Philadelphia, Ross Murphy had given me some preaching experience by sending me on occasion to a central city mission. The forlorn men there were required to attend services in return for supper, overnight, and breakfast. It was obvious to me, as a righteous young preacher, that these men were sinners, so I kept telling them they were on the road to hell. As I studied the New Testament more carefully, however, it came to me, as Pastor McCloskey had taught me in my youth, that the gospel of Jesus is a gospel of love. Hell is real enough, but hell is not what Jesus came about. My preaching changed, then and ever after.

When we moved to Spring City, I transferred my membership to the Royersford Church of the Brethren. Caleb was good not only at marrying couples, though he himself never married, but he also had a genuine love of people. Teacher of an elementary school in Lancaster, he served our church on weekends. He would eventually complete twenty years of teaching, retire, go to Millersville University for his doctorate, and become a college professor. An elementary school in Lancaster has since been named for him. Because of his love for people, he made time for a regular correspondence with all the youth from our church who were in the armed forces. As for me, he recognized my need for practice and training in the ministry, and would frequently find ways to involve me. One such involvement, very special to me, was to take his place in the community Good Friday services. Various pastors were speaking on the seven last words of Jesus from the cross, and I was to speak on, "I thirst." I proposed that Jesus' thirst included a longing for people. I have since come to believe that, although Jesus dearly loved people and longed for them to know his love, his thirst on the cross was purely physical.

Chapter Twelve

BETHANY SEMINARY; NURSING IN CHICAGO

Ordination in the Church of the Brethren at that time did not require the educational preparation for ministry common to most denominations. One's call, one's commitment to Christ, and one's (often briefly) demonstrated abilities were observed and evaluated by the congregation and the district Elders Body. In more recent times, such other qualifications as education and types of service have been added, but for that day, congregation and elders considered me qualified. I was ordained in a meaningful service at the Royersford Church of the Brethren, with Caleb Bucher; my former pastor, Ross Murphy, and Benjamin Waltz, chairman of the Elders Body, participating.

As an ordained minister, I had "authority" not only for preaching and visiting, but also for baptizing, marrying, conducting funerals, and all other ministerial services. It seemed important to me that, although it was not required, I attend Bethany Biblical Seminary in Chicago to enable me to be a better minister of Jesus. Mary Beth and I prayed and thought and sought Caleb's advice. I enrolled at Bethany in the fall of 1946. For reasons I do not now recall, we were unable to enter until after Thanksgiving, but were still accepted. Even late, I took the full seminary schedule, adding a twelve credit-hour correspondence course on the Pauline Epistles in order to catch up with the class.

I also needed a job. Not only were there living and seminary expenses, there was also that debt to Aunt Mary to be repaid. I applied for a nursing position at Chicago State Hospital, nearly an hour away. On my applying, I was temporarily, conditionally, accepted. I was asked to report early next evening for the necessary interviews. Then occurred one of the many times in my life that God has taken charge. The psychologist handed me the Otis Self-Administering Intelligence Test, the same test which I had corrected sixty or more papers for Mary Beth's fourth grade pupils.

"Er, Sir," I very mildly remonstrated, "I am familiar with that test."

"Won't make a particle of difference," he claimed. In thirty minutes I had finished the hour-long examination and returned it to him.

"Are there any more tests?" I asked.

"You aren't finished already!" he exclaimed.

"Well, yes. As I mentioned, I was familiar with that exam."

The next morning, the Directress of Nursing, Miss Perkins, stopped me as I was going off duty. "We would like you to work for us, Mr. Bieber. We can pay you $200 per month."

I was disappointed. "I'm sorry. I can't work for that."

"How much could you work for?"

I thought a moment. "I could work for $250 a month."

"But that is what we pay supervisors."

Experience at the army hospital and the state school had made me familiar with the so-many-spots-per-budget-category system, so I did not delay my reply. "I would not mind being a supervisor."

"But we don't have an opening for a supervisor. Well, I'll see what I can do. Come in tonight and I'll see you tomorrow morning."

The hospital need for a man nurse combined with my obviously high (skewed) results on the intelligence test, stood me in good stead. When we met the next morning, she said, "Well, Mr. Bieber, we'll pay you $250, but as a floor nurse."

I enjoyed my work at Chicago State. I was blessed to have as my supervisor Mrs. Minerva Maas, an elderly woman with a Danish accent, with whom I fell in love. The job was not easy; with three nursing attendants I had a ward of 200 men, about a third of them bedfast. A few of the ambulatory patients gave help so we were able to manage.

One incident merits telling. When I came on duty one evening, the supervisor reported, "You will have a big job tonight. Body lice were discovered on three of the men, and Miss Perkins wants all of the men treated. The lotion arrived only a few moments ago, so we were not able to proceed." I reluctantly accepted responsibility. When the usual evening activities had settled down, I went to examine the three "guilty" patients. I could find no lice. I did find tiny specks of dried skin, common to the dry skin of older people, and I immediately concluded that the tiny specks had been mistaken for louse eggs, or nits. In the morning, Miss Perkins came in.

"How did the delousing go?" she wondered.

"We did not do it. There were no lice. Let me show you," my explanation tumbled out. When she examined the suspected men, she realized I was right. All that good lotion, as well as the hospital reputation, was saved.

Bethany Seminary expanded and increased my faith. Even as I had become aware in Philadelphia that the gospel is not about hell but about love, so I discovered that the Bible is much more inclusive than I had ever realized. In a sense I had put God in a box of my own construction. The box was far too small. God is too big to be boxed in. My class in the life of Jesus came at 8:00 a.m., when I was weary from a night of work. Warren Slabaugh's voice was soft and rather monotonous, and I consistently fell asleep. One morning I came to class fresh after a night off duty. What Slabaugh was teaching was so moving and so meaningful that I never again went to sleep in his class.

Floyd Mallott gave new understanding to the Old Testament, making use of insights gained in Nigeria culture, and brought exciting life to church history. Chalmer Faw not only opened the New Testament to us, but also taught us how to bring our insights into Biblical passages, and into sermon outlines with current meanings. David Wieand helped to develop our prayer life and improve our spiritual health. Jesse Ziegler lifted out those psychological concepts which would be of most help in pastoral counseling. Bill Beahm worked hard at helping us to understand the basic concepts of the Christian faith, their source and validity, and those of the Church of the Brethren.

President Rufus Bowman introduced us to the essentials of church administration and, along with Al Brightbill, taught us worship planning and sermon preparation and delivery. All this, of course, took three years plus a summer practicum.

In late May 1947, first year over, I resigned from Chicago State (the job would be open in the fall) and we returned to Spring City. For the next few months, until we returned to Bethany, I worked again at Pennhurst, participating in a mumps research project of Ford Foundation, which turned out to be futile since the kids just did not react like normal kids.

Meanwhile, Mary Beth was still fertile. On July 21, Dale Ernest, assisted by some hefty pushing by his mother, made his appearance, all nine pounds, three ounces of him. There were no questions about my participation in the delivery; from the beginning it was understood that I was to be present with Mary Beth for Dale's triumphal entry. Baby Dale quickly replaced the kittens and Grandpa High's collie, "Friend" in brother Larry's affections. Once again, I gardened and assumed a considerable portion of Caleb's pastoral duties out of his desire for me to have guided experiences.

When we returned to Bethany, I was ready to return to Chicago State Hospital. I learned, however, that there might be an opening at Cook County Hospital. It was much closer—about twenty minutes by bus—the pay was a little better, and I would be doing actual psychiatric nursing rather than simply giving custodial care to old men. I would be working the night shift and, as had been my practice at CSH, I hoped to do some study at night. I shared that hope with the directress of nursing, and she saw no problem with it.

"Just so you won't neglect the patients," she responded.

Again, the need for a qualified man nurse was obvious. I did all the writing which a government institution required, and I made it a personal point to be the first to respond to even the smallest emergency.

My "study when free" understanding led to one interesting confrontation. There were student nurses with us, and one morning about five o'clock, their director of instruction came by unannounced to check on them. The ward was quite quiet, and I was studying at the desk. I had pulled out the bottom drawer and had my feet on it. The well-intentioned lady walked into the office with an opening salvo: "That is certainly a fine way for a nurse to be sitting."

I threw up the bullet-proof vest: "Well, ma'am, it would not be an appropriate way for some nurses to sit," referring of course to the lady nurses in that era when slacks had not yet been introduced as appropriate uniform.

"I shall see that this is reported," she fired back.

Just before I went off duty, Miss Skorupa, night supervisor, called me. "Oh, Mr. Bieber," she worried, "were you reading on duty?"

"I was, but do not be concerned; it is a part of my understanding with the directress."

"Oh, I hope so," she signed off.

When I came in that evening, Miss Skorupa met me with a big smile on her face. The directress assured her that I was within my rights, especially since the patients were being well attended.

Some of the patients at Cook County were there for regular treatment. Some were there for temporary treatment while they were being prepared for transfer to a state hospital. Some were drying out from drug/alcohol addiction. Some had been violent in some way and were court assigned and police delivered. Most of the attendants lacked the sensitivity and the understanding that had been drilled into us as nurses. In one sense, they feared the patients; in another they reacted to the most minor of affronts or attacks with a need for vengeance. Some of the attendants were at odds with me because of what they saw as my soft heart, and what I saw as the awareness that our patients were sick.

Late one night, as I was writing charts in the nursing office, I heard a shout from the dormitory with twenty men in it. Not wanting all the men to be aroused, I rushed in. One man, in the throes of delirium tremens ("d.t.'s") from his alcoholism, was standing on his bed, screaming, "They're coming after me!"

I seized his legs, thinking to upset him and then take him to one of the four seclusion rooms. He began to swing at me, then stopped. "Take your glasses off," he advised. "I can't hit a man with glasses on."

I laid my glasses under the bed, but by then the attendants, who had been sitting at the very door of the room, had arrived, and we had control. Next night I released him from his seclusion to the dismay and even anger of the attendants. He turned out to be one of our most important helpers with other patients during the remainder of his stay.

One night soon after, I was told of an episode with—I'll call him Mike—a Puerto Rican. I was already convinced that his problem was less a violent illness than angry frustration at difficulty with the language barrier. Meals for secluded patients were to be delivered by two persons who would remain with the patient during the meal. Then they would take the tray and ALL utensils. For some reason, a spoon had been left with Mike. He had taken the spoon, kept rubbing its handle against his bed until he had transformed it into a short dagger with the bowl as its handle. Before the evening meal, one of the student nurses was shown the dagger.

"You come, you get this," or something similar, he shouted. No one, but no one, would go into his room. He got no supper. That was the story I heard. As morning neared, I considered: information doesn't always filter to all the staff on the floor. Quite possibly, a young (female) student nurse could, unknowingly, take his breakfast in, and meet serious injury. There was nothing else but to obtain the "dagger." My once violent alcoholic friend, he of the "d.t.'s," called through Mike's window in Spanish, I think to assure him we were all right. As I stood at the door with two attendants behind me, he shouted, holding the dagger up,

"You get this." I opened the door, went cautiously in, and Mike, true to his promise, handed me the dagger.

It was midway through the first semester of that second year, I think, when Dean William Beahm asked me to stop by his office. He had been a missionary in Nigeria some years earlier. It was common knowledge that we hoped to serve there, so I anticipated some Nigeria talk. He had another agenda. After our greetings and small talk, he asked, "Bieber, how many hours are you working a week?"

"Forty hours on a regular basis," I confessed, not realizing it was a confession.

"Didn't you know that our seminary rules limit a student to twelve hours of work each week?"

I hadn't.

"What are we going to do about it?" he wondered.

I pondered. Of course, he wanted me to say that I would reduce my working hours. Still, we needed the money. It did not seem likely that I could cut to twelve hours at Cook County. Another job might not be quickly forthcoming. Besides, the long working hours did not seem to diminish my learning very much. Thence came my answer. I asked, "Have you looked at my report card?"

"I have," the dean admitted. "That's why I don't know what to do about it." He thought for a moment. Then he said, "I'll tell you what. As long as you keep your grades up, we'll let this go by."

I continued my schedule. Its three major drawbacks were these: We were depriving Mary Beth of much of the spouse portion of a seminary education. I had to find ways to make time with my family as intensely intimate as possible so we could remain close in spite of all the time we spent apart. And I simply did not get to know my classmates well outside the classroom. Still, I was glad to use my nursing skills under conditions that allowed me to do some studying. It was "reading on duty" that enabled me to double the outside reading assignments for church history. And, that second year, we were able to repay my patient Aunt Mary what she had so helpfully lent me seven years earlier.

Chapter Thirteen

PASTORAL SERVICE

Near the end of the second semester, I was again asked by Dean William Beahm to drop by his office. Why? My grades were still up. This time, maybe Nigeria. He had his own agenda. One of the requirements for graduation was an approved period of practical work, which was often a summer pastorate.

"It is time for your summer pastoral assignment," he began. "We would like you to go to the Mount Pleasant Church in Pennsylvania." I am sure that he reviewed for me the reasons the congregation was seeking a summer pastor. I am also quite certain that he reviewed with me the expectations and requirements of the summer—ten weeks of service with regular weekly reports to the seminary. Then he commented, "I want to make clear to you that this is a church with some serious problems. We are asking you to go there less because you are a seminary student than because you are a psychiatric nurse." What an introduction that was to my first pastorate except for limited assistance to Caleb Bucher. And as we will see, what an accurate one.

I wrote to the address of the person at the church whose name had been given me as the contact person. I think it was Scott Niederheiser. I let him know the day and the approximate hour we would be arriving at the parsonage, next door to and adjoining the church. I resigned from Cook County, with an assurance from them that my job would be open in the fall. We packed our belongings and the few important books I wanted to have with me and our two boys, and we took off.

We arrived at the parsonage about two hours later than we had predicted, at about eight in the evening. A short, stocky man with graying hair came to the door. When he saw us, he said, "You must be the Biebers. I am the pastor here."

"Oh," I impolitely responded. "I thought I was the pastor."

"Of course," he stammered. "I mean I was the pastor here. I have been the pastor here for ten years. When I explained to the committee that

I didn't have any place to go, they accepted my suggestion that Rose and I (names changed) live in the back half of the parsonage, and you and your family in the front." It was a sizable parsonage. There was a bedroom, study, and bathroom in the back half, with an enclosed stairway from the first floor kitchen and dining room. The front half included two bedrooms and bath on the second floor, with an open stairway leading up from the large living room. We would have to go down the steps to the church kitchen for our meals, and for play space for the boys. I would have to use the church library for my studying. Worse, how was I to bring some reconciliation to this congregation split by problems centering on a pastor who was still present? I knew, I was to trust in God that all things are possible, but . . .

The summer began. We had few contacts with Rose and O.T. Baut, except for the contacts provided by numerous anecdotes. It was not unusual for O.T. to wander through the church and drop by the library for a few (unwelcome) moments. Once he noticed my notes lying on my desk, casually picked them up and, glancing at them, exclaimed, "This is good stuff. Mind if I make use of it?"

Kitchen arrangements were very inconvenient, but the basement was a good place for the boys to play. (There wasn't any place in our half of the house.)

On my first trip to a nearby gas station, the attendant asked, "Aren't you new here?"

I explained that I was the new pastor of the Church of the Brethren. When he came to the car window and told me my bill, he sort of stepped back and waited. "Something wrong?" I wondered.

"Well, no. I was just waiting for you to ask for a clergy discount like that other guy always did."

Do you begin to catch the mood of early summer?

There were 400 members on the Mount Pleasant roll, and I determined to meet as many of them as possible. I began to make calls, and I began to hear stories. There was the plump, pleasant widow of many years who was very proud of her grape arbor. She wished it were fall, so she could give us some grapes. She told me of the time she had picked a whole basket of grapes and presented them to O.T. when he called. "He thanked me, and then he commented, 'Rose hasn't been feeling well lately, and is not able to do much in the kitchen. And we do use a lot of grape juice. I can bring you the jars. Would you mind?' So I made the grape juice for them," she concluded.

Another member, no longer active, told me of the night about eleven o'clock, when O.T. and a visiting evangelist rang her doorbell. A fire had broken out in a house four or five away, and there was a great deal of noise and commotion. The lady opened her upstairs window and shouted down, "I won't be answering the door. I've gone to bed."

"Oh, well, then we'll just pray for you from here," the shout came back, and O.T. proceeded to do so, in spite of the competition of passersby and a fire hose being stretched out along the sidewalk. And, of course, God always hears prayers. (But was that one?)

There was the episode of the enlarged stairway, described for me by Ben Black, grizzled, gray-haired deacon and retired carpenter who had kept an official eye on things while the parsonage was under construction. The congregation had approved the plans for the parsonage, including specifications for the back stairway the size it needed to be to maintain room sizes. When Ben was visiting the site one day, he noticed that the studs, the upright lumber to which treads and risers would be nailed, were out of plumb—not straight up and down. He called it to the attention of the carpenter who was at work there.

"I noticed it when I came in this morning," regretted the carpenter. "You know, that pastor of yours wanted the stairway to be wider, so I think he moved those studs to be wider, but only at the bottom."

"What are you going to do," asked Ben.

"Well," predicted the artisan, "he usually comes by after lunch, so why don't you wait and see." True to the prediction, O.T. was soon there.

Picking up his hand axe, the carpenter accused, "you are the one who knocked those studs out of plumb."

"I certainly did," boasted O. T. "A fellow needs space when he is using the stairs."

"Specifications call for them to be as they were set up," reminded the carpenter. "Now," brandishing his hand axe, "you can just proceed to put them back where they belong."

And O.T. did.

And then there was the incident in the home of the congregation's elder, the Rev. Galen Blough of Somerset (correct name). Blough had been named elder by the district mission board, which was subsidizing the Mount Pleasant program. A great many complaints about O.T. had reached Blough, and he had reviewed the pastor's career, so he was well-informed.

Late one evening, O.T. came calling. The sum of his presentation to Blough was that, although he was aware that a number of complaints had been raised, they were all brought by recalcitrant members of the church and had no basis in fact. Blough knew better, having gone into many of the matters in depth. As a result, the latening evening was essentially a verbal sparring match. Near midnight, Blough was very weary. He called the meeting to a close, saying, "It is clear that we are not going to agree on much of what we are discussing. I am afraid we will only grow angry at each other. I need to go to bed now, so you can go home."

"We must pray first," claimed O.T.

"Now, O.T., you know that neither one of us is in the mood for prayer," demurred Blough. "You go home and do your praying and I will take care of my prayers a little later."

As Blough left the room, O.T. knelt, remarking, "Maybe you aren't going to pray, but I am." He began, "God, I don't know why these things have happened. You know I never had any trouble like this before."

Turning back to the room, Blough reminded, "Why are you telling God that, O.T.? Both you and God know better. Remember . . ." and he named some of the other places where O.T. had experienced difficulty.

And of course you'll want to hear the episode of the out-of-place church seal. The church had a bank loan and, for some reason I don't understand, they needed the seal each time they would make a sizable payment and renegotiate the loan. The seal was kept by the secretary of the trustees, who for most of the ten years of O.T.'s tenure had been a good friend and admirer. Something happened—I never learned what—which drove a deep wedge between the two of them even leading to a near fist fight at council meeting. Fred Burns, the secretary, resigned his post, but kept the seal, remarking, "That preacher might use it to steal money from the church."

The Rev. Galen Blough was present one summer evening for a council meeting. The business went reasonably well, but took a long time. About 11:30, the elder said, "Well, I guess that wraps things up."

But the current secretary of the trustees raised his hand. "You said you would see that I get the church seal. I don't have it yet."

The nonplused but determined elder said, "I'll go out to Fred's house and get it tonight. Who will go along?"

The flood of volunteers proved to be nonexistent. It did not seem fitting for him to go alone, so I agreed to go along. Surprisingly enough, Fred was sitting on the porch swing when we arrived. A half hour of vituperation ensued, Fred accusing O.T., Blough accusing Fred and offering to have the sheriff out.

I did not enter into the conversation more than a somewhat untrue, "Good evening, Fred. Pleased to meet you."

Fred absolutely refused to give up the seal, even with the threat of the sheriff. We went back to the parsonage. As I got out of Blough's car and he pulled away, Mary Beth called from the door. "You are wanted on the phone."

It was Fred. "That elder wasn't very nice. But you were all right. I will see that you get the seal before you leave Mount Pleasant." Silence must, indeed, be golden. Two days before I left town, I called Fred, reminded him of his promise, went to his home, and received the seal.

I must share one more sad episode. One evening as we came over from the evening worship service, I saw O.T. at the top of "our" steps. This conversation followed: "Can we talk for a few moments?"

"Sure. Come on down."

"I was pastor of this church for ten years, and I really have them in my heart. You have been here for a month now and have had a chance to study the congregation. I want to know what I can do that will be most helpful to the congregation."

I was so overwhelmed with the stories I had heard, and with his unwitting intrusion into my efforts to bring reconciliation and prepare the congregation for a regular pastor, that I simply could not hold back.

"LEAVE!" I cried. "Tonight! Last night, if possible!"

He broke into tears. "You could say that. You could go home to your mother. But my mother is dead. Where could I go?"

Obviously there was some place he could go, for he and Rose moved out the very next morning. I heard later that he had become pastor in another denomination, about twenty-five miles away. For about five years, things had gone well in his Mount Pleasant pastorate, then, sadly, things began to fall apart. Even so, many of the members still loved him.

There were good things that happened while we were there. Attendance was good at morning and evening services and fair at mid-week prayer meeting. I had excellent practice not only at reconciliation, but also at administration and the preparing and delivery of sermons. One Sunday morning I sang, "In the Garden" to accompany a teenage lass who was taking ballet lessons, while she performed on the stage—this long before controversial "interpretive movement" became a part of some worship services. A few times, when no pianist appeared at an evening service, I picked out the hymn tune (melody only) to accompany the singing.

One faithful member was concerned about her sixty-six-year-old brother and eighty-seven-year-old mother, neither of whom had ever accepted Christ as their Savior. When I visited them, the brother, wondering why no one else had ever invited him, bowed down and accepted Christ as his own Savior. His mother made no special comment. We set an evening for his baptism, the first that I would perform, which would take place in the indoor baptistry at the church. He was diabetic, and two toes on one foot were painfully gangrenous. I got to thinking how painful it could be for those toes to bounce even lightly against the hard bottom of the baptistry. I obtained a small sofa cushion and pushed it to the bottom of the baptistry. It came zooming up, several inches above the surface. Feathers do not easily absorb moisture. To keep it down, I kept one foot on it. His hefty, three hundred pound son handed him down the steps to me. Stretching, I could fairly easily receive him, and we proceeded with the rite. Afterward, again doing the split, I handed him up the steps to his son, but my foot slipped off the pillow. Feathers or not, it had absorbed enough moisture so that it rose slowly only to the surface and did not enter the sight of the congregation. Immediately afterwards, his mother came forward. "Do me, too," she asked, so after some conversation and instruction and a confession of faith, I baptized her as well.

Visitation continued. I tried hard to get into homes of persons whose names were on the rolls but did not seem to be attending. I met many who wondered why their names were still on the rolls. They had not attended for years; they had moved away; they had transferred, but their names were still there. In ten weeks, this young preacher who wanted to see the church grow, removed over one hundred names from the rolls and left certain that there were still others who had died, quit, or moved away. Still, we made friends there with whom we continued to have contact, thanks to Mary Beth's loving insistence on never leaving anyone go. When we returned to Bethany and the dean and I reviewed the reports he had received, the most negative criticism anyone had written was that my beard was too dark and I didn't get my hair cut often enough. A few days after we returned to Bethany to continue my (formal) education, the new pastor, a graduate of Bethany Bible School, had arrived at Mount Pleasant.

I was welcomed back at Cook County. They were desperate for male nurses, and I still qualified. I think it was in early October that I got another summons from the dean. A small congregation in South Central Indiana, near Lafayette, was looking for a part-time pastor. The dean thought I could meet their need. Once again Mary Beth and I considered what was involved. It would mean a train trip or, occasionally, a motor trip, of nearly 150 miles in either direction. Sermon preparation could relate to my studies, thus making them even more practical. The experience would be good, though not related directly to missionary service. The small additional income would help. We prayed for guidance. I talked with the directress of nursing, who neatly combined her understanding nature with their need for nurses. I could continue on their staff, working as many nights as I wanted to manage, just letting them know at the beginning of each week, what nights they would be. We felt led to the completely rural Fairview Church of the Brethren. Never having heard me preach and hardly even knowing me, they accepted me.

At Cook County, I would average four nights a week. I would go south on Friday evening, work with them all day Saturday and until late Sunday, and return to Chicago again. My illegal forty hours a week became more than fifty.

Occasionally Mary Beth and the boys traveled with me to Fairview, but only when I went by auto. More commonly, I would leave the car there, to be used for visitation rather than transportation. Train travel was not expensive; besides, it was more restful and I needed the rest. We liked it at Fairview. They had been served since 1948, along with the Pyrmont and Rossville churches, by a self-supported minister. Except for a summer pastor the preceding summer, also a Bethany student, I was their first pastor. Often Ken Hartman, weekend pastor at Lafayette, and I would travel together, sharing notes and experiences enroute. I would be met at the station by my host for the weekend, usually Fishers, but at times the Brookses or the Dunks.

There were several interesting differences to me about Fairview. One regular attender, fully accepted by the congregation, was a woman who had for years had been living, unwed, with a man. Another regular attender, indeed a Sunday School teacher, had never joined. He was a member of the Christian (Disciples) Church and was principal of the Monitor School. He asked me to deliver the baccalaureate sermon for the Monitor High School and I did, the only such sermon I have ever preached. Kindly, or perhaps because he was so grateful that I didn't completely bomb out, he never tired of telling me how well I had done. I used the left lung opener which I had practiced at Juniata, and after that it didn't matter much what else I said.

The church had students at Monitor and Buck High Schools, and when a Friday night basketball game took place between them, I sat with one school during the first half and the other during the second. Plain clothes, traditional Dunker style, was part of their (changing) tradition. It was with some difficulty that we were able to bring back one good woman who had been "churched" much earlier for wearing a hat. Plain dress required the women to wear a small gauze head covering known as a prayer veil, and in cold weather a bonnet. She still wore a hat. Baptisms had been in running streams, but they were moving toward the use of a farm tank indoors.

It was a tradition of the church to have at least one revival meeting each year. In Holy Week, 1949, I was both pastor and revivalist. Mary Beth was expecting, and I definitely wanted to be there, though Chicago may have been more stringent in anti-husband rules than Phoenixville was. I alerted Albert Harshbarger, my elder, that it might be necessary for me to hurry back to Chicago at any time, and he assured me that he would fill in. Holy Week, through Easter, proved not to be delivery time. One thing that was delivered that week was a lemon meringue pie. My least favorite pie, it was served to me fifteen times of the eighteen meals I ate out.

Albert Harshbarger's alert was not completely in vain. Very early on the Sunday morning after Easter, I was awakened by the news, via Everett and Margie Dunk, that Mary Beth was in labor at Bethany Hospital. They loaded me in their Buick. Everett drove the 140 miles in 150 minutes, and I reached the hospital just five minutes after the birth of our bonny lassie, Bonnie Ruth, April 24. I missed the delivery. (How could she manage without me?) But I was quickly with my dear wife. I walked the block home from the hospital, sat down to eat some breakfast, and mentioned how glad I was that I had arrived so quickly. Mother High was boy sitting, maternity sitting, and soon baby sitting.

After a time, a neighboring student's wife came in and asked how Mary Beth was getting along. "She is doing very well," I assured them. "Oh, I forgot to tell you. We have a beautiful baby daughter."

Chapter Fourteen

MISSIONARIES, BUT WHEN?

There was not a lot of time between Bonnie's arrival and commencement, but there was time to complete a tremendously important process. A year earlier, we had made formal application to the Foreign Missions Commission, Leland Brubaker, Executive, for service in Nigeria. Largely because Stover Kulp, pioneer missionary to Nigeria and then field secretary, was a cousin to Dad High, and also because we knew Roy and Violet Pfaltzgraff, at Bethany during their first furlough, and Professors Beahm, Mallott, and Faw had all served there, our longing was for Nigeria.

In our interview by the commission, we were told that there was a need for someone to go to India. We responded that we would go wherever God sent us, but that we were really looking toward Nigeria. We were notified that we were approved as missionaries, with assignment to be made later. A letter from Stover, working in Elgin during 1948 while on furlough, hoped we would get to Nigeria, but it was still uncertain. By spring of 1949, it was clear that we would be Nigerians, and we were notified that we would be duly consecrated in Annual Conference that June to be held at Ocean Grove, New Jersey.

Graduation time arrived on May 29. It was memorable for two reasons. Reason number one: Dad was there, as well as Mother and Dad High. A graduation tradition was the holding of a Love Feast on Saturday evening before the big day. It would be at the nearby Chicago First Church of the Brethren. Dad was a loyal Methodist and not familiar with the Brethren Love Feast, so I described for him the service of feetwashing, the fellowship meal, and the bread and cup communion. He desperately wanted to be with me during that event, but as he thought about it, he felt very uncomfortable about participating in the feetwashing. I assured him that it would be quite all right for him to be present without washing feet. A while afterward he came to Dad High and me and asked for our shoes. He shined them, with the keen insight that shining shoes is an excellent modern equivalent to the washing of feet. Having done that, he joined us in the service.

Reason number two: In spite of my heavy work schedule, I was graduated magna cum laude. I was not surprised, for I had earned or argued my way to A's in all my classes for those three years. What was very special, so much so that it brought tears to my eyes, was that Wilbur Hoover, who also was older than the rest of the class, and who also had begun his first year a bit late and was our best friend on campus, was also graduated magna cum laude. Then, saying goodbye to Bethany, we loaded up our family and headed east to await God's next plan for our lives.

As had been indicated to us, God's plan included our consecration, at Ocean Grove Annual Conference, as missionaries to Nigeria. There were nine of us—Charles and Rozella Lunkley, Dr. Paul and Patricia Petcher, and us for Nigeria; and Dr. Paul and Mary Elizabeth Hoover and Mabel Claypool for India. We were close as a group. Petchers and Hoovers had been at Penn Medical School together. Lunkleys had preceded us by a year at Bethany. Hoovers and Biebers were Juniata graduates. It was a very special day for the Brethren. The entire service was around the mission of Jesus to the world.

The congregation was "armed" with white handkerchiefs. The nine of us knelt on the platform; hands of Brethren leaders were laid on our heads and prayers of consecration were lifted to God on our behalf. As we rose and embraced each other, that great crowd of nearly 9,000 were waving their white handkerchiefs in what was known as the Chatauqua salute, and they were singing, "God Be With You." How could we help being sure that we were in the center of God's will? We were READY TO GO!

We had expected rather prompt travel plans, but no word came from the mission board about arrangements for our beginning work in Nigeria. After two or three weeks of waiting, I telephoned Leland Brubaker. Patiently, he expressed his surprise that we hadn't realized that we would not be going immediately. I was puzzled. Had we been consecrated to wait? I reminded Brother Brubaker that I had a family to support and asked his advice. The best thing to do, he suggested, would be to contact the regional secretary and ask if there was a pastoral position open. For how long? Well, until there is enough money to send you out. Could be six weeks, could be a year.

Deeply disappointed, I called Levi Ziegler, regional secretary. He sent me to three different churches. One was Springfield, Pennsylvnia;

one was Champion, Pennsylvania, and the other I have forgotten. In each instance the result was the same. I would be welcomed at the door. I would be told how glad they were to see me, because they really needed a pastor. I would share with them the uncertainty of our future. I would preach. They would thank me, pay me a small stipend, and regret that they believed they had better wait for a long-term pastor. I was puzzled: was it the uncertainty or the preaching? I also earned a little traveling with Wilma Stern Lewis to counsel at several summer camps. Until fall, nothing opened, and I was ready to seek a nursing job.

Then, out of the blue—well, actually out of the green of the Cornhusker State—came a telegram. It said, in effect, "We hear you need a pastorate Stop We need a pastor Stop Come on out Stop We will pay your moving expenses and provide a place for you to live Stop."

Within days, we had purchased a small trailer, loaded it with a few belongings that we felt we would need for—who knows?—six months or a year? We moved to the beautiful city of Lincoln, Nebraska, and I served the Lincoln Church of the Brethren. There were good leaders: spiritual, administrative, musical, and educational. The congregation had purchased ground in a suburb and were planning, sometime, to move. Before we left there, the congregation would approve plans for their new parsonage and have a service of groundbreaking. Again, our stay there leaves memories.

In those youthful days, I regularly wore a bright necktie when I was dressed up. Rhoda Nebelsick, who had sent the telegram that summoned us, approached me. Would I mind wearing a black tie? Well, there were two reasons, I told her, for my not wearing a black tie.

"For one thing, I don't think it makes any difference. I even pray in my pajamas. For another, I don't have a black tie."

"If I buy you one, will you wear it?"

I would. She did. I wore that fine nylon tie until I packed it for our trip to Nigeria. Years later, when I unpacked it, the black had faded to a pale maroon. How embarrassed Rhoda would have been! Her husband operated a "Twin Kiss" ice cream stand, from which we were frequently supplied.

So that Mary Beth could accompany me on calls—she has always been a better visitor than I—a kind widow volunteered to baby-sit for us. Rhoda's sister, Ada Buch, was a gem. Not only did she entertain, teach, and protect the two boys, but she also succeeded in toilet training Bonnie much more rapidly than we had succeeded with our boys. Are girls smarter? Maybe. We also came to love Rhoda's mother, Priscilla Kilhefner, who had moved to Nebraska from Pennsylvania. She was nearly ninety years old when we met her, and bedfast, tended by Rhoda. I was deeply impressed by her beautiful spirit and her constant uttering of praise and thanksgiving. Pain in her body, joy in her heart, and a smile on her face described her. Admittedly, I had met few elderly ladies while I was a Methodist, so probably the comparison is unfair, but I have come to believe that growing old gracefully in the grace of God is a part of Brethren genius.

New forms of pastoral service opened to me. The church owned a mimeograph which operated well, but no one knew how to use it. I had never used one, but I wanted a bulletin and a newsletter, so I learned how. I was my own secretary. We had morning and evening services, and prayer meeting. It was sometimes difficult to find a chorister for the evening service so I undertook the job one evening. After all, I had often watched Al Brightbill and others. It was just a matter of swinging one's arm in the proper tempo while we sang. The singing went all right, but the pianist observed afterward, "You really looked awkward up there." No more awkward I assure you, than I felt; that was the only time I attempted that difficult task.

Nebraska Brethren liked having a future missionary among them. We were invited to speak at several of the churches. We went to Enders, where good friend Wilbur Hoover was pastor, and met the Wine family, one of Nebraska's best. We met Berwyn Oltman and his girlfriend, who would be lifelong friends. We went to the small church at Octavia. We shared in the seventy-fifth anniversary of the South Beatrice Church, pastored by Lewis Naylor and with beloved Floyd Mallott as principal speaker.

Somehow, the Nebraska District came into possession of a sizable plot of ground, including a small lake left by a former gravel pit, and decided to build a camp there. At my suggestion and on the advice that "Schwarzenau" could well be interpreted as a pretty, wooded area, that became the name of the camp. Under the able direction of Lewis Naylor, several of us, Wilbur and I included, carefully dismantled a large, wooden store structure that was donated, trucked the very usable lumber to the camp site, and erected the first building. It was an all-purpose building to serve as kitchen, dining room, classroom, meeting room, and so on. I am not a carpenter, even though I did win honors in my junior high school woodworking class. Thanks to Naylor's patient tutelage, I learned how to saw a straight line, form square corners, and nail where he told me to. The completed building was quite serviceable.

Among the leaders in our Lincoln Church were a Methodist couple, Walter and Ora Westrom. Having come from West Virginia, they were very active in the church, but had never joined. Walter taught the adult Sunday School class and shared with me in prayer meeting leadership. By summertime, they had decided to join the Church of the Brethren and undergo the required trine immersion. We decided to make their baptism part of the dedication weekend at Camp Schwarzenau. Hearing of the plan, five persons from other congregations decided that it would be good to be baptized by a missionary. So on Sunday afternoon of dedication weekend, there were a fairly large number of people present from all around the state. We had our baptismal service. The first six underwent their immersion without incident, and Ora, a rather plump lady, was the last.

Having heard her vows and with her kneeling before me, I plunged her under the water once. She had not shared it with me, but she was seriously afraid of water. She jumped up and started toward shore. I caught her arm, stopped her, and talked quietly to her, assuring her that she would not drown and that she would be grateful of the full cleansing of three dips. She acceded. She knelt again. I immersed her again. She jumped up and started for shore again; I caught her again, talked to her again, convinced her again, and immersed her the third time. As she headed for shore, I stopped her and knelt with her as we prayed for God's consecration of this one whom Jesus had redeemed, and then prayed a benediction on the whole gathering. We never talked about it again, although we were often together. Walter became a minister and pastored churches in West Virginia.

I had noticed a gray-haired elder among the congregation and feared that he would embarrass me by some remark about my inept baptizing. But he waited until the crowd had dispersed, and then came up to me. "I noticed you had trouble with that one baptism," he said.

Wondering what would come next, I answered, "I sure did, Sam."

He asked, "Do you know what I do in a case like that?"

Of course, I didn't and admitted so. "I stand on their legs," he declared. It sounded practical enough, but I could not picture myself standing on Ora's legs, and I have never followed that sage advice from Sam Forney.

The end of August drew near, and we received word from the mission board that we were to set sail in November. With some regrets—parting is rarely the sweet sorrow that Shakespeare declared it to be—we left good friends and beloved people of Lincoln and headed back to

Spring City. Last sad thought: we never did get paid for our moving expenses. Last good thought: Mary Beth corresponded for years with the Eiseles, and their son served a term in Nigeria with his family.

Arriving in the east was not only a matter of unpacking our meager possessions and moving in with the Highs. There were unbelievable details to attend to: medical exams for each member of the family; a thousand (actually, only four or five, but it felt like a thousand) injections and vaccinations for each of us; passports to obtain in an era when passports were not being easily granted; financial records to be kept; friends and relatives in the east to be visited; purchases to be made of clothing which would fit our children as they grew for the next three years; decisions about just what paraphernalia should be shipped; and similar matters.

From a commercial bakery, we purchased steel drums with removable lids, which had held shortening and needed a very complete cleansing. All the breakable things we took with us, leaving prized wedding presents behind, were carefully packed in the drums, with padding on the outside, padding between layers, padding between items. We demolished and cut sized pieces from countless cardboard boxes. The word was that, although we would have gardens, foodstuffs were in uncertain supplies from stores 500 miles away. I packed 180 glass jars of canned foods so carefully that, even though one drum was dropped about ten feet in Lagos, only three jars broke. We used boxes bought from New Windsor for the packing of clothing, equipment, books, future Christmas gifts for the children—who knows what all? And what would we want to have with us during a sea journey of nearly four weeks and travel from Lagos to our mission station? Among other things, we would need a box carefully packed for us by a friend, full of dated packages to be opened each day of the journey. We were blessed to have the High barn floor on which to do our assembling of materials and our packing.

Meanwhile, we were speaking at every nearby opportunity about our expectations of working in Nigeria (very vague) and soliciting prayers. We were in constant correspondence with Leland Brubaker, missions executive in Elgin, Illinois. We were rarely without visitors in our home, sometimes to renew old friendships that had been interrupted by years at Bethany or Lincoln, sometimes to help pack, sometimes to bring us things they thought we might need, sometimes just to be friendly. As the date for our embarkation was made more firm, more slowly because we would be traveling on a freighter rather than a passenger boat, the desire to give us a good sendoff increased. A bus was chartered and filled with friends and relatives, mostly from the Vincent Mennonite Church, but also from nearby Brethren.

The sailing date was finally set: November 11, 1950. A truck from the Brethren Service Center, New Windsor, Maryland, delivered our far too many boxes and barrels to the wharf. We got there, too, but I simply don't remember how. I do remember that Mother and Dad High and Martha were there to see us off. We did not overcome all of our qualms about the long voyage. We knew that God would care for us, but how would we keep two very active boys and their nineteen-month-old sister both safe and occupied during a long voyage? What about seasickness? So susceptible to motion sickness was I that I got queasy from riding in a porch swing. How much of that might the children have inherited? We would have to trust in God.

We set sail—well, not exactly sail—the *African Glade* was diesel-powered. There were only eight passengers other than our family: a Dutch couple headed for Liberia and work with the Farrell Line; three Canadian priests of the White Fathers Missionary Order, heading for mission work in Ghana; Max Pierce, an excited young man about to begin his missionary career in Liberia; Al Shoucar, a Lebanese businessman; and one other man whom we rarely saw. All but the last, unnamed, enjoyed our children. Ruth Unver provided some woman companionship for Mary Beth. Max was a delightful companion to all of us, and offered to take Bonnie with him to Monrovia. Al was one of those fully extroverted men loaded with friendliness for everyone. The priests, though friendly enough, were most notable for their regularly circling the ship's decks.

A freighter is not designed to provide entertainment or play equipment for children. The crew did their best to remedy that. The ship's carpenter constructed a sturdy box about eight feet long, four feet wide, three feet deep. The crew covered it with a large tarpaulin to make it waterproof. They filled it with water and behold, the kids had a swimming pool. We had with us such toys and playthings as we had remembered, and we were further aided by the daily gift openings, thanks to Mildred Kulp. There were new toys, coloring books, and books to read. Mildred seemed to know what children like. The ship also had a variety of table games and each evening, sometimes repeated on the following day, a popular movie suitable for all of us.

It does seem, too, that ships make a special effort to ensure that passengers and crew are well fed. Our food was substantial, well prepared, and varied. Illustration: the menu for our first meal, supper on the *Glade*, included Radish Roses, Hearts of Celery, Hot Consomme, Grilled Minute Steaks with Mushroom Sauce, Ham a la King en crustades, Sauted Onions and Green Peppers, Mixed Vegetables, French Fried Potatoes, Assorted Cold Cuts and Potato Salad, Tomato and Cheese Salad with French Dressing, Ice Cream with Fudge Sauce, Cookies, Chilled Melons, Cream Cheese with Guava Jelly, Crackers, Coffee, and Tea. The seasickness qualms got sick and left, but not without leaving Larry with several bouts of queasiness, and not without taking advantage of Dramamine. Still, putting it more clearly and accurately, we were only slightly affected by *mal de mer*. (Sorry. Just showing off.)

Daily, we would hear an announcement about how far we had proceeded from New York. As would be expected, we made daily progress, no storms except for occasional chilliness and brief rain showers. One day, however, we were startled. It seemed to us the sun was on the wrong side of the ship. We learned that a ship's electrician was missing and presumably was overboard. The ship followed the futile nautical regulation to turn around and return for a specific time, watching for a struggling human in the water. We did not find him.

On the tenth day out of New York, we heard a shout that land was visible. The shout came from Larry, up at 6:00 a.m. and looking ahead. We crowded our way to the rail and got our first glimpse of Africa. The seaport was Dakar, capital of Senegal and one of the westernmost points of Africa. We began what turned out to be almost a ritual. The freighter, like moving vans stateside, carried loads for several different destinations. When we anchored at a port, the process of unloading freight for that port would consume our time and take our interest. American consular representatives met us as needed, changed money for us, and helped us about the city. It seems that there were Lebanese traders in all the ports of West Africa; Dakar was no exception. Al took us to one of his trader friends. We were served refreshments, not only sweets and soft drinks, but coffee so strong in its demitasse that I feared it might dissolve my teeth. The consular reps also chauffeured the ladies and Bonnie to the shore, and the rest of us enjoyed the walk through the city in that French colony.

Let me just touch on those port stops; after all, we want to get to Lagos. We were in Dakar on November 20. Along the coast, we stopped at Conakry in Guinea, Freetown in Sierra Leone, Monrovia in Liberia, Takoradi in Ghana, and Port Bouet in Ivory Coast, before reaching Lagos.

I may have missed one or two, but those are the ones that are memorable for one reason or another. At Conakry we were invaded by swarms of insects. Where the insect landed on the skin, a red mark developed, which burned painfully. Woe to the one who swatted the bug. Crew and passenger alike were attacked by those insects which, we learned later, were Spanish beetles. Mary Beth may have been the worst afflicted of all. Not only did she have many welts over her arms, but one eye was completely swollen shut and the other she could open only with difficulty. A doctor at Freetown had made a study of the insect, but the ointment he provided was almost completely futile.

Since it was Sunday evening in Freetown, Max, Larry, and I decided to attend an evening worship service. The Anglican Church almost always has a vespers, and we thought to catch it about 6:45 p.m. Alas, the priest informed us it was long past, but he directed us to a small Methodist Church up the hill. As we approached, we heard them singing, "Make Me a Blessing" in—more or less—English. We Biebers had helped to sing that in the Lutheran Church in Watsontown on October 29. It was nice to make the connection and to notice how very welcome we were in a completely African congregation.

The beetle welts took a long time to go away. When we arrived at Monrovia, the victims were again taken to the doctor, and this man was much better equipped, with antibiotics, anti-allergics, and gentian violet. It took more than a week for Mary Beth's eyes to approach normalcy. I was frequently accused of wife beating, but I claimed self-defense. Liberia had been settled by hordes of freed slaves from America, along with those already there. It took on somewhat of an American atmosphere. Except for clerical workers, business people, and professionals, almost everyone worked for Firestone. Rubber was a principal product.

There was no true seaport in Ghana in 1950. We anchored outside the city of Takoradi, although Accra is the capital. Two factors made it interesting to be there, but for too long. There were long conveyor belts on which bauxite (aluminum ore) was loaded and conveyed across the water to the ship. And unloading was done into small boats about twenty feet long and perhaps ten feet wide. Apparently pay for unloading was based on the number of loads, for the boats kept jockeying for position. The crane would lift the load over a boat, let down close, and let go. Laborers would scurry to move the items away from the side of their boat and prepare for another load. More than once, the crane let go before the receiving boat was stable, and the load simply went to the fish.

Chapter Fifteen

MISSIONARIES, ALMOST

And then, finally, our arrival in Lagos. It was December 13, 1950; our ocean voyage had taken thirty-three days. We were met by missionaries of the Methodist Mission House who maintained a guest house there for their staff in transition and made it available for others. Even the Brethren can't get along without the Methodists! They guided us through customs, helped us collect all our personal things and were our hosts while we settled into Africa.

AFRICA!

NIGERIA!

How long we had waited, anticipated, and trusted God! The guest house was comfortable, its grounds well-kept with beautiful flowers. The children took turns being sick. Was it malaria so soon? We never knew for sure, lacking laboratory means for definitive diagnosis, but we were always thankful for their return to normal.

In Lagos, there were errands. I made six trips to the office of the police superintendent to license my small shotgun and get permits for importing it and the ammunition. We visited the American consul, the commissioner of British colonies, the bank, the post office, and the telegraph office. We made arrangements with the Barber Lines to collect our freight, deal with customs problems, and ship the loads to Jos. And then, after three days, it was time to head north, taking the train.

One hasn't lived, I wrote to my parents, until he has made a journey on the Nigerian railway. As first class (!) passengers, we had a compartment to ourselves. There were two padded leather seats, perhaps six feet long, facing each other. At night, the seat backs raised up and formed bunks. The ride was very bumpy, not conducive to good rest. Meals were substantial, and included early morning tea and afternoon refreshments which were brought to us, all for the princely sum of $13.34. There were frequent stops, also not conducive to rest. At daytime stops, local people would quickly learn there were white folks aboard and there would be a crowd outside our open window. They rarely saw white children. The trip from Lagos to Jos consumed fifty-four hours, and that meant two nights. Our children were unbelievably good travelers.

Jos, we understood, was the nearest location to mission areas of stores and shops of every believable kind and was 400 miles from mission headquarters in Garkida. Because it lies on a plateau 4,000 feet high, it is also a more comfortable city. It was there that Hillcrest School for Missionary Children was located, and there that we would be spending our vacations. The day we arrived, Claude Rupel, Hillcrest principal and house father and the mission's city "gofer," met us, along with Clara Harper, Wilma Schrag, and ample help. We knew Clara and Wilma from earlier days. We felt like long lost cousins who had just been found and were welcomed home—more so because the train was about eight hours late.

It was not only that we were welcomed. We were lodged in a comfortable (not palatial) house and fed at the guest house of the S.I.M. (Sudan Interior Mission). Like the Methodists, S.I.M. made provision for staff in transit, and when there was room, they accommodated others. We were also provided with the kind of advice we needed in order to supply the basic needs of our home in the bush (the rural areas of the country). Don't expect me to be able to list our purchases, but I do remember buying hundred pound bags of sugar and flour. There were no bakeries in the bush, and all cooking would be from scratch. We were oriented to the kind of stores, we visited the immense open air market of Jos, and we learned about S.I.M.'s Bingham Memorial Hospital, with facilities approaching those of modern American hospitals. Because five-year-old Larry would be leaving home in less than six months, we were also especially interested in visiting Hillcrest.

Would we be in Jos for Christmas? No. Herb Michael arrived in the 1947 Dodge station wagon, did his buying, got a little rest, and ensured that the car was in good condition. Now I know that I said above that one hasn't lived until he has traveled by Nigerian railway. I want to add that one hasn't lived unless he has traveled Nigerian roads in the decade of the fifties. Our luggage and loads were stored in such a way that there could be a child bed on top. Mary Beth and Clara Harper, along with Bonnie, accompanied Herb in the front seat. Larry, Dale, and I took the two-passenger back seat. At first, down the escarpment, the road was macadam, but not for long. Most of the way it was a road for my laundry-man dad, a washboard. I'd been on some rough country roads, but this one had them all beat. The kids were great travelers, although it was so bumpy that Larry and Dale could hardly stay in their bed. After eleven hours of travel, seven sojourners arrived at Marama, all brown haired because of the unavoidable dust which we had encountered. We enjoyed a good pancake breakfast at Baldwins, and left Clara off; this was her station, as well.

Enroute to Garkida, we stopped briefly at Shafa, then the newest mission station, and visited with Ann and Dick Burger. I doubt if Herb Michael had studied the AAA map; there must have been a better road to Garkida than the nightmare of hairpin curves, deep dips, and lovely bumps which we traversed too fast (for us nervous newcomers). Arriving safely, dirtily, at Garkida, we bathed, ate with Christine and Stover Kulp, and rested. It was just two days before Christmas, and we were greeted by letters from home, by all the missionaries on that largest station, including our old friends, the Lunkleys (also newly arrived), by the green trees with yellow flowers which served as Christmas trees, and by the welcome assurance that Lassa and our home there were not too far in the future. Larry seemed to be most susceptible to malaria; at least, lacking lab identification, that is what we assumed it to be. Maybe that repeated illness made him decide, at age five to be a doctor. That makes me wonder, fifty years later, whether the illnesses may have been alimentary rather than malarial, since Dale could eat almost anything and get away with it, but Larry couldn't.

I think I'll tax my mind and try to remember who were at Garkida that Christmas time. There were the Michaels, the Studebakers, the Eikenberries, Mary Dadisman, the Heckmans, Bassey Minso, and the Kulps. The Lunkleys, Bowmans, and Biebers were awaiting transportation to their assignments. We made some connections: Ivan Eikenberry's brother, Lorrel, was a classmate at Bethany. Mary Dadisman was college nurse at Juniata. Bassey Minso, from Calabar, had been a student at Bethany. It was Lucille Heckman who had pressed my wedding trousers. Kulps were relatives and our splendid hosts during the week we spent at Garkida. All but Bassey would eventually be called Aunt or Uncle by our children, reflecting the closeness of the missionary family. All of them, but especially the Kulps, made our week in Garkida a very pleasant one.

It was Thursday, December 29, when we took off from Garkida—the Bowmans, who would be going on to Gulak, and the Biebers—in two cars. Jim Bowman drove one, Herb Michael the other. We arrived at Lassa and were at home at last. Let me quote largely from my unpublished "manuscript" of those days.

"We ride into Lassa in style, perched on the front seat of the Bowman Jeep with Dale sleeping half on the floor and half on the seat, and the feet of a Nigerian servant practically surrounding me. Going through a series of farms with good crops of guinea corn still to be harvested and traveling over the new road, we suddenly see the shining roofs of the Lassa Hospital. (New road in this country is simply a motor trace newly cut through the bush; perhaps five years from now it will have been used enough to be a road.) Then, parked over at the left, we see the station wagon in which the women and children have come, together with our luggage. They are in front of OUR HOUSE. We note the slanting tiles of the roof, the mudwalled building, the large porches, and the completely barren front and backyards. We see the residence of the Pfaltzgraffs across the road, a house which we are told is a guest house and, fifty yards across an open area, the home of the Grimleys.

"But there's more. Obtaining the keys, we enter our new home. The bathroom (actually a privy with a bucket to collect you know what) is part of the house, but across the sleeping veranda. The sleeping veranda is a comfortable-looking place, and our houseboy—we haven't met him yet—is just now putting up the mosquito nets, for evening is approaching. We observe that the house has a kitchen, pantry, dining room, living room, playroom or sewing room, study, and bathroom. The walls are mud tile externally, mud brick under that, and plaster facing with white calcimine on the inside, and over a foot thick. There are ample windows. There is running water only from a tap in the kitchen and in the bathroom when our tank is full enough. There is no electricity, but someone has lent us a lamp until ours arrive, and we have two lanterns. We look over the grounds outside, see a detached storehouse/wash house, a round house where the 'boys' (servants) can stay if they wish, and the mudwalled chicken house lacking a fenced-in yard. So this is Lassa!

"Because we are practically without cooking equipment, we are fed by our genial fellow missionaries, Roy and Violet Pfaltzgraff, John and Mildred Grimley, and Evelyn Horn. For two full days they host us, and for one meal on each of several days afterward. Umoru, excellent cook for Grayce Brumbaugh, who is on furlough, helps us out until we can train our own cook. He is kept busy the first few days washing enamel dishes from the station storeroom, and boiling water. Cooking is on an iron stove burning wood. Then comes the day, almost to start the new year, when we eat lunch at home, and only supper out. Umoru has gone to market and bought a dozen eggs for about a nickel, and two live chickens to start our own flock for eighteen cents each.

"Our second day here, Roy takes me to the orchard and gardens. The dry-season gardens have irrigation ditches to each garden and into each little patch. Water is lifted into the ditches by a noria, an ancient lift first used in Spain. In the gardens we note corn, tomatoes, cabbage, and beans nearing harvest. In our own garden, planted a little later for us, there are sugar peas, soy beans, tomatoes, and other vegetables. The orchard nearby, also irrigated as necessary, provides oranges, limes, lemons, and tangerines, along with native fruits like mangos, papayas, and guavas. There are some young experimental trees which, it is hoped, will produce figs, dates, and avocado pears. So this is Lassa.

"We visit the primary school, about half a mile away. There are five or six mud brick buildings, empty at the moment because of holiday. We go to the old hospital, which is now an outpatient dispensary, also of mud brick with tile veneer. A little farther away, we come to the new hospital, for which Roy has been the architect and is the 'contractor,' as well as chief of staff. In this bush village, five hundred miles away from the source of supplies, it seems surprisingly modern. It is laid out like spokes in a wheel, with the administrative center at the hub. All the buildings are white, with aluminum roofs. Separate buildings hold a lecture room, offices and examining rooms, and the operating room, fluoroscope room, and dental center. The x-ray is to be powered by the hospital's own diesel generator, which will also provide other needed electricity, notably lighting for the operating room. There are no dietary facilities; patients' families will bring their own food. Wow! This is Lassa.

"Sleeping-in is an unattainable luxury. The young ladies, notice-ably bare-breasted, who carry five-gallon tins of water a quarter of a mile from the village well (ten tins a day for each of them) start about six. Our 'boys'—British term for servants—arrive soon afterward.

"When Roy notices a peculiar odor from our water tank, we drain it. There are four dead lizards in the bottom! Cleaned out by one of the boys, the tank should stay clean for a long time, protected by a screen over the top of the tank, but all of the drinking water must be boiled and filtered.

"Sleeping out of doors, however, is a pleasant experience. (This despite the story that this is the veranda on which Stover had once been visited by a leopard.) Larry loves his bed, which has no roof over it and lets him see myriad stars. The sky is clearer and the stars seem brighter when there is no smoke from factories and no street lights. We have arrived in the cold season, so we are glad for as many as three blankets at night. Early morning temperatures may fall below the fifties. Bonnie's bed is a screened crib.

"On market day—Monday in Lassa—we go to market. What is it like? What is sold there? We see chunks of meat, mostly goat, haphazardly chopped up and lying on cornstalk slabs, and we realize this will be our main source of meat. There are clay pots and gourds with guinea corn, rice, and groundnuts (peanuts). There are deep-fried bean cakes and peanut sticks, which sound delicious, but which we are reluctant to sample. (The bean cakes are made from flour ground from dried beans. The peanut sticks are made from the pulpy residue of the nuts after the oil has been squeezed out.)

"There is lots of cloth, both native woven and imported. There are chunks of rock, and we are told it is salt from Lake Chad, one hundred miles north. Like the salt of which Jesus spoke, it loses its savor as it lies in sun or rain and natural salt is washed away along with impurities. Most of the men wear robes or simple overall garments; most of the women wear only a tiny strap with metal thongs (Mary Beth calls them bullets) hanging from them. We observe that never in our lives have we seen so much bare skin. Babies, of course, are carried in slings on their mothers' backs, easily moved to the front for their mothers' milk. So this is Lassa! There is so much to learn and so many people to meet. Lassa. It is so important to God that God has sent missionaries here!"

Enough of Lassa description for now; let's get back to the narrative. Having renewed acquaintances with the Pfaltzgraffs and Grimleys and discovering what a special person Evelyn Horn was, having been oriented to the mission areas and programs, what would we do next? For the children, Lassa was almost a paradise. Not only was there far more room to rove than there had been on shipboard, but there were also new friends. Those not yet in school included George and David Pfaltzgfraff and Millie May Grimley. During school vacations, there would also be Roy Pfaltzgraff II and Johnny Grimley. New friends meant new toys as well as new ideas for play and, as might be expected, new ways to get in trouble. One of our "boys" was especially assigned to keep one eye on Bonnie and the other on the rest of the kids. The relationship between Nggida Gadzama and, later, Karagama Gadzama were to bring some special richness to our lives.

Chapter Sixteen

MISSIONARIES AT LAST

We began to think about our own tasks for the first year. Supposedly, the matter of learning the Margi language would be first and foremost. My reason for saying "supposedly" is that often there seemed to be something more urgent that would interrupt language study.

For Mary Beth, there would be teaching in the primary school (first four grades), visiting the women in the village, and making a home in a strange new land. For me, it would be to become acquainted with the methods of evangelism and the deeply-committed Nigerian evangelists. As persons became more familiar with my nursing background, it would also mean medical work.

How would we proceed with these three tasks? Mildred Grimley, with strong grammatical skills and a sizable Margi vocabulary, was to be our language teacher. A local teacher, at first Daniel and later Elijah, would work on our pronunciation and idioms. Six months or so after we arrived, we would be expected to take our first language exam. We did, and both passed. Within six months I had preached twice, from a manuscript that both Mildred and Elijah had reviewed, and within the first year Mary Beth had spoken to a women's meeting. Truly learning the language would take practice, practice, practice, and memory at work, although Margi grammar is simple and the vocabulary not extensive.

When John Grimley went to visit one of the several "schools" where evangelists were at work, he often invited me to go along and, barring direct conflict with a language class, I would accept. After two or three such visits, I realized that the only school in our area was at Lassa. The others were Classes in Religious Instruction and did not require government-qualified teachers. I came to believe that the two most effective tools for evangelism in those days were the leprosarium at Garkida, where patients remained for a lengthy period, and the CRI, where low-paid but very committed evangelists would share the gospel. Some of the CRIs had increased in numbers and experience so it was always being planned to establish other primary schools. Rarely was the newly committed Christian the result of direct witness by a missionary; almost always it was by the CRI evangelist or another Nigerian Christian. I enjoyed those visits and appreciated John's style, at the same time wondering when I would have enough of the language to carry on that kind of program.

At the old hospital and dispensary, there were no trained Nigerian nurses. There were a number of men and a few women who learned well without formal training and were of real help to Dr. Roy and Nurses Violet and Evelyn. There were bound to be times when one or more of them could not be present, and additional help would be needed. As often as I could, I went to the dispensary in the morning, mostly to listen and learn. The basic medical vocabulary was fairly repetitious and limited. "What hurts you? How long has it been hurting? Do you have any diarrhea?" and the like.

Medical work in Nigeria called to the front my year at Jefferson Hospital, rather than my psychiatric training. One day, for example, I served as scrub nurse for Roy as he removed an elephantiasis tumor weighing more than fifty pounds from between the poor man's legs.

Even with missionaries in the area for more than twenty years, there were still some tribes which the colonial government classified as dangerous, and we were forbidden to approach them. (In later years, Nigerian leadership would offer their suspicion that the British colonial government really did not want missionaries around.)

When the restrictions were removed, John, Jim Bowman, and I decided to trek to Kamale, a village at the foot of what we called "Finger Mountain." Close-beside was a smaller peak named "Cirgi," its Margi name—the crater of a long dead volcano from which, across the centuries, all the rest had eroded. About that time, we learned later, the *National Geographic* magazine had published a story about Houmseki, a similar crater in Cameroons, which we could see when we climbed to Cirgi. The people of Kamale welcomed us warmly. Through translators, we communicated with them that we came in peace, and the Nigerian evangelist who was with us told them about Jesus. We had hardly got past initial greetings, however, when the conversation went something like this:

Visitors: "We saw your amazing mountain here and wanted to greet the people near it."

Locals: "Are you the ones who live there where we can see the shiny roofs?"

Visitors: "Yes, we are from there. God sent us to teach them about Jesus and tell them God loves them. Some of us have lived there for many years, and we want you to know that God loves you, too."

Locals: "Well, why did you wait so long to come to greet us?"

Visitors: "The government would not let us come. They said you were dangerous."

Locals: "Us? Dangerous?" And they broke out in long-lasting peals of lusty laughter.

We stayed overnight at Kamale. We climbed to the base of Cirgi, and to the base of Cirgi's wife. We found a small cave at the foot of Cirgi, as well. It was a very interesting trip, and the best part of it was the people.

Between our house and that of Grimleys, perhaps fifty feet from us, there was a mud-walled, grass-thatched building, the guest house. It was furnished sufficiently for persons to be able to stay there for a few days, taking advantage of the missionary staff for their meals. That house provided us with excitement and conversational menu one day when it burned. One of our "boys" spied the blaze and alerted us. There was little we could do except pull out some of the furniture. The conversation for many days was to wonder how the fire had occurred. Since it is too late now to prosecute, I can safely confess that we finally settled on two missionary boys.

We came to appreciate two fruits which were new to us. Mangoes are somewhat pear-shaped, though flatter. They protect themselves with a strongly acid skin, but when they are washed and peeled or sliced past their huge seed, they are delicious. Cooked and mashed, they have much the flavor of applesauce. During one period, they were so plentiful that we were able to sell them for fourteen cents a peck to the Nigerians. The other new fruit was the guava. With the appearance of a quince, the guava is usually pale yellow when ripe. It is plentifully seeded, with seeds about the size of grape seeds and, when one eats a guava raw, the seeds are simply swallowed. The best—that is, the favorite—use of guavas to us was to mash them into a sauce, strain off the seeds, and enjoy what was very close to strawberry short cake. I was addicted!

In July, our seventh month at Lassa, the day came which we had dreaded, but for which we were making preparations. Larry, just past his sixth birthday, headed off for Hillcrest School, five hundred miles away. We were into the rainy season, so we knew we would almost certainly not get to Jos to see our boy. There was no telephone or radio communication at the time. Having friends with him, especially George and Johnny, helped make it easier for Larry to leave, and when he left, he was a sad but brave-faced boy. It was his mother and father who cried! Even for us, the separation was somewhat eased by our admiration of J.C. and Jean Wine, the houseparents, and by our certainty that we were in God's care.

During our transition from the United States to Nigeria, it seemed that Larry was most often not well. He was the one bothered by seasick episodes, the one who several times appeared to have malaria, and the Peter of our kids, rushing in where the others hesitated. (I was glad it was the older son who was bolder; I had often been embarrassed by the fact that my younger brother was bolder.) His boldness scared us several times—a gash on the head, a gash on the arm, a lacerated finger. He was a very observant and very curious boy.

One day he observed to Mary Beth, "God can really do magic!"

"What makes you say that?"

"Because he can put babies in their mother's belly."

He worried a little that Bonnie might have a baby in her belly, until Mary Beth explained that God wants babies to have a father, so God waits until the woman is married.

Another of his observations came after Mary Beth had been sick in bed for several days with malaria. He asked her, "Mama, when are you going to be boss again?"

The first letter written for him from Hillcrest gave us another quotation, which came after a heavy rain. "I looked all over, but I couldn't find any place where the water would go over my boots."

Comments from Hillcrest confirmed what we already knew, that he was a cheerful, active, and intelligent boy.

Dale's fourth birthday came on July 21, and I have rarely seen a child so excited. He loved new things and really enjoyed showing off anything he had that was new. He would dress up in the middle of the week in his once-Sunday clothes, just so he could wear (show off) his new shoes. Of course, he was always somewhat vain and wanted to dress up every day. The problem came because he did not understand what a birthday meant, except something new.

So pleasant was his celebration in 1951 that he decided to arrange another birthday a week or so later, with cake, gifts, guests, and all. His imagination stood him in good stead as he played with bricks or blocks, houses, garages, and tunnels. He loved to draw, perhaps because of his frequent association with Millie May and her talented family. Dale was the best singer in the family; already he surprised us by proudly singing our table grace as a solo. He missed Larry. Often his play was in imitation of his big brother.

After Larry's earlier reign as the sickest one, Dale took over as the one most often sick. He frequently had diarrhea and some nausea, but rarely enough to diminish his very good appetite. Most of the time he was a very happy boy and took even his bellyaches as they came. He often dreamed, and laughed or cried out in his sleep. And he was cautious; he was afraid of ants, because they bit hard.

Bonnie was very imitative. She would echo our words without, I think, knowing their meanings. She would also say Margi words to our "boys," which amused them greatly. She was also very clever for her age. She didn't eat well, and she observed that when Mother took her away from the table to "wet," she often forgot to bring her back. So there was a rare meal when she did not have to "go" at least once. She noticed that when Dale wasn't feeling well, he would sometimes go to his bed and lie down, so she would climb down from her high stool, hold up her finger, and say, "I want to lie down. My finger hurts."

When we stopped her, she was quite insulted. I think the words she said most were, "Me, too!" "Mine!" "Drink of milk."

Her favorite weapon was tears, which she used when denied something, reproved, or told to do something she didn't like. When she learned to dress herself, her comment was, "I do it my byself."

It took us awhile to develop some immunity to malaria. Larry earliest, then Dale, and then Mary Beth were attacked by the malaria bug. She was down at least two or three times with it. One time we almost got into an argument: did she have it or didn't she? She was saying how bad she felt, and then we had some company and she perked right up. After they went, I asked her how she could be so sick when we were alone and so perky when there were guests. She gave the right answer: "Honey, with you I can be completely honest!"

She had good health, except for malaria, and except for one illness which, though not worse, was more painful. The pain in her back was almost obstetrical. After two or three days of throbbing jolts of pain, it suddenly subsided and stayed away, and we became aware that she had been afflicted by a kidney stone. We were glad when that passed (pun intended), and the kids were always so glad when mother was at full function. She spent a lot of time visiting the women in the village, even though the language was new and very different.

When the rains came to an end in the first year and Evelyn Horn was on furlough, the Pfaltzgraffs took a much needed and well earned vacation in Jos. That left me as the only trained medical staff, running both the hospital and dispensary. When I knew how to treat, I treated. When I didn't know how or when my diagnosis was of a condition that Roy would have to care for, I would sometimes prescribe a hopeful cure and sometimes ask them to come back in a couple of weeks.

One case saddened me. I was treating the very sick son of one our hospital workers and sent him home, quite certain that he would be all right. It was only two days later that word came that he had died. I later learned that his mother had taken him to the local witch doctor, whose pummeling of swollen spleen and liver were almost certainly the cause of death. (Let me note here that I believe some of the medicines and therapy of the witch doctors were effective, but pummeling was not one of them.)

I also had two cases that pleased me: I delivered my first two babies. The first was a boy, whose coming out party awakened me late one night. After the birth I sent a note to Mary Beth, "It's a boy, Honey!" A day or two later, just so show my lack of sexual bias, I delivered a girl. I was greatly helped, of course, by young Titi Risku, daughter of one of the first converts to Christianity in our area.

Christmas at Lassa

Larry's first vacation, in time for Thanksgiving, was very special. All of us were tremendously happy to see that big boy. Mama was the sissy; she cried while she held and kissed him. Dale and Bonnie just could not stop following him around and trying to do the things that he did. We were amazed at how much simple maturity he had developed in those twenty weeks at Hillcrest. His table manners were careful, his appetite had improved so that he had gained some weight, and he seemed to have a new British accent.

We learned that the date for Christmas celebration was adjustable, though the date for church celebrations was normal. The "adjustable" allowed the school children who were at home, to have a little longer to take advantage of their presents before they went back to school. So we had a station-wide gift exchange early in December. Few packages from home had reached us with Christmas things, but they began coming in, and we stretched out the gift-opening for a couple of weeks. We also had a special celebration with gifts for our "boys."

The church celebration of Christmas deserves reporting. Except for the wooden pulpit and a couple of wooden chairs, all the church furniture, as well as floor and stage, were made of dried mud. Pews were about ten feet long, one foot wide, two feet high, hard, no backs. The floor was gravel. The stage was about two feet high, quite large, made of mud, squared away, dried, VERY solid.

Christmas, for our Margi brothers and sisters, meant the re-enacting of the first Christmas, with the Biblical story enhanced by sanctified imaginations. The angel—angels could be identified because their skin had been covered with flour and they wore white—made their frightening, challenging, and reassuring visits to Mary and Joseph. The tables of the census-takers/tax-collectors were set up on the stage, and while Joseph and his pregnant wife came slowly down the aisle with their donkey, others registered. "Who are you? How many goats do you have? How many cows?"

The sanctified imaginations declared that tax depended on wealth. Eventually, Joseph and Mary paid up, asked about a place to stay, searched through the village, and finally were accepted by a grudging innkeeper who let them stay in his stable. There was a great deal of price palaver about the amount of tax due, and then about the cost of the stable. The stable was a rude hut at one side of the stage into which the couple disappeared.

In the next scene, tax tables were gone, and a group of ragged men were gathered around an actual fire on the stage, with six or eight sheep and lambs nearby. Angels appeared and a loud voice called out. With one accord, the shepherds began violent trembling—so much one feared for the welfare of even that strong stage. They fell on their faces. They heard the "Fear not!" and little by little they raised their heads and listened. The angels left; the shepherds spent some time being sure just what it was they heard. Eventually, they agreed there must be some special child born in the village of Bethlehem, so they took lambs and went to see. The fire was extinguished and cleared away. The shepherds were on their way.

Now we saw a gloriously attired king sitting on his huge throne, surrounded by well-dressed courtiers loudly shouting his praises. Into the turmoil came striding three men, all regally attired, asking questions as they came. Eventually they reached the king and stated their mission: "Where is that new king being born?" The king's wise men seized their scrolls and studied. As they conferred, they agreed that some special person was to be born in Bethlehem.

"Oh, that's down that way," exclaimed the king.

"Good journey, and be sure to come back and tell me so I can pay proper honor." (No camels. Tethered outside the throne room, no doubt.)

The scene changed again, and by now the shepherds had reached that obscure stable. The glory of the moment penetrated their being, and as they approached the stable, we could hear them calling out the usual words of honor of a big chief:

"*Alvari!* (Lion)"

"*Bundi!* (Great One)"

"*Mthlagu!* (Lord) *Ciwar*! (Elephant)"

They fell down before mother and child and paid homage, presenting their lambs.

While this was going on, we heard a commotion in the back of the church. The three regally overdressed men were coming down the aisle, pointing above them to a star (rigged on a wire from back to front) which was leading them. By the time they arrived at the birthplace, the shepherds were gone. The wisemen were properly obeisant; they gave their gifts, made their speeches, and quietly left. Alone at last, the new mother and father marvelled at what had happened and we heard Mary say, "I am going to remember all these things in my heart."

With a congregational carol, the old and ever new story came to its end and we went back to our homes, deeply moved and very reflective.

Chapter Seventeen

WHAT DOES A MISSIONARY DO?

Hillcrest vacation time ended too soon. It was decided that John would take the kids back to Jos, and that I would accompany as a relief driver and for a shopping trip. We took advantage of night-time cooling and traveled at night. About a third of the way, around two in the morning, John turned the wheel over to me. Along the way, we kept seeing and driving over many night birds, too startled by our lights to get away. Occasionally one bumped the jeep and we felt a thud. As I was driving, we passed over a good-sized bird, and we felt the thud. Soon after, but not relating it to the bird incident, I noticed that our lights seemed to be growing dimmer, and the temperature gauge was rising.

I awakened John. By flashlight we discovered that the radiator hose was loose and we had lost water. We fastened the hose, poured in as much water as we felt we could spare from our canteens, and went on. The motor stayed hot, but not over-heating. The lights, however, simply were not functioning. It was a brilliant moonlit night, and John decided to drive the rest of the way to Damaturu without lights. We stopped at a petrol dump and waited until daylight to buy petrol. When John opened the hood (sorry, British friends—bonnet) he noticed feathers scattered across the motor and plastered against the hood. The generator belt, though still attached, was loose, thus explaining our loss of electricity. Naturalist John recognized owl feathers, and we concluded that an owl had taken off just at the spot to hit the radiator hose and belt, sacrificing his (her?) life. The rest of the trip, though tiring, went all right.

It was my first visit to Jos in just over a year, and I had a sizable grocery list. An impressive new department store, Kingsway, owned by Lever Brothers of soap fame, had opened. Shopping there, as I described in a letter home, was an experience:

"The shelves are pretty well stocked. You go in with a list of things you want, and name them to the clerk one at a time. He says, for example, 'Yes, we have oats. How many do you want?'

"We say, 'May we see a can?'

"He goes and fetches one can.

"We say, 'Is that the only brand?'

"He says, 'No,' and just stands there.

"So we say, 'May we see the other kind?'

"He goes and brings one can.

"Finally, you make your selection, tell him you want a dozen cans. He says all right, sets the one can on the counter and asks, 'Anything else?'

"But we say, 'Where are the other eleven tins?'

"He assures us, 'Coming.'

"We go through that process for everything we buy and when we are done, with a big list of groceries costing over $50.00, there are still only a few cans sitting on the counter. He hands us the list, with the prices, and we go to the cashier and pay. THEN, we come back and hand him our list, marked paid, and he begins to collect the things together.

"We wanted a case of twelve bottles of vinegar. Said the clerk, 'Oh, we can't sell you that many. We'd have to go to the storeroom and get more.'

"We say, 'But we want that many.'

"'Well, that makes difficulty. The manager will have to write a requisition for it and someone will have to go the store and get it.'

"We get to the manager and finally get the vinegar. We leave the clerk to gather the order while we go to another section of the store to buy some chocolate candy, in tins, for which we had all been especially hungry.

"Before we go, we tell the clerk three times, in no uncertain terms, that we want a wooden box to take all those groceries far into the bush. He doesn't get one. When we get back, he just says, 'Oh, I thought you were making a joke.'

"Again we see the manager; he hesitates when we ask for a box, but we finally get one. Shopping in that store is a great experience. Most stores are much simpler. You just go in and hope they have what you want and buy it if they do."

The "boys" who worked for us often became very special persons, and in a couple of instances, almost members of the family. Our first cook (remember?) was Umoru, who cooked for Grayce Brumbaugh. She was on furlough, so our first weeks in Lassa were made easier by Umoru's skills. The only problem we had with him was that Grayce seemed to have a lot of one-dish meals on her menu. When Mary Beth would order an entree and vegetables, we might just find them all cooked together. Keri Ali was next and had the advantage of Umoru's teaching and a smattering of English. He was very young; this was his first job, and his heart was not in it. Eventually, he left and joined the police. Mjigimtu Thliza, a schoolboy whose name means "people of death," was our houseboy, which means that he was responsible for the cleaning as well as helping Keri with serving meals.

The rest of the boys worked mostly out of doors. Musa, watchman at the hospital, was our washman, a task which meant washboard and hand wringing. Musa and Mairama, his wife, were an unusual couple. When they fell in love, they defied tribal custom of marriages arranged by parents and went ahead with their own marriage. Rajil, a Fulani whose command of English barely included garden terms, was—you guessed it— our gardener. He took care of all planting, weeding, and watering, and most of the harvesting. Our other two boys were really boys. Nggida Gadzama's main job was child care—especially Bonnie. Son of a very poor widow, he was a brilliant lad, second best student in his class. We aided him to further his education beyond the four grades at Lassa. He went to senior primary school at Garkida, became the first boy from his village to go to high school, (at Gindiri) and the first (we believe) of his whole tribe to go to college—McPherson College in Kansas. Satumari Cirarima, about the same age, kept up the firewood supply and kept the yard clear of grass and debris, thus discouraging snakes. He was even more brilliant than Nggida (first in the class), but handicapped by a father who resented his working for white folks. He, too, with our help, went on to senior primary school at Garkida and then for agriculture training; he loved the farm.

Even while Nggida was still with us, another lad, slightly younger and smaller, made himself useful by helping wherever he could, without pay. He endeared himself to us one day when disobedient Bonnie walked too close to the orchard pond and slipped in. He jumped in so quickly to save her that she did not even inhale any water. Karagama succeeded Nggida in child care and stayed with us all through our Nigeria experience.

Came March 1952, and our first vacation. We knew we were overdue one, but were uncertain about transportation. Suddenly—with only a day's notice, we were to be ready to go to Jos, and we eagerly packed up, turned over this and that, and headed out with Clarence Heckman, spouse of my wedding day pants presser. Arrived at Jos after all-night travel, we were VERY tired, but VERY eager to see Larry. Mary Beth, Dale, and Bonnie found a way to get to Hillcrest, but I had to remain to get food supplies before the stores closed. Virtue has its own reward. Wilma Schrag, Larry's teacher, brought him to the vacation compound, and I saw him first and enjoyed his wide-eyed surprise.

Having Larry with us was the best of the vacation, but there was also eating out, exploring new territories, shopping for groceries for ourselves and for others who had provided us with lists, and buying Nigerian crafts and arts. Larry and I visited the vast, open-air Jos market one day, and I was able to practice the price haggling which I had occasionally observed in my dad—that was the only way to get a fair price at market. I learned quickly that when one walked away, a lower price resulted. We were also able to enjoy worship in English, at the nearby S.I.M. chapel and at Hillcrest.

All good things—even vacations—come to an end, and we headed for the bush again, with one incident worth mentioning. At one place the laterite road was completely blocked by a fire, the burning of a ten-ton truck and its cargo, so close to a culvert as to render the road impassable. We had to skirt the road by breaking our way through the nearby bushes, to be on our way. Unfortunately, the delay kept us from some visits to other missionaries we had intended to make along the way, but it didn't keep us from arriving safely at Garkida.

All of us were so very busy after arriving back at Lassa, that it occurred to me this might be a good time to answer the question, "What does a missionary do?" At least, I can give you some idea of what this missionary was doing. Now this will take a while; I want you to think I was busy! Obviously, I learned the Margi language, with simple vocabulary and grammar, yet completely foreign to past language study. There were beautiful idioms: "Tie your heart" for "be patient," and "His heart stood up" for "He was brave."

There were useful pronouns: three different ones for "we": *nama* for the two of us who are conversing; *naya* for those of us on this side of the conversation, but not the rest of you; *namir* for all of us.

There were simple words which packed a lot of meaning: *daici* for the end, it's over, that's enough, quit it; *mdou* for I don't know, maybe nobody knows.

I learned a completely new kind of program for evangelism with a strikingly effective set of strategies. I learned to recognize new diseases and propose remedies different from any I had known. I learned how to examine persons for the covenant. They were persons who were turning toward Christ and were interested enough to spend three months of weekly classes learning specific basics—the ten commandments, the beatitudes, John 3:16, and the words of the covenant which they would recite before the congregation. Taking the covenant, they agreed to learn more about Jesus and prepare for baptism. I learned to examine candidates for baptism by seeking to discern understanding and motivation. I learned to preach in story sermons, the Jesus method. I learned to perform the feetwashing from a tiny metal bowl. I learned to eat a chunk of thick cornmeal as my communion bread, and to drink the juice of the wild cherry or perhaps, red Koolaid, as the "cup."

I learned names and faces, places, customs, patterns of greeting, tribal myths and traditions, and certain unacceptable practices. It is not acceptable to receive something with the left hand—it must be the right hand or both. One is not to wave with open fingers; an open hand held toward someone sometimes meant a curse. There was always something else to learn—and there is, still.

There were three particular lessons that the Christians in Nigeria taught me: 1) There are always persons needing to hear the story of Jesus and turn their lives to him. 2) The work of Jesus progresses better by co-operation than by competition. 3) Important though it is to learn all we can, it is more important to know God than to know theology. Simple God stories sometimes carry a powerful message. A Margi folktale has it that God used to be very close to people. All one needed to do, for example, if he was hungry was to say, "God, I'm hungry," and a calabash of food would appear. The only rule: clean the calabash when you finish eating.

One day a preoccupied eater forgot to clean the calabash. Next morning when someone was hungry, God's emissary looked for the calabash. When he scraped out the dried porridge, small cuts appeared on his fingers; they became infected, and he died. So God said, "If you can't obey me, I am going away."

But the story doesn't end there; sometime God is coming back. And the Nigerian evangelist picks up the story: "God did come back! His name is Jesus!"

I became the assistant pastor of the Lassa Church; the pastor was one who had trained in the first pastoral training class of the mission at Chibuk. I tried to interpret difficult situations, explain doctrinal nuances, solve problems, and sometimes even referee arguments. All of this I learned from good friend John Grimley, who was better at all the aspects of sharing the gospel in terms easily understood by Nigerians.

As a nurse, I examined, diagnosed, prescribed, asked Roy Pfaltzgraff's advice, assisted him as requested, and covered in his absence. That meant dealing with problems I did not understand. During one of Roy's vacations, the Pfaltzgraff cook, Palnam, fell unconscious in the road. The only information I had was that he had been complaining of a very serious headache. Could it be cerebral malaria? Could it be meningitis, which in the early stages of the annual epidemic was particularly virulent? Could he have been poisoned in some way? Not knowing, I treated all three! Injection of anti-malarial. Intravenous including antibiotic. By midnight, he still had not awakened. Imagine my relief when the Pfaltzgraffs drove in early in the morning, a day late in their return. I told Roy what had happened and left it in his capable hands. At noon, I went over to their house and asked how Palnam was getting along.

"Oh, fine," Roy reported. "I sent him home!"

The third of my diagnoses, it turned out, was the correct one; he had been spraying the pantry with chlordane and inhaled too much of the dangerous fumes.

Beyond these more regular activities and more important activities such as praying, Bible study, and all the little/big things that make a family a family, there are others:

Want eggs? Better raise chickens, even without any chicken raising experience.

Want meat? Better do some hunting. My sixteen gauge shotgun was pretty effective in scattering its pellets against guinea fowl, rock coneys, rabbits, ducks, ibis, and even a rare squirrel, but my 30-40 rifle never could overcome my inability to aim at larger game. Want the meat butchered? You were the butcher. I did know some human anatomy from nursing, and it may have reduced the amount of hapless hacking and chopping.

Bush fire causing disturbance and threatening to reach buildings? Join the busy Nigerians in wielding the green branches to beat out the flames (despite singed leg hairs!).

Repairs to property or to roads, or new carpentry or masonry to be done? Supervise the workers, even though they know their art better than you do.

And there's more: Run errands, for yourself and for others. Be the headmaster (principal) of the school, even though you never took any education classes. (After all, you are the best educated person for the time being.) Be the paymaster for teachers, artisans, hospital workers, evangelists. Keep records. Write letters home and to friends and relatives, and feature articles and stories for publication by the Brethren. Serve as appointed on committees, of which there were a variety in connection with the broadbased mission program. Attend meetings of committees; prayer meetings; mission conference, church conference; meetings. Teach. Visit. Entertain. Take pictures. Audit the mission books. Play table games. Read voraciously. Hopefully, the missionary does that for which he or she is best trained, but someone has to do all the other little tasks that come up. Get the picture?

Travel was an experience all its own. Not only were the roads quite primitive, but the available transportation was similarly primitive. Several of the mission vehicles were army surplus left over after World War II, especially several jeeps and one truck which had been an army ambulance. There were absolutely NO repair stations along the roads, and when one heard a new knock, the question was whether to stop or to hope and pray. I was riding with Roy one day when the fuel pump quit pumping. Roy detached it, fastened a bicycle pump to it, and kept me pumping. Delegated to drive the mission truck from Lassa to Garkida—for what reason I have forgotten—I could no longer get it moving past Dzonggola, about twenty-five miles to go. Towed in, it required major repairs—bearings, valves, or something. Charles Lunkley rigged up a chain hoist, removed the motor, repaired it, replaced it, kept me in town for a week assisting. Bob Bischof and I used the same truck, some months later, to get palm lumber from a site about seventy-five miles from Lassa. On the way home about ten at night, the generator got tired, and the lights went out. I sat on the hood with a flash lantern to guide us slowly to Mubi, where two relieved men spent the night and obtained repairs.

At one point, I was seriously considering the purchase of a horse. It was probably the fact that I had never ridden a horse except those ponies at amusement parks, plus the fact that I am somewhat of a coward, plus the fact that I would have had no idea about the quality of the horse, that vetoed that thought. Instead, I rode bicycle to those of the outvillage stations which were not too far away. Eventually, I bought a small motorcycle which I used extensively for the more distant visits. Mary Beth, also, used her bicycle quite regularly.

As the end of the dry season drew near, in April, the irrigation pool in the orchard was less and less. Several women from the village came with their fish nets and fished it out. Each of the five women had two nets. When a fish, disturbed by their threshing about, would jump, all five, it seemed, would head for it. Caught, it would be lowered past a draw string into the lower part of the net, and the quest would go on. It was quite a sight, especially since two of the women were very much pregnant. At the end, the fish were divided among the missionaries, and some given to the ladies for their good work.

Two of the missionary's tasks mentioned above were to solve problems and referee arguments. Both came into play in the incident of Timba and Wadzani. A twin boy, infant Timba had been discarded on the village refuse heap; after all, his mother could not provide milk for two. Stover Kulp heard the baby crying, rescued him, found foster parents in the village. His foster father was Wadzani, one of the Lassa church deacons and a teacher in the primary school. As Timba grew older, he attended school and was quite a good student. He accepted Christ as his Savior, took the covenant, and was baptized. When he was perhaps fifteen or sixteen, an unfortunate incident took place.

Wadzani came home from his teaching one late afternoon, needed some money, and reached for the tin in the ground floor under his bed, which was his bank. The tin was gone, and all of perhaps eleven pounds in coins. He reported it to the chief. Investigation took place, but there were practically no clues. The nearest to a clue was the story a small boy told, that he had seen Timba put the tinful of money into the deep pocket of his robe. No other information was forthcoming, Timba denied being involved, no money was recovered, and the case was dismissed for lack of evidence. Convinced that Timba was the thief, Wadzani ordered him out.

Timba left Lassa. He went to live in a village some fifteen miles away, the mission station of the Catholic Church, and took additional school. He married. He began to teach in the Catholic primary school. He and his wife had two sons. He kept remembering the kindness shown to him at Lassa. He found it hard to accept the local Catholic theology. He decided that he should return to Lassa, so he came to our home.

"It is bad enough that I am not following the Christian way I learned," he said, "but my wife has not accepted Christ and my boys are not learning about Him. I must come back here." As he reviewed his story for me, I remembered some of its details, and particularly Wadzani's insistence that Timba was a thief.

My observation was, "Maybe it would be better for you to settle in another village; I don't know if it would be good for you and Wadzani to be in the same church." Timba, however, not only wanted to settle at Lassa, but also to clear his name. I asked the deacons to meet that same afternoon.

It was not an easy meeting. Wadzani was obviously angry at Timba, who was not at all happy with Wadzani. Each told his story. Wadzani insisted Timba was a thief. Timba insisted he was being unfairly accused. Impasse! After some frustrated silence, we prayed. After another extended silence, someone said, "I wonder what Jesus would do. I think if Jesus were in Wadzani's place, he would forgive Timba and apologize for accusing him. If he were in Timba's place, he would forgive Wadzani for the wrongful accusation."

Again, silence. Then, Wadzani arose, went to Timba, said, "I always thought you stole my money. If you did, I forgive you. It is more important to have a brother than to have a tinful of money. If you didn't, please forgive me for accusing you."

Timba said, "*Baba* (father), I really did not take the money, and I forgive you." The following Sunday, we received Timba back into the church, and Wadzani was the first to go forward to welcome him. Was Timba guilty? I don't know. Does it matter? No.

In May 1952, the time came for Dr. Howard Bosler, superintendent of the Adamawa Provincial Leprosarium at Garkida, to retire. Lloyd Studebaker's patient load at Garkida was simply too heavy for him to cover both institutions. Roy Pfaltzgraff was just finishing the new hospital at Lassa. Velva Jane Dick was the nurse at the leprosarium, but other help was needed. In May, Mary Beth and I, with Dale and Bonnie, moved to the very nice home which the government had provided for the leprosarium head, and I assumed the bombastic title of Lay Superintendent. There were also some very helpful Nigerian staff.

The living was much more comfortable than our home at Lassa. The predominant language was Bura rather than Margi. It was just the wrong time to take advantage of a garden. Rojil did go ahead to plant for us at Lassa; we would return there after almost four months. The medical work was minimal. VJ was very efficient and much more knowledgeable. I learned to recognize the basic types of leprosy, admit and discharge patients, and prescribe treatment, which had not yet reached the effectiveness of later years. More of my time was spent in overseeing the workers, caring for maintenance, ensuring that supplies were available, and directing the farm program. I also had charge of the leprosy village at Pirkasa, where those less severely afflicted could live, and where a new church developed. On one occasion, we were host to a government supervisory committee so important that the provincial emir attended in all his pomp and circumstance.

Having had some practice at Lassa, Mary Beth now picked up her teaching skills. She taught English in the Virgwi Junior Primary School. Indeed, she became the headmistress (principal) of the school, a responsibility which she would frequently assume over the full length of our service in Nigeria. And this, mind you, along with homemaking in a strange land and fulfilling her love of people by frequent visits.

June came, and Larry's vacation. It was so good to observe how much he had developed in a year at Hillcrest. He had done so well that they advanced him a half year. We cut our service at Virgwi for three days so we could take him "home" for a while . . . and so that he and Johnny Grimley could practice their high jumps. Returned to our leprosarium home, he had a shorter trip back to school. It was also an easier one. The Hillcresters went in a lorry this time, luggage loaded as evenly as possible on the floor, covered with old mattresses, supplied with blankets, and the whole bed protected, somewhat, by a tarpaulin.

There were two important pluses of those four months. I was very pleased to be able to learn more about leprosy, particularly to understand that its initial infectious invasion was usually of small children. It is likely that most of the children did not develop leprosy even after years of incubation; only those particularly susceptible or weakened by other physical conditions. Later, I would be baptizing leprosy patients, without the slightest fear of contracting the disease. There were exceptions, of course. Long close exposure might also cause infection in adults.

The other blessing of those months was to learn to know Mai Sule Biu, a *Pabur* (Bura) prince who had developed leprosy and became a patient at the leprosarium as a child. As he learned about Jesus, he slowly but completely committed his life to Him and became one of the most powerful and highly respected of the whole Church of the Brethren in Nigeria. He had completed the pastoral class at Chibuk and was pastor of the church at Virgwi. He wrote many hymns in Bura and Hausa. He loved to tell stories and was a very dramatic preacher. I could understand only a small smattering of the Bura in which he was preaching one Sunday when he announced, "Today I will preach about sin."

He set a wide-mouthed bottle of water on the floor in front of him and began, "Once there was a man who put a fine new thatched roof on his house. He was very proud of the smooth, tight nature of his roof, and began to think it was such a tight roof it would not even burn." He took a brand from the fire, set it to the roof. It caught fire. Immediately he splashed it from a gourd of water."

At this point, Mai Sule splashed water from the bottle on all who were near the front of the church. Then he went on, telling how the man repeated his setting the roof briefly ablaze, then quenching it. Eventually the moment came when, as Mai Sule attempted to splash water on the congregation, the bottle was empty. A startled look came over his face as he realized, for the proud man in his story, that he could no longer put the fire out. Then he concluded his sermon: "You can't play with sin; it just keeps growing stronger while you grow weaker."

It was while we were living at the leprosarium that we discovered that Mary Beth was still fertile. We had hoped for a fourth child and, having learned that our return home would be delayed, this seemed a good time. So the end of August brought the announcement to families at home and gradually to missionary colleagues that Mary Beth was pregnant. The birth, we let home folks know, would certainly be on one of the February birthdays common to the Highs. Also at the end of August, Dr. Merlin and Polly Brubaker arrived, and our work at Virgwi ended. We were moved back to Lassa.

Although we were permitted a delay because of our months of absence—and there was no stringent time schedule to follow—it did seem time for us to take our second and final Margi exam. I remember some of its aspects: hearing a Margi folktale and telling it back to the Margi teacher; making a public speech in Margi; interviewing a Margi and writing his story in Margi.

At Kelle, a small village a few miles from Lassa, I had met a man named Wainda. I was very much impressed with him. He was fully committed to Jesus Christ, and he provided the basic leadership for the small Christian group at Kelle. He saw to the building and care of the small church; he arranged for the services; he taught Bible. In a technical sense, however, Wainda was not a Christian; he had three wives, so baptism was forbidden to him. Polygamy was not uncommon and brought problems to the church which could be solved only with great difficulty.

During the period when I was interviewing Wainda, I happened to read the story of a big chief in Tanganyika with seven wives. He became a Christian. He called his wives together, picked one to keep, and announced to the rest that they were no longer his wives. I told the story to Wainda, suggesting that he might consider doing the same. His first response was excitement; perhaps he would be baptized at last. Three days later, however, he came to our home with a very long face. We had hardly finished our greetings before he said, *"Mallam* Bieber, they don't want to go. And I don't think I want them to; they would take my children with them."

As I commiserated with him, I felt compelled to point out that, although baptism is very important, it is by grace that we are saved, through faith. I confidently expect to meet Wainda in heaven. I passed my Margi final . . . but never learned all there was to learn.

On a trip with John Grimley and Stover Kulp to visit the school at Wamdi, we went calling on the local witchdoctor. A very friendly chap, he was one of the fattest Nigerians I have known. He recognized Stover from a visit some years earlier and exclaimed, "White people never grow old!"

Said Stover, pointing to his white hair, "What, am I not old?" He took us to his compound to greet us and presented Stover with a capon. A young mother came to him with her baby to ask if the baby had a good life ahead of him. The witch doctor asked us to watch his answer. He called for his divining crab. We went outside his house and sat on mats on the ground. He took a half calabash, about the size of a vegetable dish, nearly filled with damp sand. He pushed several sticks carefully deep at points in the sand. If one were to be knocked down, it meant approaching death. Then he put several small carved items into the sand, each with a meaning known (?) to him, and a small piece of rope. He took the crab, rubbed it with the cactus "to wake it up," made a few magical passes and uttered an incantation, placed it in the gourd and covered it. We chatted for a while, then he lifted the lid, examined the new locations of the objects, and was able to foresee the future (very much like tarot cards). You will be pleased to know that the baby is going to have a good life. As we left, he admitted to us that his medicine was lie medicine.

Said Stover, "When are you going to leave this lie medicine and come to the Truth?"

Said the witchdoctor, "It is very hard to leave the things of my ancestors."

Said Stover, "But God was your father before anyone else."

Said the witchdoctor: nothing, either for or against. But we left in friendly spirit.

Chapter Eighteen

HOW THE KINGDOM GROWS

Missions in northern Nigeria almost all belonged to the Northern Missions Council. Respect for Stover Kulp was so high that he was its president. A few years later, I also served as president of the council, but I am sure I was riding on Stover's coattail. The eight missions decided to launch a great evangelistic campaign across northern Nigeria and set an October date for a meeting to plan. The meeting was to be at Numan, and John Grimley, one of the best of our missionary evangelists, was appointed to attend.

As the date approached, however, Mildred was sick, and I became his substitute. Along with Musa, a Lassa deacon, I made the 120-mile trip to Numan, a mission station of the Danish Lutheran Church. The trip had its moments. Even though much of it was by main highway, we were held up by mud at several places. When we reached the Benue River, it was high from recent rains, and the ferry was limited. We parked our car, went across in a small rowboat powered by Nigerian oarsmen, and spent the night in Yola with a Danish missionary. Next morning, we returned for the car and rode with it on a flat scow with room for perhaps three or four automobiles. It was propelled by several men with long poles which they pushed against the river bed. On to Numan, we enjoyed visiting the girls' school and the hospital and joined in discussions about the campaign. Major thrusts were to be in cities where Christian work had already begun.

The meeting over, we returned to Yola, performed some errands which had been delayed, and headed to the river. Our motor had developed a noticeable knock, but local mechanics believed it would not let us down. I suspected bearings, valves, or a connecting rod, but I was not a mechanic. Still, we proceeded with great caution, keeping the motor at a steady seventeen miles per hour for the whole ninety-six-mile trip. God protected us by giving us a highway less treacherous than it had been.

A mumps epidemic developed at Hillcrest School. It is a miracle that the school was ever without an epidemic of some kind in those pre-inoculation days, with children there from at least six or seven differ-ent countries. Larry, speedy in almost everything, was slow to catch the mumps, but he did. When word came that he had them, Bonnie prayed for him, "Dear God, help Larry to get over his muscles." He came home safe and sound late in November (he still had his muscles) and our household rejoiced again.

In December 1952, John took me to the village of Gashala, and one of the most thrilling experiences of my missionary career began. John and I baptized fifty that afternoon, my first baptism in Nigeria. The story, however, begins a few years earlier. A lad of the Kilba tribe, Audu, heard that there was such a thing as a school. He searched for one which would admit a tall boy of fourteen or so years along with the six-year-olds. Even-tually his quest brought him to Lassa, and a school was found for him.

After only about two years in school, however, he was "volun-teered" by Nigerian army recruiters. He was sent to Burma. In Burma, he was extremely lonely. He discovered no other Kilbas and only a few who could speak Hausa. He learned that the chaplain could speak some Hausa, so he visited with him and was given a Hausa New Testament. He assured the chaplain that he could read; do you remember how much you could read in a foreign language after two years of school? The chaplain assured him that the Son of God, Jesus, was in that book and would help his loneliness.

Army stint over, Audu went home. Learning that one of his second grade schoolmates was now a teacher, he went to visit him at his school. As Audu waited in the back of the room, he heard his friend teaching about Jesus. When school was over and he and his friend had exchanged greetings, he requested, "Tell me more about this Jesus."

The more he learned, the more convinced he became that he must give his life to Jesus. He returned to his village so filled with enthusiasm that he simply had to share it with friends. Before long there were young men and their wives gathering together to hear the little that Audu could teach from his meager reading ability. They built a small rectangular build-ing in which to study and pray, but they knew so little.

Once again, he found his way to Lassa. Couldn't the Lassa Church provide a teacher for them, so they could really know about Jesus? It was difficult to find one, because as the church grew rapidly evangelists were quickly located in new villages. Eventually, another Kilba man, Bauchi, was sent to Audu's village. The group kept growing and increased their understanding. A hitch developed. The fathers and uncles of these young seekers-after-Jesus, objected to their leaving the traditional ways. No beermaking or drinking. No second wives. No erotic dances. They tried to recall the group to the old ways. As the group met together, they realized that it would be important for them to get away from the influence of elders—whom they had been taught to respect. They left home. They found a new uninhabited area and settled there, building their houses, developing farms, and in the center of their village, erecting a small church house. Each morning before they went to their farms, they would meet for prayer. Each evening they would meet by lanternlight to hear Bauchi's teaching. It was from these events that the great day of baptism came. John and I had the very unusual, if not, indeed, unprecedented for Nigeria, experience of baptizing husband and wife—several different couples. There was now a congregation of fifty-plus.

On one trip to Gashala to examine people for covenant, I found the small church so crowded that I called Audu and Bauchi aside afterward. "Before the rains come," I told them, "you are going to need a bigger church."

"Oh yes," they assured me. "We have plans."

The next time I went to examine candidates for baptism, they had indeed enlarged their church. They had knocked out one wall and added a section surrounded with a grass mat wall. It was a great day, and we had 129 at Gashala's Love Feast. Before I left, I again took Audu and Bauchi aside. "That building was all right today, but you really must build a permanent one."

"Of course!" they cried, and they took me to show me the site they had chosen.

An old, experienced builder by now, I gave them some advice. "You have never built a big building before. When you build this one, there is one important thing to remember. Don't make it too wide. You can make it a hundred or more feet long if you want, but not more than fifteen feet wide. There is simply no wood around here long enough for rafters for a wider building."

"We understand," they assured me. Sometime later, the two men came to me at Lassa with proud news.

"We have finished our new church," they announced.

"Great! Great! How big is it?"

"Well, it is about seventy feet long and thirty feet wide."

Startled and amazed, I stammered, "How did you get a roof on it?"

"Oh, it doesn't have a roof yet. We have saved just enough money to buy palm lumber and put a proper roof on. We want you to get the mission truck and get the palm from Mubi."

Now, it is true that palm was an excellent, though splintery wood for rafters—long, straight, termite proof, but there was none in the area. Understand, too, that there are no banks, no source of loan money, and for these small farmers, money was in very short supply.

I gave them the sad news. "We have to pay for all the miles that would be needed. I would have to go to Garkida and get the truck. That's one hundred miles. I would have to drive the truck to Mubi. That's sixty miles. I would have to bring the palm here. That's fourteen miles. I would have to take the truck back to Garkida. That's about seventy miles, I would have to drive the car back to Lassa. That's 100 miles. Altogether, that's 344 miles."

When they heard how much it would cost, they looked at each other in dismay. "We just don't have that kind of money. We won't be able to get palm." They began to weep. I wept with them.

Then I had a great idea. Bamboo, though only a grass, is very plentiful. It often grows to a diameter of two or three inches. It is usually quite straight and very tall. "I think this might work," I suggested. "Get a lot of strong bamboo. Tie two or three bamboo rods together side by side to make a rafter." Put your grass roof on bamboo rafters. They thought. They grinned. They felt certain it would work. They left.

A month later, to the day, a lad came into Lassa to the hospital, bringing me a note from Audu. "Our church roof is on," he announced. "Will you come up Sunday and we'll dedicate our new building to God." Proud of my suggestion about bamboo, I drove to Gashala the next day on my motorcycle. After enthusiastic greetings by dozens of Christians, I was taken to the church. As we approached, I examined the roof. It looked smooth, even, and strong, with no hollows to catch water that could seep through or cause rotting. I entered. I looked up at the roof (no ceiling, of course).

My mouth popped open. "That's not bamboo," I exclaimed. "That's palm. Where did you get palm?"

"Well, you remember we had money to buy the palm; it was just a matter of getting it here. When we talked about it, we decided we must give God our best. We men walked fourteen miles to Mubi, bought palm, put it on our heads, walked back. We made three trips to get enough palm."

Wait! Don't go away. Let me finish the story. Some months later, a group of candidates for baptism were examined. Some sixty of them had completed their year of study and probation and appeared to have the understanding and motivation to make their public confession of faith in Jesus. We set a date. The day came. Roy Pfaltzgraff and I rode to Gashala on our motorcycle. Bob and Bea Bischof and Flossie took two Lassa deacons and two deaconesses by car. Audu, living in Lassa at the time because he was humble enough to sit in school with wee children, went with them. Six other men rode the thirty-five miles on bicycle. We worshipped in that beautiful new church. By actual count, there were 556 present, not counting children. Roy and I went into the baptismal stream and baptized nine couples. Bob joined us and we baptized the remaining forty-two persons.

Talk about miracles. Well, we weren't, but let's. From one simple schoolboy, just a very ordinary sort of fellow, God produced a church which rapidly grew to over six hundred and began to plant others. Is it that a grain of wheat, planted in faith, will grow like mustard seed; or is it that the touch of the Spirit on a person changes the ordinary person into a person of power? I don't know. I just thank God for the miracle.

And were you aware of the curative values of french fried potatoes? The missionary staff at Lassa knew that their cooks worked hard, so they always gave them Sunday evening off. We would gather together at one home or another, share foods either left over or freshly prepared, and play games together. On one particular evening in December, we caught Larry quite sick. For three days he had not been able to keep anything, even water, on his stomach. He took it in good spirit, assured that it would end sometime. So when we teasingly asked him if he would like some fries, he agreed . . . ate two big helpings and was all right from then on. Try it; you might like it. Dale and Bonnie, I think, found it hardest to see Larry go back to school. He didn't always play with them—he was busy being athletic with Johnny Grimley—but they liked having big brother around.

Late December tended to be a time with less travel, but in 1952 there was more. Chris Kulp, matriarch of the mission staff, gentle, wise, prim, finally succumbed to one of a series of heart attacks. As many of us as could made our way to Garkida for the memorial service. She was buried in the hillside cemetery which already showed markers for Stover's first wife and an infant. I well remember Stover's visit to Lassa a few days later. We talked about how special Chris was to all of us. Stover commented, "I have come to realize there is something final about death. It was final for Chris, and it is also final for all her relationships. What is left for us is memory of the past and hope for the future, but also the realization that for each of us there will be a final moment on this earth."

Not surprisingly, the principle topic of conversation during January and February was Mary Beth's pregnancy. When would that birth, originally predicted for February 1, take place? Would the new maternity ward at the hospital be ready? It was; four ladies gave birth before Mary Beth got around to it. The Margi women wondered, was there ever a mother who got bigger? We kept talking about the coming addition as another boy. It may have been a protection against disappointment. I remember my mother telling me that all the time she was carrying my sister, they called her "Marjorie June," so by the time she was born, they had tired of the name and called her Mae Hammond.

Mary Beth was very patient in spite of the increasingly hot days as March moved in. Dr. Roy tried various ways to convince that baby it was time. Castor oil. Quinine. Jumping. Finally, early on March 3, pains began . . . and then stopped. That morning Roy gave her pituitrin. No results. He ruptured her membrane. No results. Finally, we just left it to God. Bea Bischof, Roy, or I was with her every moment, taking turns to go home for such mundane tasks as instructing the cook, or eating our meal, or bringing food to our patient. At 4:00 p.m., we were all there, consulting. Roy went home; I biked home to make sure about supper for the kids. Marla decided it was about time. With Bea there alone, contractions began. Summoned, I got there to drip ether and slow the process. Roy arrived seconds later and the coming out party took place.

Marla Christine, blondish, eight pounds four ounces, announced her presence. We all rejoiced. A girl!! We brought the kids down to see their mother and sister, and Mildred Grimley came by. Then Roy went for his jeep and we somehow managed to fit the canvas stretcher into the back of the jeep, as he took her to the Bischofs. Bea was the loving nurse of mother and baby for the next few days, and then we took them home. We cabled the Highs and Biebers. Dale and Bonnie just loved their baby sister, as did Millie May and Joane Grimley. They just had to hold her, touch her, caress her. Didn't we all?

Marla's name evoked speculation. Was she named Mar for Margi and La for Lassa? Was she named Mar for Mary (High) and La for Lawrence (High)? No; we heard that name in Lincoln and liked it. The Christine was for Christine Kulp. Other names also were chosen with purpose. Larien (Larry) for Lawrence (High), George for George (Bieber). Dale was a name we liked; Ernest was for Ernest (Benner), a favorite pupil of Mary Beth who had died. Bonnie was Mary Beth's correction of my choice, Bonita, and Ruth was my favorite name for a girl.

With the coming of April, more responsibility came my way, and I realized anew what a great job John Grimley was doing. The Grimleys were due for furlough. (When the day finally came for their departure, they made several false starts, needing to return for something they had forgotten, simple things like tickets and passports.) John turned over to me three schools of which he was supervisor and eighteen outvillage evangelistic stations. Of course, Bob Bischof would be helping with them, especially among the Higi people who would be the primary opportunity for Bob's denomination, the Brethren Church.

I well remember Bob's first baptisms were near the village of Michika. The local evangelist led us along a tiny stream to a small pond in which the baptisms would take place. One of them walked into the pond to demonstrate it was of sufficient depth. When the new Christians completed their vows on shore, Bob stepped into the pond. Alas, he went in at a spot different from that which had been demonstrated and immediately disappeared. Bob couldn't swim! But in a short moment, we saw his hand come up over the edge of the bank, and we pulled him out. Already well baptized himself, he efficiently proceeded.

This would seem to be a good place to refer to some of the new staff who had joined the mission. There at Lassa, Flossie Miller became our nurse; when Grayce Brumbaugh returned from furlough, she would go to Chibuk. Bob and Bea Bischof arrived, continuing a partnership with the Brethren Church which Veda Liskey had begun a year or so earlier. Bea was a nurse, and when Flossie was reassigned to the leprosarium, Bea became the nurse for our station and hospital. Monroe and Ada Good arrived from eastern Pennsylvania and were assigned to the Shafa station. Their service to the church in Nigeria was to continue, with interruptions, into the twenty-first century. Two very able teachers who had served in China wanted to continue their missionary service. Velma Ober came to teach in the Waka Schools. Hazel Rothrock taught first at Hillcrest and later at Waka.

The prize arrival to me was Dulcie Cover. Widow of a beloved Illinois pastor, she came to Nigeria at age sixty-plus, to be the "grandmother" to little girls in an overflow home at Hillcrest. She is the only person I have ever known who could compare with Mary Beth in her unselfish love of persons. When, years later, I prepared for the message at her funeral, everyone I asked told me that the thing they remembered best about her was her love of God and of people.

This would seem to be an appropriate place, too, to mention single women who became important parts of my life and who were missionaries par excellence. There was Mary Dadisman, educator, nurse, and administrator—the backbone of Ruth Royer Kulp Hospital at Garkida. Her very good friend, Grayce Brumbaugh, was an equally able nurse who had the special kind of skill and commitment which facilitated her assignment to several different locations. Sarah Shisler, a skilled teacher, left the kind of impression that would lead former pupils, years later, to remember, "the deeper things of the Spirit which Miss Shisler taught us."

Clara Harper, had she been male, would certainly have been an elder in the church. She traveled miles and miles on horseback reaching into dozens of villages near and far with the good news of Jesus. Wilma Schrag, who had been a prime missionary in Ecuador, was an excellent teacher at Hillcrest for beginning children, and later was Hillcrest's principal. Two of the ladies who nursed at Lassa, Flossie Royer and, later, Betty Arnett, met the right men in Nigeria. Flossie and Ralph Royer and, later, Betty and Bill Hare were married in Nigeria.

Maybe we weren't paying enough attention to Dale after Marla's arrival. Less than two weeks later, he became very ill. Apparently, he had both malaria and tonsillitis. The malaria gave him nausea, which irritated his throat further, and diarrhea. His fever ran to almost 104° in the evenings. I dosed him with malaria medicine and sulfa and stayed as close to him as possible. Bonnie also kept trying to help. Finally, I added aureomycin and penicillin to his medication, and he began to recover. He was a very patient sufferer, By the time he was back to normal he had lost eleven of his fifty-two pounds, but with his great appetite he soon came back to fullback size again.

Meanwhile, a bull and I had a difference of opinion. I was returning home on my motorcycle from a village fourteen miles away. Ahead, I saw a rather large group of cattle on the left, and perhaps four or five on the right, so I slowed down. The steers on the right were moving away, so I speeded up again, and apparently the noise startled them and they chose to cross the road to their herdsman. One bull caught my headlight in his horn, part of a three-foot span, and upset me and the cycle. The bike got a few dents here and there. I got nasty brush burns which took several days to heal. The bull got up and ran on, apparently unhurt—and that's no bull!

The next months were filled with covenant examinations and services, with baptismal examinations and baptisms. Lassa's Pastor Karbam was busy enough at Lassa, and there still were no Nigerian ministers in the eastern part of the mission, so all of the rites fell to Bob and me. We also traveled a great deal to supervise the erection of new schools, pressing villagers to gather the necessary roofing grass, make the mats, and get the roof on. We took our second Jos vacation, happy to be with Larry again. One incident brought both pleasure and dismay. At one point when Larry was with us, he asked to be taken back to the school. We were pleased that he found the school such a good place, and dismayed that he was ready to leave us so quickly! Stores were well supplied this time and we were able to get all the supplies we needed. Dale was a little disappointed because he did not get a lot of new toys. Marla, of course, was a big hit with everyone, with her big smile, her habit of sleeping six to seven hours at a stretch, and the way she enjoyed her popularity. Vacation over, we traveled to bush in a kind of convoy with the school children, enjoying having Larry with us.

During the time that Larry was at home, and anticipating the fact that Dale would next be leaving us, we celebrated both birthdays early. There were always plenty of gifts available. We welcomed packages from the Highs and Biebers, from Bieber uncles and aunts, from good friends, and from the several churches which shared in our support—Mechanic Grove, Scalp Level, Clover Creek, Parkerford, and of course our home church, Royersford.

It was also a very busy time. I went with Stover, Bob, and Jim Bowman to explore areas of the Higi country for a good location for the Brethren mission station. We were almost overwhelmed by the beauty of the mountains and by large valleys which lay almost hidden among them. We were also impressed by the purity of water which came from mountain springs in good supply. Our trek was a great experience. The four of us were quite compatible, and we were cared for by some of the best "boys" in the mission, notably Audu, the Kulp cook.

On occasion we would ask for something, thinking to embarrass them for not being able to provide, but they never failed. We also were able to do some small game hunting. Near the end of our trek, we shot a large goose. My notes say that the goose went by bicycle to Gulak— I think someone else pedaled—where we celebrated the end of our trek with a great dinner.

I would not say that the antimalarial medication we took was not effective. I know that every one of us endured several sieges of malaria, so obviously it was not as preventive as we might have liked. Yet our attacks could have been much worse than they usually were. Mine did not usually disable me; I was up and down. Mary Beth's kept her aching and bedfast for several days. The little girls seemed to recover quickly. By 1953, it seemed to be Dale who was most drastically affected. As the sad day approached when we would lose our second son to Hillcrest, he was down for several days, unable to keep anything down until the day before departure. Roy Pfaltzgraff would be with him on the first leg of the journey, so we let him go, with fear and trembling and lots of prayer. Their trip was reasonably comfortable in the lorry, with luggage base and mattresses on top, but it was a full day trip. They were delayed by the need to tow Heckman's car the last two hundred of the five-hundred-mile trip. Dale's malaria was past, and it was reported to us that he arrived full of pep and vigor, even after that twenty-four-hour journey.

In August, I was able to see our boys twice—to and from Zaria. The Nigeria colonial government, recognizing that few of the more than two hundred languages in Nigeria had been committed to writing, financed a special seminar in linguistics. Margi and Bura had been reduced to writing only after the mission arrived in 1922. I was one of several from the Church of the Brethren Mission selected to go. We did learn a lot about linguistic orthography, the use of phonetic symbols to represent the sounds of primitive languages. (In English, when we spell with an "e," it may have several different sounds. In Margi, whatever different sounds there are must be represented by different symbols.) It was one of those learnings which sound good and make sense on paper. Some effort was made to use the right symbols in new translations of the Bible, but I do not believe they will ever be welcomed by anyone except the scholars. I think the seminar was effective, however, in moving the learners to the development of more literature.

Marla always seemed to be an extremely active baby. She quickly learned to roll over, and then would roll over and over, not, I think, as a means of locomotion, but just for fun. She learned to scoot along on her stomach. From about age six months, she found that she could stand by holding a chair or someone's hand. We would find her standing by a chair until—boom—she would fall. She would walk while holding a helping hand.

I jump to the last days of October. Mary Beth and I were lying on the living room floor for a brief afternoon rest. We saw Marla stand by a chair. Then, to our surprise, we saw her take four steps across the floor. Next afternoon, she repeated it, and later took six, seven steps. For a while, however, crawling was her preferred locomotion, and we seem to remember that after a couple of days she declared a two-month moratorium on walking.

FURLOUGH TIME

Our first term of missionary service drew to a close. We wrote copious transitional notes for Bea and Bob Bischof. We held an auction sale attended by about seventy-five people at which we sold everything from tin cans to items of clothing. It was quite an experience to hold an auction with bids coming in different languages. (I did know money words.) We said sad farewells to our "boys" and to close friends that we had made, as well as to the missioinary staff. Bob drove us without event to Marama, where we spent the night. Elmer Baldwin drove us from there in his Austin, by a route some one hundred miles shorter than the usual, but open for only a few months each year. It was open for us, but with difficulty.

Crossing the river, our loaded car was unable to negotiate the sand. We had sent Nggida walking ahead to test depth, and it seemed safe, but we bogged down. We were able to recruit six men to push us out of the sand, and we went on to worse problems. We went beyond where Nggida had plumbed the depths. The water drowned the motor. The car sank into the sand. Water flowed across the floorboards. We carried the kids to shore. It was covered by a layer of reeds about three inches deep, and we were able to pull up pieces of the layer to keep a fire going for the three hours we were there. Finally, men pushed the car out of the river. It agreed, reluctantly, to get to work again and we were on the way. Thankfully, none of us caught colds or suffered any after effects except for weariness for the long night.

Happily, we picked up our boys in Jos, Dale recovering from another malaria bout. We took the train to Lagos, a forty-six-hour, two-night trip. In Lagos we stayed for two nights at the Sudan Interior Mission guesthouse at Yaba. Leaving the country was almost as difficult as entering. I had to pick up our tickets, get visas for our return to Nigeria, and discover that, even leaving the country, one goes through customs. The driver who took me to town left too soon and, believe it or not, I hitchhiked back to the guesthouse.

Our boat trip was on the *Aureole*, the mail boat which followed a regular bi-monthly schedule between England and West Africa. My memory may not be fully reliable here, but I think there were several Methodist missionary families and one Lutheran Brethren family, so the kids had playmates. The cabins were comfortable, but small and not plush. There was no room at the inn (oops, I mean in the cabin with the rest of the family) for me. I was in another cabin with a roommate. The bunks were acceptable. The toilet and bathroom were around the corner. Cold water and fruit were always available. Tea for adults and fruit juice for children were served early morning and midafternoon. The meals were very good. The children had their own menu and ate early in the evening; they were expected to be in bed by the time we ate, which did not sit too well with reader Larry. Marla had one day of some identifiable illness.

As on our freighter trip, we stopped at ports along the way along the coast, but our stops were fewer and briefer. There were movies and parties along the way to help the trip seem shorter. Eventually we rounded the west side of Africa and reached the Bay of Biscay and some very rough seas. Many people were sick; my roommate did not leave the room for five days. Our family fared well except for some squeamishness; we met it by eating. The dish of apples in the cabin needed constant replenishing. Bonnie was the only seasick one; she missed just three meals. I think we learned that, for us, it would stave off *mal de mer* if we would eat a little something.

We landed safely at Liverpool and entrained to London. There we stayed for a few days at the Methodist Church Foreign Mission House. The English are friendly enough, but very formal. While we were in London, we visited a few of the high spots. I remember Westminster Abbey the best, because I was so impressed with Mary Beth's ability to keep nursing Marla, under the cover of a light blanket, as we walked through that venerable place.

Then, at last, we boarded the Queen Elizabeth II for the last lap of our journey home. We could hardly believe the size of the ship, the facilities, the crowds of people, the tireless service, and the rapid journey. Perhaps a third of the way across the North Atlantic, we ran into a powerful storm—or it ran into us—I'm not sure which. The ship rocked side to side and end to end. Crew and passengers alike were affected and afflicted. In the dining salon, we had been assigned a table for our family. During the storm, when we went for dinner, there were just two tables full in that whole salon. One was filled with about eight children whose parents were unable to overcome their seasickness. The other was ours; God enabled our whole family to weather the storm. And despite shortage of staff, we were served not only the three meals a day (four, because the children ate their evening meal early as on the *Aureole*), but the usual early morning, pre-noon, and late afternoon teas.

Arriving in New York, we made appointments with A.M.M.O., the Associated Mission Medical Office, which would eventually be responsible for our physical examinations and approval for our return to Nigeria. We were met by Dad Bieber; Mae's son, David; and Uncle Theodore; for the five of us and our loads, two cars were needed. We enjoyed crossing the East River on the renowned Staten Island Ferry. We also enjoyed stopping for lunch at an American restaurant. The kids asked for milk, and the price seemed so high that Dad asked if that also included the cow.

The second half of the High house, where we had moved shortly after Larry's birth, had become vacant and was held for us, so we were able to live there for our furlough year. The weeks after our arrival were relatively free of responsibility. We enrolled Larry and Dale in the East Vincent Elementary School and were pleased at how quickly and easily they settled in. Of course, their Aunt Martha was school nurse there, so that may have helped. We welcomed visitors; we did some small traveling of our own; and we told our story in a few of the nearby churches. We did make one trip of length, to the Fairview Church in Southern Indiana, to visit friends and former parishioners. With a great deal of financial help from the Highs and the Royersford Church, we were able to buy a Willys Jeep Station Wagon to take along to Nigeria.

For me, the easy days were not to last very long. The scheduled evangelist for the Manor Church of the Brethren in Clymer, near Indiana, Pennsylvania, was unable to fulfill his appointment, and I agreed to substitute for a week of preaching. I enjoyed the week and the privilege of preaching in English. One of the leaders bade me farewell at the end of the week with a comment that suggested I had room for improvement: "I would like to hear you when you are a few years older."

By the time my soon-to-come experience in the First West Virginia District was past, I was indeed "a few years older." Walter Van Sickle scheduled my meetings for three weeks in that district, speaking at a couple of district gatherings, but mostly speaking each night and Sunday in a series of churches. I examined my schedule, found that I would be on the docket for twenty-seven times. I wrote to Brother Van Sickle, indicating my willingness to be busy during the day as well as during the evening, and suggested schools or service clubs. He went to work again, and by the time my three weeks were past I had spoken forty-two times.

My sojourn in West Virginia left some vivid memories. I took a set of slides to use in the evening, but in two different church buildings, I found there was only one electrical outlet—one bulb for the whole room. We managed with a double socket. At every church, I told the Gashala story. It so moved one family that they later sent money to Nigeria to build a needed school. One host decided to travel with me to two additional churches. I was glad he did, for at one of those churches there were only three other persons present. (I took their addresses and wrote to them afterward.) In one home where I stayed, I boldly asked where the bathroom was and was told to just go out behind the barn.

One afternoon I located the church building where I was to speak that evening, but it was locked, so I retraced my steps (wheels) to a nearby country store. I introduced myself to the lady clerk and explained my problem. She apologized that her husband wasn't at home and suggested I wait, sitting on a nail keg in the store. Eventually, the husband showed up, and I saw the lady point me out. He came to me and, after introducing himself, he began to give me directions to the church. I thanked him, but because evening was fast approaching, I said, "I do know where the church is. I was wondering where I might go for supper."

"Oh," he said, "you'll be eating with us." For three hours, his wife had let me sit on a nail keg instead of inviting me into their home, which was connected to the store. Later in our furlough, I would also go to the churches of western Maryland.

At that time, the Brethren in Nigeria were treated almost as a district of the Church of the Brethren. That meant having delegates to the Standing Committee of Annual Conference, and the opportunity fell to whoever happened to be on furlough. This time, I was the one, and our family enjoyed Annual Conference at Ocean Grove, where Mary Beth and I had been consecrated five years earlier. William Beahm, dean of Bethany Biblical Seminary and former missionary to Nigeria, was the moderator.

The Foreign Mission Commission, in those days, had a system for promoting interest and income called the support system. Local congregations, groups, or individuals assumed the "support" of missionary families. That meant a financial commitment for the work of the missionary, and regular correspondence between the worker and the support group. The children, of course, were not working missionaries, but added to the cost of any worker, so support was assigned for each member of the family. We made it a special point to visit all the churches which supported us: Parkerford, Mechanic Grove, Scalp Level, Clover Creek, Lanark, the Foster family in Worthington, Minnesota, and the Sunday Schools of Michigan.

As autumn arrived, I was scheduled for a November trip to those Michigan Sunday Schools. It was specifically Larry that they "supported," so we arranged for a few days of absence from school for Larry and he joined me for the last few days of the tour. It was the Saturday before Thanksgiving, and we had just returned to our host's home after speaking at the Lansing Church. A telephone call came from J. Henry Long, associate executive for the mission board. He announced, "You are going to have to go to the Lansing Church in Illinois tomorrow."

"I can't go there. I am already scheduled for the Pontiac Church in the morning and the Detroit Trinity Church in the evening."

"That doesn't matter. The Lanark Church supports you and they want you tomorrow. I have booked you on a plane at noon tomorrow. They will meet you and take you to the church. You can fly back next day."

As I struggled to find my way out of that problem, it occurred to me that I had plenty of slides along. I asked nine-year-old Larry, "If I get together a set of slides and recorded comments, could you just talk a little about Hillcrest School? The church can make a special effort to get the children there."

"Sure, Dad," said the lad. We followed through. I set up the slide show, spoke at the Pontiac Church on Sunday morning, left at noon by plane for Illinois, and carried through with the good folks at Lanark. Tremendously relieved to see Larry back at the Detroit airport, I was assured by our hosts that everything had gone very well. Wanting a first hand report, I asked Larry how it went. "Oh, it was O.K., Dad. I told them a couple of things then I told them, 'I don't like to talk, but I'll be glad to answer questions.'" And we drove on home to see what kind of questions mother, brother, and sisters might have for us.

Another startling telephone call came from Henry Long. Our physicals had been completed and we assumed we were healthy enough to return to Nigeria. Well, maybe not; the gist of the call was that there was a spot of tuberculosis on my lung. I had absolutely no symptoms, so it was decided that I should see a specialist. I had a fresh chest x-ray and went to the Women's College Hospital in Philadelphia. The doctor examined me carefully, studied the x-ray, and asked, "Do you really want to get back to Nigeria?"

"I really do," I assured him.

"You have the scar of past T.B., about the size of a nickel. I do not believe it will give you any problem, and it is certainly not active. Just to be safe, get a short rest every afternoon." His report brought approval from the A.M.M.O., and we resumed our preparations to return.

There was other news before our return. With the addition of new mission stations and the increase in the number of missionaries, the work of Field Secretary Stover Kulp was growing ever more heavy. Mission conference in Nigeria decided to assign an assistant field secretary and, to my great surprise, they appointed me. All my life, the only major position I ever volunteered for was that of missionary; and how could I help that? Here again, in Garkida, the church called me. We would live in Garkida, which meant the learning of another language, Bura. Mary Beth would become headmistress of the mission's only senior primary school. I would be responsible for personnel matters, record keeping, and generally assisting Stover, while at the same time being a teacher and an evangelist. We also learned that, once again, we would be traveling by freighter to Lagos, but this time we would be accompanied by Irven and Patty Stern and daughter Gayle.

We left New York on the *S.S. Sherbro* of the Elder Dempster Line. This voyage was made different by the fact that we would be taking dynamite to Ghana for dredging out the new harbor at Accra. We were asked to sign releases indicating that we were aboard in spite of the load. From New York we sailed to Halifax, where we spent several days loading the dynamite. It was COLD in Halifax, and we enjoyed watching huge icicles develop on the ship. The boys and I went in to Halifax to see, "20,000 Leagues under the Sea."

Once loaded, the trip was a close duplication of the one we had taken five years earlier, with a different set of passengers. Irven fortified all of us against seasickness by advising that it was largely a matter of one's state of mind. He must have been in the wrong state; he was the only one seasick. We had packages to open at least once a week, so there were always new things. There were also more children—an additional Bieber and Gayle Stern, so it was a little more fun for the kids. The E.D. line had agents in more ports and had let us know in advance where mail might reach us, so we had the luxury of receiving mail several times.

The crew set up a Ping-Pong table (excuse me, sophisticates, a table tennis table) and we used it a lot. Larry fell in love with the game and before too long was beating his mother. Dale loved to make things, following directions of several kits which were in our kit of playthings. Both boys loved carrying sister Marla around. Bonnie loved playing with Gayle or her brothers. Marla became quite a chatter box. We especially enjoyed hearing her say, "I can't do it!" while vigorously shaking her head.

Once again, we enjoyed watching the unloading as we stopped at various West African ports. We did not have a Spanish fly visitation on this trip. In Monrovia, Liberia, we had a brief visit with Max Pierce, who had been a passenger with us on the *African Glade* five years earlier. At Takoradi, Ghana, there was about a nervous (for us land-lubbers) week while the dynamite was being unloaded. The men who received it into their small boats seemed so careless that we occasionally shivered. Irven and I rode a "Mammy Chair," a two-passenger cab lifted by davit into the boat, so we could go in and visit the city.

We arrived in Lagos on March 10 and were graciously received by S.I.M missionaries in their guesthouse at Yaba. After several days of impatient waiting, our Jeep was offloaded, and we took care of various business matters such as immigration, licensing, and customs. We planned for the ladies and children to fly to Jos, and for Irven and me to drive the Jeep.

So, having completed our necessary business in Lagos, including air schedules for the families, Irven and I started north in the Jeep with as much of the loads as we could manage. The Jeep had a carrier on the roof, but I was not as careful as I might have been in securing it, and after a hundred miles or so it came off. Irven and I spent a great deal of time retrieving items and securing the carrier more carefully. The loads were heavier than we should have carried for those roads, so we also broke a spring. Eventually, we reached Jos and were both puzzled and dismayed to find that our families had not yet arrived.

The day before Mary Beth and the others were to take off, there was a plane crash and several people were killed, so all planes were grounded. The train was the only public transportation north, and it was booked full. They were able to book a trip a week later. Meanwhile, planes began to be scheduled. They booked a flight. It was canceled. They booked another; it was canceled. Then, thanks to the goodness of two missionary pilots, they were flown to Ilorin and then to Jos, and we were able to collect them at the Jos airport with great relief and celebration.

Chapter Twenty

NEW ASSIGNMENTS

There was a great deal of shopping for both families to do in Jos. Sadly, we had to leave Larry and Dale behind at Hillcrest, but eventually we were on our way. This time we were able to provide our own transportation. Our initial home in Garkida was our fourth in Nigeria, after having lived in two different homes in Lassa, and one at the leprosarium. It was half of a duplex, close to the hospice for the senior primary school and the residence of Bassey Minso and his wife. Velma Ober, a teacher who had been a missionary in China, was our next door neighbor when we first arrived.

Velma's vacation was well overdue, so Mary Beth began almost on arrival to teach in the senior primary school, and I did much of my first work at home. Along with our Nigerian servants, I kept an eye on the two little girls.

The house was small for a family of six, a little easier when the boys were away at school. The dining room, living room, and bathroom were each only about 8x10, and the study was even smaller. Sleeping quarters were outside, with the toilet at the edge of the veranda. For several weeks we argued with a band of termites about whose house this was. Each morning, at the doorway to the study, there was a termite hill of about one square foot. The boys would clean it away only to find it there again next morning. Eventually chlordane discouraged the wood-eating insects.

Bura study, for both of us, was delayed and sporadic. My own schedule developed rapidly. As I began to increase my awareness of how things functioned, I compiled all the old minutes of field committee and mission conference. I did not have the direct evangelism in which I had been involved at Lassa, but I was frequently on a trip to another station or to Jos for meetings of various kinds. I kept minutes of the meetings, and Fern Baldwin, who served as secretary, saw to their distribution. With responsibilities for personnel, I tried to spend a lot of time orienting newcomers, listening, and keeping the foreign missions office informed about our morale as their staff in Nigeria.

I also spent a lot of time listening to Stover. I was to assist him in any way that I could, and I wanted to know his program as thoroughly as possible. We were in an important time of transition. An increasing number of Nigerians were reaching an educational and experiential level which would enable them to assume some of the responsibilities only missionaries had held. It was difficult to determine when the moment for such turnover had come, and there were differences of opinion about whether it had arrived. Missionaries, too, though deeply committed to Christ and the mission program, also tended to be strong-minded persons.

Stover would rather often receive a letter of criticism or complaint. He asked me to answer most of those letters, giving me a sage bit of advice: "There will always be some good in the letter. Unless the complaint is something major and urgent, just answer the good."

I had only been at work in Garkida for about a month when Stover suffered a serious automobile accident at Mubi. He was badly bruised over much of his body and had a concussion. He spent some time in the government hospital at Mubi, and then in his recently consecrated home at Mubi, with nurse Lena Wirth assigned there to give him care. As he improved, he was moved to Lassa and slowly began to pick up elements of his work, but it was several months before he was back to full activity, and his work fell to me.

It was at that period, too, that the new Waka Teacher Training College would open. There was a desperate need for teachers and evangelists, and the mission education program, though following the British pattern, emphasized filling those needs. The usual educational process went something like this: A man with from two to four years of education would gather children around him in his village. As the number of interested children increased and support of the villagers grew, the day would come when a junior primary school (first four grades) would open. In earliest days, the only such schools were in the mission stations. The next step in education would be the senior primary school, which required better trained teachers to take the students through their seventh year. For many years, the only senior primary school was at Garkida. That meant that only about a sixth of the students could go to senior primary school. The next step, with the great need for teachers, was the teachers training school, and Waka was the mission answer.

The opening of Waka meant the move of senior primary staff to become teacher training staff, so Mary Beth very quickly moved into teaching in the senior primary school. She became the headmistress (principal). I was one of her teachers, teaching Bible, health, and nature study. The young Christians had a deep longing to know more about Christianity and committed much of their time to that study; eight boys in one Bible class decided—at age about fourteen—that they would enter the ministry, and seven of them actually did.

Another of those transitions which parents both look forward to and dread came in July. Bonnie celebrated her sixth birthday in April, so when her brothers and a gang of others headed off for Hillcrest in July, Bonnie was among them. Getting a child ready for boarding school is not only a traumatic experience, but a time of busy preparations. Mary Beth had to make sure all the clothes were in order and sewed name tags on everything, from both socks in each pair, to washcloths and towels. Before Bonnie went to school, she demonstrated a strong love for flowers. She planted her own little flower garden and, with the help of two-year-old Marla, gathered stones with which to surround and protect it. A few months later, when Jean Wine, housemother, was confined by a difficult pregnancy, Bonnie took flowers to her each day.

Their going seemed to launch a very busy summer. Among other things it meant that I had to do some difficult counseling with a couple who had to go home because she was expecting a second Caesarean operation. It also meant a great deal of correspondence with the home office about staff needs and about making ready for some who would come. Fortunately, we were making more use of 1-W's—Conscientious Objectors assigned by their draft boards to meaningful civilian service.

The first to come was Earl Dibert, of near Everett, Pennsylvania, who would supervise building. That takes me back to an interesting experience during furlough. I had spoken to Middle Pennsylvania District Conference on a Friday evening, and Earl's parents came to me urging that I visit them on Sunday evening when I was to be at their church. I agreed. They asked me for supper Sunday evening, and again I agreed, but cautioned them that I would certainly have had a large dinner, so would want little to eat. Oh, of course, they understood! On Sunday evening I arrived at the Diberts. I talked with them about the good work their son was doing. We had supper. It was not particularly heavy. I noticed some fruit cocktail and was grateful for a light dessert. I ate as little as I thought I dared, and still be polite. Then I ate the fruit. Too full, but not uncomfortably so. Mother Dibert went to the kitchen—to clear up, I assumed. She soon came back in, with four pies—two on each arm.

"Which kind, or kinds, would you like?" she asked.

Stunned, I stammered, "Mother Dibert, I can hardly believe it is me saying this, but I don't believe I had better eat any pie."

Without a word, she set the pies down and retreated to the kitchen. Had I offended her? Of course not. She returned with a plate for me, with a large piece of chocolate cake and a huge dipper of ice cream.

"Well, then, you can eat this," she confidently exclaimed.

I ate. I thanked the Diberts for the great fellowship and meal, but I have never been more uncomfortable in the pulpit than I was that night at Everett.

As August approached in 1955, we were visited by two very conservative, very friendly, nicely-bearded Brethren from eastern Pennsylvania. I was their assigned chauffeur. With great cooperation from mission staff, we were able to arrange for them to visit eight of the ten mission stations, worship at a church dedication, at baptisms by a Bura pastor, at a love feast, and generally tour the area. They were outspoken and curious; they also wanted to be sure that proper doctrine was being taught. The son asked me, "What do you teach these people about the second coming of Jesus?"

Now, to be perfectly honest, that was not one of the major emphases in our teaching, but I managed an answer. "Well, Brother, we want them to know that Jesus might come at any time, so you had better be ready. On the other hand, it may be a long time yet, so keep working." It was the right answer.

The other memorable incident of their visit took place as we were driving rather slowly along a gravel road among the Higi people. The Higi women, in those days, were nude except for a decorative "modesty apron" over their loins. As a matter of cleanliness, they shaved their heads, as did the men. We passed several of these ladies with their well-exposed breasts. Finally, the father of the pair exclaimed, "I don't know how you tell the men from the women out here. They all shave their heads."

When it was time to return the brethren to Jos for their plane connection, we were delayed at several rain gates because of the muddy condition of the roads, but we arrived in time. I think God was on my side—God always is—because on the same trip I was able to pick up Iris Neff, a new nurse, and 1-W's Curtis Weddle and Ronn Moyer. They were delayed, and my stay in Jos was extended, so I enjoyed time with our children. Bonnie was getting along very well and was very proud of her first attempts at writing. She had many new friends, she let me know, but she didn't know who all of them were yet. Dale also was very content, had more friends, and was happy to be able to read well. Larry made it a point of sitting beside Bonnie at meal time and asking her questions about school.

Larry, however, who never complained, seemed to be limping as he walked. When I asked him, he said that he had a lot of pain in his knee. I remembered that he had spoken of a sore throat a few days earlier, and immediately suspected rheumatic fever. I took him to Dr. Troup at S.I.M. Bingham Memorial Hospital and a sed rate confirmed the diagnosis. We caught it in its incipient stages and except for a few weeks of precautionary limited activity, he had no aftereffects.

When I got back to Garkida with Curt and Ronn, who were to live in the other half of our duplex, I found that Mary Beth had also had a new experience. Celia Shankster had come from Waka with a son whose leg was badly abscessed. The doctor wanted them to stay for a few days, so Mary Beth and Marla went to Waka and she (Mary Beth, not Marla) taught for Celia in the Girls School.

Being assistant to Stover Kulp brought surprising responsibilities. Hillcrest School had been established by the Church of the Brethren Mission in 1941, as a school for missionary children. With the good relationship the Brethren had with other missions in northern Nigeria in the Northern Missions Council, it seemed the right thing to do to let Hillcrest expand to an inter-mission program. A Board of Governors was set up, and I was appointed, along with Stover, to represent CBM on the board. Stover was quickly elected Chairman of the Board, and I was its secretary, for three years. Later I was to serve another term as chairman.

As we moved into 1956, we were making preparations for the meeting of the Tarayyar Ekklesiyoyin Kristi A Sudan (TEKAS), The Fellowship of Churches of Christ in the Sudan, a cooperative organization of churches and missions. It took its name from the location of the churches and missions in the area just south of the Sahara known as the Sudan. Two important factors affected the 1956 meeting: there was close cooperation among the members, and missions were recognizing the growing ability of the churches to be self-governing. Likely the move toward self-government by Nigeria as a nation influenced the missions and churches in that direction.

Plans had been made and a proposed new plan of organization had been developed. It would recognize the indigenous church maturity and responsibility and the cooperation. It would emphasize that the work of

Christianity in the north was aimed at bringing people to Christ rather than to a specific denomination. A great new church would be formed. It would be called Ekklesiyar Kristi A Sudan (EKAS), The Church of Christ in the Sudan. The churches seemed ready to unite. The missions had initially indicated willingness. There were seven missions involved. They were as follows: an independent South African mission among the TIV people; five branches of the Sudan United Mission including the Evangelical, the South African, the British branch, the Dutch Reformed branch, the Danish Lutheran; and the Church of the Brethren. Local branches of EKAS would be identified only by location; the Church of the Brethren would be EKAS Lardin Gabas, or EKAS of eastern area.

Stover Kulp and Roy Pfaltzgraff were our mission representatives to the meeting. I do not know who represented the church. I attended only as a visitor; it was, after all, right there in Garkida. As the meeting progressed, it moved toward the moment of decision. Obviously union would depend upon the willingness of the missions to approve. All went well until the vote of the Danish Lutheran Mission, which included strong American influence. They declined to give approval, announcing that for their church to join EKAS would be to forfeit their American support. All of the churches continued to need mission financial and personnel support, so that one branch was forced to a negative answer. Debate continued. To go on without that branch was contrary to the sense of togetherness.

A compromise was reached: a FELLOWSHIP of Churches of Christ in Nigeria would be formed. Churches would still be in full cooperation, recognize the validity of the slightly differing doctrines and rites, but be separate denominations. (For thirteen years the churches of CBM called themselves EKAS LARDIN GABAS.) Leaders in the United States misread the name as implying the Nigerian Church did not see themselves as Brethren, and a number of misguided decisions were made as a result. In 1979, the Nigerian Church officially retitled themselves the Church of the Brethren in Nigeria (Ekklesyar Yanuwa a Nigeria - EYN).

Our mission conference in January had made me the chair of the evangelism committee, strangely, because others were doing far more evangelistic work than I was. I was serving as elder of the Virgwi Church, and Charles Lunkley and I shared the outvillage work. I did preach frequently in Bura after about eight months in Garkida, and occasionally in Margi.

The *majalisa* (church council for our whole area) had decided to set up a special Bible School so evangelists and ministers might be trained.

Local congregations were to send selected persons and their families. The entire program, except for the missionary teachers, was being financed by the church. Compounds were set up at Garkida for seventeen students and their families. I was made the principal of the school, and taught three classes. Charles Lunkley and Elmer Baldwin also taught, and later on, when Lunkleys moved to Wandali, Ira Petre taught. Most of the men in the class did become probationary ministers. In America they would have been called licensed ministers. Some of them were really good leaders.

A happy memory and a good lesson for me occurred one morning when we had an especially meaningful class and felt a real sense of the presence of God. That also made us all feel closer together. As I left the school and started up the hill to our house, Bubwa Nyamdu walked beside me.

"Let me carry your books," he requested.

Out of a feeling that I did not want the students to feel they were my servant, I declined. "Thanks, I can carry them," I said.

"That is the trouble," said Bubwa. "You don't like to let us do anything for you." I handed the books over and we went on up the hill together. Bubwa taught me that sometimes it is as important to be served as to serve.

There is also a less pleasant memory with its, eventual, happy aftermath. One student, Jilasari, was just not cut out for learning. When the church committee overseeing the school came calling, we had to report his failure to learn. His highest grade for the first term was sixty-seven, and his average was forty-two. The committee decided they could not afford to keep him there and, sadly, he was dismissed. The rest of the story comes much later, but I must tell it here.

Four years later, when we were living back at Lassa, the pastor, Ngamariju, asked me to take him to the village of Kilekasa where a group were, reportedly, ready for the covenant. I asked him who was the evangelist there, and this conversation ensued:

Ngamariju: "It is a man named Jilasari."

Me: "I had a student named Jilasari at the Bible School, but he would be too dumb to be an evangelist now."

Ngama: "This Jilasari had leprosy and lived at the leprosarium for a few years."

Me: "That's interesting. The Jilasari I know lived at Virgwi, too."

Ngama: "This man is a Margi whose home was in the village of Bagajau. He has a wife named Mairama."

Me: "Wow! The Jilasari I knew came from Bagajau and had a wife, Mairama. Let's go and see what this Jilasari is like."

You guessed it. The same Jilasari. No ill feelings at having been dismissed from Bible School. He just kept on teaching others the things he could not learn himself! There were eighteen young men reciting scriptures, singing songs, and taking the covenant. It is truly amazing how God can use people. Maybe that is why I am almost always willing to say yes to a task I am not at all sure I can do. God's strength may be made perfect in our weakness.

I don't think I mentioned that when we lived at Lassa a few years back, I built a small house of mud bricks for our monkey. When it was done, it didn't look like much, and it surely wasn't much. It took only one rainy season to knock it down. Since then, maybe from reading Amos, I learned the use of a plumb line. At Lassa, we could get small eggs at times from local people. We always put them in water. The spoiled ones were shells full of gas, so they floated. At Garkida, there were few eggs. We decided to raise chickens and I decided to build a chicken house. It was a big project; we wanted at least a couple of dozen chickens. We bought mud bricks and I laid them up, carefully using the plumb line to ensure that the wall would be exactly perpendicular. When I finished, after several weeks, I got help to put on a good roof and ended with a chicken house that lasted. We didn't; we soon moved to another home.

We enjoyed having Ronn and Curt living next to us. Ronn was quiet, but friendly and adaptable; he was my office secretary. Curt was louder and more bluff. He taught in the Senior Primary School, and sometimes seemed too rough on his pupils. Later Bob Baker came to live with them. We would feed them all their meals for a month, and then they would eat with Lunkleys—later Petres—for a month. Ronn particularly seemed to enjoy Marla. Curt had an interesting experience during one night. As for most of us, their beds were on a roofed porch, and the toilet at the side. One night, afflicted by slight diarrhea, Curt was sitting on the toilet when he heard a noise beneath him. He jumped up, grabbed his flashlight, and discovered a cobra coiled around the toilet bucket. Ever after, we inspected before sitting!

At the *majalisa* meeting after the organization of the new Fellowship of Churches, it was decided to call a general secretary for the whole church, and they elected me. My broad responsibilities involved keeping the minutes (which I did in English and, with some help, in Hausa), gathering and keeping records, keeping the churches informed, and corresponding with the home office and the TEKAN churches. I met with all the committees and helped to decide when a worshipping group was strong enough to become a new congregation. I wrote a complete new plan of organization to submit to their executive committee. With many improvements which their commitment and intelligence brought, the plan of organization was adopted and followed for nearly fifty years.

I enjoyed taking minutes of meetings. Somehow that kept me alert and aware. It was a little like being catcher on the playground softball team after high school. At one time I was taking minutes of the church meetings, the Field Committee, the mission conferences, the Northern Missions Council, and the Hillcrest Board of Governors. In the light of commonly (mistakenly) assigning women to do the secretarial work, I was an anomaly.

Once again, as the end of May came, we were delighted to welcome our school children home. Their travel was different this time. Some of them were flown by S.I.M. plane to a newly cleared landing strip at Biu, just a few miles from Waka. They had an exciting arrival. It was the first time for a plane to land there, so the big Emir of Biu and a large crowd of people joined us to welcome pilot and passengers. The children really enjoyed being home again, and little sister Marla was ecstatic.

When we were on the *S. S. Sherbro*, we had come to enjoy playing table tennis. Larry got good enough to beat his mother, no slouch at the game. Both Larry and Dale could sometimes beat me as well. Larry dearly wanted an air rifle, so I promised him that when the time came when he could beat me five games in a row, I would see that he got one. Safe offer, right? He'll be fifteen or sixteen, right? Wrong. Home on vacation from Hillcrest, he easily beat me five games in a row, and he had not quite reached his eleventh birthday.

The return of the youngsters to Hillcrest came too soon, but all three seemed to like school. Bonnie thought the second grade was a lot harder, and Dale felt overwhelmed as the only boy with fourteen girls in his class. About a month after they had arrived, measles broke out. They seemed to have been brought from the States by a recent arrival, and by the time the epidemic was past, there must have been thirty or more kids affected. It seemed to come in groups—Bonnie was in the second group—and there were only a few serious cases. We could not remember that either of our boys had ever had measles, but they were not affected.

About the same time, it became necessary for Stover to go home for an operation; he would be gone for several months. That left me with the full job of field secretary, which now involved reports to government and contact with colonial officers. Along with that, I was still teaching in the Senior Primary School and still serving as secretary to the church. About once a month the doctor would call me in to assist at an operation or a delivery. I was on the road a lot, sometimes chauffeuring families to or from their homes, sometimes for meetings, sometimes on evangelistic visits, but the Lord was with me. I wasn't having accidents and the roads were often dry enough to be passable. Of course, there was that one trip with Stover to Jos. With 270 miles still to go, we hit a rock in the road and broke the steering rod. We spent an extra day along the road while someone came to pick us up. I eventually was able to arrange an S.I.M. plane to Biu, and Waka folks took me to Garkida. The car was towed back and eventually repaired.

I am not at all sure at which annual mission meeting it took place, but at one of them we had an interesting invasion. We were meeting in one of the rooms of the Senior Primary School. Suddenly one of the missionaries cried out, "There are bees in here!" The bees in Garkida, though not deadly, stung very painfully. Someone had disturbed their hive, and they were scouting the neighborhood seeking the culprits.

All but two of us fled, most of us toward our homes, a few to a nearby darkened classroom. One of the things we had heard about bees was that they were looking for life, so they would not attack still objects. Two of us sat still. When I noticed the other jump and run, I realized bees do attack still objects, so I ran into the darkened schoolroom. Almost every person was stung at least once. The worst were a man with multiple stings on arms and legs, and a woman whose tightly wound hairdo kept bees captive so they stung her. I escaped and explained my escape by reminding that bees, of course, don't sting the flowers from which they take their nectar.

As acting field secretary, I also had the interesting job of being schools manager. In simple terms that means I had to be in constant contact with the government, from which teachers' salaries come, make sure the proper salaries reached each school, and act as the superintendent. The mission education committee, however, assigned the teachers.

Chapter Twenty-One

VISITORS—THE HIGHS AND OTHERS

As a family, we were getting more and more excited about the planned visit of Mother and Dad High. We really hoped they would arrive in time for Christmas, but, of course, we would change our personal celebration to fit. I enjoyed telling them to behave when they got here, because as the chief officer of the mission at the time, I had to send a letter to the government saying we would assume responsibility for them. Finally we learned that they would be traveling to England on the *Queen Mary*, and flying to Kano and Jos. I made plane reservations for them from Jos to Yola.

From time to time, I have been mentioning things that Mary Beth did. It is truly amazing how much she accomplished in that foreign country. She was a super homemaker. That didn't include much housecleaning or laundry, but it did include meal planning, teaching new recipes, and making sure the pantry was well supplied. It also included, obviously, caring for the children. She made dozens of garments on the sewing machine, kept the clothes mended, planned ahead for the clothes they would need (with four-hundred-mile distant stores not well supplied), and tried hard to see that they had interesting ways to spend their time. We were always generously supplied with packages from the States, and Mary Beth was the one who sorted them out and planned what toys to give what child at what holiday. And, of course, she kept wishing she could be with her children in Hillcrest, especially when Dale eventually got measles and Bonnie followed her measles a month later with mumps.

She also was in charge of the senior primary school, with its thirty-five pupils, responsible for accepting pupils and collecting fees as well as making sure all the subjects were taught. I don't know how she did it, but she loved to visit the women in the village and had an excellent ear for their language, though she could not speak it that well. She took her turn at leading our station prayer meetings. She spoke from time to time to gatherings of women and in the midweek service at the church. Mission conference recognized her ability and commitment and put her on the education committee, which meant some very long meetings. I remember one meeting at Waka that lasted all of one day up to the later hours of night and then resumed at 6:30 a.m.

And all this time, she wrote letters. She wrote weekly letters to her family at home and was also the one who kept in touch with our supporting churches. One special trait is that she finds it difficult to discontinue a relationship. She exchanged letters, for years, with persons who were members of any church where we served—even Fairview and Mount Pleasant. I was of little help in personal correspondence; I wrote so much as a part of my job that I just lacked the energy for more than a regular letter home. It is no wonder that, of all the wives (of other men) that I have known, she has always been, far and away, my favorite wife.

The date of arrival for Mother and Dad High drew near. Meanwhile, I had gone to Jos for a meeting and came out in the lorry with the school children, late in November. We made plans to use the Minso house as the guesthouse for the Highs, so we spent quite a lot of time making sure it would be comfortable for them and that the bed was properly mosquito-netted. Finally, the big day came. It was December 13, and we drove to Yola, about a hundred miles, to the airport, taking Nggida with us. I can't remember what car we took; it must have been full. I do remember that we went early because I had several business matters to care for in Yola, which was our provincial capital.

All of us were simply delighted to see Grandma and Grandpa. Each of the kids had their own plans for entertaining and/or making use of them. (Mary Beth's big one was for her mother to do a lot of sewing.) As I said, we had Nggida with us and, of course, Mary Beth's letters often mentioned him. We introduced him as our Nigerian son. Dad High, grinning, observed, "I knew you often referred to Mary Elizabeth as your favorite wife. Now I see why."

It was great to have the Highs with us over Christmas. Knowing that Larry, Dale, and Bonnie would be leaving in early January for school, we set our family Christmas about a week early so they could enjoy whatever toys they got. I was able to combine some of my trips to the stations at the east with touring for the visitors, so by the time the kids left, we had been in Uba with the Grimleys, and in Lassa for several days since much of our writing had been about Lassa. We also, excitedly, experienced the very native market in Lassa, then we visited Gulak, and even Chibuk. We were at Chibuk on Christmas Day, and we were pleased that all of us could enjoy the Nigerian-style reenactment of the birth of Jesus. We were also pleased that Nehers gave us a monkey, a duck, and a chicken to add to our passenger list.

Mother and Dad were impressed, I think, by how busy the missionaries were. Mother was quiet and just enjoyed people. She is the one who did most of the writing home to Martha. Dad was busily observant. He seemed to see everything. Each Tuesday he went alone or with one of his grandsons to Garkida market and quickly developed a number of impressions. One of them, probably accurate, was that the Nigerian women worked harder than the men. Of course, with special visitors, we were also invited out frequently. Bonnie, and especially Marla, kept Grandma busy. Larry and Dale took Grandpa walking. He also liked to sit under a tree reading, with his varicose-veined legs appreciating the sunshine. Mary Beth put her mother to sewing, and her father to shelling as many as he wanted of the two drums full of peanuts which we had.

About two dozen mission children, including our three, went off to Hillcrest the first week of January; Larry, who tended to get carsick, was one who went by air, the others by lorry. That left about another two dozen pre-schoolers to be cared for during our annual mission meeting. Stover arrived back in time for the meeting and was quickly able to assume his important responsibilities. John Grimley was our able chairman, and I sat at the table in front, taking minutes. I did not enjoy sitting there; in spite of a good cushion, the carbuncle in my gluteal cleft was extremely painful. Still, I was in a good position to see Dad High wringing his hands behind him when he responded to a request that he bring greetings. He thanked folks for the way they had been received, noted how impressed they were with the commitment of the missionaries, and embarrassed Mother with one part of his speech. He observed that Nigerian women did not wear an abundance of clothing, saying, "When a man marries, he can see what he is getting."

On the morning that we were preparing to take Highs to the airport, Mai Sule, pastor of the Virgwi Church and originator of the Boys' Brigade program in our area, came to bid them farewell. He led a group of Boys' Brigade the three miles from Virgwi, had them march and perform and sing for us, and impressed us again with his delightfully dramatic approach to Christianity. Then came the long trip to Jos, broken up by a night with the Lunkleys in Wandali. In Jos, Highs joined us in shopping and in celebrating the Hillcresters' January-February birthday party. Then came the sad moments of farewell; the flight to Jos was somewhat delayed, but in plenty of time for Kano. Later we learned that, typically, the Kano flight was delayed by harmattan. They spent a night in Kano's Airport Hotel before going on to London and home. We dearly wished we could have heard the reports of their trip!

While on furlough we had observed the warmth of Wilbur and Evelyn Martin and their easy relationships with persons of any age. We had suggested to them that they might want to consider applying to be houseparents at Hillcrest School. After praying about it, they had resigned at Royersford. Highs, going west, and Martins, with adopted son Tim, going east, just missed connections in London. We were pleased to be in Jos when they arrived, and Hillcrest staff and children all went to the airport to welcome them. It made for a wait of almost two hours as the plane was delayed, but the Martins were duly welcomed.

Boils were an epidemic. Mary Beth had one on the leg, one on the arm, one on the neck. Ronn Moyer had one. I had another three-pronged one so sore that even on a pillow I could hardly bare (oops, I mean bear) to sit for even a few moments. Marla, now four years old, tried to help. "I'm sorry you have a boil, Daddy," she said, and then sang her own song about having to sit on a pillow when you have a boil.

After the Highs had gone home, life settled into its usual busy routine. Stover was back in harness, living at Mubi, so my load was considerably less for the mission and I was able to turn more time to the church. Bible School was into its second year and Mary Petre added what had been lacking, some classes for the wives of the students. Again we had some very special visitors. They were Vernon F. Schwalm, retired president of Manchester College and then chair of Foreign Mission Commission, and his wife, Florence. This time, it was Stover who met them in Yola and did much of their touring with them, but all of us had opportunity to entertain them in our homes. Their visit was slightly reduced; it was a very hot season, and Florence suffered from the heat. When they went to Jos on their way home, she improved greatly and they were able to go to visit in Europe.

The second important visitor we had was only there for a few hours. He was the Governor-General of Nigeria, and he came with a very impressive entourage. He visited and toured the Adamawa Provincial Leprosarium at Virgwi, then he drove in to Garkida through a long line, on both sides of the road, of school children which Mary Beth had arranged. The children sang as his car moved through, and had a large sign saying, "Welcome, Governor-General!" Whether because he was impressed or it was his usual mode of operation, he stopped and spoke briefly to the large group. Afterward, he returned to the Pfaltzgraff home at Virgwi, and we joined him there for light refreshments. (I have a hunch that he was not accustomed to non-alcoholic refreshments, but that's just a hunch.)

Chapter Twenty-Two

CHANGE, TENSION, AND RELAXATION

It was also time for a change. The Baldwins were leaving for furlough in May. Elmer took care of financial matters on the station; that task fell to me. Ferne ran the junior primary school; that task fell to Mary Beth, giving her both the schools. Curt and Ronn completed their two-year term and also were heading to the States, leaving a shortage in the school and in the office. On the other hand, we were moving to a much more substantial house. The Kulps had lived there, and then the Baldwins; now it would become the Bieber house.

This would seem to be a good place to emphasize the living comforts of Garkida over Lassa. To begin with, Garkida was mission headquarters, and there was a larger staff. The staff included administration, the lone senior primary school, and the shop which tried to keep all the motors going, in addition to evangelism, teaching, and medical staff. Garkida also was served by roads which were more nearly all-season. It was a hundred miles closer to Jos, and Mubi was accessible by a regular laterite road. No road was free of delay when heavy rains came, but there was at least considerably less likelihood of being mired down in mud. The mission houses at Garkida, as well as the senior primary hostel, were electrified. A generator located in the shop ran from six until ten each evening. (Of course, generators sometimes broke down, and we would sometimes stay up after ten, so we needed our kerosene lamps as well.) All the houses had running water or pumps, backed up by cisterns and wells.

Our new home was at the top of the highest hill in our station, directly above the technical shop. It was far more spacious than our duplex had been; all the rooms were larger. Even more luxurious, there were sizable verandas front and back, and ample space around for the planting of flowers. Even the storeroom/wash house was bigger. Pindar and Bubwa, our cook and houseboy, could hardly get over the size of the kitchen and pantry. Nggida was off at secondary school, but Karagama was always with us except for brief periods when he would go back to Lassa for farming, and later to Waka Teacher Training Centre.

When the Hillcresters came home, they came to a different home. Of course, all three of them had already lived in four different Nigerian homes, so the move was not traumatic. They had more space, they could play table tennis on the front veranda, and they could even use the croquet set which had not even been unpacked in Lassa.

June 1957 brought special events both for the mission and for us personally. For the mission, it was the celebration of five years of the Waka Teacher Training Centre and ten years of teacher training, for the centre had functioned for five years at Garkida before the move to Waka. So important was teacher training that other missions and the government sent official representatives to participate in the celebration. We were able to attend, also, as a family.

The first special personal event came on June 24, our thirteenth wedding anniversary. Mary Beth announced by letter home that she was still fertile and we would be expecting our next baby in January. The second special personal event took place on Larry's birthday, when I baptized him and Dale, along with five Nigeria school boys, in the swiftly flowing Hawal River. The very next day, the lorry departed with all the school children.

The Highs had been very observant during their visit. Among their observations were the need for a piano at Hillcrest, Clara Harper's need for a new refrigerator (the old one would rarely make ice), and the need for funds to help complete the new Garkida church. They generously gave $2,000 to meet the first two needs and help toward the third, and others.

As for our heavy schedule, help was on its way. Recognizing the urgent need, our Elgin office flew Max and Loretta Baughman out. Loretta, although delayed for a few days by illness, joined Mary Beth and me in teaching in the senior primary school. Lora Mainard, nearing retirement age, was an experienced secretary, and she joined us in headquarters office. When I went to Jos to meet Lora, I also met a motorized bicycle. I bought it for Mary Beth. It made bicycling easier for her, although the motor was not quite strong enough to bring the bike up our hill; it took some additional pedaling.

To reduce the effectiveness of additional mission staff, a flu epidemic struck. Many of the staff members, two of our three children at Hillcrest along with teachers and houseparents, Garkida schoolchildren, and dozens of local citizens were affected. Mary Beth and I, surprisingly, were spared. The particular strand of flu was not deadly, but it was certainly debilitating.

I had never been afraid of thunder and lightning. I can remember how, when we were small children, Mother would sometimes take us out on the porch during a thunderstorm and let us watch the beauty of the lightning flashes. An incident at our highest-of-all-the-homes, however, at least left me with an uneasy feeling. Electricity, as I have noted, went off at 10:00 p.m., unless there was a hospital emergency.

It must have been about 3:00 a.m. when Mary Beth and I, in our mosquito-netted bed on the open veranda, were startled awake by a loud clap of thunder. Obviously, I didn't measure the distance, but I think I must have bounced at least a foot into the air. I had hardly hit the bed before I had torn the net loose and run around the bed to Marla, who was sleeping in a screened crib. No harm, she did not even awaken. I took my flashlight and explored. As I looked out from our darkened house, I saw lights at the shop down the hill, and at such houses as I could see. I found our fuse box. It was torn up, obviously having been struck by lightning. All right, that explained the loud clap of thunder. But why did everyone else have lights? An emergency at the hospital? There seemed no other explanation. I went back to bed.

Next morning, we learned that no one had turned the generator on; it had self-started. We theorized that the lightning had struck our fuse box, slid down the wires to the generator switch and turned it on. We were relieved that there seemed to be no damage to our house except to the fuse box and a small portion of chimney. Our escape was driven home to us, however, when we discovered that the cotton "ceiling" of our mosquito net was riddled with charred spots. Lightning must have come close!

Less than two weeks later, we had a more serious scare. One of the sad facts of having children away at boarding school is missing their performances in musicals, dramas, and sporting events. Hearing of a coming performance, we were able to arrange for Mary Beth and Marla to accompany me to Jos for a meeting. Marla did not enjoy the trip; she had a very sore throat and tonsillitis and had some penicillin shots. A few days after we had returned to Garkida, she began repeated vomiting. For the second time in our missionary career, the first being when I recognized Larry's rheumatic fever, I was thankful for my nurse training. As I examined Marla, I realized that her face and indeed her body was puffy. It could well be nephritis. We immediately sent a urine specimen, noting my fear.

It showed albumen, a quick sign of nephritis. Dr. Blough began treatment which, I am convinced, staved off its becoming more acute. When after three or four days she did not show significant improvement, it was decided that Mary Beth and Marla would travel along with the Studebakers when, homeward bound, they flew from Biu to Jos.

Many of us, genuinely concerned fellow missionaries, well-wishers for the Studebakers as they completed their missionary service, and the curious, awaited the S.I.M. plane on that hot October morning. We were pleased to see our latest 1-W, Sam Simmons, arrive on it. The weight load, with four adults and a child, plus some luggage, must have approached the safe limit. The plane took ALL of the mowed grass runway, and we feared for a few moments it would not be able to take off. It did.

In Jos, Marla was taken to Bingham Memorial Hospital. She already seemed on the way to recovery, but she was intensely treated there, and indeed needed several days of treatment. When she was finally discharged, Mary Beth was instructed to keep her quiet and in Jos for two weeks, and Marla slowly became her self again. Mary Beth could rejoice not only to be with the other children, but to have a little girl recovered from a dangerous illness. I could rejoice, because a shortwave radio communication had been put in place and I was able to hear the good news of Marla's recovery. Marla didn't like the doctor; how could you like someone who, every time you saw him, gave you a shot—or some similar torture! Mother and Dad, however, loved him!!!

Marla's recuperation, although complete, was just slow enough so that they were still in Jos when Stover and I came in for Hillcrest Board meeting. For the first time, we were able to see our kids in performance; Bonnie in the choir, Dale in a Scrooge skit, and Larry in a reminder of Calvary. Stover and I left afterward. The school kids went out a day or so later, but Bonnie stayed and became a help to her mother in caring for Marla. Finally, the doctors declared the little girl healthy enough to travel, and they came back home by plane.

Not long after that, Stover and I had another trip to Jos, probably for a missions council. While we were there, I was surprised to find a turkey for sale, a scrawny thing. It weighed only about ten pounds. We took Wilbur and Evelyn Martin and little Timmy along with us so they could get a taste of mission life in the bush. They had Christmas dinner with us, and all of us were surprised to be able to eat turkey. It was great having the whole family together again, even though we had to limit Marla's activities for about an additional month.

There had been so many physical problems in our family for the past two months that we felt limited in our ability to carry on. When Mary Beth and Marla came home, I was in bed and stayed there pretty much for five days. Colds, fevers, the persistent presence of white blood cells in Marla's urine, a bout of rash and discomfort for Mary Beth, all took a great deal of prayer and mutual support. We were moving about almost in a daze; physical conditions and heavy schedules contended with each other. That is probably why I remember so little of the children's vacation. As January 1958 moved in, and our new baby had not yet moved out, the days seemed to move slowly. Mary Beth was a patient waiter, but Marla kept wondering what the baby was waiting for. Henry Long, missions executive, was with us, touring all the stations, visiting the school and hospital, traveling with Stover to the meeting of the Christian Council at Ibadan, and visiting in our homes.

Other missionary mothers had new babies. The McCanns' little girl was about three months old. The Woodwards' son was a month old. The Grimleys' new daughter was two weeks old. And then, as people began to move in for annual mission meeting, Mary Beth began to have pains. We took her to the hospital. Drs. Hamer, McCann, and Pfaltzgraff all agreed it would only be another hour or so and started to leave. Mary Beth cried out, "It's coming!"

Roy, who was really our doctor, paused and checked and, sure enough, a wee lassie, all seven pounds seven ounces of her, popped out at 12:23 p.m., a really easy birth for Mary Beth after a wait not quite as long as usual. The little girl said, "Hello, you all. My name is Doreen Edith. My mamma and daddy liked the name Doreen, and the Edith is after my grandma and Mamma's close twin friend." We were happy for her explanation!

Within a couple of hours, Mary Beth and Doreen were taken by stretcher in a car, the short distance to Mary Dadisman's house, but before that I had gone home to bring Marla over to see her new sister and her mother. Mary Beth's postpartum pains were not severe, and her recovery was quick. After only three days, she came to the evening session of our conference and joined the milk bar of four nursing mothers. A day or so later she came home, to the delight of Marla, who became the new baby-sitter. Meanwhile, Mary Beth had filled in the data and addressed the twenty announcements we had prepared.

It was a special mission meeting. We were considering the need for a broad-based Bible School. We were interested in the viewpoint of the Foreign Missions Commission on various aspects of our program, and Henry Long was not hesitant to share his perceptions. It was time to elect field secretary and assistant. That Stover Kulp would be field secretary was a foregone conclusion. But I had been called to be assistant, sight unseen. One of my asssignments was personnel, which can easily produce unfriendly responses. What was the attitude of my fellow missionaries to the way I had conducted my work? Stover, Mary Beth, and I were asked to absent ourselves. The election took place. I did not electioneer for the job; I have never electioneered for any job. I enjoyed it, but the work load was sometimes extremely heavy, and it was not unusual for me to be at work before 5:00 a.m., though few of my colleagues knew that. They took the vote, and I was unanimously elected to a second term. We would stay in Garkida. A few years later, when Stover retired, the world missions commission (its name had changed), according to reports, decided to appoint a field secretary for ability rather than for popularity. My ability did not, in their judgment, measure up.

We've been working very hard. It is time out for a few games. It would be neither appropriate nor accurate to say that games were the most important part of our lives, but from childhood I had found them to be a good way to relax and enjoy. Our family played games and had fun together. As little children, we played card games like "Old Maids" and "I Doubt It" and board games like "Parcheesi" and "Sorry." A little older, we were introduced to "Rummy," "Five Hundred," and "Pinochle."

The elementary school near us had regular card parties as a fund-raising venture. Once Mother had a ticket and couldn't go, so she sent me. I was only thirteen at the time, and I well remember the dismayed looks of adults as they saw their partner was just a kid. I won no prize, but I held my own! I learned "Hassenpeffer" from my Dutch stepcousins at Hunter Station.

Grandma and Grandpa Bieber were almost addicted to "Flinch," and as they played, freely cheated on each other. They didn't care; they just enjoyed the game. At the annual Bieber reunion, the first evening included a penny-ante game with the winners treating the rest to ice cream.

When "Monopoly" came on the market, we spent many an evening over Baltic Avenue, Reading Railroad, Jail, and Boardwalk. I was introduced to chess at college, and came to enjoy it. I played checkers without really knowing the strategy, until I read a book on how to play, while I was in nurse training. Mary Beth also liked games, but in her home no one played with "the devil's cards," so we played more board games and "Rook."

Because there was no electricity at our churches in Nigeria at the time, we did not have evening meetings. The latest meetings were usually scheduled for around five o'clock, and were over before real dark. So our evenings were given to reading, writing letters, doing some studying, and GAMES, often by kerosene light. "Rook" was the most common game for a long time, until Mildred Grimley's folks introduced us to a delightful improvement, "Make a Million," and it became a favorite. We came to enjoy "Canasta" and "Samba," even though they did use the devil's cards, and "Up and Down the River," which could be played with either "Rook" or "Bridge" cards. I thought you ought to know about these games since I have worked so hard to give you the accurate impression that we worked hard!

It could hardly be true, but it was. In May 1958, Larry completed his eighth school year. Hillcrest had high school only by correspondence with some personal tutorial help, so graduation was an important event. Larry, as class president, was one of the speakers. The principle address of the evening was given by John Grimley. He was looking for an easy, light beginning, and I shared with him my "I have this trouble with my left lung BUT MY RIGHT LUNG IS O.K." approach, and he used it. The audience was delighted, except for one devout and sensitive lady who took his left lung weakness seriously. After graduation, she told John, "Oh, Mr. Grimley, I started right in to pray for you!"

Administrative work, I discovered, was not conducive to the making of good friends among the Nigerians. As I look back at the four years at Garkida, the only one I spent a lot of time with was Mai Sule, whom I have mentioned several times. The Garkida pastor, Gwanu, was probably the poorest of the six men who had completed the pastoral class at Chibuk. He lacked consistency and planning skills and may have been a bit on the lazy side. He and his wife always seemed to have trouble with their children, and one son was so naughty that one of the missionaries doubted that anything good could ever come out of him. The ones I was closest to were students at the Bible School.

As was true for each of our children, we got both entertainment and joy from Doreen. She was always smiling and cooing. She was probably the best at sleeping; Mary Beth only had to be up once a night to nurse her, usually out of her own discomfort rather than Doreen's complaint. Like Marla, she began quickly to turn over and roll around. One of our favorite pictures of her was a movie of her crawling slowly across the front veranda, quietly spitting up as she went, and just as quietly trying to lick it up again. She developed quickly, but could not take from Marla the championship in early walking. When there were four siblings at home, plus our general helper, Karagama, it would have been very easy to spoil her, but she seemed to survive all that attention well.

Chapter Twenty-Three

INSIDE FAITH, OUTSIDE HELP

I am reminded that people often asked us how we could let our children go so far away to school. In England, of course, boarding schools were common. In America, mothers often cried when they saw a child starting off to school, walking or riding the bus a short distance. We cried some, too. It was hardest when Larry went, because he was the first. Later we were aware that two or more of them were together. We derived strength for the separation from several sources. Most importantly, we were certain that we were doing God's work, and if that required some pain along the way it did not compare with the pain of the cross.

We also knew the Hillcrest staff. Jean and J.C. Wine, houseparents when Larry started school, were very caring people. They loved the children and were sensitive to the longing that parents had to know all that was going on. Jean wrote to parents frequently to report on their children. Later Wilbur and Evelyn Martin came from their service at the Royersford Church with special caring and a variety of parenting skills. Dear, dear "Grandma" (Dulcie) Cover overflowed with love. Lucile and Clarence Heckman lent a strong sense of stability to the institution.

A third help to us was the awareness that our children were receiving a really good education. Even the gentle Alice Cady who was my first grade teacher was not as effective a teacher as was Wilma Schrag at Hillcrest. In later years, Miss Vandenburg and Miss Wimberly, one from the Christian Reformed Church and one from the Assembly of God, gave excellent service. When children would make the transition from Hillcrest to a stateside school, even though there was often a time gap due to travel, they had not the least difficulty in moving with their class. To cap it all off, all of the teachers Chand staff Were staunch Christians. In later years, I came to believe that some of the Christian teaching was only at a child level and did not help the children prepare for inevitable doubts, but the Christian Spirit was powerful.

And then, all the children were away at school. We came to believe that, except for times of homesickness which were relatively brief, and perhaps during illness, our children really liked Hillcrest. It was a blessing to us when, in our second tour, news of the children could reach us quickly by our radio intercommunication system.

After our first two years in Garkida, there were enough teachers so that Mary Beth's teaching load was much smaller. She was headmistress, however, of four different schools, and that meant visiting them, meeting and working with the teachers (practically all Nigerian men), sorting the applications for senior primary school, and making reports to government. The government paid the teachers, although we made all the assignments. When payday came, I would sit in one of the rooms at the school or in the study at home, and the teachers would drop by. We talked with them about tithing, and practically all of them wanted to tithe, but knew that once they took the money away, the tithe would likely not be forthcoming. So at their request, we developed a simple system. When I paid them, I would observe, "A tithe would be ____," filling in the appropriate amount. A basket was there on the table, and most of them would leave their tithe.

I have already mentioned that one hasn't lived until he has traveled Nigerian roads. Let me add to that. The nature of my work, as assistant field secretary with special responsibility for personnel, and as the secretary to EKAS Lardin Gabas, made wide travel imperative. Dry season or rainy season, I had to visit. Main highways, of laterite, had rain gates which closed after heavy rains. I could usually manage to get through the gates. But even on main roads, there were sometimes drifts (paved fords) too deep to go through. On bush roads, which usually had simply been cleared through the bush with stones moved into swampier areas, rainy season trips were often interrupted by being mired down. Besides, all the roads were so rough that they were extremely hard on motor vehicles. That, combined with dust and heat, made it difficult to keep cars operable. The shop at Garkida was constantly busy.

The most memorable motor breakdown for me took place when we were driving Stover's Chevrolet station wagon from Jos. Almost sixty miles from Jos, we smelled rubber and stopped. One tire was hot, from dragging along the road; a rear brake had locked. I had neither the tools nor the know-how to deal with it. I flagged down a friendly lorry driver. Help along the road was an expected thing—and he stopped. He removed the wheel, unlocked the brake, replaced the wheel, and went on. Hardly two miles later, the car was pulling to the right, and we were stopped again. Once more, a lorry driver stopped to help. He removed the wheel, assessed the situation, and regretted, "The axle is broken." I could not recall a single repair station along that highway.

"Do you have any idea where I might get it fixed?" I asked.

He thought a bit. "The Public Works Department has a repair shop in Bauchi (twenty miles farther). Maybe they could help."

Reluctantly, I left the family there, at about three o'clock in the morning. The kind lorry driver delivered me to PWD Bauchi. When I explained my problem and identified the car as a Chevy wagon, they found an Opel axle. (Opel was the German-made Chevy.) How much would it cost? Nothing. It would be a service of PWD.

A mechanic picked up the Opel axle and some tools and drove out to the disabled vehicle with me. Only one of our Nigerian friends was still there, some missionaries from S. I. M. had been passing by and had taken them to their station. Meanwhile, the messenger we had sent to Jos had reached Wip Martin, and he met them at the S.I.M. station and took them on to Jos. The mechanic got busy. From time to time, he would turn to me and ask my advice at a particular stage of repair. Invariably, I would respond, "You are the mechanic. Just go ahead."

Eventually, he stood up, turned to me again, said, "Well, that's it. Now you should take it to my master and let him check my work." I thanked him heartily, but I told him that, with the uncertainty of an Opel axle in a Chevy, I had better return to Jos. I did. Before that helpful mechanic left, he offered me a dozen or so small parts which, he said, were left over. It was going to take several days to get and install the proper axle, and I had a day or two of enforced rest.

Meanwhile, I realized that it was time for the annual *majalisa* (district meeting). As the district secretary, it seemed important that I be present. I was the one who had, with the help of the executive committee, organized the agenda and planned the meeting. Tired or not, we borrowed the Hillcrest car and headed for Marama. Sam Simmons, 1-W mechanic who lived right beside us, flew to Jos to work on Stover's car, and drove out with us. He took the rest of the family on to Garkida.

My term as district secretary was nearing its three-year end. Although I enjoyed the work very much and felt that I was able to make a real contribution to the growing church, it seemed very important to me that a Nigerian become the district secretary. I proposed that the *majalisa* elect Bitrus Sawa. Son of one of the first men to be baptized in our church, he was an able teacher and had a degree from Millersville Normal School. Bitrus, however, had a speech of his own. "I want to thank you for thinking of me," he told the *majalisa*. "But I want you to know that I am simply not able to do the kind of work that *Mallam* Bieber does. You need to continue him as secretary." *Majalisa* agreed, and though I would be absent for one of the three years, I was elected for another term.

With the end of November, the happy reunion with our Hillcresters would soon take place. We were sure our Hillcresters liked school, but it was good to see how happy they were to be back in Garkida, and especially how happy Marla was to have them. They all seemed busy. Larry was typing, reading, playing games, and using his CO^2 pellet gun to shoot pigeons. He brought down six, and we had four to eat. Dale resurrected someone's old kite which had been left in our store, located twine, and was absolutely delighted to get it way up in the sky. Bonnie played with her tea set, but she and Marla spent more time with Bonnie's big boy doll. They treated him like a real baby, even to letting him wet the bed. All of the kids enjoyed Baby Doreen, and took turns carrying her around. She was almost ready to walk and would do so before they returned to school. Karagama, almost one of the family, also enjoyed having all the youngsters around.

Children home also signified Christmas coming and time for our annual Christmas letter. We sent from seventy-five to one hundred each year, taking advantage of John Grimley's artistry to have illustrated letters. With John back in the States, we were on our own. This is the blank verse greeting we sent one year:

WE SHARE these gifts with our brother this Christmas
— gifts to share, from a Father who cares:
News of an infant in manger lowly,
God come to earth to redeem his children.
News of a song by angels holy,
Peace come to earth if man will receive it.
Light for minds once shrouded in darkness;
Knowledge for living, first here, then above.
New strength for those whom disease long had weakened,
Now finding vigor for life and for living.
Hope for the soul which was shackled by fear;
Faith in a Lord who has called him to follow.
Love of a God who knows even the sparrow;

Fellowship rich with those of like mind.
These things we can share, because you care.

WE HAVE these gifts from our brother this Christmas
—gifts which he shares which help us to grow:
Knowledge that Spirits around and within
Guide and control us and shape destiny.
Strength to endure though pain be severe,
Strength to surrender without a defeat.
Heart of contentment with small earthly treasure
Will to accept what a day may bring forth.
Faith which though simple can also ask questions;
Sense to respect the experience of age.
Smile of good cheer which lightens up dark face;
Mind set to share with those who are hungry.
These gifts we have found since God called us here.

WE PRAY these prayers for our brother this Christmas
—prayers that we share that you also may pray:
Turn him forever from charms and from witchcraft;
Turn him to Christ, the truth and the life.
Nourish his soul with the Bread come from heaven
Help him to grow in knowledge and grace.
Let his heart hear the call to Your Service;
Make him the leader Your church sorely needs.
May love constrain him to seek out his brother,
Bringing to Christ each one who is lost.
Deepen and broaden the scope of his vision;
Let him know You can give strength for the way.
Praying for him, we pray for God's kingdom.

Chapter Twenty-Four

FURLOUGH COMING UP

Our family Christmas past, we talked about our coming furlough. It seemed very likely that Larry would stay in the States for his last two years of high school, and we prayed that the right home would turn up for him. Henry Long was suggesting that I might want to do some studies at Penn State. He was a sociologist, and had a great deal of interest in my studying anthropology. For several reasons, I preferred not to, but was not completely averse to the idea. It would have taken us fairly far away from our families, and we had been away from them for four years. I also was convinced that it was more important to know the person than to know the culture. My own sociology and psychology courses, plus my psychiatric experience, helped me to that understanding of people. Perhaps there would be a nearby pastorate where I could serve part time, do some deputation, and be with families. As 1959 dawned, we were uncertain, but confident that God would show the way.

The Church of the Brethren Service Commission had several programs which involved material aid. Children in the Sunday Schools and Vacation Bible Schools could be actively involved in service. It seemed to me that there ought to be some kind of program to let children be similarly involved in mission. Observing the difficulty which school children often had in providing paper, pens, notebooks, and the like, it occurred to me that school kits might be a good project. Gladys Royer listed what ought to be involved, and we proposed the idea to the Foreign Mission Commission. It took. Later we added health kits, also for the children, and sewing kits for women. Hundreds of those kits were sent out. Years later, kits of one kind or another were being gathered to meet a variety of needs in a variety of places.

On Biu Plateau between Marama and Wandali, there was a mysterious lake called Lake Tilla. It was infested—that is really the proper word—with crocodiles. The crocodiles were believed by many people to be inhabited by the spirits of the dead, especially dead chiefs or village leaders. In our eight years, we had never been there, so when the opportunity came up, we decided to take advantage of it. We drove to the lake, and stopped near it for our lunch. We understood that crocodiles forage at night. They had been reported even to invade compounds and seize small children, but that was a little much to believe. We stood near the lake and watched. In a little over an hour, we saw twenty-two crocs. Sometimes, they were little more than the image of a log floating on the water, and at other times we could see them moving around, their large mouths quite discernible. We left while it was still daylight, thanks. We were only sorry that we did not have our Hillcresters with us. Once, while we lived at Lassa, we had purchased the tail of a crocodile for meat. It tasted somewhat like fish, somewhat like pork. I would not order it in a restaurant.

For more than thirty-five years, Church of the Brethren Mission had been largely self-governing. The missionaries chose their field secretary and, later, their assistant field secretary. The field committee was responsible for assignment of individuals to their stations and/or tasks. We would submit askings to the mission board for financial needs, and they would decide which needs to respond to.

For major developments, such as the opening of a new station or the building of Waka, we needed commission approval, since those decisions would affect the need for staff and funds. In a sense, the field committee was like the manager of a professional sports team. Management, in the form of the commission, would provide the personnel and we would organize the team. Communication and reports were, of course, very important, as were occasional visits by the mission executive. The arrangement made a great deal of sense. After all, the missionaries were the professionals and they were the ones immersed in the church in Nigeria. Even executives, although men of a great deal of wisdom and commitment had only the kind of expert knowledge of the usual three weeks visitor.

We were surprised, therefore, when, after the executive visit in 1959, the commission advised us that thereafter they would appoint field secretary and assistant. Although we were not aware of it, the commission apparently asked the field committee to confirm that a given person was acceptable to them. I do not believe the criterion was ever applied. There was also a proposal that there be a business manager, rather than an assistant secretary, but that idea did not develop. When Stover Kulp indicated his intention to lay down his mantle as long-time field secretary, the commission appointed Ivan Eikenberry, without an assistant. There was no question but that Ivan was the most qualified of all our mission staff, and suited the assignment well. From our perspective, however, our mission was taking from the other missions of the northern region one of the best education advisors available.

On our return to Nigeria after furlough, we would likely return to Lassa, and I would continue in evangelistic work and as district secretary for the church. I had not sought the position of assistant secretary, but I could not help wondering at their decision to discontinue the position. I found it impossible to think I fit the case where, when a man retired and folks asked who would fill the vacancy, they would be told, "He didn't leave a vacancy."

My missionary colleagues had just, by unanimous vote, approved the way I was doing my job. Neither the executive nor any commission member had expressed an iota of criticism to me and there had been absolutely no forewarning. I could not help feeling that the whole idea of making the appointments by the commission instead of simply having their endorsement was aimed at me personally. My colleagues, though equally puzzled, did not feel the rejection or the pain that I felt. When I got up the courage to ask one commission chair what the commission had against me, he stammered, "I think it was something about the way you handled money." Strange, since I had always followed commission guidelines. I was surprised, when I wrote this story more than forty years later, to discover some pangs of puzzled pain rising to the surface. In my less humble moments, I believed that I fit my assignment.

Getting ready for furlough meant packing. The unlikelihood of returning to Garkida made packing a bit more intricate, but we managed. We also "packed" in the sense of turnover of tasks. Mary Beth turned over seven schools! Larry, taking high school only by correspondence, and always helpful Karagama were there to make the packing lighter. We made plans to travel through Europe on our way home. We corresponded about living at home, getting the children into camps and, four of them, into school. The day to depart came. We were deeply moved as we drove from Garkida with more than five hundred school children lining the road and singing, "God Be with You Till We Meet Again." It was May 13, 1959.

We traveled by lorry, schoolchildren style, with mattresses on the lorry bed and a tarp over the top. We stopped to have supper and bid farewell to Waka folks and were on our way, but not for very far. It had rained, and the gate was down at the Buni drift. Monroe Good, who was driving, tried hard to convince the gate man to let us through, to no avail. We stayed until 6:00 a.m., with Mary Beth and Doreen in the cab with Monroe. When the gatekeeper still refused to open the gate, we bypassed it and continued the remaining 320 miles to Jos. In Jos, we were reunited with Dale and Bonnie; we attended closing services at Hillcrest; and we found time to visit Nggida at Gindiri. Then, May 20, we flew to Kano and from Kano to Rome.

The commission provided funds for a direct trip home, and we supplied the difference. We landed at Rome and spent two big days visiting the famous sites of ancient history. Prices in Rome were probably the lowest anywhere, but the way Italian cabdrivers approached money made us feel as if we were being gouged. We flew to Milan, and all of us were deeply thrilled by the Sistine Chapel. We went by train to Interlocken, Switzerland, and the Alps. We took a train into the Alps. There we visited an ice cave, where carved ice statues were on display. We saw skiers and one dogsled, and the boys enjoyed throwing snowballs, but it was cold. On to Zurich, we flew to Frankfurt, Germany. While we waited for the train to Kassel, we walked the streets a bit and were interested to find a huge poster advertising the Bieberbau.

For some years, the Church of the Brethren had been maintaining a hostel at Kassel, only about fifteen miles from the East German border, for Brethren service workers in Europe. To our excited and pleasant surprise, we were met at the train station by my brother George. A chaplain major in the Air Force, he and his family were stationed in Morocco, but he was able to make use of a medical trip to Wiesbaden, rent a Volkswagen van, and be our chauffeur for a couple of days. The children just doted on their handsome uncle. Hula hoops were the American vogue at the time, and he had purchased a couple and tried rather clumsily to demonstrate. The kids were soon able to demonstrate to him. He was in civilian garb, but it was certainly unusual for pacifist Kassel House to have a military visitor.

No one could have made us feel more welcome at Kassel House than Pop and Mom Weldy of Middlebury, Indiana, who were the host and hostess. Pop (Allen) drove us to Schwarzenau, the birthplace of the Church of the Brethren, took us up the hill above the town so we could have a good view of it and showed us the ancient Alexander Mack mill and the modern school also named for him. He took us to what has been supposed to be the site of the first Brethren baptisms in 1708. The three older children waded in the Eder River, but it was only June 2, and very cold.

From Kassel we went to Amsterdam. From there we were able to visit some fantastically beautiful tulip farms. We enjoyed the windmills, and actually climbed up in one. We also enjoyed the friendly flocks of pigeons in the public square, though hoping they would remember to peep out, "Look out below!" when flying overhead.

All across Europe, whenever they were clean, we wore the bright, multicolored shirts and skirts which Mary Beth had made. In restaurants, we sang our grace, to the interest of other diners. In a restaurant in Amsterdam, we decided to seek some drinking water. The usual drink was apple cider or mineral water. I perceived that the waitress seemed to understand English well, so I asked her to bring a pitcher full of potable ice water.

"Oh," she agreed. "You want mineral water."

"No, we just want a pitcher of drinkable water with ice in it."

"Oh, you want apple cider?"

"No, just plain, cold, drinkable water."

She thought a moment, said, "No problem," and left. She soon returned with a man, apparently the manager. We explained what we wanted. We went through the same mineral water—cider sequence. Finally, he nodded, promised to meet our need, and left. We waited patiently, but honestly expected him to bring mineral water. He brought a ladder, climbed to the top of a tall china closet near us, and obtained a pitcher. He left. In a few moments, the waitress returned, with a good-sized pitcher of ice water. The pitcher, of course, was clearly labeled, "Pilsener Bier." One COULD get drinking water in Holland!

We arrived in Idlewild Airport, New York, after a fourteen-and-a-half-hour flight on KLM from Amsterdam. We were met by Biebers and by Martha High and Bob Hershberger, and therein lies a tale, but wait. The High property outside Spring City included the large farmhouse which had been divided in two, a small tenant house which had been built before 1800, and a simple, square two-story house just around the corner of the driveway. The latter was free of renters at the time, and we were pleased to be able to move in and, once again, live close to the Highs.

Now to introduce Bob Hershberger. 1-W farm boys had been assigned a few months earlier to work in the dairy at Pennhurst State School, just north of Spring City. Typically, none of the farm boys could cook, but they were surviving. At a nearby church, one of them met Jacob Kolb, neighbor just cater-corner across the road from Highs. They took him in and cooked for him. Bob wondered if Ben could find another good host, and he did. Dad High agreed to get breakfast for Bob early each morning, and Bob moved in. We heard of his arrival. Gradually, we noticed that he seemed to be mentioned more often. Then, a couple of months before we came home from Nigeria, Martha asked us to reserve June 14. Finally, we were told that was the Martha-Bob wedding day, and I was to perform the wedding. With another burst of his slyness, Dad High remarked that the Bible told us to take in strangers, but not to give them our daughter. But we all welcomed him into the family.

Problem: Annual Conference was at Ocean Grove, New Jersey, with me representing the Nigeria district on Standing Committee, which began its meetings on Thursday, June 11. When could we have a wedding rehearsal? I don't remember how we solved it, whether by a rehearsal on Wednesday evening or on Saturday evening. The wedding went very well, in the Royersford Church of the Brethren. Mary Beth (of course! who else?) was matron of honor and Marla was flower girl.

Soon afterward I drove back to Ocean Grove and rejoined the Standing Committee. It was a year of unrest in the Church of the Brethren. Three Pennsylvania ministers, one in Altoona, one in Lewistown, and one in Shamokin, believed that the Brethren were not evangelical enough and opposed their membership in the Federal Council of Churches. All three of them started independent churches and withdrew from the Brethren. Frank Carper and I were appointed by Standing Committee to seek reconciliation with one of the men, but our efforts were in vain.

Other members of the family came to conference later, and our children loved the sand and the salty waves. Ocean Grove was where we had been consecrated in 1949, and it was good to be back there again. No vehicles were allowed in the town on Sunday except emergency vehicles, so it was kind of fun just walking the streets.

After conference, we continued a busy summer by attending a missionary conference in Maryland. We were able to squeeze in a trip to the west, particularly to see Bill and Thelma McIndoe at Mt. Pleasant, visit the Fairview Church and especially the Dunks and Fishers in Indiana, call on the Eiseles in Lincoln, and see the Nehers, who were at home on furlough. In between, we visited churches, especially those from whom we were receiving support. Larry, Dale, and Bonnie went to Camp Swatara. We enjoyed the Bieber and Seriff reunions.

When fall came, Larry and Dale were enrolled at the new Owen J. Roberts Junior-Senior High School. Larry as a sophomore and Dale as a seventh grader. Bonnie was a fourth grader and Marla, unlike her brothers and sister, began school in the United States. The two girls were at East Vincent Elementary School.

The Pottstown Church of the Brethren, seven miles from our home, needed a pastor. We had often participated in youth activities of that congregation before we were married and still remembered many of the people. They asked us to serve them at least on a part-time basis, and we agreed. I enjoyed being in the pulpit and preaching in English again. Our Nigeria experiences gave us many illustrations and honed my ability to tell children's stories.

Frequently, we were on deputation visits. We had both slides and 8-mm movies, and we liked to go out as a family. We developed a pattern by which each member of the family would be involved and sang some songs in Margi or Bura. Often, we would also involve the congregation in singing with us, surprising them to learn that they could sing in dialect.

When Ivan Eikenberry had been on furlough, he had worked in the Elgin office and had written a short promotional book about the church in Nigeria. Brethren Press was unable to complete the publication before Ivan returned to Nigeria, and it needed copy reading and correction. Remaining as faithful as I could to Ivan's own language patterns, I edited his well-written book and prepared it for its final publication.

Our major concern during that furlough was the fact that we would be leaving Larry in the States. For three years we would not see that precious son. On the one hand, he was very mature for his age and well adjusted. On the other hand, he was of high school age, a very important age for character and faith shaping. We wanted him to be in a home where he would have strong Christian influence, where he would have work to perform, and where he could exercise his athletic and social skills. We also wanted him to be involved in the choosing. There may have been other possibilities, but the three I remember are these:

1) To live with Grandpa and Grandpa High. Problems: It did not seem fair for grandparents to have to go back to being parents, even though they were willing. They had never reared a son. Their location was not conducive to social activities, and he could well become lonesome.

2) He could live with a distant cousin of Mary Beth. Problems: Although he had volunteered to open his home to Larry, we did not see it as a strong invitation and did not detect any participation by the female member of the household. He was a Christian, but his view of the faith was strongly fundamentalistic and he tended to be very rigid in ideas an activities. We

did not see Larry as having the kind of freedom or the close relationships to which he had become accustomed at Hillcrest.

3) He could live with Paul and Arlene Wenger and their sons on a dairy farm in the Mechanic Grove area. Paul was a cousin to LeRoy Wenger, whose wife had been the correspondent for the congregation which "supported" Mary Beth. One son, Bob, was Larry's age; the other two years younger. There was an older daughter away from home. The idea of living and working on a farm appealed to Larry and he decided that was where he would like to live. Problems: we didn't see any. He would work hard and long hours; he would learn dairy farming; he would attend the Mechanic Grove Church and the Solanco High School just being newly built. We did not want to leave our son, but it felt like the next best arrangement to having him with us. After two years, we would plan further.

Annual Conference in 1960 was in Champaign-Urbana. Because the Nigeria district needed a delegate to Standing Committee, I was asked to continue to serve them. I have always found it difficult to speak up in any group larger than four or five, and sometimes even then, so I did not add much to the committee except to vote when called to. The moderator did not make it any easier for me. The one time when I screwed up my courage, and of course my wisdom, and made a comment on the matter we were discussing, he looked at me with a puzzled look on his face and said, "I'm afraid I'll have to move that speech out of order." Moderator Ed Ziegler was a very capable man, but I do believe his comment was out of order.

Being at conference kept us in the country a little longer. We did not return to Nigeria until July. Our assignment was in abeyance. Would we be at Gulak, where we would be the only mission staff? Mary Beth, who found a great deal of satisfaction and support in being able to visit with other missionaries, would find that very difficult, but we were committed. Would we be at Lassa, with several other mission families and many old friends among the Margi people? When we arrived in Jos, we discovered that we would have another new "home." We were asked to serve ad interim as houseparents at Hillcrest School. The Martins had left on furlough, and the Lunkleys' return was delayed. Modern America might find a conflict of interest, for I was Chair of the Hillcrest Board of Governors, and therefore my own overseer.

Houseparents at Hillcrest had all the responsibilities that parents have except saving for the future education of their children. If there were homesick children, sick children, quarreling children, naughty children, houseparents did what needed to be done. The children had homework to do, music lessons to practice for, sports to enjoy, games to play, clothes to be laundered and mended, and meals to eat. In addition, there were Sunday School and worship to plan, bedtime prayers to hear, and Christian attitudes to foster. For us, it also meant being with our children for a longer time.

When the Lunkleys did arrive, we were asked to stay in Jos and study Hausa, which we did for another month. I was able to learn enough Hausa to be able to write church minutes and records in Hausa, but not enough to understand or hear the tonal differentiations. In addition, I was kept busy, in addition to the language study, with bringing district records, particularly financial records, up to date. I came up with a simple system of bookkeeping which I taught to church treasurers. And there were always errands to run for the mission. Finally, in September, we heard our regular assignment; it was to Lassa, and we rejoiced.

It would be mid-October before we would move. Meanwhile, a whole series of events took place. Doreen developed as bad a case of chickenpox as we had ever seen; she had pox in all the least favorable places, from her ears to her bottom. She also had tonsillitis so bad that she had a whole series of penicillin shots, which did not please her immensely. Dale, though healthy enough to emcee Hillcrest's talent show and provide them with piano and vocal solos, had an increasingly troublesome hernia. Both of them went to Bingham Memorial and had the appropriate surgery, tonsils for Doreen, hernia for Dale.

Our freight was taking an inordinate amount of time to arrive. We did not need it that much in Jos, but we certainly wanted it by the time we moved to Lassa. One item we did want to use in Jos was an 8-mm movie projector. It had been with the luggage we had checked in New York, marked "Jos." The attendant in New York had assured us there would be no problem, but it was not delivered with the rest of our luggage. We reported its being among the missing and eventually, just as we were ready to give up hope, it appeared. It had been sent to "Joh," for Johannesburg.

Our Jeep station wagon, now six years old including five years on Nigeria roads (and lack of them), was still operating but needing more and more attention. We decided to buy a Volkswagen Beetle. It did not have four-wheel drive and certainly could not carry loads, but its lightness promised less bogging down in mudholes. For a time, we owned them both and used them as needed. I had trips to the bush for church events, and Mary Beth had trips from the mission vacation compound to Hillcrest. The Bischofs had brought out a VW pickup truck from their church, but it was proving to be less useful on bush roads than had been expected. We traded our Jeep to the mission for the VW truck and $150, and gave the truck to Hillcrest School.

The other important event in October was Nigeria's long-awaited self-government. The British Commonwealth, with colonies all around the world, was gradually granting self-government. For Nigeria, October 1, 1960, was the day. We celebrated with them. We had special assembly at Hillcrest, where the students sang the new Nigerian anthem, "God Save the Queen," and "The Star Spangled Banner." We attended the big celebration on one of the polo grounds. We watched the parade, mostly of notable authorities and equestrian demonstration. (We were amazed to learn, afterward, that missionaries of a "faith mission" had loaded their guns and locked their doors!)

And then we moved to Lassa, our first family trip to bush since we had left for furlough. Of course, it was essential that we exchange welcomes and "It is really good to be back" with colleagues in stations along the way. We found that Pindar, who had served us so well as our cook in Garkida, would not be able to move with his six children to Lassa. Bubwa, who had learned much and shared the cooking, did move with us, but there wasn't room in our VW, and we were without him for a while. In Lassa, we moved into the smallest—the only available—house. It was commonly the guesthouse and was not intended for long stays, but we had long since learned to accept what God provided. Our original home in Lassa in 1951 had been torn down, and Von and Elsie Hall were living in the new one. The Hamers were in what had been our second Lassa home.

About the time we arrived in Lassa, Elsie contracted a strongly virulent fever. None of the diagnoses or treatments seemed to help. She particularly had raw spots on her throat and a high fever. It was decided that she and Von and two children should fly to Jos, where better medical facilities were available. Mary Beth and I gained our sixth child. Elsie was completely unable to care for two-month-old Beverly Ann. Arrangements were made for Betty Arnett, our Lassa nurse, to bring Bev out from Jos. I met them at Garkida and Mary Beth met them at Uba. Bev was a sweet baby. Doreen enjoyed holding her on her lap. It was sad for Elsie to have to give up her baby even for a short time. I do not believe her condition was ever diagnosed. Some years later, a virulent fever broke out in Lassa, resulting in the death of nurse Laura Wine. The disease, which came to be known as Lassa fever, also caused the death of an S.I.M. doctor, Janet Troup, and several others. My own suspicion, which obviously cannot be confirmed, is that Elsie had an early case and miraculously recovered.

Elsie made some improvement in Jos, but she was left so weak that it was clear she could not continue missionary service without rehabilitation. It was decided that the Halls should return to the States. Von came to Lassa and packed very quickly. I took him and the children to Waka, where we joined in the lorry going to Jos for Hillcrest children. When, a few days later, I returned with the school children, Mary Beth met us at Garkida, because I had another committee meeting to attend. While I was gone, Mary Beth and the family cleaned and moved into the Hall house. It was quite a relief for Mary Beth, even though we were to move again in another month, to have enough room for our family.

It was great to have four of our children with us, even though their absence had been shorter this time. Doreen just doted on her big brother and sisters. Of course, when they first arrived, they were too tired for anything much. Dale had a bad cough and Bonnie had a bad fall which discouraged her walking for a few days. Marla was just worn out. Larry did not write as frequently as we would have liked, but we had news of him from the Wengers and from the Highs. As Christmas came—early in December for us—Dale and Marla had bikes and Bonnie a new watch. We sent another Christmas letter, this time to well over a hundred people.

I have wondered—
And I wonder again as dawn of another Christmas draws near:
What if the Christ Child had been born in Nigeria, with skin of soft brown velvet,
Hair of kinky black, and bright eyes shining like stars in a dark heaven?

I have wondered—
As I have noticed that stars shine brighter in Nigeria, perhaps because the
darkness is so much darker;
What if the star of the east had led wise men to a manger a few hundred
miles farther south?

I have wondered—
As I have watched little lads herding their sheep and goats and as I have
seen the tenderness with which Fulani herders tend their cattle;
What if the angel song had been to them, of "Peace on earth, good will to men"?

I have wondered—
           And especially as I saw the joy in the eyes of a dark-skinned young mother;
What if God, who is colorblind, had chosen a dark-skinned Virgin Mary to
           bear His Son?

I have wondered—
As I have seen new light dawning into the lives of God's people in Nigeria,
           to whom Salvation has come;
As I have seen puzzled doubt in the faces of many still in shadow, to whom
           such a tremendous Gift is still beyond comprehension;
As I have heard the call, again and again, for more bearers of the Light;
As I have felt the frustration of often not being able to provide for the
deep needs of God's children;

I have wondered—
What if the Christ Child had been born in Nigeria, with skin of brown velvet,
           and we whose skin shines lighter had been left in the darkness?
For Christmas is a time of Wonder, and a time to wonder.
God sent His Son that people who walked in darkness may see a great Light,
           of truth and love and Life.

As 1960 moved toward its close, we began the move to what would be our last home in Nigeria. It was the house across the road from us when we first went to Lassa. Mission houses in Nigeria tended to take the name of the missionary who lived there. Our "new" home had been known as the Parris house, then the Pfaltzgraff house. The Sterns and the Ralph Royers had been living there, but now it became the Bieber house, and has been known by that name ever since. (Strangely, our last house in Garkida, although used by a number of mission families, also has carried the name of the Bieber house.) By that time, Lassa also had the benefit of electricity in all the mission houses from six to ten each evening. A huge tank which had been set in place to provide water for the hospital also provided water to our homes by simple gravity flow. Flush toilets had also been in-stalled.

Chapter Twenty-Five

SPECIAL PERSONS

That same year, Stover Kulp, co-founder of the mission in Nigeria, whose commitment and wisdom had much to do with the successful growth of the church there, reached the age of sixty-six. It was Foreign Mission Commission policy that missionaries conclude their overseas work at age sixty-five. Ruth Utz had been retired to the States even though she had an adopted son and a granddaughter in Nigeria, and only an aged sister in the United States.

It was Stover's desire to continue to live in Nigeria, but he was not permitted to do so. Two Waka teachers, both with limited mission experience and neither with theological background, were appointed to administrative positions. Roger Ingold became Field Secretary. Stover spent as much time with him as he could and made farewell trips to mission stations in Roger's company. Dallas Oswalt became the assistant. Gladys Royer was Schools Manager. By decision of the church, I was the district secretary. I felt very strongly that I was the servant of the Nigeria church, not of the Foreign Mission Commission, although the latter, thanks to our support churches, paid my salary. I continued to represent the mission on the Board of Governors of Hillcrest and on the Board of Governors of the Theological College of Northern Nigeria.

TCNN deserves an explanation. As it became more and more clear in the latter half of the 1950s that the national churches would be assuming more and more responsibilities, it was the dream of the Northern Missions Council to leave them a special legacy. That legacy would be a school of theology. I believe that Ed Smith, of the Christian Reformed Church, originated the idea. It was given substance and direction by Harry Boer, of the same mission, a theological educator. In 1959, a Board of Governors was convened, with representatives from all five branches of the Sudan United Mission, the South African Mission to the Tivs, and the Church of the Brethren Mission. Largely, I believe, because of the tremendous respect which S.U.M. had for Stover Kulp, the C.B.M. representative was similarly respected. Ed Smith was named the Chairman of the new board, and I was named secretary. As plans developed, a site was located near Bukuru, about twelve miles from Jos. Harry Boer was to become the first principal. Funds were allocated by the supporting missions, and the dream came true. Across the years, TCNN would become the major source of advanced theological education for the ministers of eight different churches. It was a most unusual and a highly successful ecumenical venture.

Rev. Karbam Mamza, one of the men who had received special pastoral training at Chibuk, did not turn out to be a good pastor. The congregation became more and more dissatisfied with him, and in early 1961, they took the very unusual step of voting to ask him to leave. As the elder of the Lassa Church at the time, I was faced with the need to help find another pastor. God was faithful. God provided a new pastor in the form of Ngamariju Mamza.

I have mentioned Ngama earlier in connection with a story about Jilasari and his work at Kilekasa. Ngamariju was a faithful Christian, as deeply committed to Jesus Christ as anyone I have ever known. He was also a Nigeria-registered nurse, having received training at Vom, the nurse training school of the S.U.M. All of the Nigerian nurses I knew in those days were men. Dr. Roy Pfaltzgraff, and later Dr. John Hamer, then Dr. Paul Petcher were successively medical director of the hospital at Lassa. Ngamariju was, in effect, its administrator. Put together the responsibilities of a hospital administrator with serving a church of about 600 with as many as fourteen preaching points, and we begin to see what a tremendous job Ngamariju had. The preaching points, with few exceptions, did not have qualified ministers; they had qualified witnesses. They needed supervision, occasional training meetings, and the administering of covenant and baptism. Three stories of Ngamariju, my dearest friend in Nigeria, will serve to paint his picture.

In Northern Nigeria about that time, a strong evangelistic training program was under way, completely nondenominational. Ngamariju decided to attend "New Life for All," even though it meant a week or more away from home and over a thousand miles of travel. It was my privilege to meet him as he was on the way back to Lassa and transport him the last leg of the journey. Ngama could not stop talking about what a blessing "New Life for All" had been for him in his walk with Jesus. Of course, I cannot remember all he said, but I do remember very clearly his witness. "Jesus has really made me a new person." Thinking silently for a few moments, he added, "Even my wife will see how new I am!"

In the Lassa Church as, indeed, in most of our churches, the pastor was not expected to do all the preaching. We had Sunday morning worship, Sunday evening worship, and Thursday evening worship. One Sunday morning, as I entered the building, I decided to sit with the fairly large group of boys near the front of the church. Before I sat down, I glanced at the preaching schedule. Musa, watchman at the hospital, was scheduled. Time was not an important consideration; still it did seem that Musa was awfully late in arriving. Ngamariju came to me. He said, "You are our preacher today."

"No," I answered. "I looked at the bulletin board; it is Musa today."

"Well, he was supposed to preach, but they have had a problem at the hospital and he can't come."

"Then, Pastor Ngamariju, as our pastor, you can go right ahead."

"Well, you see, I led in our Thursday evening service and I will be speaking this evening, and you haven't preached for a while. I think you should do it today."

It was my turn to respond. "Brother Ngamariju, let me explain something to you. Margi is your language. All you need do is read your Margi testament and speak as God leads. On the other hand, when I preach, I have to prepare the message in English. Then I translate it into Margi and have someone check my translation. I just don't have time to do that today. I am sorry, but I can't preach today."

Ngamariju reached for my Margi testament, handed it to me and said, "*Mallam* Bieber, by the power of God you can do it."

I did; or rather, since most of the people seemed to understand, I should admit, God did.

One Saturday evening, Ngama came to our house. The next morning he needed to visit the Uba preaching point, twenty-seven miles away, because there were some ready to take the covenant and others ready for baptism. Would I take him in our Volkswagen? I would.

I arose early, packed my lunch and a flask of Koolaid and a canteen of water, picked up my Bible, and we started out. It was to be a very hot day. We reached the Wamdiu corner.

Ngamariju thought of something. "There are two brothers in Uvu (another preaching point) who are having a quarrel. We ought to stop and see if we can reconcile them."

"Well, I don't know much of the Uvu dialect," I agreed, "but I can pray for you as you work at it." We visited Uvu and met with the two brothers. Initial exchanges seemed hot and heavy, but it gradually cooled under Ngamariju's calm, but firm, mediation. Eventually, I watched the brothers shake hands warmly, and we had prayer. We went on.

We arrived at Uba—late, but no one minded. There was no church building. There was a sizable group gathered in the shade of trees. We examined candidates for the covenant. Each had to be examined individually to ascertain his or her learnings about the way of Jesus. About forty passed their "exam." They stood before the congregation and spoke their covenant together: "We think the Christian way is God's true way of life, and we will enter the six months class to prepare for baptism." We completed the service with a great deal of praise and thanksgiving, then it was time to examine the baptismal candidates. For them, we were less interested in memorized information about Christ than we were in their understanding of the Christian faith and their motivation for baptism. Ngamariju and I led the congregation to the nearby Yedseram River, and we received more than twenty new Christians by baptism.

The spiritual mood was high. Some of the local members had gone to Lassa for Love Feast, but they had never had one at Uba. Could we have one? We would need water for feetwashing; no problem. We would need food for the fellowship meal; it was just a matter of sharing the mush and greens which would be the usual meal. We would need bread and grape juice. We often used the juice of the African cherry, but there was none, nor was there grape juice. The "bread," as was usual in our Nigerian churches, was thick porridge in a lump from which pieces could be broken. Finally we remembered my red Koolaid, and we diluted it so there would be enough. Even though it was pale pink water, it was a good symbol of the shed blood of our Lord. We had our Love Feast out in the open, in the shade of protective trees, with perhaps seventy-five to eighty participating.

It was about three o'clock on that hot afternoon when Ngamariju and I started off for Lassa. Arriving there, we shared ice water at our home. Ngama went to the village, and I lay on the cement floor of our living room to cool off. In a very short time, I heard Ngama's call outside the door.

"Oh, so you need more ice water," I greeted him.

"No. It was something more serious. The teacher at our Dille School had taken a second wife. We needed to go and convince him to change and repent."

"You are the pastor," I told him. "Just go ahead." He demurred. "You are in charge of the school. You should go," he reminded me. It was hot. I was tired. I was more than reluctant. I sought a way out. "Let me explain something to you," I began. "You have lived here all your life. You have become strong enough to endure a hot day like this. But I can't stand the heat like you can. I am completely worn out. I can't go to Dille with you."

He stood silent for a moment, then he said, "*Mallam* Bieber, by the power of God you can do it." I got out my motorcycle and we went. The effort was not successful, but we worked at it together. My Margi brother taught me much about the power of God!

Mission Conference 1961, at Waka, gave us new assignments. I would not only represent the mission on Hillcrest and TCNN Boards and serve the church as district secretary, but I was also minute secretary for the meeting. I was appointed Evangelism Coordinator for the mission, a surprising appointment, for there were several others far better at evangelism than I. Mary Beth and I were responsible for schools in the eastern sector—Gulak, Mbororo, Uba, Lassa, Chibuk, Mubi, and others. For the time being, Gulak was without staff, so I went there frequently. During one period Mary Beth, Doreen, and I spent ten days there, working with the school, the church, and the dispensary.

By mission meeting time, not all of our things had been moved to our new home; some were in the store at Halls'. A radio message at Waka told us that a thief had invaded the store. We were saddened, when we returned, to discover that Dale's new bike, for which he had saved to buy some accessories, was gone. We disliked telling Dale, but he had a stolidity beyond his age. We kept hoping that the thief would be discovered and the bike returned, but that didn't happen, so we saved to buy Dale a new bike. We finally completed our last Nigeria move in March. Later in the year, Lassa missionaries were besieged by a series of thefts, involving the passport and considerable cash of one of the 1-W men, bicycles, and other items. Once a small steel safe was stolen. It was later found, chopped open. After their risk and hard work, the thieves must have been very discouraged to find it nearly empty.

Robert Zigler, familiarly known as Bob or M. R., was the prime leader for the Church of the Brethren in matters of peace, service, and interchurch relations for many years. He had hoped to be with us in time for mission meeting, but was delayed. He came later on, and was a delightful visitor. He was full of stories of his broad past experiences, as well as hopes and dreams for the future. He was used to being in places where at least a goodly number of the people knew English, but that was not true in our villages. That did not deter his friendliness. He would wander off to the village, talking with people and communicating by signs. He came to be known as the *"Ciao"* man because, when he left a group, he would wave his hand and say, *"Ciao!"* I think that was an Italian farewell. On one occasion, John Grimley took us to visit in Wamdiu. The local medicine man led us in a climb up a low mountain to see the age old cave paintings. They were in a grotto, more open than a cave. The paintings were crude drawings in *yinsidu*, the red ochre ointment with which adolescent boys painted themselves during coming-of-age ceremonies. Our guide, with a somewhat embarrassed grin, showed us the one he had done many years before. M. R. added spice to our lives for a week or more.

I suppose there are few small towns where there is not at least one person who, in past days, would have been called "odd," but in these days are simply "challenged." Garkida had a man like that. It was Yadika Aku, a man well up in years, unusually plump by the local standards, and garnished with full beard. The beard should have been white, but usually it was a bright blue; we suspected that he borrowed bluing from one of the laundry boys. He was a regular church attender. It was his wont, as Easter came, to stand before the congregation and call out something to the effect that Christ had given all for him, so he was giving all for Christ. He would sweep off his robe and lay it on the altar. Of course, he had another robe underneath. I suspect that, later in the day, he retrieved his "gift."

Tsilim, a man in Lassa, was potentially dangerous. For one thing, he did strange things. For another thing, he overindulged in the native beer, which made his behavior quite unpredictable. His constant companion, except when it strayed off, was a scrawny dog. One day Bill Hare, the 1-W teacher, and our son Dale were playing catch in an open area by our house. Neither, I think, ever saw his dog, but when Tsilim saw an arm moving in the direction of his dog and a sizable object fly from the arm, he became furious. He began screaming, "Stop throwing stones at my dog!"

Neither Bill nor Dale understood Margi, but I did. I saw him running, stumbling, in our direction, with something in his hand. "Get in the house!" I told the ballplayers. I met Tsilim as he came charging up the path, and recognized that the object in his hand was a knife.

"They have stopped." I shouted at him. "Now you stop."

He did. I tried to explain that they were not throwing stones at his dog, but were simply playing with a ball. I did not know if he understood my explanation, but at least he had protected his dog. We shook hands and he left, very proudly no doubt.

Majalisa (Nigeria District Conference) renewed my term as secretary for another term. Mary Beth was made Women's Work Chairman. I really do not know how she found time to do it, but she was already working a great deal with women's schools, teaching domestic skills. When Mary Beth took on the assignment, it was for the whole district, but women's work tended to be carried on locally. In some other Christian churches of the northern region, the woman's groups were known as Zamuntar Matan Ekklesiya, roughly translated as "Sisterhood of Women of the Church." As Mary Beth travelled extensively across the district, she took the first important steps toward drawing local groups into a strong district fellowship. Others—Mildred Grimley, Ferne Baldwin, Marianne Michael, Mary Eikenberry—ministered with power to local women, but it was Mary Beth who first welded them into a district-wide organization. Merle Bowman, who followed, extended the influence of ZME, and it became one of the most influential and important—if not, indeed, the most important—arm of the church.

Our fellow missionaries, deeply committed to Christ and the church and with a real love for Nigeria, were also special people. They were also highly skilled. Dr. Roy Pfaltzgraff was one of the two or three most qualified leprologists in the whole world. Ivan Eikenberry was an outstanding educator. Not only did he give most of the direction and impetus to the development of Waka Teacher Training Centre and, later, Waka Secondary School, but he later spent several years as the education consultant for the missions in the northern region. I have already commented on what a tremendous leader Stover Kulp was and how deeply commited were the unwed teachers and nurses. And then there were always visitors: college presidents with their spouses, mission officials, traveling students, denominational staff, and some of the highest of government officials.

It is not likely that, apart from being a missionary, I would ever have had the privilege of meeting Rosa Page Welch. I do not know by what process it happened, but Rosa volunteered to serve in Nigeria for two years. Part of her motivation was the thrill of being in the land of her family roots. She did not have a paying position, but as a volunteer she received food and lodging, medical care, and travel expenses. She loved Nigeria and the Nigerians, yet she showed some discomfort when she was alone with them (without an American colleague) except for her students at Waka. Her fame had grown out of her beautiful singing of Negro spirituals, and we took advantage of that as often as we could. On one occasion, I shared with her the Christmas letter I had sent, which began with, "What if the Christ Child had been born in Nigeria, with skin of soft brown velvet, hair of kinky black, and bright eyes shining like stars in a dark heaven." She was so delighted with it that I was deeply flattered. When she went home to Colorado, we corresponded for several years, but I never saw her again.

I am unable to pin down the date, but the event speaks for itself. As the Church of the Brethren kept growing in Nigeria, it became impossible to have a mass meeting which would encompass the whole area from Wandali to Chibuk and Waka to Gulak. For the purpose of large gatherings, only for worship and fellowship and with no business agenda, the district was divided into sections called, in Hausa, *gunduma*. The *gunduma* to which I refer took place at Uba. Area Christians worked hard to make preparations. Dozens of temporary huts were constructed of grass mats. Latrines were dug and protected. A huge cooking area was made ready with clay pots and plenty of firewood. Even the Moslem Emir of Uba gave a steer to be butchered.

For two full days, a crowd of worshipers of more than 2,500 joined together in song, in prayer, and in praise. Monroe Good and Von Hall, masters of improvisation, provided a loud speaker system powered by car batteries. All the men, Nigerian or American, educated or illiterate, leaders or followers, destitute or comfortable, slept on the same facilities, ate the same food—as did also all the women. As per local custom, meat was butchered without removing the entrails, or at least, not all of them.

On the second afternoon, a fun time was scheduled. Different tribes or clans shared their favorite songs. We white folks did not have a favorite song familiar to the people, so we made one up and sang,

"We liked the area, we liked the huts, we liked the food, but not the guts."

Our English speaking Nigerian brothers enjoyed it as much as we did. Rosa Page Welch blessed us by singing her best known song, "He's Got the Whole World in His Hands."

Make no mistake; Nigerians were equally important to us and equally a blessing of our service in Nigeria. I have already written at some length about Nggida Gadzama, Mallam Wadzani, Jabani Mambula, Mai Sule Biu, and Ngamariju Mamza. Nvwa Balami, one of the first Lardin Gabas graduates of TCNN, was one of the best pastors I have ever known. Only slightly, however, did he overshadow (for me) wise, gentle, perceptive Ibrahim Mdiriza, pastor who spent his whole life at Chibuk; or Pastor

Madu Bwala of Marama, an able officer of the Nigeria Church and later in his life, a provincial legislator as well.

Nggida was our first "son," and we were delighted to be able to help him on to his university education, but so much of his education took him away from us. Ngamariju was my dearest friend. But the one Nigerian nearest and dearest to all of our family—a genuine family member—was Karagama Apagu Gadzama. From the time he began little acts of helpfulness during our first tour in Lassa, he was never far from us when we were in Nigeria.

He made himself useful in every way he could, learning housework, learning to cook, caring for the little ones, playing with them. Not the most brilliant of students, he was still outstanding enough to keep advancing to the next educational level. When we were in Garkida, he had entered senior primary school and was there with us much of the time. He went to Waka Training Centre, but found frequent opportunities to be back in Garkida with us. He heard God's call to the ministry, and entered the Theological College. Whenever we were in Jos, he would find a way to spend time with us. After TCNN, he became the elder—then called the moderator—of four congregations, served as district treasurer for several years and, entrepreneur that he was, set up his own "egg farm." Of Karagama, there is more to come.

After Christmas in 1951 our family, with the very important assistance of Karagama, took a trip to the Waza Game Reserve in the Cameoons, about 150 miles northeast. It was in a French colony, and we anticipated some language problems, but Karagama solved them for us. He could almost always find someone to speak Fulani or Fulabi, one of the several languages in which he was fluent. He was also helpful in the preparation of food. There was no catering service; we took along the food we would need. Accommodations were round huts divided by a partition. It was much colder than we anticipated, so Marla slept with Mary Beth, Doreen with me, and Bonnie and Dale managed. I quote from Bonnie's note: "We saw lots of giraffes, wart hogs, and animals belonging to the deer family. We saw twenty-one ostriches, and lots of other people who went saw only two." In early evening, Mary Beth added, we saw jackals and monkeys. It was a great family experience, made better by the numerous animals, and by the sheer and majestic beauty of the terrain through which we passed.

Meetings, meetings, meetings. Fortunately, I do not share my brother's antipathy to meetings; actually, I usually enjoy them, and there were plenty of meetings to enjoy. As elder of the Gulak and Lassa congregations, I had council meetings, and those with various church committees. Ralph Royer had succeeded his mother as supervisor of the mission schools, but he was on furlough and I was acting, so there were plenty of consultations to take place. The Nigeria district had various committees as well as the regular annual conference, and I made a special effort to be present. For the mission, I served on the education committee, the evangelism committee, and the field committeee, and represented the mission on the Hillcrest Board, the TCNN Board, and the new Bible School Board. We added one ad hoc committee, a literature committee to engender the writing of articles for the *Messenger* and other publications. Just to be sure there would be enough meetings for me, mission meeting in 1962 elected me chairman, which meant I was ex officio on all mission committees.

On the other hand, life as a missionary in Nigeria also had its down side. The amount of disease, infection, or accidents that we worked around was almost unbelieveable. It was not only that the children suffered their full share of childhood diseases—measles, mumps, chickenpox—and childhood accidents. Larry also had rheumatic fever; Marla had nephritis. All of us succumbed repeatedly to malaria, eventually developing some immunity which reduced the severity of the attacks, but still carried aches, pains, chills, headaches, fever, and nausea. There rarely seemed to be a time when there was not at least one functioning at less than top speed. Three of the children had amoeba. Mary Beth had a kidney stone. Only a few times, however, did illness get Mary Beth down; she almost always pushed herself to continue functioning. As for me, I was stubborn enough to refuse to discontinue my activities due to migraine or malaria. In early 1962, however, I spent a good time in bed and more time at half mast. My legs, in particular, were constantly aflame, and I was successfully treated for filaria. Besides, baptizers in Nigeria were faced with parasitic invasion in much the same way that early baptizers in America had dared ice water to baptize in December waters. For us, the invasion was by schistosomiasis. The ponds and the stagnant streams in which we baptized let very few of us escape a series of schisto injections. It took a double series of treatments to overcome mine. We were constantly thankful, however, for the attentive care of our medical staff, and for the assurance of God's healing presence.

It was also in 1962 that Nigeria decided to issue new money. They announced by radio and, presumably, by newspaper in the larger cities, that all money would be replaced. We got the news by radio in Lassa that, within a month, old money would not be honored. I reflected on what that would mean. I would need to obtain a supply of the new currency in order to pay the teachers and evangelists. People who were not aware of the change would be dismayed to find that their money was useless in the market place. Eventually, they would realize that the only place where the money would not be refused would be the church offerings. I decided to do all I could to help the people, and particularly to protect the church treasury. I sent a message, by word of mouth, to all the surrounding villages. "Bring your old money to *Mallam* Bieber at Lassa. He will replace it."

Bonnie, Karagama, and I came to a new understanding of "filthy lucre." That money was dirty! We set up bins and tables on the front porch of our home. For three days we received what seemed an endless line of people. The money came in ragged cloth wrappings, in old leather bags, in tins, and simply in pockets. Some of it had obviously just been retrieved from an earthen burial. To make it interesting, we had not a pence of new money. We counted money as it was brought to us, and issued to each client a note promising to pay. We had I.O.U.s spread for miles around. When the collection slowed and we called an end to it, I knew that there was too much weight for a small car. I borrowed the mission truck, loaded up, and drove to the nearest bank, at Yola, about a hundred miles away. We had to report the weight of the load—part of the method for assessing the cost of the truck. The heaviest coin was the penny, about the size of a thinner American silver dollar, with a small hole in the middle. There were nearly TWO TONS of pennies alone! Alas, the bank in Yola had none of the new money. They gave me a receipt and promised to let me know when funds would be available. Eventually I received it, and as the word went out that the money was available, the people came in, and hopefully all were paid.

Mary Beth and I were both coming to believe, in 1962, that we had fulfilled God's call to Nigeria mission. There were several factors involved in our decision to resign. Foremost, for me, was the conviction that our Nigerian brethren needed to be the ones leading the Nigerian church. For there to be a Nigerian district secretary, for example, I needed to be off the scene. It was also more and more difficult for us to have children away. Larry had been gone for two years and would be gone a third. Dale would shortly be going home for his last three years of high school. Bonnie wasn't far behind. The negative vibrations we felt toward me from the commission were a lesser, but still a valid, consideration. My extensive bout with schistosomiasis, though victorious, was, to say the least, disturbing. We wrote a letter to the commission, resigning at the end of our tour, a year later, copying it to Roger Ingold. As the news of our resignation spread among our missionary colleagues, we were moved by the number of them who tried to persuade us to stay. We did not get such encouragement from the commission. In spite of resignation, we continued to put full time and effort into our work, even to planning for the future.

We were pleased, as I have said, with the care and the education which our children received at Hillcrest. Dale was taking his first year of high school, by correspondence, when he went home in 1962. He had a wide variety of interests. He participated in sports, but I think it was more out of a sense of duty to the school rather than eager enjoyment. He did, however, thoroughly enjoy music, and thrilled us both with his skill on the piano and with his baritone voice. He also liked drama and public speaking. He played the lead role in the Hillcrest production of "Our Town," with convincing aplomb. He was the only one of his siblings, however, who did not vie for an opportunity to hold or play with his baby sister.

Bonnie, though tending to be on the shy side like her dad, made some close friends at school who would be her friends for life. She also played the piano and had great fun in being in those skits and more comical presentations in talent nights. She was especially good at playing with her younger sisters.

Marla also was taking piano lessons. She enjoyed her schoolmates, and was proud of being the oldest one in her dorm room. She always seemed to be the first to write a letter of thanks, and her handwriting was better than her sister's.

Bonnie was quite honest to say she liked to read letters, not write them.

Meanwhile, Doreen, at home alone most of the time or traveling with her mother on many women's work trips, was providing her own education. She kept asking, "What are spoons made of? What is silver made of? What is wood made of?" and except when troubled by amoeba or malaria was a very happy lassie.

It was very hard to be away from Larry for three years. He did not write frequently enough for our needs, and sometimes our information came from grandparents or from his surrogate mother, Arlene Wenger. We learned that he was on the National Honor Society, that he was president of the youth group, that he won second place in the district speech contest, and that he was commended for a National Merit Scholarship. When he finished high school, early because he had skipped a grade at Hillcrest, we hoped he would be an exchange student, and he quickly agreed. He spent his third year away from us, in Germany. It was even harder to see Dale leave, because he would be taking much of his journey alone—with stops in Lagos and in Amsterdam. He had a great deal of maturity, however. He arrived in the U.S.A. in time to spend some time with Larry and visit his grandparents with him. A letter from him just before Larry left for Germany, assured us, "You don't have to worry about Larry. He is a fine person and a gentleman."

This would seem to be a good place to insert the story of Risku; you will soon see why. Among the first four persons to be baptized by the Brethren in 1927 was a young man by the name of Risku Madziga, a member of the Wagga tribe. The Madziga clan was royalty to the Wagga people; Risku, the oldest son, was destined to become chief, sometime in the future, of that important tribe.

When Risku was a small boy, an invading horde of warriors swept down from the north, wreaking havoc wherever they went. They reached the Wagga village, still killing and destroying as they went. All of the male members of the chiefly clan whom they could find, they killed. Small Risku, however, had been hidden away by an elderly aunt and was safe for the time being. As he grew older, his presence was still kept secret, even though the invaders gradually faded away. Except for a very few schools poorly run by the native administration, children did not have opportunity for education. The Madziga aunts learned of a school at Lassa, some seventy-five miles away, distant enough to be safe in the event of returning raiders. Risku entered the school there. He was an excellent student. He learned to know Jesus while he was in school and committed his life to Jesus. He began to serve his Lord and the church as an evangelist and dispenser, receiving training for both.

I feel compelled to interrupt here to record an incident which affected me powerfully, but which is only tangential to the Risku saga. While I was elder ot the Gulak Church, I received a message asking me to come to Wagga village. When I arrived, there were perhaps a hundred people gathered with the evangelist. He was the first messenger of Christ in that village. We rejoiced in a group of twelve who took the covenant. As I rode away on my motorcycle, my eyes were filled with tears of joy as I realized that I had been present when, for the first time in all of history, the light of Christ had come to that village.

As the years went by, young Risku returned to his natal area, married Sajo, and set up their home. He developed a process by which the sap could be pressed from sugar cane, cooked, and formed into small cakes of brown sugar tasting deliciously between sugar and sorghum. Each spring we would look forward to our purchase of cakes of Risku sugar. I came to know of him through his daughter, Titi, a practical nurse who had assisted me in my first deliveries, and his nephew, Umoru, who tended the Lassa orchard. By now an affluent man by comparison with compatriots, Risku was no longer a roving evangelist, but he was still an active and faithful Christian. When we were talking together one day at a district meeting, he talked about the pressure placed on Christians who were community leaders, by the politically powerful Moslems of the northern region. I remembered a few such men who had accepted political appointments after agreeing to be baptized as Moslems.

"My own best friend," he told me, "is the chief justice of the northern region court. He is a Moslem. Almost always, when we are together, he says to me, 'Risku, you are such a good man; you should be a Moslem.' I answer him, 'My friend, you are such a good man; you should be a Christian.'"

Again a few years passed by. We learned with a great deal of pride, that Risku Madziga had been named District Head of the Gulak District. His ancestry had become known and his current abilities were recognized. Although under colonial government, he was basically the ruler for a large area. Had he been a Moslem, he would have been named "Emir." It was only two or three years after his installation that a rumor reached us. It came repeatedly and from different sources, so we felt we would have to honor it, in spite of our reluctance.

Word came that, after all those years, Risku had become a Moslem. If he had been baptized, it was not likely that we could reclaim him; yet, John Grimley, Jim Bowman, and I went to see him in his small palace at Gulak. As was proper for visitors, we were received in his anteroom and seated on easy chairs. When he came in, we greeted each other in the traditional manner, inquiring about health and family. Then, more boldly than I would have dared, Jim said, "*Mallam* Risku, we have come because of news that we have received. We have been told that you became a Moslem. Is it true?" Risku sat looking at us. The longer he looked, the clearer it seemed that the story was true. Tears began to well up from deep within me. Then the District Head began to shake his head.

"No, no, no," he said. "I could never leave Jesus. He has done so much for me." His witness was faithful; he died several years later, still living with Jesus.

Having strayed from the more or less chronological narrative, this would seem to be the right time simply to mention some of the other things I remember from Nigeria—persons, places, or events that jump to the front of my mind at times.

First memory: the decision of Chief Jidai, of Dille, to become a Christian. The exciting news of his decision came to us at Lassa, together with a request that we have a special service at Dille where he would announce his conversion. I have never been sure whether his desire for a public announcement reflected chiefly decorum, or the feeling that he would thereby be storing up points in a heavenly record book. No matter. Church leaders at Lassa were usually such qualified people that their presence at Dille might suggest political ambition. We decided that Musa, our washboy and the watchman at the hospital, was obviously innocent of such ambition, so he and I went together in the old jeep, to Dille. A huge crowd was gathered under a spreading tamarind tree. Most of the people, I think, knew there was something special coming, but they had no hint of what it would be. I conducted the service, with scripture, song, and prayer, to the moment of Jidai's announcement.

His announcement went very much like this: "My people, I must give you some news. You remember what we used to do when the rains did not come and we were afraid that our corn would not produce? I led you seven times around Dille Mountain, and then we sacrificed three goats to the rain gods, so the gods would send rain. You remember how, when smallpox struck our village and people began to die, I led you seven times around Dille Mountain and then sacrificed seven chickens to the gods of health, so our people would be spared. Those practices are useless. We will not follow them any more. I want you to know today that I have decided to become a Christian. I will be taking the covenant and baptism."

After the sounds of astonishment and, by the Christians, rejoicing dwindled, I introduced Musa as the representative of the church who would welcome Chief Jidai.

Musa's response was so bold that I was somewhat apprehensive about the way Jidai might receive it. Musa said, "Chief Jidai, you have made an important statement which we are happy to hear. Your statement says that you will leave the religion of lies which you have followed all your life and will follow the Christian way. But Chief Jidai, how strong are you?"

"Let me show you what I mean." Looking around, Musa spied a dried cornstalk. He called a small boy to the front and asked him to break the cornstalk in two. Easily, and with a grin, the lad broke it and handed Musa the two pieces. "Chief Jidai, the devil will try to break you away from the Christian way. I hope you're stronger than a cornstalk." In the congregation, there was puzzled murmuring. Then Musa picked up a small dried branch about as big around as an adult finger and about three feet long. He went through the same process. Could the little boy break the stick? No, but a bigger boy did.

"Chief Jidai, I hope you are stronger than a small branch." He found a heavier branch, still with some life in it, and again went through the process. The big boy could not break it, but a strong young man succeeded in breaking it over his knee, and triumphantly handed the pieces to Musa.

"Chief Jidai, I hope you are stronger than the big branch, but you can see that the devil is very powerful."

Musa continued. He took out his knife and cut several strips of pliant bark from the tree. He went to the jeep and pulled out the four-foot-long jack bar. He picked up another dried cornstalk. He tied the bar alongside the cornstalk, using the strips of bark as rope.

He called the little boy up. Could he break the cornstalk? No. The iron rod got in the way. He called the bigger boy up. Again the bar got in the way. Even the strong young man was not able to overcome the iron bar and break the cornstalk. Then Musa continued his message:

"Chief Jidai, no one, no matter how strong a person he might be, is as strong as the devil. But Jesus is stronger than the devil. Jesus is like the iron bar that made a small cornstalk strong. If you will truly take Jesus into your heart and always trust in Jesus, I know that you will be so strong that the devil can never break you away."

A second memory is that of baptizing in the stagnant stream at Dille. There were several candidates, so Bob Bischof and I entered the water together and proceeded. As we were immersing the new Christians, I kept feeling what I thought were fish nibbling at my bare legs. I kept lifting the other foot and brushing them away. When we came from the water, we realized it had not been fish, but leeches. Bob had several still clinging to his legs. I had none, but one had successfully penetrated one instep. Bob wrapped his spots as best he could with our wet handkerchiefs, and as I drove blood seeped into my sneaker. We had no ill effects, unless that was one of the sources of my schistosomiasis.

A third memory is of a transition in attitude which took place in me. In those early years, a day would rarely go by when I would not see naked breasts. I was startled by such blatant nudity. There were so many bare breasts that I almost wondered if some of the men were also so endowed. Gradually, however, I came to appreciate the innocence of the young women who were carrying water to fill our tank, or the mothers singing in the church choir who would nonchalantly pull a crying baby from their back and thrust a milky breast into the infant mouth. Frequently, I would baptize bare breasted women, impressed, obviously, since I still remember, but not startled and not deterred from the meaning of the ceremony. A kind of culminating picture in my mind is of a ceremony which I observed at Wamdiu. I do not know if it was a coming of age ritual or a Margi equivalent to a lonely hearts advertisement. Forty or fifty girls, ranging in age from about ten to about twenty, bare breasted but garbed in a most colorful and beautiful arrangement of beads, bracelets, and anklets danced in slow procession past the viewing crowd, of which I was one (though not looking for a second wife, thank you!).

Fourth and fifth memories: two sermons I preached in Margi. Schooled by the way Jesus so frequently used parables, I also tried to use story sermons. One was the chicken story:

Once there was a boy who had a pet chicken. He loved his chicken. But he noticed that his chicken was eating only sand and bits of stone. He knew that his chicken would die if he did not get some proper food, and he didn't want his chicken to die. He went to his chicken. He said, "Chick, I notice that you eat only sand and stones. Now over here there are some delicious bugs and worms and guinea corn. Why don't you eat some of this good food?"

But, of course, the boy was talking boy talk, and the chicken understood only chicken talk. It kept eating sand and stones. Then the boy saw a flock of nice plump chickens, all of them eating good bugs, delicious worms, and guinea corn. He went to them. He said, "I notice that you are eating good food. Now I have a chicken that I love who eats only sand and stones. He will die if he doesn't eat proper food. Will you please go and tell him how good your food is?" But the chickens just kept on eating. They did not understand a word he said, because he was talking boy talk and they understood only chicken talk.

Of course, one can do anything in a story, so the boy thought for a while, and then he changed himself into a chicken. He pecked away along with his chicken. Then he said, "Hey, chick, I see you are eating only sand and stones. Now over here are some delicious bugs and worms and corn. Why don't you try them?" Now he was talking chicken talk, so his chicken understood and found the good food that would give him life. The story over, here is the moral: God is like that boy and we are like that chicken. Again and again God kept telling us how we could live, because he loves us, but we did not understand, because God was talking God talk and we are humans. So God changed himself into a human, a little baby named Jesus, who grew up talking human language and telling us of God's love, and now we can live, too.

The second sermon was more of an acted parable. I secured a heavy rope and laid it in the church aisle, leading from about halfway back, to behind the pulpit. I explained that the rope represented the road to heaven, and if anyone would reach the end he would have great reward. I asked for volunteers and selected a boy of about fourteen years. As I explained to him, the parable proceeded: "I want you to stand on the end of the rope. If you can stay on the rope all the way up here, you will get a reward. You realize, however, that the devil is always trying to get you to leave Jesus' road. So I will pretend to be the devil, and I will try to get you off the road. When we start, you must not believe anything I say except when I tell you to stop or go. You also know that Jesus told us to take up a cross and follow him, so here is a cross for you." And I presented him with a fairly heavy, crude cross. The talk continued: "Do you understand all the instructions? Do you still want to try to follow Jesus' road? All right. Go."

After a few steps, "Stop. Look. Here I have a shilling for you. All you have to do is come and get it." The lad remembered that he was not to believe what I said, and stayed on the rope. I commended him to the congregation: "Isn't it great that money did not tempt him from the Jesus road! Go."

After a few more steps, "Stop. I have a nice, ripe, beautiful mango here for you to eat. I know you are hungry. Here. Come and get it."

Again, shaking his head, he resisted temptation. Again I commended him to the congregation: "Isn't it great that his appetiete did not make him leave Jesus' road! Go. After a few more steps, just to the foot of the stair leading to the pulpit, "Stop. I know you like to play football. Here is a small ball that you can use. You may have this ball. Just come and get it."

Once again he resisted temptation. He saw how close he was getting to heaven. I commended him to the congregation. Pride showed on this face.

I began looking for the next temptation, but obviously something was missing. I searched my pockets. I looked around on the floor. I checked behind the pulpit. I asked Mary Beth if I left it with her. She denied it. Shaking my head, I turned to the boy. "Isn't that something? I forgot the next thing I was going to use. We'll just have to quit. Maybe we can do it some other time. Thanks a lot for your help. You were doing a good job."

I reached for the cross, which by now was pretty heavy. He handed it over. What boy wouldn't have? As he returned to his seat, I yelled, "Hey! You got off the road! Didn't I tell you not to believe anything I say except to go and stop?"

Sadly, the boy hanged his head. I concluded, "Sometimes walking with Jesus is just like that. It is when we begin to feel proud of how well we are doing that we are in most danger of going away from him." I did give the boy a reward for his helping me, and small balm for his embarrassment.

One more memory. It was Easter Sunday morning at the Virgwi Church. For the past few days, Pastor Mai Sule and I had been lifting up for the people, the cross—there was one at the front of the sanctuary—and the suffering to which Jesus' love had driven him. We had tried to make people understand the cruelty of the cross, its ugliness, and the pain it was inflicting on Jesus. I was startled, as I entered the church that Easter morning, to see a wreath of flowers on the cross, in spite of our emphasis on its cruelty. I was dismayed. For the sake of Jesus, I was offended. Then the message struck home to me. That was indeed the message of Easter: flowers on the cross!

At *majalisa* meeting in 1963, aware that I would be leaving, the delegates chose Monroe Good to fill my unexpired third term as district secretary. Later, my good friend, Ngamariju, would take the position. As the thirteen years since our first arrival in Nigeria came to an end, I reflected on the way the church had grown. There had been five congregations; now there were thirty. There had been about twenty-eight evangelists in CRI's; now there were 180 attending the evangelists' retreat. Membership had been counted at about 800; now it was well past 8,000. I had been the mission's evangelism chairman for seven of those years and district secretary for eight; yet I was well aware that what God had wrought was not the result of my work. I had formulated the decisions of the church by organizing forty pages of classified minutes. I had worked toward an accurate system of reporting. I had baptized more than a thousand because for a time there were no Nigerian ministers. Yet it was very clear to me that I could not boast of the growing church as my accomplishment. It was the result of plans carefully laid and carried out: the CRI

(Class in Religious Instruction), the provision of service programs—education, medicine, agriculture—along with strong evangelism. It was the result of truly strenuous labor, sometimes when bodies and minds were hardly able to work, by dozens of missionaries. It was the result of countless prayers and faithful financial support by the church in America. In human terms, it was the result of the enthusiasm of Nigerian Christians for sharing with others the good news of Jesus that had come to them.

Most of all—it goes without saying, but I must say it, it was the result of the movement of the Spirit of God among the people of northeastern Nigeria. On the Sunday before we left Lassa, there was an immense gathering of Christians in an open area near our house. Ngamariju had sent notices far and wide; I knew, because I had typed his notices for him. There were games, there were dramatic pieces, there were prayers, there was singing, there were expressions of gratitude, love and regret that we were leaving, and there were many tears shed. We were presented with authentic Nigerian garb for Mary Beth and me, for Bonnie, Marla, and Doreen, and to be taken to Larry and Dale. We left the next day, pausing to bid farewell to fellow missionaries along our route. We were still crying, though we felt certain that God was leading. Sometimes, a third of a century later, we still cry. We left part of our heart in Nigeria.

We had traded in our well-worn Volkswagen Beetle, to pick up a new one in Germany. We landed in Frankfurt, rested a bit, picked up our new VW, and headed as directly as we could to Rheydt and son Larry. How he had matured in the three years since we had left him! All three of his sisters decided that having a big brother like that, with a nice deep voice, was just one of the nicest things that could happen. We enjoyed visiting with the Quacks, his host family for the year, and we enjoyed some of the nearby German landmarks, notably the cathedral at Koln. Too soon, but aware it would only be a few more weeks until he, too, would be back in the States, we bade Larry farewell, and went on HOME. The VW would follow.

Expecting to need a lot of transportation during the next few months, we had also taken advantage of the kind generosity of Brethren Ford dealer John Myers, in Virginia, and ordered a new Ford station wagon. He delivered it to Spring City, and it was one of the two cars which came to Idlewild airport to meet us. We rushed through visits to the Highs and Biebers, had Dale join us, and headed for Annual Conference in Illinois. Once again, and for the last time, I was serving the Nigeria Church on Standing Committee, and Mary Beth was a delegate from the Lassa Church.

The General Brotherhood Board met at Annual Conference. They invited us in and read to us the following citation:

Charles and Mary Beth Bieber first sailed to Nigeria in 1950. Their years of service with the church in Nigeria have been filled with a variety of fruitful activities. They have become fluent in Margi and Bura, a prerequisite for the close personal fellowship which they maintained with innumerable Nigerians in both village and church activities and on both the social and official church levels. Charles obtained a working knowledge of Hausa as well.

During his first years at Lassa, Charles was occupied with language study, village visitation and, as a registered nurse, spent much time in the Lassa hospital and dispensary.

Charles has played a major role in the development of the district organization, having served the district as its secretary, and on numerous of its committees. In addition, Charles has given vigorous and imaginative leadership in Brethren missions and interdenominational boards and committees. With his great variety of skills, interests, and responsibilities, it must be said of Charles that he has been, above all else, an evangelist and a pastor of God's people. He has pioneered in evangelistic work among the Waga tribe. As moderator and advisor to many congregations, Charles has thus kept up a heavy program of village visitation even when administrative duties were most demanding.

Mary Beth has taken a healthy interest in all the people about her, showing a warm, sympathetic concern for every area of their lives. No Nigerian could be long in her presence without realizing she was deeply concerned with him as a person, anxious to help, whatever the need might be. This was especially true of her relationship with the women of the church. During the past year she has been the leader of women's work in the district.

She has spent much time in the education program of the mission and church, working as a teacher and supervisor in the primary schools and teaching and directing women's schools. In addition to this missionary activity she made a home for her family, the children of which were always divided between her own hearth and Hillcrest Boarding School.

The General Brotherhood Board expresses on behalf of the Church of the Brethren grateful appreciation for the devoted missionary service of Brother and Sister Charles Bieber, and wishes them God's richest blessing as they continue their Christian calling in the United States.

Chapter Twenty-Six

BIG SWATARA

Anticipating that we would be staying in the States, we had been in correspondence with Roy Forney, Eastern Regional Secretary. We had provided him with information about ourselves, our education, our experience, our faith, and had sent him a family picture. We heard of churches which might be interested; the supply of pastors was not that plentiful.

About six weeks before we were due to leave Lassa, a lengthy and informative letter came from Hiram Frysinger, Big Swatara's moderator. He thoroughly described the congregation, located about seven miles north of Hershey, Pennsylvania. He believed they were interested.

If we were called, would we be prepared to accept? Hiram shared with the congregaton some comments from my letter of response: "Recognizing that without opportunity for personal visits, the church is obliged to respond somewhat in the dark, we thought a few statements might help to explain the Biebers. We believe that a pastor must be a prophet as well as a shepherd. He should constantly be seeking to apply the truths of the Bible to the facts of daily life; in doing so he must speak the truth freely as God gives it to him to understand it; but he must do it in love. We believe that preaching should be from the Bible both because it is the Word of God and because it is fully relevant to our age. We believe the function of the congregation to be both witnessing and serving; both servanthood and Christian fellowship. We believe the inner strength of the church is increased by her outreach. We count ourselves to be conservative in religion, but we believe that God intends us to be constantly in thoughtful, prayerful study to keep examining how the Gospel applies to our day."

Big Swatara was a congregation of about four hundred. Its central meeting house was at Hanoverdale, and services were also held at Fishing Creek Valley and Paxton. It was an old congregation, which all through the years had been served by self-supported ministers. They had never had a paid pastor; I would be the first. It sounded like the combination of challenge and opportunity of which I had been dreaming. We prayed about it and discussed it. We indicated our willingness to accept.

Without ever having met us and without having heard a "trial sermon," they voted. By a ninety-two percent majority, we were called. We accepted. We learned, later, that the four resident ministers had been refused three times when they recommended that the congregation call a pastor. The fourth time brought acceptance, but obviously there was still opposition, so it was a safe assumption that much of the negative vote was against having a pastor rather than against having this particular pastor. Having made their decision, the congregation went all out. They began construction of a new parsonage to be completed and dedicated about mid-August. It would be a beautiful house of manufactured stone with a large living room, dining room, kitchen, three bedrooms, study, one and a half baths, and complete basement with a fireplace. The copy of the plan which they sent us increased our excitement. Not only was God giving us an opportunity; God was also providing us with a splendid place to live.

As we settled in at Highs, collected and sorted the freight which we had sent home, took inventory of what we had left in America, and continued with our end-of-service visits and worship services, Big Swatara was very much in our minds. Eastern Pennsylvania was much more conservative than our church at Royersford, both in dress and in congregational organization and polity. We would need to balance honesty about our faith position with acceptance of customs and practices which were different to us. I would, in particular, need to make clear my appreciation of the four ordained ministers already in the congregation. There were excitement and joy ahead, but we were not so naive as to expect a perfect situation. After all, heaven is still in the tomorrow!

Meanwhile, there was the summer. Three of our children were enrolled for a week at Camp Swatara. Doreen was busy being spoiled by Biebers, Highs, and Hershbergers. Grandma Bieber, whose name was Doreen's second, was pleased with the naming and gave Doreen savings bonds from time to time. There was getting re-acquainted with relatives, some of whom had been faithful supporters, by attending the Seriff and Bieber reunions. There was furniture to buy. We made weekly trips to Bonnie Brae Auction, just up the hill from the Highs. We visited Norristown and Pottstown furniture stores and bought a new sectional sofa and a new bedroom suite. We bought a sizable new freezer.

We expressed our gratitude to the Parkerford Church; it was hard to believe how much that little congregation had contributed to our missionary life. We made quiet visits to Hanoverdale, partly just to begin to learn the area and partly to watch progress on the parsonage, our soon-to-be new home.

The exciting day came when Larry returned from Germany, and once again our family was together. We visited the Wengers, who had so kindly and so wisely cared for our two boys. We made a special trip to the Mechanic Grove Church, thanking them both for their missionary support of Mary Beth and for their help to Larry's exchange student program. Larry had been accepted at Juniata College and granted what was then a sizable scholarship of $600. We were very much pleased at his choice of Juniata, our alma mater and where, in a sense, the family had begun. Then came the day, early in September, when we took him to the college. Rarely ever would we be together again as a family as we had in the past, but the mutual support we experienced in our mission years would hold us ever close together.

Even as there was no plaque identifying the house where I was born, there was no plaque identifying our first real parsonage in the States. If anything, there might have been a plaque to identify the first parsonage of the Big Swatara congregation. My pastorates to date had all had predetermined closing dates. Barring a major *faux pas*, I could have gotten away in those pastorates, with almost anything. At Big Swatara, I would constantly be under the evaluation of the congregation, sometimes formal, sometimes not; sometimes open and direct, sometimes not. With the help of the four ministers, my position needed description. The ministers were Hiram Frysinger, who was the moderator; Norman Patrick; John Patrick, his nephew; and Harold Fahnestock. One man (not one of the ministers) wondered why I needed a job description.

"I'm a farmer," he explained. "I know my job. When the cows need milking, I milk them."

"Being a pastor is different," I demurred. "All your cows want the same thing at the same time. With a congregation of four hundred, there are likely to be a lot of different wants at a lot of different times. It helps to know the general expectation."

We identified preaching, visitation, teaching, administration, and counseling to be my basic tasks. Even as the work of a missionary tended to be multi-lateral, however, so was the work of a pastor. One of the less usual opportunities came from the blind sister-in-law of one of our deacons. She caned chairs. I could hardly believe that a blind person could do that; I really needed my eyes. It happened, however, that on rare occasions she would realize she had done something wrong and would be unable to find her error. Then she would call me, and I would help her make the correction. Another potential opportunity came when one of our young mothers, expecting twins, was snowbound by a heavy blizzard. I promised to negotiate the half mile to her home and care for the delivery, if it became necessary. It did not. And, of course, other similar opportunities arose from time to time.

To open our conversation as I called on older couples, I often asked if they had grown up in this area. If not, where had their home been? In one of those calls, an incident from my boyhood leaped to the front. As a boy of fourteen, I had spent ten days with Uncle Eddy and Aunt Laura Bieber. My uncle, a Lutheran minister, was serving three churches in rural Franklin County, Pennsylvania. As I wandered around the small town of Lemasters, I often saw a man who was quite different and therefore a puzzle to me. He had a full-length beard (no mustache) in an era when facial hair was rare. He seemed always to be dressed in bib overalls and wearing a flat-brimmed black hat. One day I asked Uncle Eddy, "Who is that man?"

"Oh, that's Jake Sollenberger. He's our barber."

"Why does he have a beard and why does he dress that way?"

"That is because he is a Dunker."

That was my very first awareness of the Church of the Brethren.

One day, when I was visiting with Byron and Cora Oellig, I asked the usual question. Byron had suffered a stroke and found talking difficult, so Cora was spokesperson. No, they had not lived here all their lives; they had grown up in Franklin County. Seeing the opportunity for a connection, I told them, "I visited in Franklin County many years ago, in the home of my Uncle Eddy Bieber. He was Lutheran pastor at Lemasters, Upton, and Williamson."

They knew those towns. I went on. "Let me tell you where I first heard of the Dunkers." I told them the story as I have told it above. When I got to, "That's Jake Sollenberger," Cora blurted out, "That's my Daddy." I never did finish the Dunker part of the story; somehow, it seemed superfluous.

I believed that preaching was of prime importance and determined to make my sermons strongly Biblical, but usually topical rather than expository. The ministers confessed that the strongest plank in their platform when they electioneered for a paid pastor was visitation. "We told them that when you came you would be able to visit much better than we could, because we were all full-time employed." They were indeed. Hiram was a college professor, Norman and Harold worked at Hershey Foods, and John was a bank cashier.

Speaking of pay (we were, weren't we? See the middle of the preceding paragraph.), the Parish Ministry Commission of the Brethren had developed a recommended salary scale for pastors. Based on comparison with positions with similar educational requirements and similar responsibilities, it tried to help congregations and pastors to be fair to each other. It was based on education and experience. Big Swatara was paying me well below scale. I understood their difficulty in now paying a pastor for the first time, and I did not want to make waves, so I simply accepted. To begin with, we were in the $5,000 range, plus a parsonage with all utilities. We had all we needed for our family of seven, but very little "extra." We had a garden beside the house, but it was newly-broken sod. I fought a losing battle with the well-established crab grass until Nggida came visiting during one college vacation. He took our Nigerian hoe, with the short handle that requires the user to be down among the weeds, and proceeded to clear the garden.

Larry having departed for college, we now came to the first time since his birth, when not even one child spent all the time at home. Doreen's entering the first grade at West Hanover Elementary School, along with sister Marla who was a fifth grader, was just a little like Larry's first heading off to Hillcrest. Bonnie was a ninth grader at Lower Paxton Junior High and Dale a junior at Central Dauphin East High School. All seemed to like school, and all did well, although Bonnie would report, years later, that she felt lost by the girls' pseudo-sophisticated conversation about clothes, makeup, and the latest movies.

We had hardly arrived at Hanoverdale and settled in—actually, less than a month later—when the time arrived for our first Love Feast. I had led only two Brethren Love Feasts in America, in Lincoln in 1950 and at Pottstown in 1959. With the kind of helpfulness which would be typical of him, Hiram sat down with me and reviewed the process as followed by Eastern District elders. It had been reduced to a one-day event rather than the two-day event which was still traditional. There would be an examination service. That was the morning service on the day of the Love Feast. It involved reviewing Biblical teaching about self-examination, and confession. In the evening, the Love Feast would begin with a brief devotional period, then the feetwashing. Men sat on one side of the meetinghouse, women on the other. The pews had hinged backs which were turned up to become tables. Feetwashing took place at the tables. Water in tubs, and towels, had been provided by the deacons. One person would wash and dry the feet of the next person, they would exchange a kiss, and the washed one would proceed to the next neighbor. The last in the row would then go around and wash the feet of the first.

At Big Swatara, the feetwashing was followed by the passing of the kiss of peace, a practice not followed at Lincoln or Pottstown. The leading elder would begin, and the kiss would circulate among all the men. Hiram explained this to me.

"What about the women?" I asked.

"You will begin it with Irene (his wife)," Hiram explained. What! Me kiss a strange woman? Not so. When I went to Irene, she reached out her hand; we clasped hands, and she then started the kiss among the women. Thanks to Irene, I did not stumble over that first possible stumbling block. As a matter of record, however, let me note that I have often wondered if, when St. Paul advised Christians to greet with a kiss, it was strictly a unisex matter.

The next element was the fellowship meal, sometimes called the Agape meal. At Royersford, our meal had been rolls and cheese. At Pottstown they also added coffee. In Nigeria, people simply shared whatever the women brought, except for us shy foreigners who carried our own sandwiches. At Hanoverdale, the meal was traditional—rice soup and bread sops. We ate after a prayer seeking God's blessing and closed the meal with a prayer of thanksgiving. Strangely, to me, the meal was eaten in silence. It was strange partly because there is usually conversation at mealtime, and partly because at the first "last supper," which we were emulating, there was much talking.

The most spiritual aspect of Love Feast was the communion. The communion bread was in a strip about eight inches long, which was passed along and broken to one's neighbor. Again, the process began for the ladies when I handed a strip of bread to Irene. Then, the cup of grape juice represented the shed blood of Jesus. More traditionally, there were only two cups—one for the men, one for the ladies. A communicant would sip, then pass it on; the deacons would replenish as necessary. Big Swatara had already abandoned the common cup. Finally, we would sing a hymn and go out. I survived my first Love Feast.

Now it would be time for me to survive my first evangelistic meeting. Extended revivals, borrowed from more emotional sects and frowned on for a number of years by the Brethren, had become the practice of many congregations after the turn of the century and still continued in many. Only Fairview, of the congregations I had been associated with, had even short evangelistic meetings. Big Swatara did not have extended meetings, but annually, and sometimes semi-annually, special renewal services were held.

Our evangelist in the fall of 1953 was Perry Liskey, well known and loved both as a preacher and as a song leader. We kept him busy. Not only did he preach each evening and two Sunday mornings, but he also went visiting with me day after day. Of course, we ate out often. Perry liked gravy. A meal was really complete for him only if he could close with a piece of "gravy bread."

I well remember our visit on the day President Kennedy was assassinated. When we entered the home, the young mother said, "Have you heard the news?"

We hadn't.

"Someone in Dallas has shot the president. They don't think he will live." She paused for a moment, then added, "God bless the man who did it."

JFK was such a popular president, and she was so obviously grieving, that I could hardly believe what I had heard. Even in her emotional state, she realized I was puzzled.

"I had to say it that way," she said, "or I would keep cursing him. God doesn't want me to curse anyone."

I have mentioned that I wanted to make my sermons Biblical. I have also mentioned that evaluation of the pastor's work was sometimes direct. One precious lady made it clear to me that I must be accurate in quoting the scripture. Occasionally, as she passed me at the door after the service, she would comment, "I don't know if I agree with the way you interpreted the Bible today."

I would schedule time with her the next day. We would each present our understanding. Sometimes I would persuade her. Sometimes she would persuade me. Sometimes we would continue to disagree, but always in good spirit, and often with a laugh at the other's failure to see the "truth." Her openness was a valuable asset to me in my desire to be preaching true to the Bible. I had to be careful!

The schedule of services which had been followed with four ministers sharing the preaching responsibility included the service at Hanoverdale each Sunday, preceded in turn by a service at Fishing Creek Valley or at Paxton. Twice a month, there were also evening worship services. There was also a midweek prayer service. I determined to follow the same schedule, though I would be doing it all, myself. The Valley Church was across the mountain, about twelve miles away, and set in a beautiful area. As I preached there twice monthly and learned to know the people, I observed that only seven or eight persons really lived in the Valley; the rest were far closer to Hanoverdale. My impression was that they went to the Valley as a kind of mission project, but they were not making calls on residents there. Paxton, on the other hand, was about six miles away in a well-populated suburban area. Attenders were all local people except for one deacon couple who gave local leadership.

There was a fifth minister listed for the Big Swatara congregation, a young farmer who had been licensed, but I never seemed to be meeting him. I discovered that he had discontinued coming to worship several months earlier. I went to visit him. He was, at best, only tepid in his enthusiasm. He said that he really had trouble getting up in time on Sunday morning to get his farm work done and then get to church; he kept oversleeping. I asked him how early he would need to get up in order to get his chores done and get to church. He thought if he would get up at 5:00 a.m., he could easily make it.

I promised to call him each Sunday morning at five. He agreed. The next Sunday morning, I called. His wife answered; she said he just wasn't up to getting up, having stayed up late the preceding night. I called again the next two Sunday mornings, but got no answer. I never learned what his problem was, or if he, indeed, had a problem except for lack of commitment. His license was soon discontinued.

Within a few months, I had twice violated the principle of making no early changes. It seemed convenient to have the study in the house, but its openness to the rest of the home invited frequent interruptions from the family and made counseling difficult. I had observed one unused Sunday School room at Hanoverdale, and I proposed that it be made into a church office. Their pastor would be more efficient, I explained, if he would be in a place where he could more easily study and meditate with fewer interruptions. With minimum hesitation, they agreed.

I also believed that it was important to have a well-informed congregation, so I decided to issue a monthly newsletter. I gave it the name, *Outward*, both that it might be seen as an evangelistic possibility and that it might remind the readers of the importance of reaching out for Christ. It was gratefully received. It also gave me a chance to vent my yen for writing. Efficient secretary Alma Herr did the major job of its production.

Because we had been missionaries, there was a certain (undeserved) aura about us. The Brethren liked to hear stories of foreign mission work, and who was better equipped with such stories than recently returned workers? There were frequent opportunities for us to go out as a family, share our experiences, and tell our stories. I would not vouch for the accuracy of this impression, but it seemed to me there was less eagerness among the congregations of Eastern Pennsylvania District than elsewhere to hear the mission story.

As I remembered my two years of deputation earlier on, I noted that in 1954-55, when I had spoken 258 times, only six of them had been in Eastern Pennsylvania. One of those was Mechanic Grove, which supported Mary Beth; another was Springfield, where I had preached once in 1949. In the second furlough, visits away were sporadic. Many Eastern District congregations, I was aware, had provided missionary financial and prayer support. Perhaps the visit of their supported missionary filled their need.

There were a few opportunities within the district. I had, in the summer of 1963, spent a week as a counselor in Camp Swatara among junior highs. I also had a brief opportunity at a District Sunday School rally on Labor Day. When the leader for the day asked me to bring greetings, he observed that, aware that there were many speakers and short hours, each speaker was asked to limit his speech to three sentences. "Fine," I agreed. I pronounced one long, Pauline sentence (somewhat like many in this narrative), telling one aspect of our work. "That's one sentence," I asserted.

I repeated a second and a third time. By the time my "three sentences" were finished, I had succeeded in giving what I thought was the full, if abbreviated, story.

As I came to know more about the members of the congregation, I discovered in early 1964 that there seemed to be far more long-married couples than might be expected. Nine couples had been married for forty years or more; six couples had celebrated their golden wedding day; and three couples had been married for more than sixty years. I determined to have a marriage celebration service, both for the giving of thanks to God, and for the illustration of what marriage could be. We planned it for early May.

I contacted the local newspaper and told them our plans, suggesting that it might make a good feature article. The editor agreed. A week in advance of the scheduled service, a sensitive reporter and a skillful photographer met, after the worship service, with all the couples who were present and even went calling on some who could not be there. I remember in particular the interview with Grandma and Pop Teets. It was she who answered the questions about family. There were so many of them, and particularly great-grandchildren, that the reporter wondered.

"I may have got the count wrong," said Grandma, "but I do think there are forty-two of them."

That week, the entire back page of the newspaper was given over to telling about the special service at Hanoverdale, with brief stories of the couples and with pictures of most of them. The good feeling added to conversation for weeks to come.

Brethren organization at the time leaned heavily upon officials. Local churches were guided by "official boards" made up of the ministers and deacons. A district was largely under the control of the elders' body. When I had been interim pastor at Pottstown, for example, Bob Neff, later to be a seminary professor, the denomination's executive secretary, and president of Juniata College, came before the elders' body of Southeastern Pennsylvania for ordination.

I commented: "This man is good enough not only to be a minister, but to be a missionary." He was approved.

In Eastern Pennsylvania, I felt some distance. Perhaps it was because I did not "dress plain," although ministers who did were decreasing in number. (At Big Swatara, only one of the four did.) Slowly, I began to be invited for evangelistic meetings; in the spring of 1964, I was at Annville, which was served by self-supported ministers. Yet in seven years in the district, not once was I approached to let my name be on the ballot for a district position. Even though I was not seeking position, I was puzzled; in Nigeria I had leadership positions.

Having enjoyed six annual conferences as a family, we continued to attend each year. It was not only the deep inspiration of the messages and the music, but the feeling that we were a part of something big, plus the opportunity to be with old friends again. In 1964, conference was in Lincoln, and we were happy to be housed in the home of Bertha and Albert Eisele,

Soon after our return, we were happy to receive Lois and Gerry Neher as visitors. They were to speak at the Fredericksburg Church of the Brethren who had supported them. I was unable to go with them, but Mary Beth went, and Larry accompanied her so she wouldn't have to drive home in the dark. Nancy Meyer, daughter of the moderator at Fredericksburg, and Larry were the only youth there. They spent the evening each teasing the other about his/her sad choice of college—Juniata or Elizabethtown. Later in the summer, they met again at Camp Swatara; then, as they returned to college, they opened a correspondence. By the time Nancy visited at Juniata's Homecoming, their friendship was close enough that it would keep on—and on—and on.

By the fall of 1964, three of our family were called by district organizations. Mary Beth was added to the Women's Fellowship cabinet and immediately elected vice president for a three-year term. Later she would be president, also for a three-year term. Dale was added to the Youth Fellowship cabinet and immediately was elected vice president. Later he would be president for a term. I was appointed to the Music and Worship Committee, on which I served for six years. I was also appointed pastoral advisor to the Young Adult Cabinet, with whom I thoroughly enjoyed six years of service.

We knew that Larry was a good public speaker, but Dale had been hiding his light under a bushel. Each year, as the holiday season approached, the Harrisburg Christmas Celebration Committee of the Downtown Harrisburg Association sponsored the Christmas speech contest for high schools. More than twenty different high schools of the Harrisburg area participated in the contest. Central Dauphin East entries had won in 1962 and 1963. A third victory would retire the cup at the school. Dale Bieber was the school's entry in 1964. He did marvelously well, won the contest, won the cup for his school, earned prizes including $100.00 in scholarship money which was sent to Elizabethtown College on his behalf, and gave his parents brag material for months to come!

I do not know quite when the story of Barbara began, but it is one I must share. For me, it began one Sunday after a carry-in meal at the church when I was in a brief meeting. The church treasurer interrupted the meeting for a moment to hand me a note.

"It's from Barbara," he told me. "Don't worry about it. She is a bit different. You may not have seen her before. We had a carry-in luncheon today, and that is the only time she comes to church."

I read the penciled note: "I don't know why the preacher picks on me. I'm as good as these other people."

As I left the building a few moments later, Loretta, a deacon's wife, stopped me. "Did you get a note from Barbara?"

"Yes, I did," I confessed. "I don't quite know what to make of it."

"I read her note," the good sister said. "I told her you weren't preaching to her; you were preaching to me."

Yet I realized something had touched Barbara, so I went to see her a day or so later. Barbara lived in a very old, two-story, five-room house. There was a ramshackle back porch, but I chose the front entrance. She opened the door, and I came into a dusty, sloppy living room with very little furniture. There was a strong aroma of cats; she had two, which never went out of the house. She offered me the only cushioned chair in the room, but before I sat down, she said, "Let me turn the cushion over; there will be cat hairs on it."

Whenever I went to visit her, from then on, she would always turn that cushion over! She was a tall, very slender lady in worn garments, with a wrinkled and dirty face and soiled spots on her bare arms. She did not exude the aroma either of soap or of talcum. Her age was estimated at anywhere from sixty to ninety-five.

She recognized me as the pastor, but did not remember my name. I began our conversation—actually, after a moment or two it turned into a monologue—by saying that I had received her note and it was important to me.

"I want you to know," I assured her, "that I did not mean my message to be for you, but maybe God did."

She thought for a moment, then she launched: "People have picked on me for many years. They make fun of me; the children throw stones at me; they won't take me to the store to buy groceries; one neighbor always threw trash in my yard until I screamed at her."

Those are only samples of a very long list of ways which Barbara described of how people had been unkind and even cruel to her. She had been a member of the Big Swatara Church in her youth, but then she and her sister had done something out of line. She could not remember what it was—wear a hat? ride in a fringed buggy? Whatever. They were summoned before the church officials.

Barbara said, "I didn't think I had done anything wrong and I didn't go. They chased me out and said I couldn't be a member any more."

I could not distinguish between anger and anguish as she concluded. I do not believe anyone had sat down and listened to her before.

We sat silent for a few moments. Then I said, "Barbara, I can see that you have some very unhappy memories. But, you know, those things are all in the past. You can leave them there. What is important now is that God touched your heart on Sunday. What is important is having the right relationship with Jesus today."

Tears began to wash down through the dirt on her face. "I really want to be right with God," she said. "What can I do?"

"First of all," I said, "Let's pray together." We held hands and prayed. We thanked God for never having stopped loving her and for having now touched her heart.

Then I said, "At the end of church Sunday, I will ask anyone who wants to get right with Jesus to come forward. Can you do that?" Eagerly, she said she could. I was ready to receive her as she was, old clothes, dirty face, disheveled hair; what mattered, after all, was her heart.

I shared the good news with Loretta, asking her to keep Barbara's decision confidential. I had not realized what a good sister Loretta was. She went to Barbara's house, found some clean—although not fancy—clothes. She took Barbara home, got her into the tub of warm water with wash cloth and soap. She took the old clothes and washed them. She washed her hair. She combed it and arranged it. Without mentioning that she knew of Barbara's decision, she picked her up and took her with her to church that Sunday. Barbara came forward and recommitted her life to Jesus, before an almost stunned congregation. More than half a century of separation came to an end.

Members of the congregation made special efforts to show kindness to Barbara: bring her to church, take her places, help her with laundry, and the like. I made regular visits. I learned that she did not have a bathroom. Her toilet was on the back porch. There was one spigot in the kitchen, no water heater. She cooked on a small electric plate, and she had a small refrigerator. When she knew she was going somewhere, she would make a special effort to be clean, but day unto day uttered dirt, and her house was simply not clean. She would often offer me some tidbit to eat, but I managed not to be hungry unless there was a freshly opened box. I remember accepting milk from her in an obviously dirty glass, and drinking without comment except a thank you. She also gave me antique dishes, a stool, a kerosene lamp. When I remonstrated, she explained, "If I give you something, you will keep coming!"

Barbara's age continued to be an interesting mystery. Often we would wonder just how old she was. Leighton Ford, one of the Billy Graham evangelists, had a campaign in Harrisburg. On one of the several evenings when she was with us, the worship leader announced that he was going to find out who was the oldest person there. "If you are over seventy," he called out, "Please stand up." Looking around, she saw people standing all around. She jumped up.

If you are over seventy-five, stay standing. The rest of you, sit down." He continued that pattern until he reached eighty-five, then went on a year at a time. Barbara stood until he told the eighty-seven-year-olds to be seated. Now we knew her age, and now she discovered there is something special about getting older. It seemed to me that, from then on, whenever she climbed into the car to go somewhere, she would comment, "Pretty good for eighty-seven years, not?"

The most important moment in Barbara's story, of course, was the moment she decided for Jesus. A kind of culminating time, however, came several years later. Jeanette Rodriguez Arce, a Costa Rica exchange student who lived with us, found Barbara to be a different kind of person. She had a number of questions about her. The more she heard, the more she wanted to meet her personally. Could she go calling? I wasn't sure how Barbara might react to a young Costa Rican girl, but we decided to make the effort. We went in, we were welcomed, and we conversed, although Barbara did have some problem with Jeanette's accent.

When we were on our way home, Jeanette, whose home in Costa Rica was simple but very clean, remarked on how dirty the home was we just visited. I had my doubts that Barbara would, or even could, clean it.

Jeanette said, "Why don't we get the youth to go in and clean it for her?" Again, I wasn't sure that a cleaning crew of youths would be welcome.

First, Jeanette talked with the youth; it sounded like a different, but fun-to-do-together kind of project. Then I talked with Barbara. The youth knew that she was up in years, and they were looking for a way to help her. Would she mind if they would come in and clean her house? They would be welcome.

Six or eight young people, led by Marla and Jeanette and with two adult advisors, invaded the old house. They carried with them brooms, soap, detergent, mops, rags, and furniture polish. One room, for whatever reason, was not to be entered; otherwise the kids had free rein. When several of them were on the floor in the living room, it did not seem very stable. The youth called in one of the handymen of the church. He inspected, and it was decided to lay a new, heavy plywood floor over the old floor. Barbara never got over the kind and gentle caring which people showed her. I do not believe she knew what a blessing she was to the congregation.

Once again, in 1965, we went to Annual Conference. It was at Ocean Grove and brought back memories of the conference in 1949 when we had been consecrated.

We made special efforts to increase attendance at both Valley and Paxton. We spent a lot of time visiting in the Valley. The local folks never turned us away, but either they said they worshipped regularly elsewhere, or they just didn't want to hear our message. The nearest we came to a convert, I believe, was an old man with a full white beard.

After we talked with him for a while and seemingly he listened, he remarked, "Well, I'll tell you. I just can't come to church. I'm afraid if I did the building would fall down."

I advised him to come anyway, just let me know when so I could get out of the way. He did not come. When the official board reviewed the situation, they agreed that seven or eight persons were hardly enough to keep a church going. In 1966, services at Valley were discontinued. As it turned out, the building may, indeed, have fallen down if the old man had come; we discovered it to be badly infested with termites.

Paxton was different. The usual pattern at Paxton was for the local people to come until their children were old enough to come themselves, then stop. As the children grew older, they would follow parental example and quit. We visited. People would say words about what a nice little church it was. Most of the members and attenders were from the local community. Only Earl and Naomi Kuntz, loyal deacons, worked with the church for many years.

One effort we made was to hold outdoor vesper services. The space was limited, and some of the seats were simply logs. At one vespers, a heavy thunderstorm quickly swept into the area. We fled indoors. I was doing a series on mountain tops in the Bible, and that evening it was to be Mt. Sinai and the thundering voice of God. Electricity went out. I think we had some sense of the awe and fear which the Israelites felt as we went on with our service. God chose a good evening for his thunderstorm.

When fall 1965 came, we had two sons in college. Larry was a junior at Juniata. He continued to do well in his courses. From early childhood, he wanted to be a doctor, so he was taking pre-med courses. He also played tennis for four years, in the number one singles position. In his senior year he was captain. Juniata had its best tennis year ever. At the same time, the football coach had seen Larry kicking off, soccer style, for a touch football game. Larry had never played football, but he responded to the coach's invitation and became Juniata's first soccer-style kicker. He often thrilled the crowd by kicking off over the goal posts, and his toe was always a field goal threat.

Dale was a freshman at Elizabethtown. Less certain than Larry about his choice of career, he still did well in his studies. Elizabethtown did not have a football team, but his first sports love was soccer. He played first team for four years and was captain as a senior. The team made play-offs several times, but did not quite reach national championship level. We saw the conference final game, which Elizabethtown won; Dale and Ron Good, another "missionary kid," were named MVP. In the spring, Dale also went out for tennis and played second on the Elizabethtown team.

Chapter Twenty-Seven

BEYOND THE LOCAL

A surprise came to me in the spring of 1966. Earl Hostetter, who had been pastor at Everett when I visited there, was on the nominating committee of Standing Committee. He called one evening and asked if I would be willing to let my name go on the ballet for General Brotherhood Board. I had been in nominating committee position sometimes when it was hard to get candidates. Sympathetic to Earl's problem, I agreed to "run," ONLY in order to help fill out the ballot. To my great surprise, I was elected to a five-year term.

Annual Conference that summer was in Louisville, Kentucky, and for the first time in history a lay person was moderator. It was Dan West, whose experience in war relief in Spain had led him to develop the Heifer Project. Rather than simply sending milk to hungry families, a fresh heifer was presented and the milk would be forthcoming. The major topic for discussion was whether the Brethren should join the Consultation on Church Union, which if it reached its ultimate intention would unite a number of congregations, abandoning their separate existence. Emotions were high. The compromise decision to send only observers to the consultation did not satisfy, and the Brethren lost a significant number of leaders. West, a peacemaker, was unable to exert the kind of forceful leadership that conference required. Still, I have known peacemakers who were forceful leaders as well.

When October came, I attended my first board meeting. Norman Baugher, executive secretary, met with me. He commented that Henry Long was now Foreign Missions Commission executive. Apparently Norman was aware of my earlier tensions with the commission. He asked if I would be willing to serve on the Parish Ministry Commission. I agreed, though I felt that my foreign mission studies and experience might have been better used. As a board member, I was almost completely useless. I simply could not muster up the courage to speak up in that assemblage of wise men and women. On commission, with six members, I could hold my own, though my experience as a pastor was certainly limited.

Brethren practice through the years required that members be received only by trine immersion or by transfer from another Church of the Brethren. We were also quite exclusive. In some congregations, participation in the Love Feast was limited not only to members of the Church of the Brethren, but even to membership in that particular congregation. Annual Conference in 1964 had passed a ruling that allowed the receiving of Christians from other denominations, even though they had not been "properly" baptized. Congregations could exercise their own judgment on whether or not to receive the ruling.

After a year or two, I proposed to the official board at Big Swatara that we adopt the new ruling and receive members by transfer from any Christian denomination. I believed there were persons in our neighborhood who would join us if they were not required to undergo a second baptism. I reminded the board that Brethren would not be the only inhabitants of heaven, so baptism was certainly not the only key. The board refused, and a few board members were actually offended.

One of the sad days of my ministry at Big Swatara came when a delightful young family—the father was a deacon—decided to leave. When I visited with them, they assured me repeatedly that it had nothing to do with me; they appreciated my sermons and my Bible study. I seemed to sense a break with some other members of the congregation, although they never said so, and I was unable to dissuade them from leaving. Another sad day was the death of Sam Wagner, a deacon who had been very supportive. It had been his sly practice to knock on our back door, shout, "Baker!" and disappear, leaving behind a roast, a bag of apples, a freezer of ice cream, and a lot of good feeling.

One of the expectations of my contract with Big Swatara was that I would spend a week each summer as a volunteer at Camp Swatara. For two summers, I suffered—that is the right word—with junior campers. For the third year, I asked and was granted the opportunity to counsel on mountainside. We slept on cots in tents. We did all our own cooking. Our hikes were longer and more strenuous. We learned, afresh, how much we could rely on each other and how much we needed that reliance. For my last four years on the mountainside, I was director of junior highs. I slept alone on the porch of the cabin-store-room where we could gather in case of rain. I loved it. Thirty years later, men and women have come to me and remembered those days on the mountainside.

In 1967, Annual Conference was scheduled for Eugene, Oregon. We recognized an opportunity for a camping vacation west. We planned to drive a northern route, visit in California, and return across the southern states. We would be tenting, so Dale and I practiced setting up the tent. Mary Beth, meanwhile, aware of our planned route, was also aware of friends we could visit along the way. Thanks to the hospitality of friends, we would not begin tenting until Laramie, Wyoming. When we arrrived there, we were in a heavy rainfall. We found a motel. The next night, we were in Yellowstone, with its ample campgrounds. Alas, it was far colder than we expected in early June. We discovered that the park had some cabins with ample bed space at a low price. We slept inside. Of course, we did have to go out to the rest rooms, and there was a bear working over the trash can, but it was a good night.

At last, our first night of camping came. It was on the volcanic, stick-to-the-soles soil of Craters of the Moon National Monument in Montana. We set up tent. Mary Beth was preparing supper as we all went for a walk. We arrived back. Just as Mary Beth announced that supper was ready, the clouds burst open and the rain poured down. We hastily, and dirtily, moved into the tent. The night was all right after that, but somehow it was a bit spoiled. We traveled on without incident to Eugene, enjoying along the way the most beautiful falls we had ever seen, just east of Bend, Oregon.

A study of our maps had shown us a small town in northern California named, "Bieber." After we drove through Lasser Volcanic National Park with snow piled up alongside the road higher than our car, we arrived at Bieber. All of us wrote cards or letters in anticipation. Driving into town, we passed a large water tank, a College Avenue, and a jail with the grass three feet high in front of it. We found the post office.

"We want everyone to know we were in Bieber. Would you mind handstamping our mail?"

"Friends, all the mail here is handstamped."

"Do you know how this town got its name?"

"Maybe if you go to the town hall over in Clara Bieber Memorial Park, they could tell you."

We found the small park and the town hall. Just inside the front door there was a sign, "Library." I have always known librarians to be well informed, so I asked the librarian the origin of the name.

"Why don't you ask Judge Bieber. He is just down the hall." We found the office, accepted his invitation, and trooped in. Judge Aubrey Bieber was the son of the founder of the town. I think it was in 1883 that he arrived there. Clara had been Aubrey's mother. We could find no connection with our branch; their branch had not come to the States until about 1850, ours in 1731. We went on our way. Three miles down the road there was another small town, Nubieber. What! These Biebers had a big disagreement and left? Surely not! But???

Continuing on our way, we visited Yosemite, loving its waterfalls and surprised by the road which went through a tree trunk. We crossed the desert without air conditioning, hanging out wet towels to provide our own cooling system. We were awed by the Grand Canyon, moved by the rich Indian heritage manifested at Mesa Verde and Canyon du Chelly, impressed by the wide fields of Kansas, and glad to get home.

Larry did not accompany us on the trip because 1967 was a busy summer for him. He was earning money, planning marriage with Nancy on August 19, and making preparations to enter Hershey Medical School (Penn State University) in the fall in their first class. In June, we purchased a small house on Duke Street in Hummelstown, which was less expensive housing for them. As Larry entered medical school, Nancy continued her teaching of English at Lower Dauphin High School.

Then came the big day. We were delighted to welcome that new member to our family and to share Larry with the Meyers. Nancy's father, Ammon, and I were pleased to perform the ceremony in the Meyer House of the Fredericksburg Church.

When fall came that year, my work on the General Board changed. Henry Long had talked with Norman Baugher about our relationship. He believed my experience would be of help on his commission. He was sure, as was I, that we would have no personal difficulties. We were right. I was transferred to the Foreign Mission Commission, where I was to serve for seven years, four of them as chairperson.

Chapter Twenty-Eight

THE BIAFRA EXPERIENCE

In Nigeria, a civil war had broken out. In the March 1968 meeting of the commission, we heard reports of the war. It was being fought mostly in the southern parts of Nigeria and did not affect our mission or church directly. The Missouri Synod Lutheran Church, which had mission work in the area directly involved in the war, was sending a medical relief team under the leadership of Dr. Wolf Bulle. The MS Lutherans are far more strict than we, and far less pietistic. They were appealing to other churches to assist with medical staff. Reports carefully prepared and widely distributed by Biafran leadership implied that Nigeria was at war to annihilate the Ibo tribe—reports I found hard to believe. As I sat in commission and heard the reports, I knew immediately that I had to respond to the appeal. I loved the people of Nigeria and had medical experience there. I volunteered to go.

The Big Swatara congregation readily granted me a leave of absence for the months of July, August, and September 1968. At my request, it was without pay. The congregation called William Longenecker to serve them during the interim. I also asked no pay from the General Board, except that they finance a brief trip to the Brethren mission area at the close of my medical assignment. They agreed. I would still carry on some of my work through Mary Beth and through copious correspondence.

On July 3, I flew from Kennedy Airport by Swissair to Geneva. I had probably heard, but forgotten, that all the relief teams were being coordinated by International Committee of the Red Cross and working under their umbrella. I was met in Geneva by their representative. For the next week plus, I was being provided with necessary papers and documents, being oriented to relief work in war areas, and being exposed to a great deal of information about the Red Cross. I heard Wolf Bulle's name and it was clear that I was on his team, but planned relief work was just beginning, was needed in so many different areas, and was still being developed. Meanwhile, I was doing very little of consequence; I kept hearing different reports of where I would be located, and I was impatient to get to work.

I drove one of the land rovers to Enugu, still uncertain where I would be assigned. At Enugu the team had rather comfortable quarters, the home of an Ibo obstetrician who had left. A euphemistic term was used about homes, equipment, furniture, even autos that had been left behind and which we now used; we were "liberating" them. Because we took good care of the items, we also said we were "storing" them until the owners' return. Enugu had been the capital of the Eastern Region, a city of over 300,000. Now there were about 2,000 there, many of them police or army.

Marion Bricker, a Brethren 1-W, had been spending his vacation there, doing maintenance kinds of things. Tom Dauterbahn, a Lutheran, ousted for the time being from his missionary residence a hundred miles or so away, was called the administrator of the team.

Therein lay a problem. Both Tom and Marion were leaving. I was assigned to Enugu, and Bulle kept calling me the administrator. It took me a while to realize that was just a glorified term for custodian. My skills did not lie in maintenance, though I did work at ordering supplies and having them available. It took a while for me to make it clear that my skills were medical rather than custodial. Bulle traveled quite a bit, which meant he was not always with us; he was trying to set up teams elsewhere and doing a good job. Still, there was always some tension between us, so I was not unhappy for his absences.

It seemed strange to be doing normal things in a wartime, but they were necessary as well—normal things like registering our presence and getting residential permits at the state capitol, Makurdi. To reach there, we went through the town of Oturkpo. Roy and Doris Frysinger, members of the Big Swatara congregation, were doing a teachers abroad stint there; it was certainly the most distant pastoral call I ever made!

Still, aware of the tensions with which we were surrounded, we watched for little things which would ease our own tension. We were well aware of the tremendous medical needs and were still not quite sure how we would work at them. One tension-easer came when one of the men spied a huge scorpion about six inches long. A small toad came over to check it out, decided it was too big a mouthful, and scurried away—did you ever see a toad scurry? Our houseboy killed the scorpion with a stick, saying, "You naughty boy, I beat you because you not come to school on time."

Another tension-easer was Glen Haydon, from Iowa, an ICRC staffer who was assigned to our team in late July. Perhaps because he had been in war zones on other assignments or perhaps it was just his sense of humor, at the sound of gunfire, he instantly slid down in his armchair and became a smaller target. Gunfire was almost always target practice by the Nigerian army; there were no longer any free Biafran soldiers in the area.

There was, in Enugu, a kind of internment camp. It was the Dayspring Hotel, fairly comfortable but very crowded, and always with sick or injured men. We visited there once a week, encouraged by the Nigerian army to care for these who were, technically, their enemies. I made it a personal project and occasionally made an extra visit. The men were not in fatal condition, but could become so without help.

All the time I was in Enugu, I kept seeing signs that this was not a war to annihilate the Ibo tribe; it was, instead, a war to protect the oil resources which were in Ibo territory. In one village I saw a lassie of about five with a bandage on her head and on her arm. Her story: She had been riding on her father's shoulders when a Nigerian bullet hit him in the head, first striking the little girl's upper arm and skinning her head. The father fell down dead. Bleeding, the little girl just kept on walking until a Nigerian soldier saw her and picked her up. The whole platoon adopted her.

Let me try to describe our medical efforts. We were a team of six. There was a doctor, usually on short-term loan from some mission or from stateside. There were three American nurses, Olive and Dorlie, both experienced Lutheran missionaries and both very skillful, and me, somewhat rusty; and one Swedish nurse whose name I have forgotten. There were also two young Ibo women who had Nigeria nurse training. Six days a week we started out, usually in two vehicles, with whatever supplies we were able to muster and visited villages as far as a hundred miles away. The villages were notified in advance that we were coming, and there was always a crowd. The most common conditions were related to malnutrition, but there were also injuries, infections, and such dread diseases as typhoid or cholera. With children, it was kwashiorkor. Apart from us, there was simply no medical care.

A typical day went like this: we arrived, set up tables—usually in an abandoned schoolroom or schoolyard. The crowd gathered, sometimes as many as 5,000 people milling about. With two or three of us making snap diagnoses, referring the more difficult ones to the doctor, we could treat any number from three hundred and up. The most, according to one of my letters home, was seven hundred and thirty-six, an unbelievable number for six people to have treated. Knowing that when we returned next week, many whom we did not treat would have died, we still left as darkness approached. Back at Enugu, we unpacked and stored supplies, remembering that tomorrow was still coming. We cleaned up. We ate. Meals were tasty and substantial, but being surrounded by starving people does not induce good appetite. Weary as we were, we often had guests, missionaries, or other expatriates who found their way to visit us, army officials, police, a few locals, and Father Coleman, Irish, the resident Roman priest. We enjoyed the company, but their presence and the frequent parties to which army officials invited us, drastically reduced our rest time.

From time to time, I saw men from the Church of the Brethren Mission area. Most memorable were two men at the army motor depot, where I took a car over for some tire work. I could hear their talk. "Looks like him." "Yes, but it's a different man."

I heard their Margi, and shouted, "*Jangu, niyu!*" (I'm the one.)

They grinned, and we exchanged chatter for a few moments. It felt good to unlimber my five years of rusty Margi again. I also would recognize names on military i.d. badges as being Margi, Higi, or Bura, and would speak to them, locating several. It was fun, too, using my meager Hausa with the soldiers, most of whom were from the north and did not expect a man in the south to talk their language.

The best incident of that kind occurred at Nkalaga. A number of patients came with cards indicating that an army medical man had tried to treat them. One was especially interesting. The card said, "This man come to me because he is no able to use his wife proper. And I have no testosterone. Can you help him?" It was signed by Cpl. Mari Tarfa, whose name I immediately recognized. A practical nurse by that name had refused to work for CBM when another student was chosen over him to go to Vom for training. I remembered his brother, Ali, who worked in Garkida Hospital for many years. Mari had joined the army, received two years of medical training, and was now serving. Now, in addition to his duties to the army, he was operating a clinic for (enemy) civilians at his own expense. When I told him I expected to visit Garkida, he asked me to explain to his wife that he could not send money home because his clinic used it all.

While I was talking with Mari, a Bura from Biu, and a Margi from Lassa, a Fulani man came up. I greeted them all. I did not know Fulani, but I had learned from our Lassa gardener the elaborate greetings and used them. His face lit up like neon. He walked back and forth talking to himself and laughing. Then he thanked me in Hausa for "knowing" his language, and promised to bring me a Bornu knife next time. Alas, that was my last visit to that village.

Although we were the first medical relief team in the area, others were gradually coming and being assigned by the Red Cross. One located in the general area was a Swiss team of five men. Two of the men, a nurse/medical student and a young Catholic priest, had been killed when a Biafra land mine exploded under them. Both their team leader and the army liaison officer reported that the men had been instructed not to use that road, but they only had one-fourth of a mile farther, so they had gone on. The explosion left a large hole in the road and well-scattered debris. It was a miracle that two bodies could even be recovered. One, the medic, was so badly charred that his later identification would read, "nursing sister."

The bodies were taken to the army morgue, where there were coffins. The funeral was planned for the very next morning. Cemeteries were riddled by battle marks, so it was decided to bury on the grounds of the cathedral. Father Coleman promised to place a plaque for identification. The army provided grave-diggers. As the time for the service in the cathedral neared, we observed that the graves seemed small. I went to the morgue and, stepping carefully in the odorous seepage, I measured the bodies. The graves were, indeed, too small. Father Coleman proceeded with the service to the noise of pick and shovel enlarging the graves.

When we came out, the bodies had not yet arrived. We waited. Police and military personnel waited to form their honor guard. We waited. A police officer left in his car to investigate the delay, returning to tell us, "They are coming."

We waited. An army officer left in his car to expedite proceedings. At last, a large army ambulance drove up with both bodies in coffins in the rear. Ten or twelve men, all wearing rubber gloves and cotton masks and carrying huge wads of cotton and bottles of disinfectant, hung on around the front of the vehicle. They alighted and stood silent. Their corporal screamed at them and, I am certain, cursed them roundly.

They finally moved the coffins to the graves, setting them on pipes suspended by rope. As they were lowed, by rope, into the grave, Father Coleman brought the funeral to its close. I have never been sure whether the whole procedure reminded me more of Grand Central Station or of an old Keystone Kops film; the latter gets the edge.

I dislike shaving and actually enjoy having a beard. Since Mary Beth does not share my attitude, however, I have usually kept beards for a relatively short time. During my Biafra experience, I decided not to shave. One unanticipated result was that, with their usual respect for age, Nigerian officers would often turn to me first, rather than to Dr. Bulle, with their business. Whether it was that or his Austrian army experience, Bulle did not like my beard. He approached me with it (not with the beard, dummy, but with his dislike of it).

"Mr. Bieber, you are going to have to shave off your beard."

"I have no intention of shaving off my beard."

"I am afraid I must insist.

"Wolf, I will take your advice on medical and team business, but the beard is a personal matter and entirely my own affair."

"Then I may have to recommend that your church recall you."

Exerting patience beyond my usual, but as adamant as ever, I observed, "Wolf, first off, you have no real reason for making such a recommendation. You are fully aware that my work has been adequate. For another thing, for you to ask that I be recalled would jeopardize your relationship with our church." I kept my beard.

Occasionally we had official visitors—from ICRC, from local or state authorities, and others. We also had other visitors. One day two British missionaries from the north came in with three Nigerians. Let me quote what I wrote home about the coming of David Wilmshurst, the executive of Sudan United Mission British Branch, who had been on the Hillcrest Board of Governors when I was chair:

It was a surprise to see David Wilmshurst; he looks older and grayer. He and Moyer came walking in with Olive. I said, "I know you. I'm Charles Bieber."

He peered at me more closely and said, "Why, so you are."

It seems that he had written to the governor of Plateau State, in Jos, showing some strong Biafran leanings and asking questions. So his nibs requested Wilmshurst and Moyer to be his special fact-finding team. They are out for two weeks, are touring in different areas looking and asking questions. I think a number of the things we told them really impressed them—the numbers of people we treat, the numbers being fed, the many still unreached in Biafra, the genuine concern of the army in this area for the local people, the hundreds of gallons of petrol the army gives us, etc. I think Wilmshurst went away nearly satisfied that this was indeed an economic war rather than a genocide of the Ibo people.

As the number of relief teams grew and the amount of food and medical supplies became more adequate, ICRC recognized the need for a central distribution center. (I cannot resist reporting this data: Choice of food to contribute was sometimes idiotic. On one occasion, a plane delivered thirteen tons of tinned vanilla, strawberry, and chocolate pudding to Enugu. Of course, we did receive tons of usable food, as well.) It was also expected that, any day, the Nigerian army would start a big push, which would drastically increase the number of refugees. ICRC reassigned me to Lagos to set up that distribution depot.

During my work at Enugu and its surrounding villages, I had set up a kind of protective psychological wall around my emotions. Otherwise, there was simply no way that I could have endured the tremendous suffering I was seeing and our ability to meet only a small part of it. As I drove out of Enugu, alone, on my way to Lagos, the wall broke down. Tears gushed from my eyes so I could not see to drive. I stopped at the top of a low hill and wept. I thanked God for letting me help, even infinitesimally. I prayed for greater response to the desperate need. I prayed for peace of mind. Gradually, God gave it to me, in spite of the painful pictures which persisted in my memory, and I went on to Lagos.

I had been in Lagos several times. It was a crowded, dirty city, but there was a huge task to be done and I felt honored to have been entrusted its supervision. Our work was to center in a warehouse provided by the Christian Council of Nigeria (CCN). To my surprise, I was to stay in a very comfortable hotel. As direct ICRC staff, I was also to receive "per diem," a substantial daily allowance for food, lodging, and necessities. It was ample enough to pay for my later trip to CBM, relieving the Foreign Mission Commission of that expense. There were three or four others regularly assigned to work with me and a flow of temporary workers—pharmacists on leave, nurses awaiting transportation to their relief teams, and the like.

Supplies came from many, many different places, in amounts which would have seemed enormous had I forgotten the crowds in the village dispensaries. Medical supplies were identified in various languages, depending on the country which sent them. I remembered having unpacked, at Enugu a huge box from Russia and identifying bandages and several kinds of medicines. We were able to organize the drugs and the supplies into their probable uses. As the depot began to show some order, we planned to send to the relief teams weekly lists of what was available.

One day, in particular, is memorable. A new group was at work. One man came up to me and identified himself as an American (we had

German, Swedish, Swiss, and English). I asked, "Is there anyone here from Pennsylvania?" He thought there was one girl.

I shouted, "Hello there, Pennsylvania girl. Which one are you?" She came up and introduced herself as Barbara Souder, from Spring City.

"Oh, I know you! I know your father, Norman, too!" I did, indeed know Norman, but only by name. He was one of many Mennonites I had met when Mary Beth and I had occasionally attended Vincent Mennonite services. Barbara was a nurse and soon left on assignment.

When, eventually, my stint with ICRC came to an end, I made reservations for my Pan-Am flight to America two weeks later and took off for CBM. Those two weeks were extremely busy, filled with nostalgia, with renewal of friendships, with reporting on my experiences and impressions, with meetings in which I urged response to the relief needs, and with the answering of questions. I will not attempt to name missionary colleagues except to mention Roger Ingold's seeing that I got around. But it was very special to be with Nigerian brothers again—Karagama, who immediately commandeered a portion of my letter home so he could write to Mary Beth; Jabani, then principal of Waka Secondary School; Martha; one-time houseboy Mjigimtu, a student in teacher training; Ngamariju, and Rachel.

Everywhere I went, I was warmly welcomed, partly, I like to think on my own right, but more because of the intense curiosity people had about the war and its effects. As often as four or five times a day I met with teachers, students, church groups, or missionaries to tell my story and to answer their questions. I suggested that the entire Waka student body be dispatched to the south to do relief work—an impractical suggestion but one which did show the extent of the need. I urged the Executive Committee to request of the commission in America that some staff be seconded to the ICRC. Several did go on short assignments.

My visitation time came to an end and my flight schedules loomed. An S.I.M. plane from Biu to Jos was late, having responded to an emergency which delayed them. I was desperately afraid we would miss the Jos-to-Lagos flight, and I was relieved to discover I was in time because the Jos plane was late. That brought another concern: would I reach Lagos in time? Pan-Am flights to America were only twice weekly.

I sent a note to the pilot as we flew toward Lagos: "I am booked on the Pan-Am flight to the United States. Would you please request them to wait for me?"

A few moments later his reply came: "You should have no problem; that flight is being delayed."

I had kept my one heavy suitcase with me. As we landed, I disregarded the instructions to remain seated until . . . and moved to the front. I disembarked. I was not sure, but I thought that, almost immediately, I heard a call for boarding by Pan-Am. Disregarding immigration authorities, customs, and army who were body searching all passengers, I kept flashing my Red Cross Identification, shouting "Red Cross!" and escaped. I reached the gate just as the attendant was closing it and, breathless and exhausted, found my seat.

Via Idylwild (later Kennedy), shuttle, and La Guardia, I reached Harrisburg airport at Middletown. Twenty-five pounds lighter than when I had left, one full beard heavier, and wearing a raincoat and a Nigerian hat, I alighted. No one came forward to meet me. Hadn't the information of my arrival reached them? I spied Mary Beth and the children across the waiting room. They hadn't recognized me! The joy of our reunion was delayed for a few moments, but not diminished. Had it been only three months?

They were, without question, the three most useful months of my life. Not only had I changed, so had the whole family. Larry was in medical school. Dale was in college. Bonnie had just entered Juniata. Having a perfect math score in her PSAT, she was a National Merit Scholar and a National Honor Society scholar. Marla was in Central Dauphin East High. Doreen was a big sixth grader.

Chapter Twenty-Nine

BACK AT BIG SWATARA

I arrived on Friday, with baptism, worship, and Love Feast coming on Sunday. I preached on Sunday morning, still bearded; after all, I had to display it. However, yielding to my good wife's pressure, I shaved that afternoon. Bare-faced, I led in our Love Feast. Many a comment came to me: "You really got younger in the past few hours."

Among the effects of Biafra on my faith journey were these: I could never give thanks for a meal without adding a prayer that God would show me how to help others. And, at the first official board meeting, I announced to the board that I had developed a new impatience with nonessentials.

"I want us to concentrate on that which is important," I told them. "That is so true that if I notice the board wasting their time on something not essential—the color of the drapes, the right song to sing, the dress requirements to adhere to, I will almost certainly get up and leave." It was firm, but unloving, which was called to my attention a day or so later by one of the younger board members.

I entered into a tremendously busy year. The work of a pastor was itself a full-time job. In addition, however, I had a series of revival meetings at Midway; I participated in three meetings of the General Board; I was interviewed by Lancaster radio about the Biafra situation; I wrote letters to congressmen urging that Biafra not be recognized as a country; and I told the Biafra story approximately fifty times.

The most memorable of those times came when Dad, proud of his boy, arranged for me to speak at a men's meeting at our old home church, East Third Street Methodist in Williamsport. We went there on a wintry evening; I met Dad at Camp Hill and he drove. The evening went well and both Dad and I enjoyed being with the men again. Now let it be known that by that stage of his life, Dad had very shaky hands. When he was emotional for any reason, they were worse. That evening, he was emotional. He was so happy to be with his old friends; he was so proud of his son; and then it began to snow hard and we had a snowy trip of more than a hundred miles to anticipate. Dad was shaky! The men served oyster soup. Dad kept putting his spoon into his bowl and taking it out, shaking so much there was only that which stuck to the spoon. Eventually he used a cup. Being Dad, he just laughed it off.

We did find time to take the whole family to a figure skating exhibition at Hershey arena, the whole "family" including Dale's latest girl friend, one Judy Brown. During a comical sequence in the exhibition, the streamer shot from a toy gun caught Judy's glasses and took them to the ice. For the rest of the show, our group was fairly central as they kept checking on Judy's welfare.

Sam Wagner, Bud (Earl, Jr.) Light, and I decided to attend the Citizenship Seminar in Washington one year. To save money we arranged to stay with my Aunt Mary, whose home was there, and with cousin Bill Pettis and family next door. After the events of the first day, which had included a small banquet, we arrived at Aunt Mary's home late in the evening. On the way, I told the men, "Aunt Mary will want to give us some supper. Is it all right with you if I say, 'No, thanks, Aunt Mary, we did eat awhile ago. But we would enjoy some ice cream'?"

It sounded good to them, and we did indeed go through that conversational sequence. The next evening, we went through the same sequence with Bill and Madeline next door. On the third evening, as we were leaving the city, we stopped at a restaurant operated by one of Sam's hunting lodge friends. His friend offered us menus, but Sam interrupted. "No, thanks," he said, "but we would enjoy some ice cream." We got it. Typical Sam Wagner.

Dale was graduated from Elizabethtown in 1969 with a science degree and qualified to teach high school math. He and Judy both volunteered for Brethren Volunteer Service. BVS did not allow marriage at the beginning of service, considering the adjustment to a new assignment to be difficult enough. Dale went to Poland on an agricultural exchange program, in which he worked with a veterinarian. Some months later, Judy followed; they were married in Poland and brought great publicity as an American couple wed in Poland. Dale's job paid him more than he dared take from the country, so he bought me an eight-year collection of Polish stamps.

That summer, 1969, began another pleasant interlude for our family. We had appreciated Larry's experience overseas under ICYE— International Christian Youth Exchange—and applied to host a student. The student we received, Jeanette Rodriguez Arce, I have mentioned above in Barbara's story. Jeanette was a delight. She was deeply committed to Christ. She was effervescent, always happy, unembarrassed by lapses of language, and fit well into our family. She was a "special" student at CDE, where Marla was a junior in advanced classes. Jeanette was named Homecoming Queen for her school. She was granted a diploma with the class in 1970. There are three other episodes of her stay with us that I want to recount.

At Big Swatara's Love Feast, the ladies always wore the prayer covering, a small white gauze cover on their head. Remembering that too late to instruct Jeanette, I simply asked her to wear one because I asked her to, and I would explain the rationale later. She agreed. A few days after the Love Feast, she came to me. "Daddy, you didn't explain why I must wear that little white cap."

I got my English Bible and she got her Spanish and we turned to I Corinthians 11. I pointed to the fifth verse: ". . . any woman who prays or prophesies with her head uncovered disgraces her head. . . . That is why the ladies wear coverings at Love Feast," I explained.

Jeanette nodded. She read on. Then she said, "But, Daddy, look what the fifteenth verse says: "If a woman has long hair, it is her glory, for her hair is given to her for a covering." She placed her finger on a long-standing Brethren debate!

Near the end of December 1969, the area was inundated by one of the worst of snowstorms. We were snowed in for days. I searched diligently for the mailbox in front of our house, but simply couldn't find it. I devised a snow box of the snowbank nearest the plowed portion of the road. We did not find the mailbox, in its proper location, until February. Jeanette loved the snow. There was none in Costa Rica.

As spring came, the snow finally disappeared. Easter was approaching as Jeanette asked, "Daddy, when will it snow again?"

"I do not think there will be any more." I told her.

"I am going to pray for snow this Sunday," she said.

"Jeanette! It is Easter, everyone wants a nice Easter."

But she prayed. Was it God answering her prayer that brought eight inches that April Easter Sunday? It was warm enough so it did not last long, but it was there!

The close-knit Arce family saved up, pooled their resources, and made it possible for Mama to come visiting. She knew no English, but she was a great talker. Marla and Jeanette could translate. The language barrier was no barrier to Mama Arce. She would talk along at a great rate, suddenly realize people weren't hearing her, and shout, "Jeanette!" so the chat could go on.

For most of our lives after Nigeria, we had two vehicles. We loved the Volkswagens. Over the years, I think we had twenty-two of them. Two of them were "totaled" while we were at Big Swatara. I was guilty one time. I was driving from the hospital after visiting a lovely young mother whose face would ever be distorted by the scar left by a tumor. Struggling with emotion, I was hardly aware of driving and turned at a wrong time. The second was the result of an icy stretch on an otherwise clear road. Marla hit the ice, skidded across, and wedged the car between two steel posts. I was on my way to look for her—she was only a sixteen-year-old driver—and found her almost immediately after her accident.

"Are you all right?" I shouted. "Don't worry about the car. You are the one who is important."

She was safe but bumped.

Dale always seemed to have some project going. One that I remember was the impossible, to me, project of making a kayak. He had a plan to follow, I think, from the *Popular Mechanics* magazine. He borrowed tools that he needed. He purchased the wood, the paint, the solution, everything that the project required, and set to work in the back part of our sizable basement. From time to time we wandered in to inspect his progress, but none of us really understood if he was making progress or not. I was afraid, when he started, that the kayak would be too large to get through the door, but kayaks are really not wide, and that turned out to be no problem. On the other hand, how could he make the wood so tight it would not leak? He couldn't. He covered the frame with canvas, treated the canvas to make it waterproof, painted it green, fitted a seat, and had his kayak. He tried it, successfully, in the Swatara Creek at Union Deposit. I did not ride along.

One spring Saturday, a group of Elizabethtown students, together with one of the faculty, decided to take a canoe hike. There were three canoes, loaded safely with camping eqipment, beverages, and a picnic lunch. Starting on the Little Swatara, they planned a stop to cook supper, then go on, eventually to a campsite. They didn't make it. The lead canoe glided under a tree; one of the paddlers grabbed a branch to help steady them, causing just enough imbalance that the canoe turned over. The other canoes were near enough that they bumped into the first and were themselves capsized. Food was dumped out and mostly lost. Sleeping bags were dumped out, recovered, but wet. The campers were all soaked by the time they had rescued what they could, recaptured the canoes, and gone on to Union Deposit. Wet, tired, and hungry, they came to our house. Bonnie was away at some event, and Bonnie, a beautiful girl, was slight. Still, Dale took the girls to Bonnie's room, told them to pick out clothes that would fit. He helped the boys. We fed them. About half the group had already gone home, but the rest stayed with us for the night. No kayaks, this time, but real aluminum, rented canoes.

I enjoyed singing in the choir at Hanoverdale. We had two good tenors, both solo quality, and two good basses, and I sang either, depending on which was needed. Dale, who sang in the college choir, joined us when he was at home. We particularly enjoyed singing a Christmas cantata each year. When Dale was at home, he sang in the cantata with us. He also took organ lessons and occasionally played.

It has been easy to love the people in all the congregations I served, and Big Swatara was no exception. Unavoidably, some people stand out in my memory. How could I forget Grandma Teets, she of the many grandchildren?

A slender woman past eighty, she had a genuine love for people and for God. She also loved gardening, and each spring she was out planting, weeding, tending her small plot. She had some kind of allergy that each spring caused a serious rash in her legs, but that did not deter her. When I visited her, she always reviewed the health of the family for me, noting especially that "Pop isn't getting along too well," and "My boys aren't as faithful in church as I wish," and perhaps some financial squeeze. She always brought her recital to its own end by observing, "Isn't it great we can go to the Lord? Where else could we go?"

Grandma's heart, though big and warm, was not strong. Each winter, it seemed, she would come down with pneumonia and be hospitalized. My very favorite memory of her is of one visit to her in the hospital. I unzipped her oxygen tent and put my head in. "How are you getting along, Grandma?" I asked.

"Well, I still seem to have a lot of pain, and I just can't sleep here in this place, but I can still go to the Lord. So tell me, Charles, how are all the sick folks getting along?" I would have been hard pressed to find anyone sicker than she.

There were also negatives. One of the ministers stopped talking to me. He kept coming to church, but when he went out, though he shook my hand, he said nary a word and turned his face away from me. One day he had a serious motorcycle accident resulting in multiple fractures to his leg. He was to be in the hospital for several weeks. I went to see him. I asked how he was; he did not answer. I commented that he must be having a lot of pain. No answer. I asked what care was being planned. No answer. I told him we would be glad when he could be back at church again. No answer. I prayed. I did not keep my eyes open to see if he was praying with me.

Every couple of days, I returned to the hospital, and the same one-sided conversation took place. One day, I asked him what was the problem that kept him from talking to me. No answer. I said his name, and said, "I really would like to make things right between us, but I honestly don't know what it is that I have done."

He shouted at me, "Here I am in a hospital bed and you come and bother me with that!"

A deacon who was visiting when I went in one day told me afterward, "The room got cold when you came in." Neither he nor I ever discovered the difficulty.

Another plus memory is the group of local ministers with whom we had fellowship. For the small town of Hummelstown, it was an unusually gifted group. Dan Shaffer, Methodist, was later a District Superintendent. John Bernheisel, Lutheran, went from Hummelstown to an important church in York. Ubel Frost, U.C.C., was to move, later, to a parish at New Salem where he stayed for many years. High school baccalaureate services were still the usual practice. In 1970, Ubel and I were asked to conduct the service and bring the message. We both felt that involvement by the students was important. We worked with a group of students to adapt portions of "My Fair Lady" and make it the message for that baccalaureate. I wonder if any of the kids remember!

We also shared, while we were at Big Swatara, in a cooperative fellowship of the four Church of the Brethren congregations in the Harrisburg area—Harrisburg First Church, Harrisburg Ridgeway, Mechanicsburg, and Big Swatara. We exchanged pastors and choirs and occasionally had four-church gatherings for fellowship or fun.

For about a century, the Church of the Brethren had been making use of the deacon's visit. Most of the congregations had discontinued its use, but some, particularly those served by self-supported ministers, still adhered to it. Although Big Swatara no longer had self-supported ministers, they did still have the old style official board. We had heard no discussion about the program. We were surprised one afternoon when a deacon and his wife stopped in for an unannounced visit. What did they want?

Did they have an idea for a new church program that they wanted to discuss? Were they about to invite us to some special event? None of the above. They were making the formal deacon visit on our family. They proceeded with the three questions which had been prescribed in the Annual Meeting of 1867.

Were we still adhering to our baptismal vows? We thought we were. Were we in peace with the church (which primarily meant were we in peace with the brothers and sisters)? We thought we were. Were we continuing to work toward an individual and congregational "increase in holiness"? Well, I wasn't satisfied with my personal devotions, but otherwise we thought we were. The deacon couple thanked us; they prayed with us, we chatted briefly about the church, and they went on their way. It was to be the only deacon visit I ever experienced.

A more recent program of the Brethren in which we participated was Mission Twelve. Developed by the Christian Education Commission of the General Brotherhood Board, it aimed for release of the potential of individuals and groups to live and witness effectively. A group from Big Swatara went to New Windsor for three weekends, sharing with those from other congregations in small mixed groups. A major emphasis was mutual trust which would enable open, honest sharing of relationships, likes and dislikes, and faith positions or lack of them. We struggled together with the deeper meanings of faith—how to live it and share it with our own personhood, and with human relationships. For those of our congregation, which had tended to be somewhat separatist from the world, it was a meaningful growing experience. Our group continued to meet at intervals from time to time, seeking also to continue the growth in faith that had begun at New Windsor.

In Mission Twelve, we were thrown into groups of persons from varied, though always Brethren, backgrounds. One woman from the Ephrata Church of the Brethren, in particular, became a lifelong friend. The friendship was cemented one day when, as I was driving through Ephrata, I stopped to visit a new discount store. I was in the back of the store and had just turned toward the front. Far ahead I saw a woman raise her arm and wave; nearsighted, I could not see who it was. She began to run toward me, and I moved toward her. We met; we embraced. It was Millie Eisemann, strong Christian spirit and influence for years to come in the Ephrata area and well beyond.

In a new house at Hanoverdale, it was some time before we obtained a pet dog. As a matter of record, we did not obtain the first one. It was a very friendly Manchester terrier which we kept for a few months of transition in the life of a cousin, Mary (Lengel) Sherman. We missed the friendly dog when it was gone, so we decided to get one of our own. We found a pedigreed black dachshund and named her Hildi. She dog-loved all of us and gave us much pleasure. She gave birth to one litter of puppies, which we unselfishly shared.

One evening, as we were playing games in our basement family room, Hildi became very disturbed. She ran to the wall below one basement window and barked furiously. When we went outside to investigate, we discovered that a skunk had fallen in to the window wall and was unable to get out. What to do? On the advice of church custodian George Kuntz, we put a small piece of lumber as an escape ramp for the skunk, and skedaddled before it did. Sometime during the night it escaped. We learned later that it was the denatured pet of a neighbor. Hildi's long dachshund back eventually was too much for her; she developed chronic, painful inflammation and we lost her.

Our extended family was making changes. Mother and Dad High sold their property in 1967, dividing the proceeds between their two daughters (that gift enabled our purchase of the house at Hummelstown), and moved into the Brethren Home at Neffsville. Their move brought them closer to us. They went into one room, taking with them only an easy chair, their grandfather clock, and Dad's radio. They liked it at the home, where they were relieved of all the responsibilities which had been theirs through the years. Mary Beth was particularly glad for their move, for she had been concerned about care they might need in coming years.

My own parents had already reached the point of needing care. Dad had learned, in early 1969, that he had prostate cancer which had already begun some metastasis. We had met around the kitchen table in their home to plan together, aware that Dad had not long to live. He underwent an operation and a urinary ostomy, but continued to lose strength. I took over their financial management. We sold their home and contents at auction. They moved into two rooms in a nursing home at Manchester, Maryland.

Chapter Thirty

THE MOVE TO BLACK ROCK

Although things were going fairly well at Big Swatara, my Methodist heritage left me with an unconscious feeling that seven or eight years was long enough for a pastorate. When Joe Long, TriDistrict Secretary, approached me in the spring of 1970 with the possibility of a move, I agreed to consider it. Earl Ziegler, the first paid pastor of the rural Black Rock Church ten miles south of Hanover, was leaving. Mary Beth and I had never gone through the pastoral placement procedures. They were interesting. I reviewed my faith journey, education, and experience with them, and tried to answer their questions. They shared their perception of the strengths and needs of that healthy congregation of five hundred. They were in a beautiful new building only two or three years old. The church board, which conducted the initial interview with Joe Long's supervision, recommended to the congregation that we be called.

I remember three things about our considering a call to Black Rock. For one thing, Earl Ziegler, an excellent pastor, had been there for ten years. Friends advised, "Don't go there. The people really love Earl."

I responded, "If they can't love me too, he hasn't done a good job."

One comment of the board in our interview was of their pride in their stewardship. I answered that I had examined their stewardship record and they had a long way to go. They had scheduled a Lay Witness Mission for that fall. With changing pastors, they would have to determine the better wisdom: postpone it or go ahead with a newcomer.

We met the congregation in a semi-formal setting one Saturday evening. After refreshments, Joe Long interviewed me. He asked tough questions. I told him afterward I thought he had some tough ones, and he commented that he was confident I could answer them. Questions from the congregation were much simpler. I led the gathering in a worship experience of about ten minutes, and Mary Beth and I withdrew while they voted. We were accepted!!! Even though it would mean changing schools for Marla and Doreen, we were confident that God was calling us to Black Rock. We wrote and sent to the Big Swatara members a letter of resignation to take effect at the end of August 1970.

The worst moments of any congregation, for us, have always been the leaving. We loved the people. Despite the common recommendation that pastors not form personal relationships, some were very difficult to leave. We had grown close to Lou and Louise Bocian, partly because of Lou's tendency to try new things and partly because of my ministry to Louise's parents and half sister. Alma Herr, church secretary, and her husband Carl, then a manual arts teacher, had been with us in Mission Twelve. Hiram Frysinger had been such a helpful moderator for transition from Nigeria and from less traditional Brethren usage. His mother, who lived down the hill about a hundred yards, was one of those persons who was always there when needed; she would even come tromping up with a paring knife and pan to help Mary Beth with canning.

How could we leave Barbara, cleaned up and loyal, soon to go into a nursing home? She told me she was leaving her money to me. When I could not dissuade her, I determined that whatever it was would simply go to the church. Actually, it was quickly used up by the nursing home. I left them as a pastor and discontinued all pastoral relationships, but I never left them as brothers and sisters.

The men of the Black Rock Church took care of our moving. When they talked about it later on, they would best remember moving the fifteen-foot nearly-full freezer. Our move took us farther away from the Highs, but much closer to the nursing home with my parents. Even as we moved, Dad was growing weaker, and I visited him and Mother daily. Three days before my first Sunday at Black Rock, Dad died. He was seventy-six.

I went ahead with my participation in the service, sharing my sense of loss and grief with the congregation and letting them minister to me. My sermon that day was, "Life Begins with Jesus." Dad's life had begun and was just going on. The memorial service was next day at Westminster, and Dad's body was buried in the Bieber plot at Watsontown. Mother had a longing to be back "home" in the Williamsport area, so we moved her to a nursing home in familiar territory on East Third Street.

Dad loved his family and was proud of his Bieber forbears. He worked hard from the time he was twelve or thirteen, until leaving the hospital laundry when he was seventy-four. He was a very patient man, rarely becoming angry, constantly showing concern for others. He remonstrated with the laundry owner for decent working conditions for the "girls" whose boss he was. His patience stood him in good stead at times when Mother's frequent and chronic illnesses made her irritable and demanding. He loved gardening. He loved baseball. He loved the church and was frequently the "cook" for men's breakfast meetings. He loved to work with wood, and it is possible that the strong solutions he used in refinishing wooden furniture may have contributed to his getting cancer. He enjoyed teasing. I remember one time when he had taken Dale to the basement and they were working together. Dale hit his thumb with a hammer, but he didn't cry. Dad reported it later. He said, "The poor kid hurt, and he didn't know what to say, but I taught him some choice words."

Several months before his death, my parents had made me their agent, giving me a power of attorney. With the sale of their small house in Westminster for $9,400, the auction of their furniture, and insurance, Dad's estate was about $25,000. Mother had a small social security income. Thanks to high interest rates at that time on certificates of deposit (14%+), we were able to provide for Mother's care for the nearly five years left in her life.

In many respects, Black Rock was not unlike Big Swatara. It was in the open country of southern York County, a mile from the Maryland state line. The beautiful new church building was set on a hillside. Across the parking lot was the new parsonage, about fifty yards up the hill from the road. The first Church of the Brethren west of the Susquehanna, it had been served by self-supported ministers until the Zieglers arrival. All three of the ministers were schoolteachers. They were Henry Miller, who also did carpentry and construction; Mark Wildasin; and Noah Sellers. Many— perhaps most—of the 570 members had been pupils of one or another of these three. About a fifth of the members lived in Maryland.

The location of the Black Rock Church made for some interesting differences. Less than half the members could be reached by telephone without a toll call. Young Maryland couples, having obtained their marriage license in Carroll County, Maryland, could not have a full wedding in the church. Our custom was to have the wedding service, then go with the couple across the line into Maryland and let them take their vows to each other—at the florist's home, the home of a friend, or just in the auto. Best remembered is one such wedding on a snowy November evening. We drove across the state line; the couple took their vows. As we returned, we found the parking lot so icy we could not drive up it. We left the car where it was and stepped gingerly to the basement entrance near the foot of the hill.

When we moved to Brodbecks and the Black Rock Church, our family had made some changes. Larry and Nancy spent ten weeks on medical work in Nigeria, he as a part of his training, she to sense his boyhood. Dale was still in Poland, working with a veterinarian and beginning to get a yen toward medical school. Bonnie was at Juniata. We moved without our paying enough attention to the needs of Marla and Doreen, who were still in school.

Marla had completed her junior year at Central Dauphin East as a junior in advanced studies. To our dismay, we learned that there were few classes at Southwestern which would take her further in her studies. She enrolled at Western Maryland College, Westminster, for a term, spent fourteen weeks in school with Jeannette Rodriguez in Costa Rica, and was graduated from Central Dauphin East in 1971. It was in Costa Rica that Marla had her first deep conversion experience. Indeed, the group of Christian youth with whom she shared reported to her their special revelation. The Holy Spirit had advised them, they said, that Marla and Jorge were destined for marriage sometime in the future. More of that later.

Doreen, who had been in Lower Paxton Junior High, found no difficulty in moving to Southwestern. A year or two after our move, however, when she and I were in the Hanoverdale area, she confided in me. "Daddy, I was angry when we moved from here, but now I see it as a blessing. My friends were beginning to do things which made me uncomfortable, and it was good that we moved away." A graceful God brought good from our own thoughtlessness.

Getting under way with a congregation of five-hundred-plus and its scattered membership brought its challenges. The congregation had planned for a Lay Witness Mission that fall, and there was disappointment when it could not be carried through. We rescheduled it for a year later. I had been elected chair of the Foreign Missions Commission, which placed me on the Executive Committee of the General Brotherhood Board and made Elgin visits several days longer. In accepting the call to Black Rock, I had indicated that I had two evangelistic meetings scheduled. It was agreed that I should fulfill them, so I spent a week at Greensburg, Pennsylvania, with Jimmy D'Amico, and a week at Nokesville, Virginia, with Paul Crumley. I also led a retreat at the Indian Creek Church.

Routine visitation has always been one of the most difficult pastoral tasks for me; I do not find it easy to meet new people. Hospital visitation, on the other hand, has come easy, probably related to my nursing background. Black Rock members usually went to the Hanover Hospital, but also to the York Hospital, the Carroll County Hospital in Westminster, Maryland and, on occasion, to the Johns Hopkins Hospital in Baltimore.

I tried hard to get the deacons involved in visitation. They were faithful and efficient in making preparations for Love Feast or baptism and in assisting in anointing services, but they fell short in visiting. Mary Beth and I invited them to the parsonage for a curried chicken supper. That Bieber favorite, involving rice under curried chicken and gravy and covered (ad lib) with chopped celery, peanuts, pineapple, peaches, onions, pickles, coconut, tomatoes, oranges, apples, eggs, and chutney, was foreign to them, but they seemed to enjoy it. Afterward, we talked about the work of deacons. They saw their tasks as making the preparations for the ordinances, assistance to the poor and needy, visitation, and helping the pastor as needed. I zeroed in on visitation. Were they doing it? Not much. Could I help them? Probably. I handed to each deacon couple a list of four homes to be visited in the next month, when we would meet again.

When we met again, I asked them how the visitation had gone. Only one of them had worked at it, visiting two of the homes. I asked if they could visit one home each during the next month. They thought they could. A month later, in another meeting, I asked again about their progress. None. I told them I would place on my study door at the church a list of persons needing a visit. As they felt led, they could consult the list, mark off the visits they would make and go on. Month after month, no marks.

Deacons did go with me at my invitation for anointing services, but that seemed to be all. On the one hand, I found it hard to understand; this was a church which had practiced the annual deacon visit! On the other hand, I could understand; did not I, also, find visitation difficult?

Once I reached a home for a visit, however, I found it an enjoyable experience. Once past my original reluctance, I found people to be pleasant and welcoming, and we were able to talk about the work of the church. I suspect that I was more uplifted than those whom I visited. There were, of course, the regular Sunday services and a weekly Bible study. I also thoroughly enjoyed singing with the choir, which produced both a Christmas and an Easter cantata each year.

I also did much more pastoral counseling than, I have come to believe, was wise. Again, one memory persists, that of a woman in depression with whom I spent an hour or more weekly for many weeks. I do not honestly believe that I was of much help beyond giving her an hour or two a week of a listening ear and assurance of a caring God.

Perhaps because I came to the Brethren from a setting unfamiliar with the Love Feast, that ordinance has always been very special to me. I wanted to make a special effort to increase others' appreciation for it. I sent an invitation to all the membership: "The Father invites you to a banquet in honor of His Son, Jesus Christ" (with the time and date and a brief note identifying the "banquet" as the Love Feast and Communion). The idea was not original. I am not known for originality, but I do make use of others' wisdom at times. I tried other announcements: "Meet Jesus personally!" and miniature headlines: "Jesus to be present at Black Rock Love Feast." I do not remember that it made significant difference in attendance!

By the time spring 1971 had arrived, I had become aware that Black Rock, like Big Swatara, had many long-married couples. The carefully kept records of the congregation listed fifty-seven couples who had been married for more than twenty-five years. We made personal contact. The oldest couple had been married for sixty years, and there were four others who had celebrated their golden anniversary. As a congregation, we worshiped with them, singing, "O Perfect Love." Most of them reaffirmed their vows. Richard Bradford, whose beautiful baritone voice blessed us all during my years at Black Rock, sang, "Because." Of course, not all the couples were present, but some were present who rarely attended services otherwise. For many years afterward, one or both of a couple would recall for me that very special service. Neither the Hanover nor the York papers, however, made a big story of it.

Chapter Thirty-One

LAY WITNESS MISSION

In spring and summer 1971, we were making preparations for our first Lay Witness Mission. LWM had first appeared in the United Methodist Church and was made available to any interested congregation. The design called for the appointment of a whole series of committees to make the necessary preparation. There was broad publicity, made as personal as possible. A list of possible witnesses was provided to us, and invitations were sent to them. LWM appointed a coordinator, Jay Wallace. As the title implies, it was totally a lay program.

In addition to the logistical preparations, serious effort was made to be prepared in spirit. We used a daily devotional guide called *Forty Days of Love*. The six weeks placed emphasis on Christian love in its varying relationships. Then, a week in advance of the Lay Witness Mission, Black Rock had a twenty-four-hour prayer vigil, during which there was someone at the church in prayer—in half-hour segments—for the entire period.

The weekend, Friday evening through Sunday evening, began with a gathering of the witnesses with the local steering committee, continued through a congregational dinner, and went on into a Friday evening time of witness and sharing. Three things impressed us greatly on that first evening: the number of persons who had responded to our invitation and traveled at their own expense to share in the weekend; the immediate positive response of any of the witnesses, not forewarned, to stand nervously before the gathering and tell what Jesus meant to them; and the frequently repeated assurance, "God loves you and I love you, too."

Saturday morning, members of the congregation joined the witnesses in "coffees," informal gatherings in the homes of various members, in which there was a more intimate time of sharing. Witnesses shared the stories of their faith journeys, and—for the first time for many—local people shared theirs.

As evening approached, the witnesses and steering committee met to review plans for the evening and the events of next morning. Jay asked me what my sermon topic and scripture would be. Surprised, I commented,

"Jay, this is a LAY witness mission. I understand that it is all in your hands, but I will be glad to help in any way."

Jay had not expected to "preach," but he reluctantly agreed. As I sat as an observer in the planning meeting, I observed, "I have a strange feeling of not deserving to be with you. You are all lay persons; I am a pastor. Perhaps I should not even be in the meeting."

Immediately, someone proposed, "Let's make Charles an honorary layman," and I was promoted.

Sunday morning came, and Jay accepted his responsibility for the morning message. I sat in the far back of the crowded church. Had Jay been in a preaching class, he would have flunked. He stumbled and stammered. He forgot the scriptures he had intended to use; he did not even have a text. Even so, after about fifteen minutes, he invited all who wished to commit—or recommit—their lives to Jesus, to come forward. I was afraid he would be embarrassed when no one came, so I stood up and started toward the front. To my surprised delight, I could not even get front. The aisles quickly filled with persons with a new sense of the Spirit of God within them.

After our Sunday dinner at the church, we bade fond and reluctant farewells to our (that is, Christ's) witnesses. That evening, we met again as a congregation for reflection on what had happened among us. One man, I recall, observed that he had felt outside the flow of events. Otherwise, there was a constant series of testimonies, from men, women, older persons, youth. I particularly remember two sequences: One high school girl told how she was at first turned off, then suddenly found herself filled with joy and surrounded with love. A high school boy, better known for mischief than for commitment, rose to say, "I saw that P___ was having trouble, so I prayed for her."

Two sisters, both divorced mothers, came to me. "We want to sing," they said, "but we are afraid our knees would shake too much."

"Stand with your backs against the choir loft," I recommended. They did, and moved us by their song.

Due largely, I believe, to the loving nature of the three men who had been serving as self-supported ministers and the nourishment of that love in Earl Ziegler's ministry, Black Rock had a continuing good spirit. Lay Witness Mission built on that by the open sharing of agape love and by the renewed commitment to Christ by a great many persons. Another of the many conversion experiences in my own life took place. On returning from Biafra to the Big Swatara congregation three years earlier, I had bluntly announced that I would follow God's will no matter what. After LWM, I realized that it was impossible to follow God's will without a genuine love for God's people!

Chapter Thirty-Two

MORE OF THE
BLACK ROCK CHURCH

One of the blessings of our location at Black Rock was the privilege of sharing in weekly gatherings of Brethren pastors from the area. We were free both to support and encourage one another and to be equally supportive in negative reactions and criticisms. We learned from each other. All of us participated in an annual professional growth event which was, without question, the best I ever experienced. It was the Institute on Ministry to the Sick at Johns Hopkins Hospital in Baltimore. Clyde Shallenberger, a Brethren minister who headed the chaplaincy service, developed plans for a continuing series of excellent presentations by Hopkins staff personnel—administrators, physicians, nurses, social workers, psychologists.

Because Black Rock was somewhat more open to new ideas than Big Swatara had been, I tried new worship ventures. One of them was what I came to call the Popcorn Service. The New Testament word for Spirit, I had learned, is the same as the word for wind. I saw a relationship between the way air explodes the popcorn seed and the way the Spirit expands the Christian spirit. On a stand beside the pulpit, I placed an electric popper with a see-through top which doubled as lid and serving dish. I loaded it with popcorn and butter. As I began my sermon, I turned on the popper. The message reflected explosion and expansion, our own need for personal and congregational expansion, and our need for God's Spirit to produce the necessary explosion. Sermon and popper finished together. I took the bowl of popcorn with me to the door as I left, and persons helped themselves. My favorite comment: "That was certainly the best smelling sermon we have ever heard."

The second service I discovered in reading Lay Witness materials. It was a catacomb communion service. The only light in the sanctuary as people arrived that evening were from the rheostatically-dimmed light on the cross and from two candles on the communion table. Also on the table were two pewter tumblers, a pitcher of grape juice, and a broken-in-two loaf of Vienna bread.

As we began, I explained that the darkness was to simulate that of the Roman catacombs in which early Christians worshipped. We would commune with God and each other, I suggested, by offering a short prayer, by starting a hymn, by reciting a verse, or by sharing a thought. We would continue as long as persons shared in those ways. We would share with God as individuals moved to the communion table, prayed their own prayers of dedication, and served themselves to broken bread and the cup of "wine."

Having explained, I sat down, very nervous. Would anything happen at all? YES! There was a steady flow of shared Bible verses, prayers, comments, and songs. Youth started popular youth choruses; we joined in. One man loved old German (Pennsylvania Dutch) songs and started several; those who remembered, joined. Young or old alike moved at intervals to the communion table, sometimes going beyond to kneel at the foot of the cross. If a person went alone to the table, someone would get up and join him or her; it didn't feel right for an individual to be communing alone.

I had no clue as to how the service was expected to end. Finally, after about ninety minutes, there came a lull in our communing. I did as I felt led—moved to the side, took the hand of a person and asked her to stand. Soon we were gathered around the sanctuary, holding hands with one another—and certainly with Christ—as we sang, "Blest Be the Tie That Binds."

As might be expected in a congregation of nearly six hundred, Black Rock had an excellent musical program. There were three—sometimes four—different organists, as well as a large group of pianists and other instrumentalists. There was a senior choir, a youth choir, and a junior choir, all of whom performed beautifully.

The first mistake I recall came one Sunday when the junior choir were to sing. They were robed and ready, standing just behind me, and I FORGOT THEM!!! Patiently, they returned and sang the next Sunday.

The senior choir produced Christmas and Easter cantatas, occasionally sharing them with other congregations or in a commercial mall. Most memorable is the youth cantata, "God Is Here, We are Here, Now We Can Start" led by Jan Croasmun. A semi-dramatic production, it helped not only those at Black Rock, but in several other places, to a deeper sense of God's presence. Another of the mistakes I made came when a high school girl, serving as interim director of the youth choir, declared that she would be happy when that chore was finished. I took her at her word and found another director, thus offending her parents, who felt I was removing her unfairly!

Black Rock also had several able singing groups and some outstanding soloists, notably Jan Croasmun, Mary Ellen Bachman, Lloyd Sackett, Laura Six, and Richard Bradford.

The Bradfords had two sons, one, Bruce, about five; and the other, Danny, an afflicted infant. From the time Danny was only a few weeks old, he would develop diarrhea and vomiting whenever he ate anything other than four kinds of meat. Even with that regimen, he became ill several times and was taken to Carroll County Hospital in Westminster for intravenous replenishing of fluids. When he was several months old, he became very ill, even though still eating only the proper foods. His parents asked that he be anointed, and Deacon Bill Sunday and I went to the Bradford home. My prayer during the anointing was for his healing and for calm faith by the parents. Mother and baby went, that Sunday afternoon, to Johns Hopkins. I visited next day. Mother was staying with her baby and studies were beginning. Next day I went again.

Mother was extremely agitated. She said, "They won't believe he was sick. They even called Carroll County and asked for their records. They can't find anything wrong with him." Short of the faith that God would bring healing as a result of our anointing, I assured her, "Don't worry! They'll find what is wrong." They never did, for there was no longer anything wrong! Danny was fully healed. A week or so later, after Danny had been brought home, Rich told their story to the congregation, and we praised God for the miraculous healing. As Rich finished, big brother Bruce shouted from a few seats back in the congregation, "Yeah! He even eats ice cream!"

As I began to suggest above, a third mistake I made at Black Rock was to spend too much time in counseling. My counseling skills had been honed by my training as a psychiatric nurse and considerable experience, and I was comfortable with them, but a pastor simply does not have the time for extensive counseling. Nonetheless, I undertook it. I spent, literally, hours with one depressed woman with a problem husband and problem children, who never did come to realize she was the problem. I may have been a little more successful with another woman who came to my office one morning, slightly tipsy. As she began her story, she explained, "Vodka makes you tell the truth." I soon appropriated her bottle of vodka and the pistol with which she was threatening suicide, took her to the parsonage, and let her sleep it off.

There was, however, one counseling incident which I prize. Donna had called me to share a frightening experience. A good friend had entered a two-couple arrangement with free swapping of mates and was feeling guilty about it. When Donna called her one morning, she got no answer. Believing she would not have gone out and left the children, Donna went over and found Marilyn near death from gas inhalation. Marilyn was taken to the hospital and recovered from the gas, but was then in the psychiatric section.

Would I go to see her? I would. "But don't be a pastor," Donna advised. "Pastors turn her off." I agreed.

I went. When I met Marilyn, I had hardly got from my mouth the words which identified me as Charles Bieber, Donna's friend, before she jumped up and hugged me. "Oh, you are Donna's pastor!" she exclaimed.

I confessed, but cautiously added, "I didn't come as a pastor. I came as a friend because Donna loves you and I love you, too." We talked. She shared a little of her background. She had come from the Altoona area; her husband was a Lutheran minister being shared back and forth with another woman. She wanted me to know that she had been a woman of faith.

She said, "I felt deep pain within me. I tried to pray, but I kept getting a busy signal. I figured that God wouldn't be busy at two o'clock in the morning, so I got up and prayed. All that happened was a voice coming out of the corner with loud laughter. I don't know if I believe in prayer."

"I do," I said, "and I feel the need for prayer. Do you mind?"

We joined hands, and I prayed . . . words to the effect that I knew God loved Marilyn and nothing at all could separate her from that love.

When she left the hospital, we continued to visit. I reminded her that I was her friend, not a pastor, but offered to help as she was restoring her relationship with God. I did not once give even a hint that she would be better off at Black Rock Church. Still, she began to worship with us regularly and to attend our Sunday evening prayer group.

She came to me one day, asking if she could become a member of our church. I stammered about getting her letter of transfer and receiving her, but she said, "NO! I want to be baptized!"

So she and her two children became active participants at Black Rock. Out of her own pastor's wife experience, she often gave me valuable suggestions. Eventually I conducted the wedding of her and the "other" of the former two-couple menage. Counselor? Not really. God and Donna did the counseling. God just let me love.

It was not my custom, as a pastor, to issue regular invitations at the close of my sermon. It seemed to me that there was no record of Jesus having issued public invitations, so it did not seem appropriate. Invitations were private. Yet at Black Rock, it was not at all unusual for someone to come forward at the end. I would approach them, ask what was moving them, and pray. I want to share the story of two of those incidents.

Bob, a high school senior with a brilliant mind, was a constant renegade. He would have been a thorn in the flesh for any other youth teacher, but Marian refused to be offended by his tactics and accepted him as he was. Despite her loving interest, he persistently refused to admit to being a Christian.

One Sunday morning, Bob came marching forward. "Something special, Bob?" I asked.

"Yes," he blurted. "I fell out of an eighteen-story window." Puzzled, I looked him over. He looked uninjured. It would not have been beyond him, I thought, to be making a joke of some kind. Still uncertain, I went to the pulpit and commented, "Bob has had a special experience," and prayed for him.

Three evenings later, I caught Bob as he came for youth choir practice and pulled him into my office. "Bob," I said, intending to reprimand him, "what was that eighteen-story business about?"

"Oh," he explained, "in our Sunday School class I asked Marian how I would know that I wanted to follow Jesus. She said, 'Bob, when it happens, you will know it, just as clearly as you would know you fell from an eighteen-story window.'"

A longer and even more beautiful story is that of Gladys. Afflicted for many years by debilitating rheumatoid arthritis, Gladys had difficulty in making any kind of movement. She sang in the choir, so we walked in slowly to let her keep up, sat down slowly to keep her with us. She could hardly eat; it was painful to raise her arms to mouth level. One week she was getting colloidal gold injections, new to her and to me. As I was driving by her house later that week, I slowed, as was my wont, and looked toward her window. I thought that she waved, but knew she could not raise her arms. Sunday came and we were in worship. The choir did not sing that day. Gladys was seated about four rows from the front as we began our closing hymn, "Joyful, Joyful, We Adore Thee," singing too slowly. Just before we ended the first verse, I saw Gladys move out from the pew and start forward.

I interrupted the hymn and met her at the foot of the chancel steps. "Something special, Gladys?" I asked.

"Yes! They are not singing that song right. Tell them!"

"No, Gladys. You tell them," I insisted.

I helped her up the steps and to the pulpit.

"We are not singing that song right," she informed us. "That is a happy song. That is a joyful song. Look! I can raise my hands! Now sing it with joy." And she led us, waving her arms like an old-time chorister. As the days went by, the colloidal gold effect wore off and Gladys lost the motions, but she never lost the joy!

In the fall of 1971 Marla, a National Merit Scholar in spite of her changing of schools, entered Manchester College. Jorge, the Costa Rican youth who, according to the reading of the Holy Spirit by the Christian group there, was to wed Marla sometime, had come to Goshen College. He had nowhere to go during the Christmas holidays, so it seemed appropriate for Marla to invite him to our home. Now I admit that I was looking at him through the eyes of a father, but I must say that he seemed to be about the dullest person I had ever met. Marla is vivacious, energetic, always on the go, always thinking of others. As nearly as I could determine, the only things Jorge and Marla had in common were that they were both human beings and they were both Christians. Someone—it could not be the Holy Spirit, so it must have been those Costa Rican youth—had read the wrong message. Yet there would be time ahead, I was sure, so I did not relay my negative feelings to Marla, unless she was unusually perceptive.

Immediately, I suspect, and continuing after Marla returned to Manchester, Mary Beth prayed. If we had not believed in prayer earlier on, we would have when we had a letter from Marla, not long after her return to college, saying she had met a young man who was becoming special to her, Jim Abe, a Brethren student from northeastern Ohio. By the time the next fall came, they were close enough so it was hard for Marla to carry through on her plans to spend a study year abroad. She was one of a small group who were the first to go to Barcelona under the Brethren Colleges Abroad program.

Marla and the others of the Barcelona group were quite compatible, but her stay there brought one negative and one positive event. Early in December, she became ill with, as I recall, some kind of abdominal distress. Diagnoses by the doctors there did not seem to us to fit the symptoms Marla described, and we arranged for her to come home. Treated here, she soon recovered, apparently completely, and returned to her studies in Spain.

Chapter Thirty-Three

GOLDEN ANNIVERSARY IN NIGERIA

The second event was much more pleasant and came in connection with a memorable trip by six of us to attend the fiftieth anniversary of the first Brethren worship service in Nigeria. Charles and Rozella Lunkley, their son Jim and his wife, Judy, and Mary Beth and I were able to plan our trip so a visit to Barcelona would fit with minimal added expenses. So, our first stop on that very special trip was in Barcelona, joyfully spending time with Marla and letting her be our tour guide to local attractions.

Our next stop was to be Rome, but a strike by French air controllers made it necessary for us to detour to Milan. The stay there was limited to the airport; there was not enough time for touring. We had lunch, which Marla had packed for us, and ate there in the airport. Eventually the moment came when my visit to the counter brought news that our plane was coming in. As I returned to the group, I passed a very British couple who seemed to be waiting for the same plane.

"I think our plane has arrived," I told them. The man looked at me, looked at his wife, looked at me, turned to her and asked, "Do we know that person?"

The short hop to Rome, although arriving much later than we had anticipated, was uneventful, but then—ah, then. Charles and I went to the counter of Nigeria Airways. It was closed, but a small placard advised that after hours a call could be made. I listened as Charles called.

"We have just arrived and wonder what we ought to do until our plane for Kano leaves. . . . Yes sir, to Kano, Nigeria. But sir, we have tickets for the plane which leaves early in the morning. There isn't? What do you suggest that we do?" He hung up, and we reviewed the chat. In simple terms, we had tickets for a flight on Thursday that had taken off on Wednesday. There was no Thursday flight; the next would be Saturday.

Jim and Judy had planned to spend a few days in Rome on the return journey, so they had the address of a hotel in downtown Rome. We contacted them; they had rooms for us. We contacted the baggage people; they took us into the bowels of the airport (it even smelled like bowels!) and we searched out our baggage, which had, of course, been checked through. We boarded a bus to the bus depot in downtown Rome, close, we understood, to Hotel Canada. Arriving there, past midnight, weary travelers, we asked directions. Hotel Canada is just a couple of blocks from the bus depot. Oh, sure. We lugged all our baggage through the depot, itself about two blocks long, passing taxi drivers that we could have called. Outside the depot, we were on the right street and struggled on. After a block, we were so weary we stopped, rested, and laughed hilariously at our predicament. That was a twice-repeated occurrence, but we did finally reach refuge—the Canada.

After we slowly came to, next morning, I inquired and discovered the Pan-Am Office was quite close.

"Come on," I said to Charles and Jim. "Get your tickets and let's see if we can get some help."

The scene: Pan-Am Office.

The conversation: "What can I do for you gentlemen?" (in English; apparently we had an American look about us.)

"Well, sir, you can arrange for the cost of our hotel stay here in Rome, provide us with meal vouchers, and get us tickets for the Saturday morning flight to Kano, Nigeria." (Usually unassertive me, so fed up that I had become very assertive.)

"What's that? What do you mean?"

"Your company sold us tickets for a flight that doesn't exist. We are delayed here for three days because of the mistake of your company. We believe your company is responsible for our expenses here."

"Do you have your tickets?"

"We certainly do!!!"

He took the tickets, disappeared for a few moments, came back, and said, "You are quite right!" He prepared meal vouchers for the three days, called Hotel Canada and assumed our room cost, provided new tickets, regretted Pan-Am's error, and wished us well. Our three days in Rome with no expense except tourist trips, were offset by the fact that our Nigeria stay would be three days shorter.

Eventually, we arrived in Kano, met there by beloved friends. How does one describe a totally nostalgic visit like that to Nigeria in 1973?

Sketchily! For some of our trip, our touring group split; the Lunkleys wanting to visit in Wandali where they had spent much of their service; the Biebers wanting to be in Garkida and Lassa. A few things stand out. We felt welcome; we felt loved. People were simply delighted so see us, as we were delighted to see them. Mary Beth showed an amazing ability to recognize people whom we had not seen for ten years or more, especially those who had been teenagers and now were adults with all the changes that entailed. We could not help feeling pride in those who had been our students in primary school or in the Bible School.

The high moments of the trip, of course, came in the celebration of fifty years of the church. Nigerians have a special sense of celebration. It involved remembering, giving thanks to God and to those who had gone before, enjoying tribal songs as well as choirs, the exchanging of gifts, and the expression of hope. The major event took place under the wide-spreading tamarind tree at Garkida, where on March 17, 1923, Stover Kulp and Albert Helser had led in that first public Christian service. Great emphasis was placed on the passage from Ephesians which declared, "You are no longer strangers, but fellow citizens with the saints and members of the household of God."

The most notable gift of the day was that of a Land Rover (auto) to the church in Nigeria, a gift from the Church of the Brethren General Board which, in a sense, recognized the church there as a self-standing organization. Changes were about to take place, some by new perceptions and planning, some by misunderstanding. One misunderstanding brought serious separation of relationships between the church in Nigeria and that in the United States. I have already referred to the naming of various Christian churches in Northern Nigeria by their geographical location. The church which had been planted by the Church of the Brethren Mission came to be known as the "Church of Christ of the Sudan, Eastern Region" or, in Hausa, *Ekklesiyar Kristi a Sudan, Lardin Gabas.*

That name was sadly misread by leaders in the United States to indicate a Nigerian intention to sever the kind of close relationship which had made the Nigeria church a district of the church in America. In fact, the name was in no way intended to imply separation. Its purpose was to signify togetherness with other Christian bodies of Northern Nigeria. Such togetherness was not new; it had been an integral part of mission polity through the years, as expressed especially in the former Northern Missions Council and the founding of the Theological College of Northern Nigeria. Church leaders in Nigeria only gradually became aware that, in a very real sense, they had been cut off from their founding mother *while carrying out the policy that "Mother" had established*. Other "indigenous" churches underwent somewhat the same experience. They gradually began to adopt names for themselves which reflected their full heritage, and the church in Nigeria adopted the name, "Ekklesiyar 'Yanuwa a Nigeria," i.e., "Church of the Brethren in Nigeria." Interestingly enough, the literal translation would be "Church of Children of the Same Mother in Nigeria," an even closer intimacy.

Her independence having been recognized was, however, a real blessing. The old plan of organization, most of which I had written in 1960-1963, continued. Programs which were begun by the mission became programs of the church, initially with some financial support from the church in America. And as we will see later, the church took some new strides.

Another interesting occurrence came as we were about to leave Nigeria. Bob Greiner, General Board Treasurer for many years, had attended the golden anniversary celebration along with his wife, Edna. A mite nervous about being on time for their flight home, they had traveled to Maiduguri by car and flown to Kano. Our own itinerary was by way of Jos to Kano, from which international flights were to take off. When we arrived in Kano, there was very heavy harmattan, the foglike dust which swept down from the Sahara. Informed that our flight to Rome could not take off, we were taken to the Kano Hotel. When I registered (by writing our names in the registry), I noticed that Bob and Edna were already there. We went to their room to greet them. Uncomfortable about being in a strange country in a strange land with a strange language, they opened their door very carefully—until they saw us, and the most beautiful expression of relief and reassurance spread across their faces. When, the next morning, our flight took off, we were told it would need to go south to Lagos to avoid the harmattan. We went to Lagos, picked up passengers, flew back to Kano—harmattan or no—took on more passengers, and headed to Rome, and then to New York.

Chapter Thirty-Four

SOUTHERN DISTRICT YOUTH

Southern Pennsylvania, even as Eastern Pennsylvania, did not nominate me for any district office—appropriately enough, since I was heavily involved in the national General Board. Mary Beth's abilities were recognized, however, and she was elected to the District Board. Doreen became a member of the District Youth Cabinet. I was appointed to the Evangelism Committee. It did seem difficult to find persons who were willing to serve on the board of the Children's Aid Society, so I accepted that nomination and was elected. A year later I became its president. I succeeded in opening the Children's Aid Society influence to new areas, making personal visits to places of possible need. I also was able to point them in the direction of a full-time executive.

At the same time, I was appointed the pastoral advisor to the District Youth Cabinet, along with Larry Hassinger, an active layman from Huntsdale. I was fifty-four years old, but I felt comfortable, having read a study done by Lyle Shaller which suggested that high school youth leaned toward advisors in their fifties. There were three exciting years from which I cull two experiences, both of which I was pushed into by the Black Rock youth.

The Lay Witness Mission at Black Rock in 1971 was still having positive results. Some of the members became witnesses, including several youth. Tim Nace and Doreen told the LWM story to the district youth cabinet. Would it be possible, they wondered, to plan a Lay Witness Mission as the annual "Hilltop" of the district youth? Several factors mitigated against the idea: Attendance at Hilltop rarely surpassed fifty. LWM was set up for the intimacy of one congregation; could it be revised to touch congregations fifty or more miles apart? Was there a sufficient source of youth witnesses? Could it be done? We would try.

With the Hilltop scheduled for March 8-10, we set about reaching the youth. We asked each congregation for a list of their youth, names and addresses. Handwritten letters went from cabinet members to all of them, inviting them to Hilltop at Black Rock. Letters to youth advisors and pastors informed them of what the Hilltop would be like and enlisted their personal and prayer support. Second and third letters went to all the youth by bulk mailing. "Guests" were solicited to be visitors in each of the churches three weeks in advance of the weekend to enlist interest and attendance. Black Rock and Hanover youth planned menus and recruited hosts for overnights and breakfasts. Letters went to youth witnesses asking for their sharing. Bill Cox of Pikesville, Maryland, and Doug Maxwell of Mount Joy, Pennsylvania, were our witness leaders.

The undergirding of prayer was essential. We sent prayer cards to all the youth in the district, provided a booklet, *The Great Discovery*, to guide prayer and discussion, and proposed prayer vigils. Prayer vigils involved groups of churches, assigned for their nearness to each other and taking place by scheduled periods in each of the participating churches.

Only one past Hilltop had attracted more than fifty participants. We did not reach our goal of 200, but we had more than 120. Friday evening brought registration, home assignments, witness team meeting with district cabinet, fellowship meal with witnessing, and small group discussions on what persons hoped for or expected from the weekend. On Saturday morning we continued our discussion on what the weekend might mean, pointing it to our personal hopes. In the afternoon there was free time, visitation, a work project, and a discussion on being a Christian at school.

As we entered into our evening gathering, in semi-darkness and with singing and witnessing making it one of the most important hours, I was called away. A young woman called with the fear that her mother and father, then in a deep fight, might kill each other. I asked the group to pray for me and left. When I returned, the Spirit was still at work. I spied Tami, for whom her whole group was praying, sitting alone, weeping. I sat beside her, put my arms around her, reminded her that God loved her, as did I, but she had much difficulty believing anyone could love her.

Next morning, visiting youth infiltrated all the Sunday School classes from junior high on, and team leaders led in the classes. The youth planned and led in a moving service with tremendous response in the congregation. As the youth returned to their homes, they took with them the suggestion that they meet together that evening just to reflect on what had happened at Hilltop. Letters to the Black Rock youth, the congregation, or to me, poured back. The best was one in which we received the report that dear Tami had given her life to God—and another some months later affirming her commitment.

We sent our own letters to participating congregations, reviewing the weekend and lifting up the ways in which God had shown loving power. Let me close the story—you could hardly stop me—with this poem by Kathy Kaucher, cabinet member and daughter of the Huntsdale pastor (there were others, but I liked hers best):

We came from afar, Seeing each other as we are
We came as sinners, We left as winners.
We came to Hilltop, Perhaps as a flop,
But when we left, The movement was deft.
For if we would look back,
We would remember that Christ we did lack.
Our problems we could discuss, And try to solve them with no fuss
We've met many a trial, And left all the while,
But when we came to Hilltop, Those practices we tried to stop.
We learned that God's grace we cannot borrow;
We have to trust Him to face tomorrow.
For our sins we did repent
As we realized our lives were bent,
The joy of Hilltop in words we cannot express,
But our futures are no longer a guess.
This news, please share 'round.
We must spread this love we have found.

The second event with the district youth was also urged by the Black Rock youth. They remembered our Catacomb Communion Service and wondered if it could take place with the youth. It could—and did. After the LWM Hilltop, it was relatively easy to attract a goodly number of youth to a special service at Camp Eder. Lacking a more traditional communion table, we simply transformed the piano bench. On our new "communion table" we laid a cover, a "common cup" borrowed from the Black Rock Church, a broken loaf of Vienna bread, and a pitcher of grape juice. Dim light came from two candles on the piano and soft reflection from the outside night light.

All of us sat on the floor. I reviewed for the youth the way the service would proceed, recalling the catacomb atmosphere in old Rome. We would commune with each other, I explained, by sharing our songs, prayers, Bible verses, or sentences of joy or concern. We would commune with God as persons felt led to go to the communion table, pray their prayers of consecration, and serve themselves the communion elements. Would it work? Weren't we expecting a little much of the youth? Would they respond? They responded. I had hardly sat down before songs began, prayers, verses, personal thoughts, in an endless out-pouring. Youth knelt before the communion table/altar in personal communion with God. Wow! What a powerful sense of the presence of the Holy Spirit!

At one point in the service, the daughter of one of the youth advisors whispered to me that her dad would like to have the closing prayer. I had no plans for a closing prayer; we would close with, "Blest Be the Tie."

I thought for a moment, then advised, "Your dad will recognize when I start a closing song. Tell him that he should pray as soon as the song ends."

I knew that parents would be coming to pick up some of the youth, so I tried to be aware of the time. There was no clear break in the movement of the Spirit among those young people, but when it seemed to be getting late, I took the hands of nearby youth and pulled them to their feet. As we rose, we joined hands. We sang, "Blest Be . . ."

At the close of the prayer, the advisor prayed. Our service was over. No, it wasn't. Immediately on the close of his prayer, one of the youth recited a verse; another started a song. I have rarely felt so moved as I was by the response of those young people to the Spirit of Christ. As I heard cars approaching outside, I turned on the room lights and shouted, "Hallelujah! God loves you and I love you, too! Go with God and we'll see you next time."

We did a lot of hugging, and we took our enthusiasm with us.

Chapter Thirty-Five

GETTING PERSONAL

After Dad's death, as I have mentioned, we settled Mother in a nursing home on East Third Street in Williamsport. I made it a point to visit her at least monthly and take her out for lunch. She always liked our visits and would almost always comment, "I'm glad you come, Charles. No one else ever visits me." That seemed strange to me, because sister Mae and her gentle Greek husband, George, lived just north of the city. I was sure that they, as well as Uncles Bob and Myles, came calling.

One day we took Mae with us. Mae had hardly left the room to confer with the nursing staff, which she was obviously accustomed to doing, when Mom said to me, "I'm glad you come, Charles. Nobody else ever does."

Mom was confused often, but seemed happy and content. Late in 1974, she became more ill and was admitted to a nursing center. She died quietly on January 25, 1975, and her body was laid along that of Dad in Watsontown. In spite of the fact that her only income was from social security and Dad had left a limited amount, careful management left each of her children with about $6,500. Mom and Dad would have been pleased!

Mom went to school for eight years, but she was afflicted with terrible myopia, and good grades came hard. She loved Dad and her children dearly, and was constantly giving up something so she could provide for the kids. Whenever we had even the most minor accomplishment, she was very proud of us. She loved to sing and whistle, and we would often hear her around the house. She had a number of illnesses, usually related to gastro-intestinal problems, but she also reported to us other problems which existed only in her mind. She worked hard; she was a meticulous housekeeper and a very good cook, and she managed our meager household finances with amazing skill.

She was very serious about her faith in Jesus and about her longing for her children to know Him. Thanks, Mom.

In the widespread Bieber household, other kinds of activities were taking place. I am sure they will not be recorded in proper chronological order. For one thing, Larry completed his studies at Pennsylvania State University Medical College. Thanks to the thoughtfulness of Grandfather and Father in passing on a name beginning with B, he was the first medical graduate of the new program. He entered a resident program at Case Western Reserve, and he and Nancy moved to Cleveland.

Dale and Judy returned from Poland. Dale entered a Master's program in Physiology at Penn State and then entered medical school at Hershey.

For another thing, Bonnie was graduated summa cum laude from Juniata. Although the college years had splashed some cold water on her Christian faith, she continued with a strong commitment to serving people. She entered Brethren Volunteer Service and was assigned to work in a religiously conservative Afro-American social service program in Jackson, Mississippi. A year later she was transferred to Bloomington, Indiana. Completing her service there, she accepted a fellowship in psychology at Purdue University. She took her Master's degree to a position in Owatonna, Minnesota.

Larry and Nancy produced our first two grandchildren, very welcome granddaughters, with the birth of Diana in 1973 and Alisa a year later.

A second exchange student, Kyung Wan Lee, came into our home from Korea. Daughter of two professors in Seoul, she was a bright high school student. Her command of English left much to be desired. She was friendly enough and cooperative enough, but she lacked the personal spark that we had experienced with Jeanette. She was a voracious shopper, and we were often puzzled to know where she found enough money for all her purchases. Near the end of her stay with us, we learned that she had not always paid for her "purchases."

Marla returned from Barcelona to Manchester, completed her degree in three years with transfers from Western Maryland, and was graduated in 1974. That wasn't enough excitement for the year. The wedding of Marla Christine Bieber and LeRoy James Abe took place that June in the Black Rock Church. Typically Marla, she wanted a carry-in luncheon at the church for their reception. The congregation, she said, were family. They responded beautifully, and it was a pleasant reception. Marla's Aunt Martha, however, was puzzled by our inability to afford a reception!

Doreen was the only one of our children to become involved in high school sports. The boys, of course, were away from us, and the other girls had no interest. Doreen played on Southwestern's Field Hockey and Women's Basketball teams, and we thoroughly enjoyed watching. Team-minded, she agreed to play goalie in hockey, in spite of skills which would have let her be a good forward. In basketball, I found myself frequently disagreeing with the referees, as did the father of one of the other students. Both of us were kind enough to offer advice to the referee, but the advice was not graciously received. At one game, he, a teacher in the school, was sitting some rows in front of me when I made a thoughtful suggestion to the referee. Not seeing it as thoughtful, she took umbrage, thought it was my teacher colleague, and ousted him. I decided she did not deserve my advice, and I kept it to myself for the rest of the game.

In the summer of 1974, I think it was, Doreen went on a bike hike with a group, mostly of Mennonite youth. She was so impressed with, particularly, the leader of the hike that she decided to visit her college, Goshen, Indiana. With some trepidation, we put her on a bus. She was so favorably impressed with her reception there and the girls she met that she decided to enroll there. Another of our children to be merit-scholar favored, she started in the fall of 1975. Our nest was empty, and we missed her. At home for Christmas vacation, she reported loving Goshen, but lacking a "best friend." (In the parlance of the day, we understood that to be another girl with whom she could share almost as a sister.) Would we pray for her? We did. She got her "best friend." Soon after she returned to Goshen, a letter came mentioning a young Mennonite a year or two older, her biology lab assistant. They clicked. That fall, we had a phone call from Myron Miller soliciting our blessing on his marrying our daughter. As long as she finishes college, Mary Beth agreed, and they were engaged.

The three Church of the Brethren congregations in Akron, Ohio, had a regular autumn event which they called their "Adventure Series." Outstanding leaders from across the denomination were invited to preach on a fall weekend in each of their three services. I was invited to be their speaker in the fall of 1975. The only reason I could figure out for my being invited was their sense of need for some missionary flavor. I could provide it, even though we had "retired" from Nigeria in 1963. Our 1973 visit had added fuel to our continuing embers of interest.

Through exchange students hosted by the Zieglers when Earl was pastor, an exchange experience in Korea by Mary Ellen Baughman, and Kyung's presence, Black Rock became very open to persons from other cultures. They sponsored several Vietnam refugees. Two of them became close to some of our members, and it was hard to see them move to Utah, where they had found some old friends and relatives. We were blessed by the visits of several Nigerians to our congregation, particularly my good friend Jabani, Mamadu Kwaya, who would become a teacher at the Theological College of Northern Nigeria, and Nvwa Balami, one time principal of Waka Secondary School and an outstanding pastor.

My philosophy of pastoral service involved making use of the skills and the commitment of lay persons. Black Rock had many of them, willing, able Christians who enjoyed serving their Lord and the church. Still, it seemed appropriate to involve college or seminary students in summer work programs. Mark Bowser, son of Pastor Harold Bowser, and Nina Bowman, daughter of Pastor Walter Bowman, were both loved by both youth and adults during their summers with us. In the summer of 1975, the congregation was blessed by the service of Rod and Marvis Custer. They had special relational skills and genuine love for people which let them fit well at Black Rock.

Chapter Thirty-Six

MODERATOR ELECT!

It was on a Saturday evening in June 1975, that another phone call came from Earl Hostetter—he who had placed my name in nomination years earlier for General Board. Earl was again on the nominating committee of Standing Committee. He surprised and startled me by asking if I would let my name be entered as a candidate for moderator-elect of Annual Conference.

I have never longed for high office or had the least ambition toward prestigious positions. My first reaction to Earl's request was to express a combination of gratitude and regret. Earl talked about the difficulty of getting four acceptances, from which Standing Committee would choose two. Sympathetic to his problem, I gave tentative agreement. There was no chance, I felt, that I would be elected. I would need the approval of Black Rock's Executive Committee.

I called Bob Schlegel, able businessman who was our moderator at the time. He called a special meeting of the executive committee next morning. The committee approved, with the frequently repeated observation, that it was an honor to be on the ballot and I'd never make it anyway—exactly my own sentiments.

Annual Conference was in Dayton, Ohio. Mary Beth and I stayed with John and Mildred Grimley at Brookville. At conference, I learned, to my great surprise, that I was one of the two nominees for moderator-elect. With a sense of relief, I learned that the other was Leon Neher, well-known Manchester College professor, Christian social activist. Obviously, he would be elected. There was much dissatisfaction with the ballot that the Standing Committee had chosen. Three additional nominees for moderator-elect were added to the ballot from the floor. Two votes eliminated the three, and it came down to Leon and me. By that time, I was surprised to be having new feelings. In spite of having no ambitions earlier in that direction, I found myself wanting to be elected. I suddenly remembered that I had never lost an election. At last, the results were made known: I received a majority of the votes after all the extra candidates were eliminated.

Mary Beth was sitting beside someone who commented, "That is a BIG job. It will take a lot from the winner, and I certainly wouldn't want it."

Mary Beth said, briefly, "It was my husband who was elected."

John was delighted. He immediately invited all the ex-missionaries he could find to a celebration supper at a nearby restaurant. He awakened a special sense of pride and responsibility within me. I was the first former missionary since Desmond Bittinger to be elected, and I felt responsible to all my missionary colleagues.

We would not get home until Monday after conference, and we wanted Black Rock to get the news from us. I called Bob Schlegel after we heard the report of the elections, and asked him to announce it to the congregation. We heard later how he made the announcement. After reporting my election, he added, "We never thought Charles would make it, but he did. Now we will have to help him."

Stan Earhart, our district executive, was a huge help. He visited the congregation one Sunday morning a few weeks later and reflected with them what it means to be Annual Conference Moderator. My Uncle Theodore read the report in the *Washington Post* and wrote to congratulate me.

Moderator 1975-76 was Blair Helman, president of Manchester College and a brilliant man with outstanding service in education and broad experience behind him. He had an unusual knack of reflection, by which he was able to analyze, assort, organize, and to some extent, predict. An administrator, he was incisive and directive. From the first meeting of Annual Conference Central Committee in August, he was clearly the one in charge. We reviewed the evaluation sheets from the 1975 conference, planned the theme for the year, and began to choose speakers and pertinent committees. Hubert Newcomer was Annual Conference Manager, and Bill Eberly was clerk.

Meanwhile, back at the ranch—that is, at Black Rock. Being pastor there had the most important claim on my time and energies. In the interest of challenge, I gave the newsletter a new name. It had been *The Black Rock Flock* which had a good sound but felt more custodial and paternal than I felt a congregation should be. Intending to convey the feeling of a church on the move with God and for God, I proposed *THE JOURNEY* of the Black Rock Church of the Brethren. I was aware that in another year, much of my energy would become denominational, so I determined to work extra hard during this year, serving Black Rock.

Also in anticipation, I made a special effort to make them feel a partner-ship with me in the moderatorship. (After all, Bob Schlegel had proclaimed, "Now we must help him.")

Panama

Spring 1976 arrived, preceded only a couple of weeks by the important arrival of our third granddaughter, Kirsten, born to Dale and Judy. Less important, but certainly with higher temporary priority was a trip I made to Panama in April. I went as one of three persons from the Church of the Brethren and one of the fourteen sent as a delegation of the National Council of Churches of Christ in the U.S.A.

We were asked to get the facts on the United States position in Panama. The treaty of 1903 was still in effect. Was it being followed? Was it fair? Should a new treaty be negotiated? Did Panama receive a fair portion of Panama Canal income? Had the time come for the United States to return Canal Zone—and of course, canal—to the people of Panama?

We met with a wide variety of spokespersons, some official, some American, some Panamanian, one group under the cover of darkness, reli-gious leaders, military leaders, students.

My personal conclusion closely followed that of the delegation as a whole:

As a Christian, I do not want my country to continue an unjust, power-controlled policy toward a small neighbor; I do not want my country to continue to deprive that neighbor of the full benefits of her principal natural resource, her geography. I believe that, in the best inter-ests of good relationship between U.S. and Panama, as well as with the rest of Latin America; for the purpose of maintaining world peace in what is a potentially explosive situation; but most of all because of the sheer demands of justice and international brotherhood, the Panama Canal treaty should be renegotiated with a view to early United States withdrawal.

Meanwhile, among the Brethren, a growing number of persons were being attracted by the Pentecostal revival, with emphasis on the gifts of the Holy Spirit, in particular speaking in tongues. It was decided to hold a Holy Spirit Conference, the first of several such annual Holy Spirit Conferences. It was scheduled for Valparaiso University, with its ample facilities and beautiful chapel. I understood that Blair Helman, Annual

Conference Moderator, was invited to give the closing message. I do not know whether because of his lack of enthusiasm for the charismatic movement or because of his heavy schedule, but he declined the opportunity. As moderator-elect, I was next choice, and I agreed, though not without considerable trepidation. In theory, the closing message would send us off all empowered by the Holy Spirit.

Russ Bixler, in many respects the prime leader of those sponsoring the conference, pointed out to me that planned worship services assumed the message would be about forty-five minutes in length. A few years earlier I had preached in the church where Russ was pastor, and he may have remembered that my sermons were half that.

Mary Beth and I attended all the services, along with Marla, whose conversion in Costa Rica included a strong charismatic flavor. We were impressed by the sincerity of those participating, especially enjoying the soft harmony of what was called singing in tongues, but what seemed to us to be too regimented to have been spontaneous.

Did Russ and others realize I was not a fully committed charismatic, that I had never once spoken in tongues? The conference was to close near noon on Saturday. Russ came to me on Friday evening. His request went very much like this: "We are finding that the worship service tomorrow morning is getting rather long. Do you suppose you could shorten your sermon to about twenty minutes or so?"

"I think I might be able," I responded, "but I am not sure the Holy Spirit will go that way." My observation of the charismatic movement, rightly or wrongly, was that it tended to be self-centered and inner-directed. I felt a strong need to lift up the ACTION of the Spirit. The message I brought was that the Holy Spirit is a MISSIONARY Spirit in deed as well as in speech.

Annual Conference 1976 in Wichita, Kansas, was upon us, with Standing Committee meetings, sessions of the Central Committee, and then conference itself. I was almost overwhelmed by Blair's skill and particularly by his self-assurance. I did not have that same kind of self-confidence. Yet I did have some things going for me.

Thanks very much to the spirit of Black Rock, I loved people and felt loved. I had experienced the power of prayer. And I had a sense of humor which could give me relief in difficult moments. The traditional service of consecration and laying on of hands was held, with John Grimley the agent of God that I called upon. Blair turned the gavel over to me with a speech lengthier than, in my nervousness, I wanted to listen to.

Chapter Thirty-Seven

ANNUAL CONFERENCE MODERATOR

My acceptance speech was much briefer. I spoke of my surprise at the trust the conference was placing on me, and promised to be faithful to the trust. I leaned heavily upon the promise in II Corinthians 12:9, "My grace is sufficient for you, for my power is made perfect in weakness."

At Black Rock, their help had already begun. The visit of Stan Earhart a year earlier had reminded them how important their support would be. Ammon and Lucille Meyer, parents of Larry's Nancy, had volunteered for Brethren Service.

On the request of the Black Rock congregation, they were assigned as assistant pastors. An apartment was provided for them. They were not only very pleasant folks to be around, but were adaptable and able for almost any situation. When moderator duties would take us away, they would stay at the parsonage, take care of preaching and visitation and be, in fact, the pastor. Lucille did a great deal of the work of preparing the newsletter. Even before Annual Conference, with my much needed vacation and my first visit to a district conference, Ammon was beginning his preaching ministry.

Two convictions entered into planning for the moderator year. I believed it to be important for the moderator to visit as many as possible of the twenty-four districts of the Brethren. I also wanted to be at Black Rock as consistently as possible, both in the usual pastoral activities and in letting them be a part of my moderatorship. As the year developed, I was able—usually with Mary Beth—to visit in all but one district.

Let me try to indicate what the schedule for 1976-77 involved. Every month I preached at Black Rock on at least two Sundays, during November and December on all four Sundays. Almost all of the district conferences took place in August to October, sometimes two of them at exactly the same time. (Sometimes I would be the speaker; sometimes I would hardly be noticed.) There were three meetings of Annual Conference Central Committee and two of the General Board. There was one week-long series of revival meetings which I had promised. There were local churches which wanted very much to be visited by the moderator. There were special events in which the planners hoped for moderator participation—union services, rally days, centennial celebrations.

It was essential to care for personal needs such as the weekly pastoral support group, ministerial meetings, and professional growth events. There were conferences of sister Brethren denominations to attend. There were piles of correspondence to which to respond. And surrounding it all, there was the family I loved and wanted to be with.

Several of the moderator visits deserve further mention. Going to Goshen, in Northern Indiana, came after another telephone call from Earl Hostetter. This time he was speaking for the district board, inviting me to consider their need for a new district minister. We loved Black Rock so much that my initial response was quite negative. Still, I was to be in the district, and I agreed to sit down with their search committee.

Two factors led me to keep the option open. They called their executive, the district minister, expecting ministry to pastors and congregations. And there appeared to be a challenging amount of intra-congregational conflict. At one point in our discussion, they asked, "How do you feel about conflict?"

I said, "I don't like it, I don't look for it, and I don't run from it." It was enough for them to keep me on their list.

A second memorable visit was one to the Missouri-Arkansas District Conference in Springfield, Missouri. What makes it memorable is the fact that they were considering the sending of a query to annual conference. As I recall, there were only twenty-one delegates present from the small congregations in that district. A few years earlier, action by Annual Conference had eliminated the office of elder in the church. One of the Arkansas congregations proposed a recommendation to Annual Conference that the elders body be restored. As I listened, I observed that every speech made seemed to oppose the proposal. Then when a vote was taken, it passed by a 17-4 vote. I was impressed and actually pleased that even a tiny congregation and district had the right and the gumption to send a query to the whole denomination.

In Western Pennsylvania, I was privileged to provide leadership in November for the District Women's Meeting in the Walnut Grove Church.

I was very much impressed with the District Youth Choir. So far as I knew, that was the only district with a youth choir, and they were justifiably proud of it. I was able to arrange for the choir to sing in one of the evening services at Richmond and to present one of the early evening concerts.

By far the outstanding trip of the year was one arranged for six days in February to the Pacific Southwest Conference. Truman Northup, the Executive Secretary, had been arranging a similar tour of the district for the moderator, and now it was my turn. Mary Beth and I visited in thirteen different churches. Three times there were meetings involving several congregations, and the others were in more usual settings. By that time, the conference theme, "To Serve in a Changing World," had been adopted and was widely known.

In group meetings, I spoke on "Our Changing Mission" or "To Share the Dream." In local churches I was just another preacher. One special result of the tour was to be able to visit with former missionaries, Irven and Patty Stern, Max and Loretta Baughman, Lawrence and Ruth Clark, Esther (Bowman) Gregory, and Lena Wirth. In the Pomona Fellowship Church, we were presented clever badges, "Charley's Angel" and "Leave it to Bieber."

On the Pacific trip, I became acquainted with Bob Earhart, pastor of the Pasadena Church, and learned that the vice-mayor was a member of his church. The information would come in handy.

The resignation of Loren Bowman after several years of able leadership as the denomination's General Secretary made necessary a search for his successor. I was asked to chair the Search Committee. We solicited names from across the Brotherhood for our consideration. (Surprisingly, my own name was one which had been submitted, and I quickly had it removed.) After long consideration, the committee almost surprised themselves when we came to a unanimous decision to recommend Robert Neff, Old Testament Professor at Bethany Seminary. The General Board was even more surprised. We could read the surprise on their faces. Then we began to hear comments, on what a great choice that was, and Bob became our new General Secretary.

As the time for conference approached, I prepared a tentative moderator's address. I preached it to the Black Rock congregation, asking them for any comments for suggestions. It would be their sermon too. Two or three valuable suggestions came, and I made use of them. I felt led to make the message both a "state-of-the-church" review and a challenge to service with Christ.

With the coming of June 18, 1977, and the beginning of Standing Committee meetings, I expected to feel nervous and unsure. Certainly people would discover that they had made a poor choice for moderator! I had none of those feelings. My feeling was one of being almost bathed in the prayers of the Brethren, not because it was Charles Bieber, but because of the widespread respect for the moderatorship. I felt as if God was literally carrying me in His arms. My own calm confidence amazed me.

Standing Committee brought together delegates from all the districts, many of whom were old friends. Bill Eberly, conference secretary, was an old hand at his job; it was really Bill who led me through what might have been the wilds of newness. Ira Peters, Virginia layman, an executive with Shenandoah Power, was a supportive moderator-elect. Galen Heckman, pastor of the West Richmond Church, and Janet, gave strong local orientation and support. The agenda which would come before conference was the heaviest in decades; none since has been as heavy.

When the time came for my message on Tuesday evening, good friend Charles Lunkley prayed for the Spirit to guide and enable me. Members of the Black Rock Church sat in front to give me encouragement. Marla and Jim, by then having left Bethany and become pastors at Oklahoma City, were present with the very youngest conference attender, their nine-day-old son, Troy. I had given a copy of my message to a reviewer for the daily news sheet, and he had made a special effort to tell me, "That is the kind of message we need." I think it went well; after all, Black Rock had let me practice on them.

Another day was not only the continuing of conference business, but also our thirty-third wedding anniversary. I asked Mary Beth to lead in our opening prayer. When she had finished, I put my arm around her and announced that the day was our anniversary. I added, "These years with Mary Beth have been as sweet as could be. I want to share some of that sweetness with you." And the tellers distributed to all the delegates and as many as possible of other attenders, the thousand lollipops for which Galen Heckman had been my purchaser. How could the moment help adding to the calmness I felt? When I returned to my position after the noontime break, I found a HUGE all-day sucker awaiting me, with an anonymous note: "This compares with the lollipops you gave, as your job compares with ours." An additional boost came from the youth of the Huntsdale Church, who surprised me with the gift of a wall hanging, "Huntsdale Youth Love Charlie." And then, as a part of the worship service that evening, conference presented us with a bouquet of roses, and beloved balladeer Andy Murray sang an original song in our honor.

However, all was not gold and glory! As I have suggested, there was a very heavy agenda, and some of the items were laden with emotion. There was the matter of Marriage and Divorce, with the tensions of Biblical teachings versus societal practice and painful personal experience. There was the report of the Review and Evaluation Committee, a pentennial study of denominational organization and program. There was, "Ethical Teachings of Jesus in the Public Schools," less controversial but important enough to deserve and use a large block of time, and a simpler matter, "Christian Ethics and Law and Order." There were a whole series of polity statements developed by various General Board entities and meriting careful study and adoption by the delegate body.

At only one point was there a snag in parliamentary procedure. It could have come at any time, but I believe it came during the discussion of "Equality for Women in the Church of the Brethren." Remember that this was in 1977, and society had hardly begun to make the changes which would give to women their rightful status. *Roberts' Rules of Order* do not cover every situation except by granting leeway to the moderator or chairperson. One such situation developed and I made my declaration. There was a whole series of "points of order," asking for interpretation; I handled them in turn.

(Without all my prayer support, I would by then have become angry!!) Finally, I reiterated my decision, offered to allow the delegate body to challenge it, received no challenge, and went on.

In addition to these "unfinished business" items, there were reports from all the varied organizations related to and responsible to the conference, the time-consuming elections, and twelve new items of business, including seven queries. One of them (remember?) was that query on reinstatement of the elders body, from Missouri-Arkansas; it was returned.

One problem which had come to me from earlier conferences was that worship services were growing longer and longer and tended to include elements which would not adapt to congregational worship "back home." I strongly urged our worship committee to plan services which would continue to be meaningful, but would also be adaptable. They responded successfully. It felt good, in later weeks, to be able to use at Black Rock some of the same elements from conference worship experiences. The speakers, of course, could not be transported, but their messages could be summarized.

In addition to the moderator, speakers included Loren Bowman, soon to retire after his years as General Secretary; and Ruby Rhoades, former missionary to Ecuador and staff member for women's programs. The Friday evening service was "A Celebration of Joy," a glorious festival of music. (The idea, if not the actual singing groups, could be taken home.)

On Saturday evening, our speaker was Andrew Young, long time friend of the Brethren and kindred spirit, and a strong leader in the civil rights movement, then United States Ambassador to the United Nations. We welcomed him at the Richmond airport and awaited his message. I doubt if anyone else ever introduced him as I did, in this manner: "I could tell you about his great influence as a civil rights leader—but you already know that. I could tell you of his extensive education and myriad honors, but you already know about them. I could mention that his wife, Jean, was May Queen at Manchester College, but you've heard that before. I could speak of his important influence in government and his service to the country as ambassador to the United Nations, but that's old knowledge. Tonight I just want to introduce Andrew Young as our brother in Christ, whose message we eagerly await."

Whether because of the sheer weight of business or because I was not skilled at expediting it, we needed a late Saturday evening session to complete our work. Then came Sunday morning, with an inspiring message by Duane Ramsey, pastor of the Washington City Church of the Brethren. We made brass lapel pins of the theme for all who would commit themselves to serve Christ in a changing world. (A quarter century later, I still see those pins on occasion.) We participated in a moving service of laying-on-of-hands and prayer for new moderator Ira Peters and newly-elected moderator-elect Warren Groff. I turned over the gavel, which I had hardly used, to Ira.

It is worth mentioning, I think, that when the moderatorship ends, there is a sharp collapse. Very little attention was paid to the moderator just past, except that a great many kind persons wrote letters of appreciation. Among them, the one I prize the most came from Loren Bowman, from which I quote a few lines:

You were a very useful moderator for the church at this particular point in time. Your visits across the brotherhood and the candor with which you were able to discuss the issues and concerns of the members produced an open and positive attitude when we reached Richmond. Although there was a heavy docket of business—and some of the items became rather voluminous and complicated—the sessions were handled well and the people were able to express their judgments without undue pressure from the officers. So please accept my personal appreciation for your leadership and for the "positive mood" of the Richmond Conference.

Just let me close the conference saga with the note that we went to Chincoteague for some rest and relaxation, and I stopped shaving for a couple of months!

Vacation over and rested up, we were back home again. We had a farewell party for Ammon and Lucille, all of us tremendously grateful for the unstinting giving of themselves during their year of volunteer service to us. With the coming of August, the day came for Myron Miller and Doreen to be wed. It took place at the Black Rock Church, with the two fathers officiating. Doreen had been so active in the youth group that it seemed very appropriate to make the reception a carry-in meal, as had been done for Marla and Jim. Doreen gathered Queen Anne's Lace for the wedding bouquets. We provided a large variety of cheeses for the carry-in.

Chapter Thirty-Eight

FROM BLACK ROCK TO NORTHERN INDIANA

And then there was the request from Northern Indiana that we consider their need. Very reluctant, but not wanting to close our minds to a possible call from God, we agreed to a further interview. We sat down, first, with our own district executive, Stan Earhart. Always thoughtful and analytic, he did not give us advice, but succeeded in helping us to see what was involved. Principally, it would mean separation from the close congregational ties which we loved, but also it would be one of the important tasks of the denomination. We felt the call. It had to be a strong call, because Black Rock was so very special to us. The fact that Doreen and Myron were at Goshen College may have helped Mary Beth to be more positive. We announced our resignation from Black Rock, effective at the end of the year (1977).

Reluctantly, but feeling led, we took our leave from Black Rock, having enjoyed the joys of Christmas with them. We followed the truck from the Brethren Service Center as it proceeded merrily out the turnpike. As we approached Somerset, we also approached a snowstorm and found it a very nervous time to be on the highway. Once across the mountains, however, all was clear again and we arrived safely at the district parsonage in Nappanee, Indiana. Feeling that it was about time to build an equity in a home of our own, we intended to buy, so we settled in only partially. Much of our substance was stored in the garage, leaving room for only one of our two cars.

We had other things in mind. We had a long time longing to see the Rose Bowl game in Pasadena and the Rose Parade. We flew to Los Angeles, were met by Max and Loretta Baughman, and were graciously provided with the use of their VW Rabbit for the duration of our trip. Thanks to the help of Bob Earhart and his politician parishioner, we were able to get tickets for the game. We stayed with the Earharts. We found that the district youth had an annual all-night party in the Pasadena Church. They set up chairs along the parade route so that next morning we were able to view the exciting parade in comfort. It lived up to all our expectations!

Next, of course, was the football game. Parking was limited for that huge crowd. By the time we arrived they were shuttling drivers to an adjacent golf course. It did not have the kind of lane markings that are usual in parking areas. We were in a strange car and a strange place. Mary Beth and I oriented ourselves by sighting on some houses up the hill. Seated about as high up as we could be, we watched Michigan lose to Washington. We enjoyed it, although we would have had a better view of the game, as well as instant replays, on television. By the time we left the stadium, it was dark. We simply could not see the houses on which we had sighted. Would we ever find the Baughman car? Would we be the last ones there, wandering around at two o'clock in the morning in vain search? No, we wouldn't. Mary Beth's amazing sense of direction served her well.

Our pleasurable transition to Indiana completed, there was work to be done. Very soon I undertook my first pastoral placement process. On a quiet January evening I drove east a few miles along U.S. 6 to the Bethany Church of the Brethren. Two hours later, as I went to my car, I found that a heavy snowstorm had begun. When I arrived at the parsonage, enough snow had accumulated so that I could not ascend the small ramp to the garage. No matter. I could take care of it next morning. No, I couldn't.

Next morning the Rabbit would not jump. I let it roll down the ramp far enough so I could pull the other one around after I had shoveled the whole way. When I opened the hood, I found snow packed solid inside. I tried jumping the ignition. Nothing. I cleaned away as much of the snow as I could. I tried jumping the ignition from a more powerful car. I called the garage. It sounded, they said, as if the packed snow may have thrown the timing off. I would have to tow it to the service station. Next morning I got in the car, informed it: "This is your last chance. If you don't start now, you go to the doctor." Stern words worked. It started immediately, but it did leave me aware of the potential interruptions which lake-effect snow could cause.

As I resumed my work in the district office, ably guided and assisted by Anita Metzler, Mary Beth took up her personal assignment—for the benefit of both of us—of finding a house we liked and could afford. Houses were less expensive in Indiana than back at Hummelstown, but sale of our house there helped our eventual purchase. Having visited a dozen or more homes, only two of which were attractive enough so she wanted me to see them, we settled on a lovely home on Goshen's Main Street, just a block from the college. With its picture windows, one fronting the street and one at the side, its finished basement, the trees which shaded it, and the large yard, it easily took Mary Beth's heart, and I easily followed. We bought our first home for $35,000 and moved to Goshen in July 1978.

By that time, Marla and Jim had accepted a call to the Rock Run Church, just a few miles east of Goshen. (In spite of their strenuous efforts, the church in Oklahoma City did not survive. Their influence, however, led two men to accept a call to the ministry.) They settled with Troy into a very nice parsonage across from the church.

Bonnie came from Minnesota to spend a few days with them. Doreen and Myron were at the college. We decided to have a picnic at the park in Milford as a kind of housewarming outside the house. As it happened, Bonnie had to leave. Marla and Jim were counseling at Camp Mack, also at Milford, but they could get away for lunch. The Millers could come. We decided to go ahead with the picnic. When we got out of our car at the park and started to carry food to the table, we were startled and thrilled by persons appearing from behind the massive trees—Larry and Nancy, with Diana and Alisa. Dale and Judy with Kirsten. Bonnie, who hadn't flown off after all and, of course, the Millers and Abes. It was the best housewarming we ever had!!!

Chapter Thirty-Nine

THE DISTRICT MINISTER

Carroll (Kaydo) Petre, who had been a missionary in Nigeria after we left there and was then the executive for South Central Indiana, taught me the ropes of my new job. Possibly the most visible aspect of the job was the placement of pastors—not by direct assignment but by bringing congregations and pastors together until they recognized compatibility. The ministry office in Elgin provided us with profiles of pastors open to a call and congregations seeking. There were always more congregations needing a pastor than pastors seeking. Besides, often as many as a third of the pastors on the list did not really belong in the ministry. There were also women and a few minority persons on the list, and most congregations were reluctant to consider them.

I have long had a high opinion of women in ministry. It likely began with Anna Mow, whose speaking, writing, and committed Christian personality made her one of the denomination's oustanding leaders. It was nourished by the work of missionary teachers and nurses. I was (perhaps with bias) impressed by Marla's work. If there was the least opportunity, I included women among pastoral candidates which I presented to search committees.

My memory does not provide even one search committee whose first response was positive. The common response was, "Oh, our congregation would not want a woman."

My speech to them went something like this: "It takes more courage and character for a woman to accept God's call to ministry these days than it does a man. For that reason alone, there may be better woman pastors available right now than men. Ten years down the road, when women are more common, that won't be true, but just now it is. Besides, these women have a hard time getting intreviews. Why don't you just give this one a break? You won't have any commitment to her and you can't lose anything except your time and the relatively small cost of bringing her here."

Almost invariably, the committee would agree to invite some woman. Without exception, the results were that when they met the woman and perceived her skill and commitment, they recommended her, and the congregation accepted. Some of the exchanges during the interviews are illustrative:

Question: "You are only a single woman. How could you handle counseling with couples planning to be married?"

Answer: "That should not be a problem; priests have been doing it for years!"

Question: "There are probably some people in our congregation who would find it hard to have a woman minister? How would you respond?"

Answer: "If they are looking for a male body, I don't have it. If they must hear a male voice, I can't provide it. But if they are looking for someone who has heard and answered the call of Jesus, I will be there."

On two occasions, the woman candidate declined to go farther with the search committee. During my nine years in Indiana, I helped in the placement of sixteen women. I also helped to place three minority persons.

Let me go a little farther by describing some of what was involved in being a district minister. Central, as I have implied, was pastoral placement. The process required the district minister to write an evaluation of each congregation and each pastor. In order to do that with integrity, I needed to experience worship in various places and hear various preachers. (When we joined the Goshen Church of the Brethren, the moderator observed that we were becoming members, but folks wouldn't see us very often.) Because I was expected to be involved in decisions by the commissions on ministry, witness, and stewardship, I tried to hone those skills, but even more I tried to make use of the skills of others. (Anita Metzler carried Nurture/Christian Education responsibilities.)

In addition to meetings located within the district, it was important that I attend meetings of the Indiana Council of Churches, the local ministerium, the three annual meetings of the denominational General Board, Annual Conference, and meetings of the Council of District Executives. Participating in the human resources committee, then known as the nominating committee, I needed to know as much as possible about as many people across the state. I was the one to whom pastoral or congregational problems came first. The district provided scholarship help to their students at Bethany, so I visited with them at intervals. That also gave me an opportunity to meet Bethany seniors, some of whom might fit our pastoral vacancies. Apparently I fooled enough people into thinking I was doing the job well, because when the six years of my original contract expired, they asked me to stay on. At age sixty-four, in 1983, I agreed. When I became eligible for social security, I accepted only the social security salary limit, plus some small annuities.

It was also important to have sharp tools for the job, so I continued to take advantage of professional growth opportunities. Annually the Bethel Temple in South Bend had an Institute on Judaism for Gentile religious workers. I found it to be very meaningful. I was particularly impressed by the New Testament knowledge of the lecturers, and by the prayers in the Hebrew hymnal. The Johns Hopkins Institute on Ministry to the Sick was also a valued annual affair. Often I stayed with Black Rock friends or, later, with the Grimleys. And then there was the Forum, open-to-all, which originated at Oaklawn, a Mennonite mental health center. And then there was the annual State Pastors Conference in Indianapolis and frequent special events for district executives. But let's get back to the work.

In a very real sense, search committees became my congregations. God guided us into compatible arrangements, but with a few exceptions. The search committee from one large congregation met four candidates. Each one was presented with information as open and complete as I was able to provide. On the basis of that information, there was not a large difference among the candidates. All the interviews went well. In one case, however, when the moment came for the candidate to ask questions of the committee, he asked, "Would each of you tell me, please, how you have seen God at work in your life in the past two weeks?" They were deeply impressed by that question, and in that moment I could see their mood swing toward him. They recommended him and he was called by a large majority. In little more than a year, however, it became clear that it was not a match. When he declined to resign, a vote was taken and he was dismissed.

And then there was the committee which met with me to discuss the process by which they would find a pastor. When we came to the place where I told them I would be with them in their interviews, they said, "We don't think we want you in our interviews."

I said, "It will be important for me to be there to ensure that all the questions are asked that need to be asked." It happened that I was the speaker for their midweek service that evening, and apparently what I said was compatible with their faith, for they agreed that I would share in their interviews. They called a man. They were so pleased with the way he began that they took Mary Beth and me out to dinner one evening. Even though it transpired after only a few months that he simply did not fit their congregation, they still welcomed my help in seeking his successor.

Their next interview was with a young man from Idaho; he and his wife were doing well in their responses. Then one of the three men asked, "Would you be willing to preach a sermon on wearing the covering?" "Well, to be honest," he said, "we did not follow that practice closely in Idaho, and I am not very familiar with it. But if you will help me, I would be willing to preach on it."

When we left the room, we visited the church fellowship hall, where a mother-and-daughter banquet was being prepared. To our surprise, hats hung from the ceiling. In that church where the women were all required to wear no hat but the covering and its bonnet, the decor was hats. They hung down all around the ceiling.

In two situations, I presented to the search committee a man who had been divorced. The idea was foreign to me, and I was negative. Yet as I met the men, I came to believe they were meant to be shepherds of Christ's flock. In both cases the divorce had come, according to my perception, by the wife's disinclination to be a minister's wife. The minister was driven to decide between Christ and the wife. It was a painful decision, and took months of personal doubt before being resolved.

Personally convinced of Christ's approval, I developed a pattern. I presented the candidate to a search committee without mentioning the divorce. When it seemed clear that they knew the candidate as a called person, I asked the candidate to review his marriage history. The result was the decision to recommend the candidate to the congregation. There we followed the same procedure. I particularly remember the second of the two. After the congregation had expressed a strong call, one good lady came to me. She objected, "You made me do something I said I would never do."

"What was that?" I asked, innocently.

"You made me vote for a divorced person to be our pastor." In both cases, I am pleased to report, the men proved to be faithful leaders, were loved by their people, and are still in the ministry today.

In March 1978, I fulfilled an assignment I had accepted several months earlier—to provide leadership for the Pennsylvania Men's Retreat. The fourteenth annual retreat had kept pace with the renewed perceptions of the time and become a retreat for both men and women. As I read the list of very distinguished persons who had provided leadership in preceding years, I felt humbled and uncertain. I remembered, however, that God's strength could be manifest in my weakness, and I went ahead with four different messages. Nancy Faus, coming into her own both as a musician and a leader of worship, was invaluable in opening our minds to the presence of God.

The Bieber family was making its own changes. They had discovered in their surprise housewarming for us that they really liked being together. From then on, each Thanksgiving weekend that busy group of people reserved time to enjoy that togetherness. Meanwhile, the family was growing. The Brown-Biebers presented us with our second grandson, Ben, in March 1979.

Bonnie had been single long enough, and when she and Dan Corcoran found each other, we were delighted to have their wedding out of doors beside Goshen's stream.

It was May 25, 1980. Dale and Judy had by then moved from Rochester and Dale's residency there, and Dale had begun a new practice at Fredericksburg, Pennsylvania.

At Bonnie's wedding they introduced us to the two children they were adopting, Twyla, aged nine, and Damond, aged seven. Then in July 1980, Joel presented himself to the Abe family. It is truly miraculous how love keeps expanding!

Mary Beth and I had been in Europe on several occasions, but we had never been to Scandinavia and had never seen the famous passion play at Oberammergau. When good friends Earl and Vivian Ziegler planned a tour, we decided to join them, despite my pride in having planned all our former trips without tour guides. I was pleasantly surprised to find I was very comfortable with a tour group. We enjoyed thoroughly the natural beauty of Norway; the snowy mountains; the narrow, serpentine roads; and the mountain-sheltered fiords. We also appreciated the unusual, wooden beauty of many of the church houses. When our bus driver took us on a small detour, we were thrilled by a sizable herd of reindeer. Although we enjoyed the Swiss Alps in 1959, Norway is the most beautiful of the European countries I have visited.

Our trip took us briefly into Sweden, then into Denmark, the home of Hans Christian Anderson (and, shh, Danny Kaye), the quiet beauty of the lonely mermaid, the more exuberant beauty of Tivoli Gardens, and even the small cemeteries carefully laid out (pun intended) in small garden plots. We arrived by train in West Berlin. It was still the period of the cold war, but we were able to cross through Check-point Charlie after careful inspection to visit in East Berlin. Sadly, the Berlin wall was still there and in some places we could read rebellious graffiti.

And then, Oberammergau. We appreciated the opportunity to stay in the home of two of the characters in the passion play; most of the citizens of Oberammergau are involved in one way or another. I do not have the words to describe how moving was the dramatization of the last days of our Lord. I will say only that it was bluntly and boldly done and stayed close to the Biblical record. One thing which surprised and impressed me was the amount of choral music. I do not know the composer, but it was the kind of strong, vigorous music that I associate with Wagner.

The play is produced out-of-doors, and we would have been exposed to rain had there been any. During one intermission, a bee found his way to Mary Beth and stung her, despite my opinion that bees don't sting flowers. She is allergic to bee stings, so I hastened to a nearby apothecary and obtained anti-histamine for her. My nurse experience had to do me some good!

Back to Goshen and Nappanee and to work again. One disappointment came in connection with the placement of Jim and Marla. Although they were few, the number of persons who did not appreciate their ministry was very vocal. It became very clear that there were a few women in the congregation who felt that a woman pastor was competition to them. They accused me of having used undue influence. I invited the district discipleship and reconciliation committee to work with them, but in vain. At my request, Olden Mitchell replaced me in the pastoral placement process. He was very favorably impressed with Jim and Marla, and when they left in 1980, he gave them a strong commendation. They found not the least difficulty in finding a congregation where they could continue to serve, and were actually invited to consider each of the four congregations where they interviewed.

The committee which had originally interviewed me for their district minister had informed me of considerable conflict in their congregations. I did, indeed, spend an inordinate amount of time working at reconciliation. Several of the congregations were afflicted. On the surface it would appear to be a conflict between pastor and people. Closer examination and review would confirm that the conflict was between groups within the church, one very well pleased with the pastor, one very negative. The differences may have been decades long! I urged each congregation to adopt a position description for their pastor, so they could more objectively evaluate him or her. One good farmer raised a question with me. "Doesn't the pastor know his job? I am a dairy farmer. I know my job. I don't need a job description."

"There is a big difference between you and a pastor," I told him. "All of your cows want the same thing at the same time. But people within a congregation want all kinds of things at all kinds of times." I think he got the point.

The need for job descriptions was affirmed by the variety of complaints which came concerning a pastor. Almost always there were defenders as well as complainers. This pastor and spouse did not seem to know how to care for their children. That pastor simply did not have any substance to his sermons. This pastor did very little visiting, spending much time just loafing about town. This pastor frightened some members into thinking he was too charismatic when he had an anointing service as a part of the worship. In some other congregations, this was a regular practice. I do not honestly know how successful I was in helping the congregations through those kinds of differences. In two of the instances I tended to agree with the critics, but was adamant in insisting that members come to agreement. I absolutely refused to allow "votes of confidence." Such a vote, I felt, let the minority rule. A two-thirds vote would have been required for approval, which meant that one third of the congregation could dismiss a pastor. Instead, I urged the pastor to resign. If it was successful, it was probably because I was more stubborn and dared to assume authority I did not really have.

I remember two different congregations in which the pastor felt some negative vibrations. In both cases, we took a kind of straw vote, and in both cases the pastor was strongly affirmed. Still, there were negative votes and criticism. In the one congregation, the pastor said, "They don't like me," though there were only a very few strong criticisms, so he resigned. In the other, the pastor said, "Neither Jesus nor Paul pleased everybody," and stayed on successfully.

In two other instances, the problem was the reaction of the pastor to his predecessor. One pastor kept complaining about interference by the former pastor who lived in the town but did not attend that church. I was firmly convinced that there was no interference, only some lack of self-confidence by the new shepherd. In the other case, the new pastor said, "I have a lot to learn from his experience after twenty-five years. I hope he won't mind my calling on him for help."

My own practice has always been to absent myself from a congregation when I left it. For Mary Beth, that is an impossibility. Her love for people simply does not allow her to say any permanent good-byes to living people. She has kept up correspondence and/or telephone connection with dozens of former parishioners, but never in a pastoral way. Still, I was pleased to accept an invitation from the Black Rock Church to hold a five-day series of pre-Easter meetings with them in 1982.

With the shortage of qualified pastors which I have described, it seemed to me that special efforts should be made to recruit persons for the ministry. My own experience—considering a call to the ministry only when my pastor suggested it—made me believe persons might be helped by a nudge. As I visited in congregations of Northern Indiana, I would seek opportunities to ask persons, "Is there anyone in this congregation that seems to have the commitment to Christ and the leadership abilities to be a minister?"—or a similar question.

Often I was given a name. I would then write a personal letter, telling the individual, "Persons in your congregation think you should be listening for God's call to the ministry. Would you be willing to talk with me about it?"

Olden Mitchell and I also developed a monthly class in lay ministry. We followed what was known as the Three Year Reading Program, but emphasized that it was for any one who wanted to learn about serving in the church. I was delighted by the large number of persons who responded to that class and to the call to ministry. In the nine years I was in the district, we licensed seventy-nine persons to the ministry. We celebrated each year with a "Church Vocations Dinner," to which we invited persons who appeared to have ministerial potential, as well as the new licensees. Almost all who were licensed, eventually were ordained, both men and women.

Because I was not a congregational pastor, I missed many of the pastoral services I enjoyed: weddings, baptisms, infant dedications, leading Love Feast. I did perform the wedding ceremony for one pastoral couple whose wedding day was our own anniversary. There were also three Love Feast experiences. One took place when one of my Hanoverdale kids, Eileen Herr, was a student at Manchester. The Brethren students asked me to lead them in a Love Feast. They made the arrangements for feetwashing; I provided the elements. The fellowship meal? Well, that was made up of whatever snacks the students happened to have in their rooms and brought to the service. I thought it was beautifully appropriate. The second was a

Love Feast which Kaydo Petre and I arranged for Brethren students and their invited friends at Purdue University.

The third took place as a result of the interest of Myron's dad, Mahlon Miller, and some others to experience a Brethren Love Feast. It was held at the Mennonite Seminary, and I was careful to give what Brethren understand to be the Biblical basis for the service. The participants expressed appreciation. I am aware that some Mennonite groups do practice feetwashing, but I do not believe our worship that day, though well received, was a very strong influence toward change.

Chapter Forty

TRAVEL, TRAUMA, AND TRIUMPH

Marla had been in Costa Rica during her senior year in high school. Both Myron and Doreen had spent time there in Goshen College's program for third-world experience. In June 1982, the Abes and Millers went with us for an eighteen-day visit in that beautiful country, with our one-time exchange student, Jeanette, and her family. By no means an affluent family, they were certainly affluent in their hospitality. Our group split into three different homes most of the time we were there. I recall an all-day boat trip arranged with an Arce relative to a nearby sandy island where we picnicked and where we met our first iguana. I remember a train ride through the banana orchards and the coffee groves. I remember walking with the Millers in the lushly beautiful rain forests of Monteverde, helped by the Quaker community centered there.

I remember being advised not to flush the toilet paper, lest the sewage system be clogged. Wrap it in newspaper and eventually burn it. I remember the beautiful seaside town of Limon, where we enjoyed a picnic in a natural park. I remember the soldiers at the airport inviting us to take their picture. In Nigeria in those days, picture-taking was strictly limited. (It happened while we were in Costa Rica that President Reagan offered two war planes to the Costa Rican president. They were refused. Costa Rica is a peaceful country. Some years later their President Arias received the Nobel Peace Prize.) It was a great trip. Can you tell?

When Myron graduated from Goshen, he took a job for a while, giving Doreen a chance to catch up. When he was accepted at University of Illinois Medical School, Doreen laid aside her plans to be a doctor and went into a social work plan. When summer and her internship in social work came, it came clear that was not where she belonged. Reading Myron's medical texts reawakened her long time interest in medicine. She decided to take the entrance exam, laying out a "Gideon fleece." (Don't know what that is? Look it up in Judges 6:36-40). If she was accepted, God approved. If not, she would find another road. Her fleece was wet when supposedly dry, dry when supposedly wet. She followed Myron into medical school.

The Millers wanted to start their family. They reasoned that Doreen could take a leave of six months during her last year and still finish with her class. Pregnant, she went to Lancaster as a learner to work with Larry. She had hardly begun when symptoms of toxemia appeared, and she rushed back to Peoria and the doctor's care. A sonogram revealed she was carrying twins. When the first pregnancy is with twins, toxemia very frequently results. She would need to do almost nothing, spend a great deal of time in bed, and eventually be hospitalized. Five months went by and she was admitted to St. Francis Hospital and full bed rest.

Mary Beth and I had long planned a rail trip to Florida, and we decided to carry through. Near the end of the trip, on December 9, we were visiting my Uncle Harold and Aunt Patty in Fort Myers. How was the mother-to-be getting on? Mary Beth called St. Francis Hospital.

"Oh, Mrs. Miller was transferred to the Methodist Hospital," Peoria's location for premature births. We reached her room at Methodist and the phone was picked up by a roommate.

"Well, I don't know. They took her out several hours ago and she isn't back from recovery yet?"

Aware that the pregnancy had been preserved barely past the most dangerous miscarriage time, we had a whole series of questions. Had the twins arrived or had it been possible to postpone delivery? If they had arrived, were they all right? Had it been a natural birth or a Caesarean? Above all, how was Doreen doing? And could we even find out? Had we given Myron the correct phone number for the Fort Myers Biebers? Finding it almost impossible to be patient, we prayed and hoped. We decided to wait for four hours, then call again. Doreen answered, obviously very weak. The twins had been delivered by Caesarean, Rebekah weighing two pounds and ten ounces, and Amaris at only one pound and fourteen ounces. Still having serious breathing problems, they were in neonatal intensive care. Doreen was very weak, but recovering and with a strong sense of hope.

Trip aborted, we flew home. As soon as we could, we planned a trip to Peoria—actually suburban Morton, where the parental Millers lived. Both of our cars were off the road, so we rented a car. A friend took us to the rental agency. On the way back to Goshen, I was running through a snowstorm—brief, I hoped. Not brief. Next morning we awakened to the worst snowstorm of the year. Churches were closed. Police wanted people to stay home. There we were, desperately wanting to see our new, tiny granddaugters, and with a rental car we could not use. About noon, I thought I heard a possible opening. I called the State Police. Would it be possible to reach the Indiana toll road? Would it be open west? There was one ramp entry open, and the toll road was open, though it was slippery and great caution was advised.

We started out. I knew how nervous Mary Beth was on slippery roads and how the trip could be spoiled by her repeated cautions and my repeated rebuffs. I resolved NOT to respond to any fear. On that whole six-hour journey, she did not express even one fear, although she did report how many tractor trailers—103—had slid off the highway. We arrived at the senior Millers' home, were welcomed, saw that Doreen seemed to be progressing well, heard full descriptions of the birth and current status of the twins, and relaxed. Relaxed? Well, the temperature in the wood fire warmed room was eighty-four, and Mary Beth sat there shivering vigorously. The tension of the trip finally caught up.

Next morning we were taken to the hospital and saw our new twin granddaughters. It would be dishonest to say that they were beautiful, even though beauty is in the eye of the beholder. The fact that they were there was most beautiful, and the loving God who was still protecting them was most beautiful. Tubes here, tubes there, Myron or Doreen taking opportunity to hold one or the other, softly caress, and form those essential bonds. Eventually—years later, it seemed, but short months in fact, Rebekah, then Amaris came home. With monitors attached to protect against crib death syndrome and with gentle loving care (Mary Beth also learned the procedures and helped), they gained slowly but surely. And then, they truly became beautiful.

Graduation came for Doreen. Myron had Rebekah and Amaris there in a basket. As the capped and gowned new doctors were greeting folks afterward, Doreen took the twins and carried them around. "What beautiful babies!" people would comment. "Whose are they?"

"Mine," came the response, with a happy grin.

The next big event for the Bieber family came in June 1984, when our five families invited friends to celebrate our fortieth wedding anniversary. The big event was preceded by four days of family reunion—every one of our family present—at Camp Mack's new Wampler Retreat Center.

Then our kids did a great job at the New Paris Church of the Brethren. Mary Beth counted 140 guests at the open house, including seven good friends who had traveled all the way from Black Rock. Our pastor, Phyllis Carter, led us in a service in which we renewed our wedding vows, and our five children renewed their vows with us. A Miller-Abe quartet sang, "O Jesus, We Have Promised."

That old married couple was the center of attraction, of course, but tiny, smiley Rebekah and Amaris were a close second. Decorations featured flowers, balloons, and Mary Beth's wedding dress. (No, friend, I did not hang my wedding suit there, nor was there a second wedding night.) The day after the open house, we drove to Carbondale, Illinois, for Annual Conference.

Two of the sad events during my tenure in Northern Indiana were the closing of two congregations. The idea is to plant new churches, not close them! One was the Auburn Church located in the town where the Auburn car had been made famous. The congregation, a mission point of Cedar Creek, had begun to meet in 1914 and had been in their own building since 1917. It never grew beyond fifty or sixty members, and by 1980, it was made up almost entirely of elderly persons. In 1982, with an average attendance of less than a dozen, they made the wise but painful decision to disorganize. Brent Driver, a licensed minister who served part time, led them in a love feast as their closing service. The South Bend City Church, by then known as South Bend Second, made serious efforts to meet the needs of central city for more than eighty years. In spite of carefully planned programs to reach the changing ethnic community in which it was located, it became necessary to close its doors in 1984.

My extended service in Northern Indiana was coming to an end. I must say again that departure is the worst aspect of pastoral service; I think a piece of my heart was left behind in each place where God allowed me to serve. Northern Indiana is no exception: English Prairie, known for its mushroom production and its popcorn fields; Little Pine, kept serving by the sheer energy of Tom and Anne Clark and Janet Ryman; Wawaka, discovering the special quality of woman ministers; Blue River, traditionally Brethren conservative with genuine concern for people; Pleasant Chapel, with beautiful people in the most beautiful spot in the district; and Pine Creek, daring to build anew—and with success—when attendance was dwindling. Busy churches in South Bend, Goshen, Fort Wayne, and persistent churches like Turkey Creek and Union. Faithful to their Lord enough to influence new persons to hear God's call to ministry. And on. . . .

Chapter Forty-One

FROM DISTRICT MINISTER TO LOCAL PASTOR

They said farewell to us in September 1986 with a special celebration of our years with them and the gift of an Amana Radarange, a result of my frequent comment that I would like to use one. By then Ron Finney, who had been teacher of the year for the state a few years earlier, had heard God's call to ministry and was serving well as associate secretary. We sold our loved home in Goshen and moved to the Mingo parsonage in Montgomery County, Pennsylvania—the twenty-fourth home in which we have lived.

Anticipating our move, I had been corresponding with Earl Ziegler, district executive for Atlantic Northeast, which included Pennsylvania east of the Susquehanna River. I let him know that we would be available for interim service on a part-time basis for an indefinite period, preferably in a congregation struggling to deal with some differences. We met with the Mingo search committee. Possibly the location appealed to us more than anything, because it was just two miles from the Royersford Church, where Mary Beth had grown up. Although that close, they had been in two different districts. Our interview went well. We negotiated a part-time schedule with specific days and hours and the appropriate part-time salary. Still under seventy years of age, I would have been penalized by too large an earning.

One thing Earl forgot until after I had left the meeting was vacation time. Then he observed that since I was on half-time I should take half a vacation. When the chatter came up later, I pointed out that if I were to take a half-time vacation, it would really be only one-fourth vacation. I said, "Why don't we just leave it that if I need a vacation I will let you know." They agreed with that unusual arrangement. It was my full intention to be at Mingo for only a year, but in the light of pastoral shortage and the fact that I was still in good health, I was willing to stay on. They asked us to stay, and we did—for nearly six years.

When we had lived in the Eastern District earlier on, I had never been nominated for anything. Now I was nominated for District Board and was elected, eventually to become board chair. It was while I was chair of the board that Earl Ziegler resigned to return to pastoral duties, and we called Allen Hansell to be the new executive. Also during that period, I was elected to an Annual Conference Committee of three, to review and possibly rewrite the world mission philosophy of the Brethren. When we came to conference with our report, we became the only conference committee in history whose report did not come to the floor. We had taken a bold step, suggesting, "As the Father has sent me, so I send you," as a more appropriate, universal, and timely basis for mission than the usual, "Go into all the world and preach the gospel." The motion which came to the floor, without our having a chance to give our rationale, was to dismiss the committee and name a new one. It passed. I still believe, however, that John 20:21 is a far more inclusive directive from Jesus than Matthew 28:19, 20. No matter. The conference action still rankles a little.

Aware that Mingo had strong differences of opinion about their preceding pastor, I determined to surpass my agreed-upon assignment of three and one-half days per week, to pay absolutely no attention to complaints from the past, and to proceed as if I had full authority from God. Although I consider myself to be conservative in theology, I was reasonably certain that Mingo leadership was more conservative than I. They likely needed lessons in joining Biblical and leaning liberal.

Years before, a funeral director in Manchester, Maryland, had presented to local pastors a collection of one artist's portrayals of the twelve apostles. For a few of them there is little more in the Bible or ancient writings than the names. Yet I was able to preach a series of sermons on the apostles and distribute copies of their "portraits." The series was so well received that I determined to do others—the Ten Commandments; the Beatitudes, and the prophet, Amos.

I also developed a newsletter, producing bulletin and newsletter myself. It was while we were at Mingo that I bought my first computer and printer and began to learn its operation. My skills are even yet very limited and confined almost completely to word processing. With a congregation of only a few more than a hundred, it was easy to do the visitation, even in half time.

There were some changes that Mingo needed to make, as it seemed to me. One had to do with their insistence on trine immersion. Early Brethren polity had required that any person who had not experienced trine immersion baptism, wishing to transfer to a Brethren congregation, must be properly baptized. About 1967, Annual Conference had approved receiving any Christians, regardless of their type of baptism, if the congregation wished to do so. Mingo had not wished to do so. I proposed to them that they receive members from any Christian denomination, teaching them the Biblical basis for trine immersion but not requiring it. They balked. I asked some questions. "Do you think Brethren are the only ones who will get to heaven?"

"No, of course not."

"Do you think God will accept Lutherans and Methodists even though they were not properly baptized?"

"Well, yes."

"But you won't accept them at Mingo unless they are re-baptized?"

"No, we won't."

"Oh, then it must be easier to get into heaven than into the Mingo Church of the Brethren!"

"Oh, we never thought of it that way before."

They revised their membership requirements.

Practice of Love Feast brought some plus and some minus from my own perspective. The plus came in an unusual cooperation with the local Lutheran Church. The wife of our board chair was Lutheran, and they alternated in attendance at worship. She appreciated the Love Feast and told her pastor about it.

"Would they let my catechism class take Love Feast with them?" he asked. We would. There was a small deterrent; the young ladies would be required to wear the prayer covering. No problem. After a brief explanation of their meaning, prayer coverings were lent, and the young ladies wore them.

The minus came in the physical arrangements for Love Feast. It was set up with tables at one side for the males, on the other side for the females, and one set apart for two deacons and the pastor. It was improper, I felt, to make three seem more important than all the rest. I spoke to the chair of the deacons. I told him how improper it seemed to me to set three persons apart. Could we not all sit together (albeit gender-divided)?

No problem, I was assured. Came Love Feast time. I was there early to ensure arrangements were complete. The small table had again been set aside for the three of us.

"That is the table I do not want there," I remonstrated.

"Well, I talked with the deacons and they wanted it there," he explained. I was angry.

"You can go to the deacons," I said, "and tell them they will need to get someone else to lead the Love Feast. I can no longer do it with that kind of separation of the family."

God wouldn't let me act that way. God calmed me down. This was to be a Love Feast. "Wait a moment," I said. "Let me talk to them."

I went to the deacons and raised my concern. The small table was removed. After the service several deacons came to me and expressed their appreciation for the new setting. I had serious doubts, which I kept to myself until now, that the deacon chair had ever brought the matter up.

We tried other services at Mingo. We had a "Popcorn Service" and a catacomb communion, which we had at Black Rock and which I have described. One couple refused to come because the communion did not include feetwashing and the fellowship meal. Later, it would become a regular practice to have two "bread-and-cup" communion services each year, but that couple always stayed away on those Sundays.

By the time we moved to Royersford, our annual family Thanksgiving reunion had also moved. We tried one year at Akron, then we made use of the Northern Ohio District Camp at Inspiration Hills. From the very beginning, our reunions included preparing our own meals, playing table games, reading, and, very early, volleyball.

At Inspiration Hills we added bedtime stories for the children. Years before, on our freighter trips to Nigeria, I had begun making up stories for our children, usually animal stories with alliterative titles based on the town we were near. Now I had a chance again to make up stories, this time for grandchildren. Others, however, shared the talent and the story telling.

With three families in Pennsylvania, we decided to move our reunion as well. A site was discovered in the Poconos on what was known as "God's Mountain," which served us for three years. Volleyball there was still being played out-of-doors and occasionally was played with snow on the ground.

Chapter Forty-Two

VISITS TO ZAMBIA

Myron and Doreen had long been planning to serve as missionaries. They made contact with several mission boards, including the Brethren and Mennonites, and in 1987 accepted a call to serve with the Brethren in Christ Mission in Zambia. Our earliest news from Zambia reported that just as they were preparing to leave the capital, Lusaka, to proceed to their station at Macha, Myron was struck by a car and suffered multiple fractures of his leg. Settling in and orientation would rest largely on Doreen, aided by loads of prayers.

For the first time, Mary Beth and I could appreciate what it had meant to our parents to see their children and grandchildren leave for long periods. We missed the Millers, all five of them, desperately. Our homesickness weakened us so badly that we caught a new-to-us disease called wanderlust. Our stateside progeny aggravated the condition. At our Millerless reunion at Thanksgiving time, the other four families presented us with a one-way ticket to Zambia. What a great bunch! Their gift card read, "We think they would benefit by a period when their hearts and heads are on the same continent. We love you."

We were pleased when in January 1988, Dale joined the annual work camp in Nigeria. I had frequently wondered: "Does our children's love for Nigeria stem from their own experience or simply reflect what they see in us?" Dale's action, as well as that of Larry and Nancy on medical assignment a few years earlier, made us feel that their love was their own.

Easter at Mingo in 1988 was a joyous time, including 5:00 a.m. caroling by twenty-four singers at twenty homes. A week later, we returned to Black Rock to celebrate with them one of the Sundays of their 250th anniversary celebration, rushing from the fellowship meal to the Philadelphia Airport. Our safari began as we flew to Lusaka, Zambia. Our Zambia Air flight from London, we were surprised to discover, had been rescheduled for two days later, but we were able to book a flight on another airline and arrived at Lusaka only an hour late.

Zambia, which had been part of Cecil Rhodes' vast land holding at first known as Rhodesia, had also been a British colony, so the language we met, though accented, was usually not a problem. Nervous because of flight changes, we were especially relieved—and overjoyed—to see Doreen and Charis enter through the back door of the customs shed, followed by Rebekah and Amaris and Carolyn Horst. When we went through customs, we encountered only a small delay. All of our luggage was opened, but the young lady only threatened: "We won't charge you anything this time, but the next time you come we will get you!" After a day or so at Lusaka, we traveled to the central mission station at Macha.

Myron, meanwhile, was back in the States. When his broken leg refused to heal, he had returned there for treatment. Apparently a small sliver of bone had wedged in the place where knitting should have occurred and prevented the knitting. It was clear that God had chosen the time for our visit, so we could help in their home while Doreen was carrying an extra load.

For the first week or so, we just enjoyed being grandparents to curly-headed one-and-one-half-year-old Charis and the lovable twins. I wonder if Charis still remembers that her kneecap is her patella. Maybe a week after we arrived, as we were sleeping on mattresses in the living room, Mary Beth's bladder awakened her. Hearing someone in the twins' room, she spoke and scared away a thief who had invaded the home. We were also scared but grateful that no one was hurt and nothing lost.

The Brethren in Christ began their work in Zambia (then Rhodesia) early in the century, I think about 1910. Macha, where Millers were stationed, was their largest station. It included evangelism, schools, and the well-equipped hospital. Doreen and Myron (even with his broken leg) worked in the hospital where about a fourth of their patients were afflicted with AIDS. Doreen was also teaching Amaris and Rebekah in a schoolroom that was already set up and in use for other children. They seemed well adjusted to their new location. It was not essential that they learn the local language, but they did, feeling that it would help them to feel closer to the people and would be useful in out-village evangelism. They had begun evangelistic work in the hospital and found time to visit some nearby villages.

I was impressed by the excellent medical facilities at Macha, which compared favorably with those of the Brethren in Nigeria, and by the deep commitment of the missionaries. I was dismayed, however, by the fact that the Macha Church had been built of brick by American masons. Its fiberglass steeple had fallen and lay, unrepaired, nearby. One principle of our work in Nigeria had been for the Christian community to build their own church buildings. I was also puzzled by the fact that the church was only half full until I reflected that Zambia is far less densely populated than Nigeria.

We were blessed by the fact that our visit coincided in part with the annual gathering of missionaries at Macha. Myron arrived in time for most of the event with a screw-fastened steel rod in his leg and wearing a removable Velcro-fastened cast which allowed him more mobility. We enjoyed worship services and fun time. The best of those memories is of Rebekah and Amaris singing, "God's Still Working on Me," and "The Little Drummer Boy."

Our visit approached its ending too soon. We said goodbye to new friends, and rode in a new Toyota van on the bush roads to Choma, where we spent the night. The next day we went on to Livingstone, located across the Zambezi River from Zimbabwe. We were delayed at the border for two hours or so by what seemed to us to be an unwarranted need for security (first emigration, then immigration), but finally crossed the Zambezi into Victoria Falls, Zimbabwe.

Victoria Falls could be spelled t-o-u-r-i-s-t, but with good reason. Much of our stay was in a park-like motel. The motel had a strange clientele; five wild boars cavorted on the lawn outside our lodge rooms. It was outside that tourist town that we viewed the spectacular, powerful beauty of Victoria Falls. From high school days and the flood in Williamsport, I have been overwhelmed by the power of water, and cascades are my favorite natural sight. A life-sized statue of Livingstone greeted us as we approached the falls. Mary Beth, having been weakened by dysentery, decided to forgo the walk to the falls and viewed it from an airplane. It was also outside Victoria Falls that we enjoyed a game reserve where we were thrilled by the elephants. There, too, we bought carvings and lace tablecloths, after having watched the women doing their intricate crocheting.

Returning to Zambia with the same delay in crossing the border, we had another view of the falls, impressed this time by their extent rather than their height. With what natural beauty and power God has blessed us! Outside Livingstone we visited a Zambian game reserve, where we were particularly impressed by the fearlessness of giraffes with regard to automobile and human visitors. As we sat quietly in the car, giraffes came close to us, and one came very near to thrusting an investigative nose into the car. We also saw impala, zebra, baboons, and one hartebeest, but it was the giraffes that were best remembered.

We spent that night with a devoted Christian ranching family who had been in the area for two generations, raising steers, sheep, chickens, pigs, and fish. From there, we took off for Lusaka. Myron was still on crutches, so the driving was up to Doreen and a missionary colleague. The van was full, with six adults, three children, and our luggage.

On the way, there occurred another of those unforgettable incidents. As we drove around a lengthy but sharp curve, another car attempted to pass us. They were going too fast to negotiate the curve. They jammed on their brakes, lost control, and went over a steep bank, turning over several times. The car was demolished. At least two passengers were badly hurt, one man with extensive cuts on face and forehead and a woman with a badly wrenched back. Myron, disabled, could not help. Doreen proceeded to the spot and did what she could which, lacking equipment, was temporary at best. We had thought our vehicle was already full, but we re-loaded, took on the two injured persons and a helper, and went on, sixty miles or so to Lusaka. The accident victims were bleeding, one in particular from a head wound which rendered him unconscious. With such high incidence of AIDS, the blood caused extra concern, but for the victims to receive quick care and possibly even to live, they had to reach the hospital in Lusaka. We made room, somehow, and delivered them. I have a vague memory that one of the nurses remembered Myron from his own accident some months earlier.

After we had left them at the hospital, we went to a rest home which the Mennonite Central Committee maintained in Lusaka, and Doreen, as carefully and thoroughly as possible, cleaned the blood from the car. We found a fairly modern accommodation at the Ridgeway Hotel, a good meal and comfortable beds to close that long and eventful day.

Too soon, it was time for us to return home. Seeing Doreen and Myron and the girls in their missionary home made it easier for us to picture them in their activities and be confident of their happiness, but there would still be emptiness. The next evening we said our tearful good-byes at the airport, leaving those loved ones to serve God in Zambia while we returned to serve stateside. How good that God is with us wherever we serve!

Back at Mingo, plans had already been announced and invitations issued to all the congregation for an "Adventure Weekend," a Friday evening through Sunday program of personal spiritual involvement and excitement. It would be less than two weeks after our return and would take hours of preparation by pastor and congregational leaders. Meanwhile, for us, there was another adventure. We were able to invite Dale to report on his experience in the Nigeria work camp. Always a good speaker, he taught our adult Sunday school classes, with enthusiastic response.

This would seem an appropriate spot for an important interlude. Through the years, Mary Beth and I have continued to love Juniata College. Not only did we make annual gifts; not only did we influence two of our children to matriculate there, but we attended alumni gatherings, participated in promotional efforts, and stayed in contact with Juniata friends. I had been overwhelmed when, in 1977, I was awarded the "Juniata College National Alumni Association Achievement Award." It is also worth repeating that I have never been a seeker for office. Yet I had long buried one secret longing which I never really expected to be fulfilled: to be a member of the board of trustees at Juniata. In the fall of 1987, the college nominated me and the Atlantic Northeast District Conference elected me, to a three-year term as trustee, representing the district. Almost a year later, on September 1, 1988, I became a trustee. I attended all the meetings, participated in committee planning, and rubbed elbows with outstanding people for three years. To be quite honest about it, however, I made very little meaningful contribution to the important decisions the board was making.

As a trustee, I was also a member of the Juniata Church-College Council, on which I served for more than nine years. It was the purpose of the council to promote good relationships between the college and the Church of the Brethren and also to strengthen all church connections with the college. At its founding in 1876, Juniata had been closely related to the Brethren, but through the decades, the connection had eroded and was now more tangential than actual. Still, it was at Juniata that I had met the Brethren, and I was delighted to work at re-developing that relationship. For two years, 1995 to 1997, I would serve as council president. In 1997, I was honored with the Church-College Service Award.

Interlude over, we were back at Mingo. We re-entered our work there with renewed vigor. We had already joined in their annual spring retreat at Camp Swatara, a weekend which included inspiration, fellowship, and the hard work of thoroughly scrubbing the camp swimming pool. (We also took advantage of the delicious nut-rolls which the ladies made to help finance the retreat.) I had begun in 1986 to participate in the ten-kilometer Crop Walk, a practice I continued for ten years, even when at Ephrata it grew to a ten-mile walk.

We helped develop two important relationships with other congregations. One was with the Royersford Church of the Brethren. We began looking for things to do together as two groups of Brethren with only two miles between them. Along with Larry Wolfgang, Royersford pastor, we carried through each June a joint Sunday service in a Royersford park and a picnic together. The second was with the Royersford Lutheran Church, whose sharing in our Love Feast I have described above. The gift they gave to us in exchange was to visit our Sunday School on several occasions with their delightful clown ministry. They also contributed when, at Earl Rarich's death later on, we launched a fund drive to place an illuminated sign in front of the Mingo Church in his memory.

"Passing on the Promise," a process for improving evangelistic outreach, swept across the denomination in 1988 and 1989. Mingo decided to take part in the process, led by Pastor John Hess of the neighboring Skippack congregation as coordinator. I was also a coordinator, thoroughly enjoying my work with the Springfield Church of the Brethren. I was very sure that none of them remembered, but that had been one of the congregations I visited in 1949. I had been hoping for interim pastoral work while awaiting our move to Nigeria.

The Mingo congregation, after many years of holding fast to tradition, seemed very open to new ideas. I remember a number of what were, for them, innovations: the catacomb communion which I have mentioned; gathering clothing, preparing food, and going to Philadelphia monthly to assist the Germantown Church in caring for the homeless; a pictorial church directory; the beginnings of a ministry to prisoners involving the provision of Lydia Kits for women prisoners, and correspondence with three different men in prison; "Bring a Friend" Sunday, an effort to build upon the statistic that most people begin to worship in a given congregation as a result of invitations by friends or relatives; and the use of a Christmas greeting tree on which members placed their greeting to all the others and then contributed the "savings" to some worthwhile project.

Along with the part-time pastoral work, I also had opportunity for two spiritual emphasis meetings a year; I taught a course in mission philosophy in the Keystone Bible Institute, and I provided the leadership for Women's Camp in 1990. We also continued to attend Annual Conference each year.

Dale's work-camp experience awakened a nostalgia and a desire that his family also have Nigeria experience. He was able to obtain an appointment to teach pediatrics at the University of Maiduguri, one of the important institutions of the north. Maiduguri is the capital of Bornu Province and the location of the first real city congregation of the Church of the Brethren in Nigeria. Located there, the family could be involved in the largest Church of the Brethren in the world, and all four children—Kirsten, Twyla, Damond, and Benjamin—could attend Hillcrest School. At the same time, Dale was able frequently to visit in areas where we had lived, and provide assistance in the Rural Health Program.

At the same time, our reports of our visit to the Millers in Zambia awakened some excited interest in Bonnie. The possibility of visiting Millers again, along with Bonnie, and coming home by way of Nigeria to visit the Brown-Biebers, led to our plans. We set the time, arranged with a travel agent for flight plans, and left it to him to secure the necessary visas. They would be no problem, he assured us. He was half right. Zambia visas were readily granted. Three days before we were due to leave, the travel agent informed us he had been unable to secure visas for Nigeria. We learned that he simply had not followed the correct procedures, one of which was to have an official invitation from Nigerians.

Our itinerary was to take us first to London, then to Lusaka. Leaving Zambia, we would go to London, then to Kano, Nigeria, back to London, and home. We tried in Zambia for a Nigeria visa. No luck. We tried in London and were informed, "There is no way you can get a visa." The uncertainty of a Nigeria stop would not detract in the least from our thorough enjoyment of the Millers.

First, Zambia. For Mary Beth and me, it was primarily the sheer joy of being with the Millers, enriched by seeing Bonnie's enjoyment. Charis remembered her "patella." Amaris and Rebekah were relaxed schoolgirls. Myron was getting around well, having had a year of healing and strengthening on his leg. Doreen was seven months more pregnant than when we had left her. With both doctors sharing in the hospital work, the load was not as terribly heavy as it had been for Doreen alone.

We were able to greet other missionaries as old friends. We were able to spend time visiting in the hospital, and even visiting in the secondary school. We made one trip with Doreen to an outvillage where the pastor was guiding his people in the erection of a new church building. We accepted invitations to meals in the homes of several of the staff. And we repeated our vacation itinerary to Livingstone and Victoria Falls. We were able to visit a Botswanian game reserve, where the elephants at one point were close enough to frighten the little girls. We liked a presentation of Zimbabwean music and dancing which would not have qualified for Kennedy Center, but was still very entertaining. We indulged in some high-class restaurant eating in Lusaka. We were undisturbed by any dreadful accidents on our journey. We headed off to London, pleased to think that about two-thirds of the three-year commitment of the Millers was now past and carrying video films which would bring them back in memory. Our whole trip was made much better by Bonnie's presence.

Aware that we might not be able to make the Nigeria arm of our trip, Mary Beth had remembered some childhood friends who had relatives in London. With their help, we were able to arrange very comfortable bed-and-breakfast accommodations. We enjoyed visiting rural England for three days, particularly viewing the sheep on a dozen hills and seeing some very-much-like-Stonehenge monuments. When we went to Gatwick to take the plane home, we discovered an interesting phenomenon. One can take more free luggage into England than from England! As a result, we were considerably overweight and had to pay excess baggage charges. Fortunately, we discovered we could pay by credit card, else we might still be there!

Chapter Forty-Three

FROM MINGO TO EPHRATA

As September approached in 1989, my seventieth birthday also approached. As it happened, Mary Beth's nephew, Doug Hershberger, was marrying Leasie Esbenshade on the same weekend as my birthday. Aware of Mary Beth's love of surprises, and knowing that all of our stateside families would be at the wedding, I was quite certain that a "surprise" would be planned. The most logical time was obviously Sunday at Mingo. A week or so in advance, I called my sister, Mae.

"They are having a surprise party for me next Sunday," I told her. "I want you and as many of your kids as possible to be there."

"Oh, yes!" responded Mae. "They did invite me and I told them I'd be there."

So it was definitely not a surprise, but I put on my surprise act when, sitting behind the pulpit at Mingo, I watched the front seats fill with family. The way they handled it was, however, full of surprise. I was ordered to sit with the congregation. Jim and Marla took over the service, he leading, she to preach. Dale played the organ and sang. Bonnie read scripture. Larry prayed. Wow! The service was followed by a dinner in the church basement, and my seventieth had been duly celebrated.

Annual Conference in 1991 was scheduled for Portland, Oregon. We contacted good friends John and Mildred Grimley. Would they be going to conference? Would they be interested in a trip to Hawaii afterward? When they gave positive answers to both questions, we went ahead with plans. Our own travel cost was halved by my accumulated mileage. Our flight across the Pacific took us to Honolulu, capital of Hawaii, on the island of Oahu.

Warm, comfortable, beautiful Hawaii. Mennonite Travel Service had found for us a bed-and-breakfast with a young Mennonite family. It was on a hillside giving us a good view of the city and easy access. We walked along the shores of Waikiki and appreciated the beach front, but we did not go swimming. We motored to Diamond Head State Park, from which there were fantastic views of the island and the ocean. We enjoyed the Polynesian Cultural Center so much that we made two trips to it. There were multiple displays—a drama of Polynesian history carried out in native canoes, craftsmanship, the undulating dances with expressive use of hands and arms as well as legs and feet. The evening trip to P. C. C. took us to a beautiful shoreside restaurant with delicious Polynesian cuisine; with our experience of Nigerian foods, we were game for any kind of food. There was fresh fruit, especially delicious pineapple. We visited pineapple farms. Discovering that there is strong Mormon influence in Hawaii, we visited a Latter Day Saints tabernacle, obviously not the one in Salt Lake City to which Gentiles are not admitted.

The state of Hawaii, we were reminded, consists of a number of islands, of which five are inhabited. Oahu is the most heavily populated island and is the most touristic. Molokai had for us the attraction of being the site of a historical leprosy mission, but we did not visit there. Maui is the luxury island; its facilities were much too expensive for our pocketbooks, and the attractions there did not draw us. Lanai is the smallest, and we did visit there for a day to catch some of the feel of a less touristic island. Hawaii itself, known as the large island, provided the most beautiful scenery.

We landed at Hilo, county seat of Hawaii county and an important commercial center, and found our motel there. We rented a car and on our only Sunday looked for a place to join in worship. We passed a Presbyterian Church, kept looking, and finally returned there. We were a few moments late, and as we went in we heard the pastor instruct the people to "Greet and welcome each other." Several folks welcomed us as a result of that admonition. In spite of the vigorous welcome moments and the sign outside claiming that this was the friendliest church in town, we were all impressed by the fact that when the service was over not one person spoke to us. We invited the pastor's attention to that lack. (As a matter of fact, people on Hawaiian streets were more friendly than the people at that church.)

Taking advantage of Mary Beth's love of driving, we circled the big island. I was thrilled by the large number of waterfalls, some of them quite large; falls are my favorite natural wonder. We were also impressed by the volcanic scenery, Mauna Loa, Mauna Kea, and, particularly, Kilauea. When we learned that one of the Kilauea volcanoes was even then in active eruption, John and Mildred and I joined those walking toward the seashore where the eruption could be seen. It was hard walking, about two miles over jagged volcanic rocks with the utmost care required. But I did get near enough to shore to see the red-hot lava pouring out, feel the heat, and realize afresh how the islands had been formed.

I have three other memories of our journey. Our motel was near the ocean. We walked to the shore and the two ladies waded briefly, but we were impressed by the rocky, rough, no-fun-swimming nature of the Pacific shore. Mildred and I discovered the delicious quality of Kona coffee; sadly, it is too expensive for us poor folks to indulge. During some of our chats during the trip, we learned that the Grimleys were buying a double-wide mobile home at Ephrata, into which they would move when they closed their pastorate in the fall.

Therein lies another tale. One of the ways in which I continuously teased Mary Beth when she talked about moving into Brethren Village, the retirement facility at Neffsville, was to suggest that we live in a mobile home. When she would demur, I would respond by suggesting she go ahead to the Village and I would live in a mobile home, and she could visit me sometimes. By late spring 1991, when I announced to the Mingo congregation our plan to retire, I had stopped that teasing. In early fall, Melody Rupel, who lived in the Ephrata suburb of Akron, invited former missionary colleagues to an open house for her parents, Mary and Ivan Eikenberry. John and Mildred Grimley were there. I was unable to enjoy that rich fellowship. As the afternoon drew to a close, Mildred invited folks to go with them to see the mobile home into which they would shortly be moving. When Mary Beth left the Grimley home-to-be, she noticed a sign announcing an open house next door.

"It was like a St. Paul style light came on," she reported afterward. Two days later, on our way to Akron, Ohio, to visit the Abes, we visited the open house. Mary Beth fell for it. She, who never agreed to my helpful suggestion that we live in a mobile home, decided that would be where we should live. On the way home from Abes, we bought that bright and roomy mobile home and lived there for the next six and a half years.

We moved in December 1991. Aware of the shortage of pastors and especially the reluctance of pastoral families to move in wintertime, I agreed, if Mingo wished, to commute until after Easter 1992. Mingo agreed. They rented the parsonage to the Royersford pastor. I used a small corner of the basement. I drove down Saturday night or Sunday morning and went back to Ephrata Tuesday or Wednesday, finally closing my service at Mingo on May 1. As was true in all our pastorates, we left good friends, brothers and sisters, behind and moving was sweet sorrow.

For the next two months, we visited nearby congregations. I felt strongly attracted to the Middle Creek Church of the Brethren, served by a group of self-supported ministers with whom I felt strong kinship. God had a different idea. Albert Sauls, whom I knew as the chair of the district board and who had served as pastor at Ephrata for thirteen years, had given a full year of notice that he would retire at the end of August 1992. A search committee was in place, but no successor had been found. The Ministry and Evangelism Committee invited me to an interview in early July, and Mary Beth and I accepted. As a result of the interview we agreed to accept a call to be their interim pastor for six months if the church board would extend such a call. The church board at that time included about sixty persons, but only seven were present for their special August meeting. We accepted the unanimous call and began our service on September 1. Not until that day did I actually make a tour of inspection and discover what tremendous facilities there were.

I was not aware when we accepted the call that Ephrata was the largest congregation in the district and one of the largest in the denomination. We recognized a real need, were favorably impressed by the committee members, recognized some real similarities to Black Rock, which we had loved, enjoyed being in service and, of course, welcomed the income. As I began, however, I insisted that they expect me to serve as a permanent pastor, even though I would be there for only six months. I would not simply be filling in time. The six months went on and on and on; pastor and congregation joked often about it.

The interim lasted exactly four years. My own frequent explanation has been that I work slowly, so it took me four years to get the six months finished. Actually, the interim itself lasted twenty months. In April 1994, District Executive Albert Hansell, in a letter to the congregation, recommended that they "name Charlie as pastor."

At a special council on May 1, Moderator Darvin Boyd commented, "They have not sought nor are they seeking a longer tenure at our church, but they have willingly agreed to continue to serve until another pastor is found."

The vote was ninety-eight percent favorable; I became Ephrata's "regular" pastor. The delay in finding their regular pastor was due to two factors. For one thing, there were relatively few well-qualified pastors and even fewer with a desire to move. For another thing, the search committee had become psychologically committed to one particular person who kept delaying a final response to their interest.

Meanwhile, I had set about trying to achieve some personal goals for the congregation. My first responsibility (indeed, that of every interim pastor) was to provide a comfortable transition from a long term, beloved pastor to a nearly unknown newcomer. And then, as I reflected on what I knew of the Ephrata congregation, it seemed important to help them be more closely related; in such large groups intimacy is almost always in short supply. I also wanted to help them to grow spiritually and to extend their vision outside the local front. And after they had heard good preaching for thirteen years from the same pastor, I wanted to provide them with a wide variety of sermons—another way of helping them to prepare for someone whose preaching might be quite different.

My priority was to draw the congregation closer together. The church records gave me a path. When I examined the records, I was impressed with how carefully they had been kept and how complete they seemed to be. There were birth dates, marriage dates, family data, dates and means of becoming members at Ephrata, and the like.

Very early in my pastorate I began to write personal letters to all the members on the anniversary of their having become members at Ephrata, and inviting their recommitment to Christ. It was such a simple idea that I was amazed by its enthusiastic response. Also in the interest of intimacy, but also because I love babies, I made it a point to visit in the home of each new baby and then to invite members of their family to join us at the dedication of parents and their little ones. I cannot resist recording the fact that I never had a child cry for me when I took one in my arms at those dedication services. I boastfully credited my calming personality until some kind friend suggested that the poor kids may simply have been scared out of voice!

Chapter Forty-Four

GOLDEN WEDDING ANNIVERSARY

1994 was the year of our golden wedding anniversary. Mary Beth—with my support had often observed that she wanted a "big bash." Together with our family and some of the church members, we planned for the celebration in the fellowship hall of the church on Saturday, June 18, a few days before the anniversary date (June 24), for obvious reasons. Early that week, Dale called with the welcome news that Ben was receiving some kind of an award. He was an outstanding student, and it was easy to believe that he would get an award. There would be an awards banquet at a nearby restaurant on Friday evening. Could we come? We could. We went to the Brown-Bieber house and Dale drove us to the restaurant. We went in the front entrance, asked where the awards banquet was being held, and were directed to the banquet rooms.

Are you surprised? We were! There were no awards being granted. Instead, we entered a banquet room peopled with family and friends. It was a complete SURPRISE! All of the family were there, along with the Grimleys, Xinia Tobias, Lucille Meyers, and likely someone I can't recall. We exclaimed, hugged, thanked, had pictures taken, and prepared to sit down to the banquet. Larry began looking around, said, "I thought there was someone else here." He opened a door at the side of the room and out walked Karagama, our dearly loved Nigerian "son." It would have been utterly impossible for the family to present us with a more welcome gift than his being brought over for a two-week visit. The first week of it he spent with our family, then flew to Kansas for the wedding of the Elliots' daughter, and then to Annual Conference.

On Saturday the fellowship hall had been carefully arranged and decorated with the special help of Joanne Phillips. There was no need for us to stand at the door in a receiving line. We wandered about at will, sometimes together, sometimes not. Granddaughters received and welcomed persons. Off at one corner was a continuous showing of old Nigeria movies, without sound. That great family of ours provided several sequences of entertainment, with music, reminiscences, a poetic "history" by Dale, and a prose, somewhat fictionalized history by Marla. We were overwhelmed by the persons who came. They were not only local folks like Ephrata members, but beloved missionary colleagues, members from congregations we had served, childhood friends, nursing school and college mates, and relatives. That which we enjoyed most, without question, was showing off our family, fifty years of proud accumulation. The prized gift was a scrapbook of letters and greetings, beautifully calligraphed by Diana.

The two cakes which had been provided were not completely consumed on Saturday, and we had a Sunday postscript after worship services, when our family joined us again and added their own loving post-script.

Then it was off to conference in Wichita, where in 1976 I had been moderator-elect. Even though good friend Earl Ziegler was moderator in 1994, it was necessary for us to leave conference a day early in order to join the Mennonite-Your-Way tour to Alaska, our second (third? fourth? twentieth? continuous?) honeymoon. We flew from Harrisburg to Chicago to Vancouver to Anchorage.

Mary Beth's diary of the trip, typed up later, took eight and one-half pages. It seems inappropriate for that long a report here, so let me just list enough items to give a flavor and evoke some nostalgia. There were a variety of overnight accommodations, from a small semi-primitive room to a suite with kitchen (fridge, microwave, stove, coffee makings), bathroom with jacuzzi, kingsize bed with tall metal fittings, and two television sets.

—Scenery: broad vistas; an amazing variety and quantity of flowers; Portage, Mendenhall, Glacier bay and other glaciers; Denali—Mt. McKinley; mountains and valleys; the Alaska oil pipeline.

—Worship: with the Prince of Peace Mennonite Fellowship in Anchorage, with fellow passengers sharing faith or faith experiences on several occasions.

—Food: too much and in great, often unfamiliar variety; Alaskan lox; salmon; haddock; biscuits and gravy; Chinese cuisine; baked Alaska; rich desserts including, one evening, a "Dutch chocolate extravaganza"; sandwiches and snacks; a great variety of fresh fruits even to bananas, mangoes, and papaya; served on bus, on train, on ship, in restaurants, in our rooms.

—Wildlife: We saw dahl sheep, caribou, moose, golden eagles, salmon leaping up a "ladder" to reach their spawning spot, black bear, brown bear, bison, elk, muledeer, sea otters, hump-backed whales.

—Transportation: planes, domed trains, buses, a coach with articulated lounge for games or refreshments, small ships and cruise liners, riverboats, and one train which found its way along the very edge of the mountainside with valley FAR below.

—People: Leon and Nancy Stauffer were superb tour guides; passengers were very compatible; workers along the way were always friendly; coach drivers and hostesses were superior; one local guide was a young man from Souderton.

—Experiences: seeing Denali twice; enjoying an Indian village; learning about dog sleds from the first woman to win the Iditarod; watching a Russian dance routine; laughing at a stand-up comedian with tour jokes; stomping our feet to the music of an expert pianist playing, among other things, "Rhapsody in Blue"; movies for entertainment and for enlightenment; phone conversation with Carol Diehl, one of Bonnie's college roommates; sharing the embarrassment of one driver of an articulated coach whose vehicle got hung up and needed considerable expertise to be released; full days with no darkness (four hours of twilight). One experience deserves special mention. In Juneau on the last leg of our journey, we were walking to find a recommended restaurant. We heard voices behind us. "Yes, that IS the Biebers!" Turning around, we found Ron and Marge Hendricks on the first leg of their trip. Ron had been a fourth grade pupil of Mary Beth in Harleysville. We dined together.

—Locations: Vancouver, Anchorage, Denali Park, Fairbanks, Beaver Valley and White-horse in Yukon Territory, Frazer, Skagway, Juneau, Glacier Bay, Sitka.

It was not easy to leave Alaska behind us, though we returned home weary. Nor was it easy to get back into the routines and non-routines of the pastoral ministry. Still, August is not a difficult month in the church, and things went smoothly. I took some liberties not expected of a pastor: I met with the search committee, partly to suggest some names and partly to advise them to accept a negative response from a candidate as being final.

We were also looking forward to a very special event planned and developed by ABC, the Association of Brethren Caregivers. It was the National Older Adults Conference and took place on the beautiful campus of Lake Junaluska in North Carolina. A bus was chartered which collected passengers at Brethren Village and made a one-day trip to North Carolina.

We arrived just as the dining room was getting ready to close after the evening meal, ate quickly but lightly, settled into our room in Lambert, and rode the shuttle down to the great auditorium. NOAC became, for many of us, an event superior to Annual Conference. It brought together some deep fellowship, some growing experiences, some inspirational worship, and a horde of memories, all without the necessity for carrying out intricate—or any—business items. ABC planned to have other conferences every three years, but the response of attenders was so enthusiastic that it became a biennial event.

There were special blessings in the congregation in 1994. Licensed minister John Snader was named Minister of Outreach. Mike Fletcher was newly licensed to the ministry. Fifty-three new members were received into the congregation. The congregation participated with the Foreign Study League in hosting Spanish high school students. We experienced our first "Bring-A-Friend Sunday." We continued our exchange relationship with the Brightside Baptist Church in Lancaster, with their excellent pastor, Lewis Butcher, preaching for us and I filling the pulpit for them. We attempted a Catacomb Communion service, with low attendance, but high appreciation.

Members of the congregation also became aware of some serious health problems for one young mother, Susan Kulp. She was afflicted with, among other things, TMJ, TemperoMandibularJoint, a deterioration of the jaw which made it impossible for her to open her mouth more than a half inch or so or to chew. Necessary treatment, corrective surgery, was available only in New Orleans. We began a fund drive which would involve benefit concerts, sales, luncheons, personal gifts, and an all-day auction and would continue until more than $75,000 was raised. The condition was not fully corrected, but there was enough improvement so she could at least eat soft foods.

The fall of 1995 brought other events. Akron Eastwood Church, where Jim and Marla were serving, had a surprise celebration of their twenty years since ordination. It was on a Saturday evening, and I had to preach at Ephrata next morning, but Dale came to the rescue. He flew me out, then flew me back home. We landed at the Lancaster Airport about one o'clock on a cold morning. He took off, and I went to my car. I found a locked gate in the way.

The only way to the car was to climb the five foot—seemed like ten—chainlink fence, so I did. My heart pounding, I could barely unlock the car door and start the motor for warmth. I had been experienced some breathlessness with rapid or uphill walking and knew that could mean a heart problem. The thought ran through my head: "Who will find me here?" Slowly, strength returned, and I drove home. End of story? No. Wait.

It was a long-time practice of the district to recognize ministers who had been ordained for fifty years, and this was my year. John Grimley wrote the citation, which was flattering but welcome, and which was read and presented to me at district conference. That wasn't enough for the Ephrata Church. (I have never been quite sure whether their appreciation was for me as a pastor or for me as a gap-filler in their need for pastoral leadership.) It was impossible for them to surprise me with the celebrative service, but they did surprise me with the speakers. I heard kind expressions from John Grimley; from our Ephrata moderator, Darvin Boyd; and from the district executive, Allen Hansell. The preacher for the morning was Bob Neff, the president of Juniata College, and that was a surprise. I had been Bob's pastor when he was ordained. I had been on the search committee which called him to be the Executive Secretary of our denomination and had chaired the committee which called Al Hansell to his position. There were gifts and pictures, a beautiful plaque, and a meaningful bulletin cover produced by Mark Herr. At the dinner afterward, I reported my near-death episode.

Short weeks afterward, a light snow—about an inch covered the ground. Early in the morning, I took the snow shovel and with almost no effort was pushing the snow off the driveway. I felt dizzy, so I stopped and found my way into the house. Nauseated, I crept into the bathroom. I simply could not get up, and I had almost no voice. I wriggled my way to our bedroom door, rapped, called as well as I could, crept to the sofa and managed to get into it. You've recognized it: this healthy specimen of virile manhood was having a heart attack. We need no further details. Akron ambulance with CPR arrived; I was taken to St. Joseph Hospital. I had since boyhood, been aware of a weak aortic valve; now it was so diseased that it required open heart surgery. We scheduled it for a few days later, when Larry would be back from one of his trips. My miserable valve was replaced with that of a healthy, but obviously deceased, cow. Five days in the hospital, a month of limited activity, and I was moooving normally again. Deep gratitude to God, to the surgeon, and to the excellent hospital care, which was skillful, firm, and gentle.

Chapter Forty-Five

FROM EPHRATA TO CHINA

We had planned to make a trip to Australia and New Zealand in early 1996, but my heart problems prevented it. I was feeling fine, but it wasn't until Dr. Zadeh, reviewing my sonogram, predicted another twenty years for me that I really picked up my ministry again. One event that bears reporting: John Snader was leading in the consecration of several parents and their infants. I was standing with one unmarried mother, just to show my support for her. When John took the first child in his arms, he —the baby, not John—began to squall loudly. That seemed to awaken all the others, and soon we had a male choir of infant voices. John handled it with both nervousness and relaxation. Looking toward me, he asked, "Charlie, why doesn't this happen to you?"

It must have been in late January that another interesting episode intruded into our lives. A telephone call came from someone in Albuquerque, New Mexico.

"Are you Charles Bieber?"

I confessed.

"Is your address . . .?" and they repeated it.

Again, I confessed.

"Thank you. We have mail for you."

A few days later, the mail came. Two letters from a finance company, both of them addressed to Charles R. Bieber, were enclosed in an envelope addressed simply to Charles Bieber. I marked them missent, put them in an envelope, and returned them to the return address on the original envelope.

A week or so later, a note came from Transamerica Financial Services, stating, among other things, "We have transferred your account to our Lancaster office."

Looking up their Lancaster office, I telephoned.

"This is Charles Bieber," I boasted. "I want to report a miracle."

"What kind of miracle?" they wondered.

"I have a letter stating that my account has been transferred to your office. That is a miracle, because I do not have an account with you."

Stammered expressions of thanks.

End of story. No. There's more. Telephone calls came.

One of them asked me, "Is this Charles Bieber?"

I admitted it.

"Do you have a woman living with you whose name is Ruth who is not your wife?"

"No, Ma'am," I replied. "It is obvious that I am not the person you are looking for. He is Charles R., I am Charles M., and have been that for more than seventy-five years."

End of story. No. A few days later a registered letter to Ruth Bieber appeared in our box.

Mary Beth handed it back to the mailman. "This doesn't belong to me."

There were no more letters, but telephone calls kept coming. Finally, I got fed up.

Answering one of those calls, I said words like these: "I am Charles M. Bieber. I am not the person you are looking for, and I have repeatedly told you that. I am tired of your harassment. The next time I hear from you, you will hear from my lawyer."

End of story. I wonder what ever happened to that other Charles and his live-in Ruth.

In preparation for Easter, I wrote a dialogue between the late-believing Thomas and the deeply committed Mary Magdalene of their meeting on the first Easter morning. Delores Neuber and I acted the parts, and it was our Easter Sunday message. It was one of the variety of sermons I had promised myself as a way of preparing the congregation for a different pastor. Among them were a series of sermons: Amos, Jonah, the Ten Commandments with banners, the Beatitudes, the twelve apostles with one artist's depiction of how they may have looked. There were monologue sermons in which I spoke as Judas or as a self-righteous Pharisee. There were dialogues in which each of us helped the other to interpret the scriptures. There were times when the sermon was introduced with a brief skit. There were times when I would close my sermon with an invitation, patterned after my brother George: "You have always sung, 'Jesus Loves Me.' Do you believe it?" During my last summer as Ephrata's pastor, I preached a series on the "Door" references in the scriptures with a door standing on the platform. Some of them went well, some of them not; so what else is new?

In May 1996, our family welcomed a new addition. Kirsten was wed to Darryl Reinford in a lovely ceremony at Camp Swatara; it was my privilege to be the officiating minister with help from Darryl's grandfather. The Reinfords, both students at Eastern Mennonite University, returned there for their next two years and their eventual graduation with honors.

As summer approached, the church's pastoral search committee reported that they were ready to present a candidate. When the date approached for his being considered by the congregation, Mary Beth and I wrote to them, inviting them to have lunch with us so we could answer any pastor-to-pastor questions they had about the Ephrata congregation. We met. We conversed. They did not ask even one question about the church; their one and only topic of conversation was themselves, as if they had to sell themselves to us. The congregation met them, were impressed, issued them a call, and on the first Sunday of September, he was to assume the pastorate. We did not vote for him.

I reflected on my four years of ministry at Ephrata. What, after all, had God enabled me to do? I listed things in my mind: personal birthday letters inviting recommitment to Christ; a purposeful name for the newsletter, *The Upward Call*; family involvement in child dedication services; catacomb communion; variety of sermon styles; inclusion in the directory of married women's maiden names; several articles monthly for the newsletter; a fresh awareness of overseas missions, especially Nigeria; (One anonymous note to me asked if I didn't know anything but Nigeria, since I used so many Nigeria stories.); a pastoral team involving Mark Herr, Christ Arndt, John Snader, and Mike Fletcher; sharing of opportunities to baptize new believers, especially that Mark Herr, with responsibility for youth, would baptize the youth; two congregational spiritual retreats; a successful $75,000 campaign to assist Susan Kulp; financial stability—the treasury went from a $17,000 shortage to more than $40,000 surplus; and receiving nearly 150 new members. God had been good to us.

My last message as a pastor emphasized the fact that we are all co-workers with God. Both with me and with any newcomer, we would want to let God be in charge as we worked together. The congregation, who had done so many things for us, gave us a farewell picnic. I wore a badge which asked, "Have you hugged your retired minister today?" which had been given to their pensioners by the Brethren Benefit Trust. Those hundreds of hugs still squeeze my heart.

Time doesn't stand still. The third NOAC —National Older Adults Conference—took place in early September, again at Junaluska, and again we were among the appreciative participants. In October, we took advantage of the excellent leadership provided by Earl and Vivian Ziegler, and joined the group that they were guiding on a sixteen-day trip to China.

Where do I go from here? This is an autobiography, not a travelogue. Yet it does seem appropriate to note at least some of the sights, observations, and experiences of that trip. They would seem to be personal enough to qualify.

Shanghai was our first China stop, from Philadelphia via Detroit and Norita (Japan), about twenty-two hours altogether. It is a city of thirteen million people, nine million bikes, and at least a trillion taxis, with modern high-rise buildings contrasted by tin-roofed shacks. We were impressed by the beautiful four-century-old Yu Yuan Gardens and by the jade factory, where we saw delicate, artistic carving in process. The highlight of Shanghai for most of us was the "Children's Palace," an old apartment building with a playground outside and arts and craft classes inside for children aged five to nine. I remember one concert by nine accordionists playing "Jingle Bells." On a one-day side trip by train, we visited Suzhou and its silk and embroidery establishment.

Much of the food we ate in China was served with nine or ten persons seated at a round table with a large Lazy Susan about three feet in diameter, in the center. One glass of water. Small cupsized bowl with ceramic spoon. One plate, saucer size. Forks by request. Food, usually nine or ten different kinds, served one after the other on the Lazy Susan, either twirled or passed on. Always rice, though served late. Almost always soup, usually egg-drop. Five to six kinds of meat; fish and Chinese vegetables. Sometimes hot-spiced, though usually not overly hot. It took less than two weeks to tire us of approximately the same daily dinner.

Enroute to the Shanghai airport to emplane for Beijing, we noted a line of taxicabs waiting, There must have been at least 500, perhaps a thousand, lined up for passengers at the airport. Then, by China Air, we reached the capital city, a metropolis of eleven million with eight million bicycles, and at least two hundred traffic miracles per day. The Temple of Heaven was a host of large Buddhas, with incense burners, candles, and a few devout worshipers. We visited the Imperial Palace and discovered we were in Tian An'Men Square, once a gate to the palace. A few years earlier, perhaps a million dissenters against communism had been killed here. There were huge buildings: museum, Parliament, Monument to the People's Heroes, and Mao's tomb, but wide open spaces now filled with Sunday crowds.

Out from Beijing, we were impressed by the Cloisonne Ware factory, where is made that beautiful pottery with base hammering, copper-wire intricately shaped, soldering, enamel filling and firing, polishing, and gilding. Then there was the Great Wall, its story remembered from grade school days. At Badaling, one of the reconstructed sections was open to tourists, and we climbed the wall (for me, 200-plus tiring steps, worse coming down than up).

The next city stop was Xi'an, ancient city, former capital. I remember being among those interested in visiting a Chinese hospital. As the doctor displayed items of native medicine, I noticed with amusement that among his books was the 1994 edition of the *Physicians Desk Reference*, of which I had a copy at home. At Xi'an came one of the most memorable moments of the tour. A few years earlier, farmers digging a well had come across pieces of clay (terra cotta) figures, which they simply discarded. Someone else saw them and realized they were part of a larger event. Eventually, about 3,000 of those terra cotta warriors were excavated, including horses, carriages, and groups of soldiers. They had been constructed at the order of Emperor Qin Shu Huang for his entombed protection. Hundreds have been restored and replaced in their original pits. When we entered "Pit No. 1" about 200 yards long and 100 yards wide, carefully roofed for preservation, we were startled to be confronted by a whole array of 800 warriors.

When we went by bus to Guilin, we viewed natural beauty in God's world, but we also passed extensive rice or corn fields being harvested by hand. One of my high moments came in the nearby Reed Flute Cave. In more or less the center of the cave, there is a very large chamber, including what appears to be a spring-fed pond. Our guide, leading us by flashlight, paused here, apparently waiting for a large group of people to move away from the pond.

Surprisingly, I thought I heard Christian music, vibrating like a keyboard or small accordion. I could see only silhouettes, but deep under ground in that pagan land, I heard one unnamed hymn, then, "What a Friend We Have in Jesus" and "The Old Rugged Cross." Of course God is everywhere, but hearing God's praise there made the Presence more vivid.

Now we went via Guangzhou (Canton) to Hongkong, a British city then about eight months from becoming Chinese. Traveling by train, we were warned that, a half hour before arrival the toilets would be locked.

Explanation: "They don't want to take our—somethings—into Hongkong." The forest of skyscrapers in that modern city was overwhelming! I also noted, as we awaited our bus from the train station, large advertisements for cigarettes, the death which the U.S. exports. With each ad, in LARGE letters, there was a warning against cancer.

One day when, having purchased a few stamps, I turned away from the philatelic window in one of Hongkong's two large post offices, I was met by a smallish gentlemen. With a slight accent, he observed, "You must be a stamp collector."

I admitted it.

"So am I," he said.

"Why don't we exchange?" So there began a five-year period of stamp exchange with Joseph Dumuk, then about to become president of the Philippines Rotary Club.

The only other Hongkong event I want to report is an expensive one. In our tours we had seen the "Jumbo Floating Restaurant," brilliantly lighted, brilliantly decorated, and, as it turned out, brilliantly priced. In addition to the pork and beef and rice served on the Lazy Susan, we were lent at least three different warm washcloths which kept us and our napkins clean. We were entertained by singing and dancing ladies. Cost: almost $40 each, but it was our farewell-to-China dinner.

As I was finishing the packing early next morning, Mary Beth noticed long lines of people on the streets below. Probably as many as 2,000 people were, we thought, waiting for buses. While we were wondering about what seemed a dreadful delay, a phone call came from Earl.

"Did you notice those long lines?"

We had. "What's going on? A bus drivers' strike, maybe?"

Earl explained. "A new stamp was issued today, and they are on their way to the post office, three blocks away."

Hongkong was honoring the woman who had won their only ever gold Olympic medal. (Sometime later, friend Dumuk sent me one of those stamps.)

Our last stop in that visit in the orient was at Bangkok, capital of Thailand, a rare country that has never been a colony, always free. The Orchid Farm was beautiful with its vast variety of orchids and orchid products, including delicate pins which were simply gilded orchid blossoms. The ride up and down the river in longtail canoes where we sat on cushions on the floor, was tiring even for a young man like me. The Rose Garden Resort provided delicious food plus traditional Thai entertainment. "The Grand Palace" proved to be not one, but thirty-three different pretentious structures, including the Temple of the Emerald Buddha. The buddha was far inside, hardly visible to a non-worshipper from outside the door.

I report one last incident. On the way to Bangkok Airport, Ms. Jim, our local guide, collected tickets and passports, our usual pattern, to facilitate the obtaining of boarding passes. When she returned to the bus and distributed passports and passes, Marianne's passport was missing. Every effort to locate it failed. Obviously it had been stolen. She was forced to remain in Bangkok (Vivian Ziegler stayed with her) while a new passport was issued. Four days late, the two ladies made it home.

It was a great trip, tremendously interesting, highly entertaining, very satisfying, and extremely wearing (walk, walk, walk, walk). The Zieglers are very good tour directors. We expressed our gratitude to God, then spent about a week to feel recovered and back to normal.

Chapter Forty-Six

STILL TRYING TO SERVE

Normal for us meant being free to visit neighboring congregations, which we did. We found inspiration and fellowship as we joined in worship with brothers and sisters from congregations both near and far. We found more time to visit relatives in the Williamsport area, in Delaware, and in Baltimore. We went to Florida for a few days in early 1997. Mary Beth, loving person that she is, looked up addresses of Bieber cousins in Florida. Two years earlier, that had led to a first, small Bieber reunion in Florida. The cousins enjoyed it so much that they met again in 1996, and in '97, we were able to join them. Returning from there, I had one of the dwindling number of evangelistic meetings, enjoying fellowship with the nearby Cocalico Church of the Brethren.

For me, however, other tasks were looming. 1999 would bring the celebration of the centennial of the Ephrata Church of the Brethren, and I agreed to serve on the planning committee. Among other things, I volunteered to arrange the dates with our pastor, and to be responsible for inviting, as many as possible, former pastors and ministers who had been called by the Ephrata Church to preach during our anniversary year. The committee also decided there should be a history of the congregation. They asked me to do it. I declined, respectfully, I hope. They seemed not to have heard my refusal. At the next meeting they asked what progress I had made. None. They reiterated that a history was essential and that I was the one to do it. Adamantly, I again indicated my unwillingness.

Still, they were right; a history would be important. I enjoyed writing, having been well taught in English and journalism by my high school teacher, Miriam Wendle. I had even been an editor, and nearly a hundred of my articles had been published. Perhaps I should try. But where does one begin? Were there old minutes? There were. The historical file contained the minute books from the very beginning, all handwritten, sometimes faded, not easy reading, but with a great deal of information. I read them carefully. At first it was simply a matter of interest and exploration. Perhaps I could at least write a series of articles for our newsletter.

Then I came to the report of a fire in the church, even as plans were under way to build a new church. Careful studies led to the decision to build at a new, more spacious location. A site was purchased. In September 1970, a groundbreaking service was celebrated. Building would begin. It wouldn't! A day or two after the groundbreaking, the church received an injunction forbidding them to begin building. A lawsuit had been instituted claiming certain deed restrictions on the title of the new site.

When the fire occurred in February 1971, the suit had not yet been settled. The disastrous fire ruined the sanctuary of the old church building. Studies were reinstituted. Was the fire God's way of telling the congregation to stay where they were? Should they rebuild on the same site? There would already be considerable cost to repair the fire damage, essential to an eventual sale of the building. Would the suit be settled soon; would the decision allow building on the new site? Sentiment was strong in favor of going ahead as soon as possible, whenever that would be. Refurbishing the old was done with much less expense than anticipated. By fall the suit had been settled. The title was clear.

Having found that story to be interesting, I wrote it; others may also find it interesting. Writing it was not difficult. Perhaps I could, after all, produce a written history. I made copies of what might be a chapter and took it to the committee. When they read it, they were enthusiastic. They insisted that I go ahead, and I did. The minute books, the newsletter which had begun in the late 1960s, interviews and conversations with long-time members, and material that had already been published for one reason or another became my sources.

The computer became my method, first in the listing of data, then in the writing. The computer and I had many arguments. The computer always won; three times it struck down (to be fair, it was my ineptness that struck down) four or five pages of my incipient manuscript. I had to review the research and rewrite.

At last, aided by committee members in locating pictures which would enhance the prose, the manuscript was ready—the prose on computer disk, the pictures by location and caption. The big day came. *Keeping the Embers Aglow* went to press. A banner by Todd Ream, depicting the old and the new buildings, proved to be an excellent cover. In August of the anniversary year, the book became available to the congregation and I guarded against writers' cramp as I signed copies for count-less purchasers.

But the book was not my only activity. In 1990, Annual Conference had approved exploring mission possibilities in Korea. An American of Korean birth, ordained by the Brethren, became the center of the effort to plant the Church of the Brethren in Korea.

Several plantings failed to take root, but the effort continued. Our district, Atlantic Northeast, accepted the assignment to be responsible for, among other things, ministerial credentialing. Denominational funds were in short supply. By 1997, there was so little money and progress was so unsatisfying that the General Board decided to close—or at least put in abeyance—the mission effort in Korea. A committee of three was sent to Korea to make the regrettable announcement. David Radcliff was the national staff member, Lori Knepp went as chair of the General Board, and I went to represent the Atlantic Northeast District. I flew from Harrisburg on Monday, October 6, met the others at Washington/Dulles, and flew via San Francisco to Seoul, nineteen hours of flying time.

It was a brief trip, an intense trip, a difficult trip, and a learning trip. We were in Korea less than three days. During that period, we visited with persons in major cities, spoke to a university class, looked across the border at North Korea, and brought the sad news that the Brethren were discontinuing their support. Already on Tuesday evening, with no time to recuperate from the long journey, we developed the agenda for our visit. In Seoul we worshipped in their church, a sizable second-floor room in an apartment building. We met with a group of about ten men and women who identified themselves as pastors or church leaders. David was our spokesperson, bringing what to them was unwelcome news. Lori and I could do little more than confirm his statements.

I made mental notes of their responses, of which I recall the two most vocal. One—only one—pastor regretted the loss of relationship with the Brethren. When he met them, he said he felt he had found the church he had long sought. One man reflected what appeared to be the more common reaction. His regret was that now there would be no seminary. We motored to Taegu, where we visited with the pastor of a church who had been considering joining the Brethren. From there we went, early next morning, to Kwangjoo, visiting the university and meeting with a professor who seemed to be a strong Christian and had studied in the United States. We drove back to Seoul to spend the night there.

On Friday, October 10, we had time for a brief visit to a site looking across the border into North Korea, and felt the pain and uncertainty
of persons who were also looking across, hoping somehow to catch a
glimpse of relatives long separated.

Our visit took us from the extreme north to the extreme south of
Korea. Escorted by Dan Kim, who had been the Brethren missionary, we
met and had serious conversation with perhaps forty or fifty different
persons. None of them appeared to want the separation from the Brethren
in United States; all of them seemed to accept stoically. I confess that I
had not been enthusiastic about the Korea mission. My perception was
that a large percentage of Koreans were already Christian. Our motivation
seemed to be more a desire to plant our denomination than a desire to
plant the Kingdom. The visit did not significantly change that perception,
yet I felt real regret at the discontinuation of our effort there.

Another activity which began in late 1996 for Mary Beth and me
and continues, was our being called to serve on the Publications Committee of the Brethren Disaster Relief Auction. The auction, a program by
Atlantic Northeast and Southern Districts, has as its purpose to bring honor
and glory to God while raising money to assist victims of disaster nearby
and worldwide. Each year a tabloid-style booklet of sixty-four to sixty-
eight pages is published. The Publications Committee suggests, collects,
writes and edits articles, and sells advertisements. I became involved in
writing and eventually in editing, and Mary Beth became an expert in selling the ads. During the first half of the year, it can be a time-consuming
program. We also helped the auction in other ways, Mary Beth by making
and selling shoo-fly pies, and I by caning chairs with the income going to
the auction.

During May 1997, we accepted a call to be part-time interim
pastor of the Mt. Zion Road Church of the Brethren, not far from Camp
Swatara. We enjoyed the opportunity to serve, making use of furniture
that had been lent for our use during the days and nights we spent at the
parsonage. Somehow, part-time interim work leads more to friend and
friend or brother-sister than to pastor-laity. When we left at the end of the
year as friend rather than as pastor, I had the unusual responsibility of
conducting the election by which David Ulm was called to be their pastor.

Other events into the fall brought both light and shadow for us.
There was a mixture of light and shadow when, in August, the Miller
family left for an eight-month ministry in the back country of Honduras.
We were joyful at their commitment to Christ, but saddened by the en-

forced absence. In October, we shared the pain of suffering and death for John Grimley, best friend for many years, co-worker in Nigeria, and next door neighbor. Again, however, there was light in the confidence that his pain was gone and he would be busy in heaven getting ready to welcome others.

Also near the end of 1997, Allen Hansell completed his service as district executive to accept a position on national staff. It took two of us, both working part time, to replace him until a full successor could be found. Mark Bushong was, in a sense, senior, and I junior. He had responsibility for administration and stewardship. Beginning in October, I accepted responsibility for pastoral matters. Interestingly enough, our district executive is a regular member of the Board of Trustees of Elizabethtown College. Mark was on college staff, so I became the trustee for all of three months! I was no more effective for the Elizabethtown board, alas, than I had been for Juniata's.

With the conclusion of our pleasant experience with the Mt. Zion Road Church of the Brethren, we had been away from the Ephrata Church for four months, although we were still members there. The pastor had indicated to the moderator, Darvin Boyd—probably when Darvin asked him—that he would be glad to have us back in action. (Brethren practice is that a pastor not be involved in a pastorate he or she leaves, for at least six months, and preferably longer.) Darvin proposed to the congregation, and they, reportedly, approved by a large majority, that I be made "Pastor Emeritus." I had already been designated "Minister Emeritus," simply implying retirement, when we left Northern Indiana. Pastor Emeritus, I thought, was an expression of appreciation for past work. Besides, with district work still on my lap and with two months of travel ahead, I did not see myself in the new pastor's way. I gratefully accepted the honor. It was officially bestowed early in February. When asked, I usually explain that "emeritus" is Latin for "on the shelf."

Chapter Forty-Seven

AUSTRALIA AT LAST

We had already been forced by my heart problems to forgo one Australia jaunt. We had signed up for another, this one with Mennonite Your Way and their excellent leaders, Leon and Nancy Stauffer. We did not let the interim district position deter us; we simply postponed or referred pastoral matters during our absence, and we took off on a twenty-eight-day trip to see how people stand up on the bottom of the world—or are they at the top? The eve of our departure, we stayed in a Day's Inn outside Harrisburg, because there were predictions of a snowstorm. It came, all right, but we were safely borne to the airport. From Harrisburg to San Francisco to Sydney we flew, almost a full day of flying time.

And, almost immediately on our arrival in Sydney, we were off again, to Cairns, from which we could see the Great Barrier Reef. Of course, we weren't there to rest, but we needed more than we got before the prospect of snorkeling, next morning. Learning that breakfast at the motel would cost $12.50, we located a small convenience store, purchased Weetabix and milk. (Weetabix became our substitute for Shredded Wheat.)

Did we sleep? I guess we must have, but we were up at 6:30, joined the group, and boarded a catamaran for the trip to a suitable island. There we took the instructions, we found flippers and oxygen masks to fit, were delivered to the proper spot, and snorkeled. Well, at least, we tried. For three reasons, it was a fiasco. One, we were, putting it bluntly, inept. Two, the waves were quite strong. Three, the combination of our age and our lack of rest rendered our legs too weak really to control those flippers. For me, there was a fourth alibi: I couldn't wear my glasses under the mask, and I couldn't see without them. (I have long had a personal fear of swimming without my glasses, lest I reach out to touch Mary Beth and find I am touching some other lady, maybe in a not-to-be-touched spot.) We soon flip-flopped our way to the sandy beach, where we watched, waited, and chatted with other snorkelers who had also failed the test.

The afternoon went better. We were on a kind of semi-submarine. The passenger part of the boat was under water, and we could see well through the glass windows which were the sides of the boat. The beauty, variety, and quantity of coral is simply indescribable. Who was God's designer, and how did God ever find time for all those brilliant, intricate designs? Oh, of course. A thousand years is as a day.

The next day was one of the best of our trip. We traveled by train, maybe that which is the oldest in use, via twisting, turning railway through fifteen tunnels and past some magnificent scenery including waterfalls. We visited a butterfly sanctuary where the beautiful insects displayed their colors. Who was God's designer and how did God find time? We walked through an aboriginal village with its tourist displays and learned how to throw a boomerang or blow a hornpipe. We watched men producing Pamagirri dances. They were marked not only by music and rhythm, but by the dramatic way in which their motions told stories. Of course, we were helped by comments, but the interpretative movements were clear. Still another enjoyable episode, probably because I so much enjoy rain forests, was the swampy ride in the "Ducks," amphibian vehicles from World War II.

The Great Barrier Reef portion of our Australia visit, for which we paid $670 each and found it a bargain, was over, and we flew back to Sydney to rejoin the newly-arrived remainder of our group. When I went to a money changer at the airport, I happened to be next to a man in uniform. As we talked, it turned out that he was a flight attendant on our Sydney flight. He remembered me, took us to the business flight deck and into the pilot's room, and treated Mary Beth to cup after cup of orange juice.

Again I am faced with a balance between travelogue and life story. Of course, I have already begun the effort, in Cairns. Now to Sydney. Having joined the rest of our group who had chosen to forgo the Great Barrier Reefs addition, we first enjoyed a luncheon cruise which took us past some luxurious riverside homes, as well as the humble abodes of fishermen and farmers. We could not know it at first, though it took only a few days, but our coach driver, Robert Nutt, was one of the most important blessings of our Australia stay. A friendly, talkative, knowledgeable redheaded man of about fifty summers, he was a great storyteller. He shared native lore with great clarity, and from time to time would even demonstrate some aboriginal customs. A staunch Christian, he loved the hymnsinging with which our coach frequently reverberated and often joined us. Unlike any other coach driver I have known, he also attended worship services with us. When we learned that he was a singer and guitarist, we prevailed on him for "special music" at one such service.

In the Sydney area, we were treated to some fantastically beautiful scenery, culminating in what Robert called Australia's Grand Canyon. We passed by a great deal of busy building in preparation for the Olympic games, which Sydney was to host in 2000. We visited the world-famous Sydney Opera House. Its sharply curved roof sections gave it the look, from a distance, of a frigate in full sail. One story of the architect, however, reports that the roof was inspired by shape of the peels he observed as he peeled an orange!

We visited large cities—Canberra, Melbourne—and strangely named smaller ones—Echua, Coonabarrabran, Dubbo, Ballarat. We experienced Old Sydney Village, with its preserved or reconstructed buildings and with dramatized echoes of the past, reminding us of Williamsburg. We worshipped at the one organized Mennonite Church in Australia, and were provided there not only the worship, but rich fellowship and a plenteous breakfast.

We were instructed about farm life on a huge plantation, more than 20,000 acres and two centuries of history. We were delighted by the bird sanctuaries and zoological gardens at Warrabangle National Park, Western Plains Zoo, and Healesville Sanctuary. What did we see? Well, there were kangaroo, snakes, lizards, reptiles, dingos, wombats, echidna, platypus, and the playful koala, and we were close enough so we could have shaken hands (didn't) with wallaby. One evening we saw the dwarf penguins, smallest in the world, coming in to their nests on the shore, carrying food for their young. We learned how to make Billy Tea, by heating water in an open gallon tin, adding the leaves, and then swinging the tin in an overhead circle to settle the tea leaves.

As the time neared for our departure, we had a most unusual experience. Our whole group had grown fond of Robert, Mary Beth and I more than the rest because he seemed to pay special attention to us. When Robert, in telephone conversation with is wife, mentioned how he was enjoying the group, she wanted to meet us. We accepted their invitation to their country home for a high tea. We were welcomed by his lovely daughter, Stefanie, and his wife, Joan, and by his mother, Beth. He introduced us to the family, again with special attention to Mary Beth and me. Then we learned the reason for his special attention: his father, now gone, had been named Charles, and his mother Beth. Robert said I reminded him of his father, and I told him I could not remember a better compliment. Our visit there was a most enjoyable interlude, though a prelude to our sad parting.

What do I remember best about Australia beyond the comments above which were enhanced by my journal? I remember both its modern cities and its friendly small towns and villages. I remember the massive grandeur of its mountains, rock formations, deep-hewn canyons, wide rivers. I remember the sinuous movements of the Pamagirri dancers. I remember the amazing variety of beautiful colors in coral and in butterfly. I remember the pride of the people in their country which had early been the place to which English prisoners were banished. And I remember Robert Nutt and our sad farewell.

Now, however, it was time for New Zealand. The day was marked by food—a very nice breakfast at the hotel at five o'clock, then a huge brunch on the plane to Christchurch. Once settled into our hotel, we appreciated a tradition which may be unique to Christchurch. Divided into groups, we were entertained for dinner in the homes of New Zealand hosts/hostesses. Mary Beth and I, among others, were in the home of Barry and Andrea Gwynne. Barry is a Gideon. He was interested that we are Brethren, observing that he was also a Brethren. By his description, I recognized the Plymouth Brethren, also known as Darbyites, a somewhat Adventist sect. They gave us a great welcome to their country.

New Zealand is indeed a beautiful country. Its beauty is that of delicate lace, a contrast to the ruggedness of Australia. There were snowcapped mountains and broad blue lakes. One commentator insisted that there are more ski runs in New Zealand than in Switzerland, unbelievable though it seems. A special day of sightseeing took us to Milford Sound, which should be Milford Fiord, set as it is in Fiordland National Park and hemmed in by tall, snow-topped cliffs. Below the snow lines there are trees and rocks, the rock covered with moss and lichen and providing a seed bed for new trees. On other days, we also saw the bubbling mud pools and the geysers of Whakarewarewa Thermal Reserve. And there was the eerie feeling of being in Glowworm Cave, with its sandstone formations dimly lit up by countless glowworms.

There were great ranches, with herds of Black Angus cattle and Hereford cows, as well as deer farms. The big farm industry, however, is sheep, and it is for wool that the islands are best known commercially. At Timbertop Farm, Bruce Peterson told us about the four related families who work there. He described their sheep farm, demonstrating sheep shearing and showing off the wisdom of his sheep dogs. He told us they have

5,500 sheep, 400 deer, 100 goats, fifteen ostriches, seven sheep dogs, and one pet dog. Watching how cleverly (instinctively?) the dogs tended the sheep was a real delight.

At the Agrodome we were introduced to nineteen different breeds of sheep and provided with information we will never use about the advantages of each separate breed. We were impressed by angora rabbits, with such abundant, fluffy fur that they are sheared four times per year. Their wool is softer than that of the sheep.

I knew that New Zealand aboriginals were the Maori. I had heard an old tale of what happened when the British military invaded. The Maori, a peace loving people, made it clear that they were not resisting, simply by parading their women and children in front. Our last evening in the rustic countryside we were fed a sumptuous buffet dinner and royally entertained by dances and music typically Maori.

Then, by way of Queensland, we were delivered to Auckland, New Zealand's capital. I will forgo sightseeing there to report one very unusual incident. With an hour or two to wait until we were taken to the airport for the homeward flight, we visited a modern indoor shopping mall, just browsing, maybe looking for some ice cream. Suddenly, all around us, the bright lights went out and the emergency lighting system began to function. Electrically operated doors to the stores slid shut. Elevators and escalators stopped functioning. No one seemed to know what had happened or how long we might be imprisoned. Making the best of it, we walked up a stalled escalator and found an ice-cream dealer glad to sell before his product melted. Just as we began seriously wondering if we would be freed in time for our airport trip, lights came on and normal conditions were restored. We learned that electricity for Auckland arrives by large cables. To cool them, they run under a sizable lake. However, this was a hot summer day and air conditioners were hard at work. The city was using too much electricity for what coolness the lake could provide, and the system was automatically shut off for a cooling down period.

What do I remember best of New Zealand? I remember its delicate beauty. I remember its rustic nature. I remember deer, Angora rabbits, sheep, and, especially, sheep dogs. I remember the friendly hospitality of the Gwynnes on our first evening. And I remember the Auckland shopping mall. Were I to return to the far south Pacific again, I would spend more time quietly enjoying the New Zealand beauty.

Arriving at Ephrata again, there were scattered pieces of my district pastoral duties to pick up, none urgent, but all waiting. Now my body, for whatever reason, has never paid much attention to western-bound jet lag. Eastern-bound jet lag, on the other hand, is a different story. I rested a day and assumed I had won over the time change. Monroe Good and I had developed a tour to Nigeria to celebrate the seventy-fifth anniversary of the first worship in our church there. Indeed, within short hours of our arrival home, I had to deliver my passport to him so he could obtain the necessary visa. Meanwhile, aware that in less than two weeks I would be leaving for Nigeria, I went about my work.

On my way to the office at Elizabethtown and with only another mile or so to go, my body objected. As I drove along Campus Road, I fell sound asleep. I awakened suddenly, to see a telephone pole approaching directly in front of me. No time to react, I crashed. The seat belt seized me, the airbag exploded on me, the car crashed. I may have been unconscious for a moment; at least I was disoriented. Glasses were gone. I looked for them. Then I stood outside the wreck wondering what I ought to do. Two young ladies who were driving by, saw what had happened and stopped. Could they help me?

"Please, find my glasses for me."

They did. They used their cell phone to notify Mary Beth, the office, and the police. David Longenecker arrived from the office. Police arrived and took down information. They wanted to take me to the hospital, but I demurred. I had a serious abrasion on my left arm and pain in chest muscles, which I did not believe warranted hospitalization. Mary Beth arrived. She and David worked out some details. Mary Beth took me to the Norlanco Medical Office. The staff bandaged the abrasion and, because of my record of heart surgery, they took an EKG. After the medical staff were assured that I had no dizziness and I did not lose consciousness, Mary Beth took me home.

Chapter Forty-Eight

NIGERIA CHURCH DIAMOND JUBILEE

When I left for Nigeria some days later, the abrasion was not yet completely healed and there were patterned bruises on my chest, obviously left there by the seat belt. The police thought the airbag had saved me, but I think all it did was rip off my glasses. It was the seat belt which held me firm. I think that, in spite of my lacking good sense, God really did want me to make that Nigeria trip.

It was Monroe who did practically all the planning for the trip. I was his backup, support, and publicity agent. I wrote to all former missionaries or Brethren Service workers whose addresses I could find and to all the district offices. Larry, Mary Beth, and I helped Bonnie and Marla to find enough money to afford the trip. There were, in all, thirty-one of us, of whom all but five had been in Nigeria before. It had been twenty-five years since my own last visit, which was on the occasion of the golden anniversary of the church.

Arriving in Kano, we found absolutely no problems related to customs or immigration. I was simply delighted to be met by our "son," the Rev. Karagama Gadzama, as well as a good friend, the Rev. Nvwa Balami, and Daniel Dibal, a Bura businessman who gave us a great deal of assistance in the trip's logistics. After a very late supper and a short night of rest, we boarded a twenty-four-passenger bus, a twelve-passenger van, and Daniel's Peugeot sedan and toured the city. We visited the Kano Church of the Brethren, which was without question the ugliest church building I have ever seen. Its walls were made entirely of rusty, rough, unpainted sheets of metal, probably discarded sheets of roofing metal from earlier days. We met in a nearby Sunday School building, which had the same kind of walls. Karagama and Nvwa gave us some helpful initial orientation to Ekklesiyar Yan'uwa A Nigeria (EYN—the Church of the Brethren in Nigeria) and our anticipated tour. They led us, then, into that unattractive church building.

Inside, we found more than 600 enthusiastic Nigerian brothers and sisters. The building was just as unpretentious inside as outside. Walls were the framework on which the metal sheets had been nailed. There were choirs of women, youth, and children. The pastor welcomed us on behalf of the congregation. He explained the state of the building. The original had been twice burned by the Moslems, and once bulldozed by the city government, possibly as an eyesore. Again rebuilt, it could hold 1,500 worshippers on Sunday, had planted three other congregations in the area, and was looking forward to a new location and a new building. I was reminded that man looks on the outward appearance, but God looks on the heart.

Our journey took us by way of Kaduna to Abuja, Nigeria's Federal Capitol Territory. We were to visit the Kaduna EYN in the former Northern Region Capitol, but Nvwa was catching up on sleep, and we missed our stop. We did visit Suleja, outside Abuja; we experienced a "launching" in behalf of additions and renovations to their building. (When I was a boy, our small Methodist Church had held just such "launchings" but we called them fund drives. Givers came forward to announce their pledges or make their gifts.)

The congregation in Abuja was worshipping in a block-walled building set among dozens (no exaggeration) of similar buildings of other worshiping groups. An area had been set aside by government for religious groups, but there were no planned streets, and our approach took us through piles of trash and construction debris. We were pleasantly pleased by a site which the congregation had obtained on the edge of the city along an important highway, for the building of a more permanent structure and auxiliary facilities.

While we were in Abuja, we visited in the lovely home of Daniel Dibal, whom I mentioned above. I asked him how he had managed to get our visas so easily—a year earlier they had been delayed so long that the work camp had been aborted. He explained that he had gone to the Minister of Foreign Affairs, a Garkida man who had received his early education in the mission school. Though now a Moslem, he was grateful to the mission, and without ado sent a letter to the consulate in Washington instructing prompt issue of our visas. Daniel also took us to visit the Minister of Transportation, another Garkida man with his early education in the mission school. He, too, was appreciative and showed it by providing the transportation vehicles and drivers for our visit.

From Abuja, the journey became, for me and presumably for Bonnie and Marla, more nostalgic. When we left the bus in what used to be the Jos vacation compound of the mission, we were welcomed by smiling faces, singing voices, clasping hands, and hugging arms. One lovely young lady hugged me, introduced herself as Titi Risku. (Young? She had to be at least seventy!) How well I remembered! It was she who assisted in my first infant deliveries at Lassa (actually, I think I assisted her). The girls loved their visit to Hillcrest School; Bonnie, in particular, was full of questions for the houseparents.

We drove out to Bukuru, to the Theological College of Northern Nigeria. I had been the secretary of the Board of Governors when the college first opened and was very much pleased to see how it had developed. I was able to give them the information that the colored glass in the chapel windows had come from Coventry Cathedral in England, bombed during World War II. It was also good to know that twelve students from EYN were at TCNN, though we were not currently providing any staff.

Our journey took us by way of Maiduguri, capitol of Bornu Province. I had been there only once in missionary days, but I remembered that Dale and family had lived there during his teaching at the university. Maiduguri was the first EYN church in a big city and had become the largest Church of the Brethren in the world, with more than 4,000 attending each Sunday. While there, we also visited the University of Maiduguri. Nggida Gadzama, who worked for us as a small boy in Lassa, had just completed a five-year term as vice chancellor, and Dale had taught pediatrics there for a year.

Then we reached EYN Headquarters, along the highway in front of the Kulp Bible College. We spent several days there, both to visit KBC and to hear reports from program directors of the broad aspects of the church—programs which they efficiently adopted from missionary days. While we were there, Bonnie, Marla, and I stayed with Karagama and his family and enjoyed their special hospitality including COLD drinking water and HOT coffee. Karagama had twenty or so peacocks, and I well remember the peacock "choir," which began to function after two in the morning, repeatedly being called back by their director for further rehearsal. The choir never did seem to get it right.

On the weekend, our group visited various villages and churches. The girls and I, of course, chose to go to Lassa. We discovered that Nggida, though living in Maiduguri, had built a retirement house there in his home town. He opened his home to us, and we spent the night there. We were especially pleased that he and his lovely wife, Alisabatu, came down from Maiduguri especially to welcome us and spend time with us. Although Bonnie hardly remembered, Nggida had carried her around a lot when she was two. The next morning, the girls found their way to the "Bieber house," still known by that name despite the fact that we had left it thirty-five years earlier.

Karagama had told me that the people at Lassa wanted me to preach. I regretted that my grasp of the Margi language had sadly deteriorated in the thirty-six years since we had left. I thought I could manage a greeting, so I proposed that I introduce Marla, who had been born at Lassa and was a pastor. She would preach, with a translator.

"Oh, that's a good idea, *Baba*," responded our "son."

"And then you preach."

I could not evade it. God took over. I recalled a story sermon I had preached many years before. It was a simple story, with a great deal of repetition of vocabulary. I rehearsed it and it became my message and hopefully, even God's.

Rejoining the group, we moved on to Garkida. The three of us were hosted in the home of another old—though less known—friend, Paul Gadzama. The air conditioning was not operating, but fans were, when Nigeria electricity was on, so it made for comfortable sleeping.

March 17 dawned hot and clear; late March is Nigeria's hottest time. It was Celebration Day, and we were guided to the site in front of the great tamarind tree where, seventy-five years earlier, Stover Kulp and Albert Helser had conducted the first worship service. The text from Ephesians, "You are no longer strangers and aliens, but fellow citizens," was engraved in English and Hausa on a monument under the tree. The crowd, which would exceed 5,000, was already gathering on folding chairs and under tents which, we learned, had been rented from Daniel. The program was conducted both in English and Hausa and was easy to follow.

Let me quote a description which I wrote, earlier, of the Diamond Jubilee Celebration:

Dignitaries—in particular traditional rulers, government officials, and military administrators, about twenty of them—arrived in their chauffeur-driven autos.

Ordained ministers of EYN, in pale blue robes and carrying briefcases which had just been presented to them, followed EYN president Bitrus Kwaghui Tizhe and vice president Karagama Apagu Gadzama in an impressive procession. The special dignitaries were introduced and a warm welcome extended to the tour group.

The Zamuntar Mattan Ekklesiya (Association of Women of the Church) from Garkida and from the whole of EYN, sang in their stirring, rhythmic fashion.

Their presence was a reminder that almost half the members of EYN are women, and they are a powerful evangelistic force. Other musical groups sang, notably a choir of young men and women and the EYN national choir.

The Boys Brigade, Girls Life Brigade, Mason Technical School students, and Comprehensive Secondary School students marched and sang. Speakers reviewed the history of EYN and noted the church's broad current influence, as well as pointing into the future. A new book, *The Progressive History of the Ekklesiyar Yan'uwa A Nigeria*, by five different authors, was presented.

Finally, dances from their tribal traditions were performed by groups from nearby villages. Official greetings to the assembly were brought by Wilhelm Scheydt of Basel Mission. I read the official letter of greeting from Church of the Brethren Annual Conference moderator Elaine Sollenberger, interim executive director Joseph Mason, and the director of Global Mission Partnerships, Mervin Keeney. Personal gifts to each of the tour group were presented by the traditional ruler, the head of the Garkida District.

In appreciation for founder Stover Kulp and his wife, Christina, the assemblage honored their daughter, Naomi Kulp Keeney, who had been born at Lassa, receiving her greetings and presenting her with a decorated cake.

In his address reviewing the years from 1923 to date, Musa Mambula also pointed to the future. "The 1997 church statistics," he reported, "have revealed to us that from 1973 until now, ordained ministers have risen from 51 to 250. The districts have risen from 6 to 36, communicant members from 18,000 to 140,000, while the average number of worshipers on Sunday has risen from 40,000 to 240,000 with about 1,070 preaching points from the earlier 430."

He added, "The EYN now has a new vision of looking into the possibility of extending her evangelistic outreach to neighboring countries like Cameroon, Chad, Niger, and Ghana."

The thought went through my mind: "We appear to have moved from, 'You are no longer strangers and aliens' to 'The earth will be filled with the glory of God as the waters cover the sea.'" Following the celebration, we enjoyed tea with John and Janice Tubbs, in the Nigerian home where we had lived when the lightning struck.

With reluctance, we had left the tamarind tree and the six-hour celebration of EYN's Diamond Anniversary. With a mixture of even greater reluctance at leaving and happy expectation of being home again, we left Garkida. We spent an evening, overnight, and a morning at Yankari Game Reserve and headed off for Kano, Amsterdam, and the United States of America.

Chapter Forty-Nine

FAMILY, BRETHREN VILLAGE, AND NIGERIA

Before going on with events in my life, this would seem a good place for an important interlude. We do not know how it happened except to give God all the credit, but we have simply tremendous children. For one thing, every one of them is deeply committed to helping others, both personally and vocationally. For another, they are all such attractive personalities, which I dare to say despite probable accusations that I am prejudiced. For still another, all of them have college degrees, four with graduate degrees and the fifth with graduate credits. They are the kind of people that, if I were just beginning to have children, I would want my children to be. For still another, along with their spouses, whom we also love, they have produced for us some great grandchildren.

My dad, when he was proud of his family or had another emotional moment, would control his emotions by an uncontrolled quivering of his nostrils. I am one of those whose eyes quickly fill with tears. How very, very often that has happened when, with grandparental pride, we have attended sports events, countless musical renditions, dramatic presentations, graduations from high school with "our kids" among the speakers, and graduations from college; or read newspaper reports honoring one or another of them. . . . Every single one of them has awakened loving pride in our hearts and brought proud tears to my eyes!

Okay! I'm back from Nigeria. The high spirits to which I was lifted by the genuine compatibility of our travel group, the real affection I felt from so many Nigerian brothers fand sisters (sometimes for me, more often because they remembered Mary Beth), and the strong appreciation so often expressed to the Brethren for their mission work in Nigeria, all lifted me, and the high lasted for a long time.

Hardly more than a month after my return home, Mary Beth and I flew to Minnesota to help Bonnie and Dan celebrate his retirement. Again a month or so later, we flew to Orlando for Annual Conference. Our first evening there was our fifty-fourth wedding anniversary and when Mary Beth mentioned it in the International House of Pancakes where we went for supper, our supper was free. While in Florida, we took advantage of their presence to visit with some of our Bieber cousins and some old friends.

When August came, we enjoyed the wedding of Ben and Jen on the sandy shores of Rehobeth Beach, Delaware, and the reception, afterwards, in a pizza restaurant. In September, we flew to Albuquerque, rented a car, and drove to Alamosa, Colorado, for a very pleasant visit with granddaughter Diana. With her, we rode on a narrow gauge railway into higher grounds where we could fully appreciate the brilliant golden yellow of aspens in full leaf amid bright green firs.

Across the years, we had owned more than twenty different Volkswagens, from two "Bugs" and a pickup in Nigeria to a camper van while we were at Black Rock, and then to VW Diesel Rabbits. By 1999 we had changed to Japanese cars. In January, we were selling some stock to help pay for a new Nissan. It was then that Mary Beth announced to the broker what she had not yet discussed with me, "our" intention to move to the Brethren Village. Having made our decision for us, she had in mind a particular apartment. It must have been God's intention that we contract for the apartment then, because the stock we sold was $15 higher than we could ever remember it, and a few months later had returned to its usual level.

On April 1—no fool's day for us—we moved into our newly refurbished apartment. It was a good move. It meant, for us, that we were assured of facilities where we could receive health care if that became necessary in later years. It meant comfortable living facilities among many pleasant people, although it also meant distancing ourselves from Mildred Grimley and Esther Haller. Cars do still run. For Mary Beth, it became an almost ideal situation. She could indulge her genuine love for people by being, likely, the most available helper of others in the whole campus. For me, it meant little change. I was still spending most of my time in my study, with stamp collection, chair caning, Bible study preparations, work with the Disaster Relief Auction, the computer, and this writing.

June 1999 found us once again attending Annual Conference, this time in Milwaukee. It was made special for us, because Marla was elected to the Program and Arrangements Committee of conference. We went on to Minnesota to spend time with the Corcorans. On the way home, we visited friends, especially former missionaries, in Indiana. Through all the years they have continued to be as close as our extended family. Then, in the fall, we flew to beautiful, busy, rainy Seattle to enjoy a too-short visit with granddaughter Alisa and her friend Sam.

Meanwhile, two other interests were developing, both of them Nigeria-related. For a number of years, the Brethren had sponsored work camps to Nigeria. Most of the United States workers, who were usually joined by volunteers from Germany and Nigeria, came from our district. Monroe Good planned and directed the work camps for a number of years, and then Jeff Mummau, also from our district. Added to the interest which that engendered were three other factors. A number of former missionaries to Nigeria were living in the district. Besides, there were a sizable number of persons in the district dissatisfied with the denominational mission programs and determined to support programs with which they felt some relationship. At the same time, EYN leadership were seeking additional work camps and had actually asked Monroe to lead some again.

An important result of those factors was the gathering of a group of about fifteen persons to discuss whether or not the Atlantic Northeast District and EYN could develop a program which would be mutually beneficial and which would complement, rather than compete with, denominational programs. To explore the possibilities, the district raised money to send a delegation of five to Nigeria to study the church there and to discuss possible programs with EYN leadership. Four of the delegation had never been in Nigeria. It was considered important to have along someone experienced in Nigeria, and I was blessed to become the fifth delegate. (They needed an "old hand.")

Our trip in March 2000 took us via London to Abuja. Unlike alighting at Kano, we did encounter some minor difficulties at Abuja. We were carrying a good-sized box of medicines for an EYN doctor in Maiduguri, Dr. Hedima. It took a great deal of persuasion to convince the official that these were indeed legitimate medicaments. Finally, he decided to take down my name and passport number, just in case any problem may develop later.

A work camp sponsored by the Atlantic Northeast District and EYN had functioned in the preceding summer, assisting in construction of the new Abuja church. We understood that the walls of the building had been erected almost to roof level, and this year's work camp would complete it and prepare for roofing. When we approached the building, we found it much farther along. I was particularly impressed when I entered the building. It was so full of wooden scaffolding in preparation for placing the roof that it felt like a jungle. Ayuba, moderator of EYN Abuja, observed our pleased surprise. It was entirely because of the first work camp, he explained, that the building had progressed so far. He explained with two stories and an observation, which I share.

When the work campers had been at work laying block, a Nigerian mason came by, seeking employment. "What are these white people doing here?" he wondered.

When he understood that they were helping to build a church, he said he would help at the same pay those white folks were getting. When he discovered that they had actually paid for the privilege of that hard work, he decided to help without pay.

"When our church is ready," he asked, "you can come and tell us how you worked this out." After three days, he said he would have to quit. He was hungry, not having eaten for those three days. When he discovered that food was provided, he kept on working, at least until those white folks left.

On another day, a muscular young man approached, with the same question about those white folks and black folks working together. When it was explained, he spent several days helping. When he found it necessary to move on, the local Nigerians explained to the visiting Americans that he was Nigeria's heavyweight wrestling champion.

More significant than either of these events, Ayuba wanted us to know, was the impact the progress had on the congregation. Members who had previously done very little to aid in the construction now became busily involved. Members whose cash contributions had not been particularly generous now found money they could give for the purchase of materials and the payment of artisans. What would the next work camp do, we wondered. Mostly plaster, we were told. The church was completed by the end of 2000, for use, and was dedicated in a great service in June 2001. How I wished that I could have been there!

Accompanied, indeed guided, by the Rev. Toma Ragnjiya, EYN president, we moved on to Jos. When I stepped down from the bus, there was dear Karagama waiting. He rushed up to me and we hugged.

"*Baba*," he exclaimed, "I didn't think I would ever see you again, but here you are!" I learned that he represented EYN on the Tarayya—Fellowship of Churches of Christ—and was in Jos for a meeting. Our group had twin purposes: to greet our brothers and sisters in Nigeria and move toward a closer relationship, and to seek the kind of reliable data and personal impression that would enable us to report wisely to the District Witness Commission. Therefore, our trip involved talking with as many as possible of persons in leadership. In Jos, it was the local EYN pastor and the Tarayya secretary. Outside Jos, at the Theological College of Northern Nigeria, it was the principal.

We moved on to Garkida. There we visited what has almost become a shrine, the tamarind tree under which it all began. We visited the small cemetery where had been buried the bodies of missionaries or missionary children. We visited the Mason Technical School. We entered carved doors into the beautiful, stone Garkida EYN. Again too soon, we moved on.

When we arrived at EYN headquarters, a goodly number of people were waiting. Two ladies rushed up and hugged me warmly. They identified themselves as old friends of Mary Beth and I realized it was really Mary Beth they were hugging! Eventually, after having found our sleeping quarters and had a night of sleep, we met all the program directors of EYN, as well as some regional secretaries. Each of them handed to us a carefully prepared report of what was being done in their program and what were their needs, hopes, and dreams. I was particularly interested in the report of Dr. Isiah Tari about the Rural Health Program since part of the cost of my trip was paid so I could bring a report on RHP. We visited Kulp Bible College, where we were greeted by the principal, the Rev. Jinatu Wamdeo, who had frequently visited us at Ephrata when he was a student at the seminary in Myerstown. We visited the Comprehensive Secondary School and heard the principal review the extensive construction which would be necessary before the   school would be fully completed.

On Saturday, we again went to churches and locations away from Headquarters, and I went again to Lassa. Karagama drove me there in the car he had obtained from Dale ten years earlier. We found that we were unexpected and no arrangements had been made for lodging, so Karagama simply took me back to his home for the night. Back in Lassa next morning, Karagama took me to greet Keri Ali, the retired policeman, now somewhat lame, who had been our first cook. We visited and had lunch with my very dear brother, the Rev. Ngamariju Mamza. I was able to bring "official" greetings to the congregation. With difficulty, I repressed tears as I met numerous friends from the past. And then, in the late afternoon as we returned to Headquarters, we stopped in the compound of Mjigimtu Thliza, who had been our houseboy (the male equivalent of a house maid) when we first arrived at Lassa, and now was a retired teacher and headmaster.

Our journey to Maiduguri next morning took us by way of Gavva, The station there was one which had been established by the Basel Mission, now a full partner with the Brethren, with an important EYN congregation located there. I was deeply impressed by the literacy program which centered there. It being hot March weather, the trip on to Maiduguri seemed extra long. Arrived there, Jere Cassel, who was my roommate much of the time, and I were taken to the home of the Rev. Dr. Musa Mambula. His son, Chris, had spent a year with Dale's family, and was now in medical school.

At last, I thought, we could dispose of that pesky but very important box of medicines. I asked Musa to contact the doctor for whom it was intended, and whom I had never met. We were assured he would be there later. Later got to be after 11:00, and after the hot journey I was worn out. I decided to make bed-time preparations, and went to brush my teeth. I thought I heard Musa say, "Come in, doctor!"

So I went back to the living room Sure enough, a strange man was there. I went up to him, placed my hands on his shoulders, said, "I'm glad to see you. I really need a doctor."

He grinned and said, "You don't need me. I'm a gynecologist." It was not Dr. Hedima, but a very devout Christian and a delightful person, whose wife, Klara, had grown up at Lassa and was now a local judge.

The next evening, which would be our last in Nigeria, Nggida came and took us to his university-provided residence, to meet his family, and we had a brief but very pleasant time with them. He and his son, Ibrahim, drove us to Nggida's future home, which was fully and comfortably furnished. A brick house, it had been completely closed, in that 110-degree heat, until the houseboy opened the door for us to enter. It was stiflingly hot. I noticed, however, that ceiling fans were in operation over both our beds. Just as Nggida and Ibrahim drove out the driveway, Nigeria's electricity went off. No fan. No light. Our last night, so extensive repacking needed to be done. The houseboy brought me a six-inch candle. I packed my large suitcase and my carry-on by candle and flashlight. By the time I finished, the floor around me was wet with my sweat.

I went to the bathroom, took out my teeth, returned to the room, took off my glasses and took out my hearing aid, blew out the candle, and lay down clad in pajama bottoms. In moments, the bed was wet. I prayed. I asked God's protection of Mary Beth and family, gave thanks for our trip, and then realized I could use some personal prayer as well. My prayer went like this. "God, you know that I can manage heat during the daytime by extra water and seeking shady spots. But you also know that I can't sleep when it is so hot. I have that plane to Lagos to get in the morning, and I'll just leave it to you to see that I get some rest." As I said "Amen!"

the lights came on, the fan began to spin, and my faith in prayer was renewed.

Next morning, we flew to Lagos, surely one of the most unpleasant cities in the world. I had lived in a plush hotel in a Lagos suburb during a month or so of my Biafran experience in 1968. I have three very good and one unpleasant memory of that one day in Lagos. First, we were hosted by Paul and Asta Thlahal. Paul, retired, had been the Nigerian Air pilot who piloted Stover Kulp when he left Nigeria, and Asta was another Lassa girl. Asta had opened a nursery school. The new congregation in Lagos, established there as a jumping-off spot for mission in other African countries, met first in their home. The growth of the congregation and the need for additional school space coincided, so Asta arranged for the erection of a building with five side-by-side rooms, with partitions which were removed for worship services.

Second, I was able to visit with another longtime friend, Nvwa Balami. Nvwa was pastor of EYN Lagos and, in my judgment, the best of all EYN pastors. He was already making plans for mission to Togo. He guided us to the site which had been purchased on the outskirts of the city for their new, more permanent church building, and we could rejoice with him on the prospects it held.

Third, we met an outstanding physician, Dr. Mangga. I recognized his name and asked. Yes, he was the grandson of the chief of Ngurthlavu, a village about seven miles from Lassa, whom I had met in 1952. The report was that Ptil Mangga had numerous wives and back in 1952, forty-two children. Dr. Mangga had worked with the Rural Health Program in past years. Now he was national director of the Planned Parenthood Association. Asked about abortion, which has caused much resistance to the association in America, he assured us that abortion is not permitted in Nigeria.

The fourth memory, the unpleasant one, is of long waiting in the airport in almost unendurable heat. Both Nvwa and Mangga were with us till the last moment, however, making the unbearable bearable.

Our fact-finding visit over, I reflected on what we had been told. Every report had lifted up the need for money and for personnel, both of them denominational responsibilities into which we would not venture. TCNN and KBC wanted books and possibly magazines. There was enthusiasm expressed for the work camps, and there were enough places which could be helped by them that both the denomination and the district could work at it. The technical school wanted typewriters. There was a big need for improvement in communication equipment and for office equipment. The Rural Health Program desperately needed vehicles, refrigerators, and laboratory equipment, as well as trained medical personnel. Could a pastoral exchange program be developed? How about sister churches? From the perspective of our district, the most important contribution EYN could make was their enthusiasm for sharing the good news of Jesus Christ. Development and coordination of programs involving EYN, the national office, and district leadership, still lay ahead of us.

It would be dishonest, I think, not to admit some negative feelings which influenced much of my activities that year. As I have reflected these "glimmers," I think this was the only time in my life when I was personally at odds with two different persons for extensive periods of time. It would also be unfair to them for me to comment on what I saw their problems to be, but in both instances I had attempted personal communication. In simple terms, my activities were affected in two ways: I sought outlets for my spiritual energy outside my local church, even while accepting fringe opportunities to serve there. And I spent countless hours, along with others, seeking ways by which our district could respond to expressed needs of EYN without threatening or diminishing our denominational programs.

The long flights to and from Australia in 1998 had seriously dampened Mary Beth's interest in overseas travel; perhaps she gave her interest to our children and grandchildren. For me, there were still places I would like to visit, although travel without Mary Beth would not be nearly as much fun. Would I ever get to Iceland? Would I ever be able to compare the reported beauty of Austria with the Norwegian beauty I had seen? Would I ever be able to experience the enormity of the Amazon River and the rain forests and jungles which surround much of it? Well, maybe. Meanwhile, there were several times during the year when four or five of our offspring were outside the country at any given time. They were affected by the travel gene. At the same time, Bonnie and Dan were echoing the family enjoyment of travel and new experiences, by a fifteen-month jaunt around the country in their recreational vehicle.

There were three other special events in 2000. We enjoyed another Annual Conference, this one in Kansas City, Missouri, even though it was foreshortened and some of our socially enjoyable events were eliminated. We attended our fifth National Older Adults Conference at Lake Junaluska and were pleasantly surprised by the number of persons who had been present for all five. And we had another of those Thanksgiving weekend family reunions which have been such an important part of our lives. The "significant other" of five our family were also present with us, so we could look forward to a family growing—by marriage, if not, to that date, by reproduction.

Chapter Fifty

MACHU PICCHU AND THE AMAZON

When long time friend Bob Neff visited his mother at Brethren Village in the fall, he mentioned that he would be guiding a tour to Peru in March, and I decided to indulge one of my long time hopes. I would be able to see the famous Inca village, Machu Picchu, and spend three days in the upper Amazon Valley. I was aware that might be a strenuous trip for an old man, particularly with high altitudes in Peru, but I also knew that God was continuing to grant me good health. I joined the group.

It was only a nine-day trip, landing at Lima and leaving from there, with trips to Cuzco, Machu Picchu, and the Amazon filling the days in between. Several things impressed me about Lima. I remembered that Diana had spent a year there, teaching, and wondered where her schoolroom may have been. It is a modern city, of about 800,000, and had for many years been the capital of Spanish territories in South America. An election for president was in the offing, and buildings were plastered with political signs. I learned that ballots would be cast by the number assigned to the candidates' party, and observed numbers at least as high as forty.

Wow! Forty political parties!? We climbed the Huaca Huallamarca, a 500-foot adobe pyramid from Inca days. We visited the Park of Love, impressed by the many statues and formations of loving couples. Most impressive, as I look back, were the catacombs. I had visited the catacombs in Rome, where skeletons lay, still reasonably whole, in their crypts. Lima was much more space-efficient. The skeletons were dismantled and bones of a kind all piled together. The most impressive spot was a large circular pit, with concentric circles, all lined with skulls.

Cuzco, next stop, had been Inca capitol in ancient times. With its altitude of 11,500 feet, it threatened altitude sickness. Tourists were fortified by drinking demitasses of coca tea, so named, we assumed, from its small cocaine content. In the city, we marveled at both the architectural genius and the incredible masonry of the Incas as we visited the Temple of the Sun. Stone blocks had been laid up in massive walls. The blocks were huge; each must have weighed a ton or more. They had been so carefully hewn that when they were laid up, without mortar, a sheet of paper could not be thrust between them. Equally awe-inspiring was the religious motif, which we would see repeatedly. Openings were planned into the walls to catch the rays of the sun—a center of worship—at propitious moments. Obviously, the Incas were deeply religious.

We took an all-day coach trip through the "Sacred Valley of the Incas," the valley of the Volconota River. We visited Inca ruins outside the city of Pisac, noting particularly the well preserved terraces in which farming took place. Usually the terraces had been built of stone blocks, much smaller than those at the Temple of the sun, and smoothly but not as closely laid up. Isolated near the top of the mountain were a row of what looked like small huts, described to us as grain storage bins. Most of our group climbed a rocky trail, sometimes with stone steps sometimes with rocky path, to the fortress above Ollantaytambo. I climbed along for about a fifth of the way before discretion overcame valor, or else I just got lazy, and returned to the base. In some areas, the valley was hardly more than a football field wide, and in other areas very broad. Lining the road for mile after mile were potato fields (Peru grows 400 different varieties) and corn fields of a similarly astronomic number of varieties.

Then came what was, for almost all the group, the *pièce de resistance*, Machu Picchu. We reached the village below Machu Picchu by train. We traveled by coach up several miles of hairpin curves until suddenly the great ruins burst into sight before us. It would have been enough just to see that great sight—hundreds of stone-built houses, some still with their thatched roofs, and layer after layer of terrace. We walked. It was a day threatening rain, but we were spared any but a few drops until we had completed our tour. I thoroughly enjoyed the strenuous climbing up long stone stairways without the aid of banisters, even as I felt some nervousness and became very weary. The many, many stone houses varied in the quality of the workmanship of the artisans. Terraces, too, were defined by stone walls, the arable land in strips about two yards wide. At one place, the terrace had been carefully widened to provide room, surprisingly, for an orchard about fifteen feet by forty feet. Passages between the houses (and small temples, as well) were narrow. Certainly this was not horse country.

Again I was moved by the spiritual nature of the Incas. Their search for God apparently involved three important elements: the sun, represented by the condor, the earth, represented by the llama, and water, represented by a snake. In one small inlet we found a stone formation much like a condor. A stone had been placed to reflect the sun so it would precisely strike the head. In a central area of the ruins was a round building, a temple, again so constructed that at the summer equinox the sun's rays would strike the altar.

With an altitude of 13,900 feet, the strenuous climbing and descending, and the high humidity of the day, I was ready for a rest. But the day was not over yet. When we left our coach at the station, we stepped out into a warm, steady rain. By the time we reached our restaurant, those of us, like me, who had disdained umbrellas and rainwear, were nicely dampened, but harmlessly so.

Buffet dinner over, we entered once again into the train. We returned by almost the same track, along rushing river waters and long stretches of farmland. At one place, it seemed to me we were in new territory. Evening was approaching and if was difficult to see very much, but suddenly we stopped. I thought nothing of it; there were frequent switchings along the way. This was not a switching. A huge boulder had been dislodged from the mountain beside us, and lay on the track directly in front of us. What to do? This was the only track. Train men, with the assistance of some of the more rugged passengers, took sledge hammers and pounded away at the boulder. After at least an hour, it was reduced to a size that made it moveable, and we were able to proceed.

Now, at last, it was time for the Amazon. Or was it? We emplaned in Cuzco early in the morning to go to Lima. There we were to board a plane to Iquito, arriving there in early afternoon. Alas, planes were not leaving Lima because of heavy fog to the north. We languished in the Lima airport. This afternoon was to have been spent in Amazon country. What were we missing? Finally our plane took off, and we did reach Iquito about nine hours late. When a coach took us to the shore of the Amazon— yes, the Amazon—we boarded two speedboats. I had no sense of excitement. Here I was on the storied Amazon, but with fatigue, darkness, and the speed of the boat, I could hardly think, let alone feel.

We arrived at the foot of a long series of steps, lighted only by small kerosene lamps strategically placed. We arrived at the lodge, one of the Jungle Lodges of Paseos Amazonicos. We found it to be a well constructed lodge with a central dining and fellowship area and covered walkways to the sleeping quarters, but no electricity. We ate supper by lamplight, found our way to quarters by lantern light, prepared for bed in the dimness, and the day was over. Only two days left. Oh, Amazon.

Our visit compressed, what would we miss? Well, as it turned out, the only thing we would miss was rest! Early next morning, some of the group boated through jungle waters for bird watching. With my lack of propensity even to see a bird, let alone identify it, I declined. The bird watchers back, we had breakfast and prepared for the jungle walk we had missed the preceding afternoon. I dressed in hiking garments. Each of us was presented with a strong walking stick. A boat took us—boats the ONLY way of travel except by foot—to the spot from which we would challenge (?) the jungle. More realistically, the jungle was challenging us! There was no path. Indeed, the man who went before us with a machete to clear the way was essential. We SLOGGED through mud. By the time we finished, mud was spattered on my trousers almost to knee level. There were clouds of mosquitoes. The person behind me commented that my back was almost black with mosquitoes. I didn't notice the back of the person ahead of me; I was busy looking where to put my foot. There must have been chiggers, too, though it was not until three days after I reached home before those intensely itching bites covered my legs.

It sounds like real fun, doesn't it? No, it doesn't! But I enjoyed every moment of it, even to slipping and almost falling into the stream as I was entering the boat! It was such a different experience, and quite likely such thoughts were passing through my mind as, "Ha! They think an old man can't do this."

Adding immensely to our enjoyment was our uniquely qualified guide, Jaco. A native Indian, he was steeped in Indian lore. From time to time he would stop us and while we stood in our muddy footprints he would share information. "This plant is one with much iodine content. Squeeze a few drops from it to purify the water." (And I had iodine tablets in my kit!)

"Mash the roots of this plant, make a paste, and smear it over pain— headache, menstrual cramps—the pain goes away." (I remembered that Roy Pfaltzgraff, as a doctor in Nigeria, believed that much of the native medicine might be efficacious.)

"Use the long, slender leaves of this plant to weave a hat to protect you from the sun." Besides, Jaco had degrees in sociology and biology which enabled him to analyze Indian customs and give scientific names to the flora. A skillful artist, he would occasionally sketch a drawing to illustrate his oral description.

We reached another of the Jungle Lodges and found lunch had been prepared for us. It didn't take long; we were filling a lot into that day.

Again into the boat, we went to our next landing, by a wide path which led us a quarter of a mile into the village of the Yagua Indians. The chief and a cohort, both attired in their traditional, company best, welcomed us with a handshake. We were guided into a large round hut about thirty feet in diameter. Mud walled, grass roofed and ground floored, its only light came from a narrow space between the roof and the wall, and two small doorways. Low benches lined the wall. Jaco gave us a lengthy spiel about the chief, standing beside him, touching his arm or, in one instance, his nose. I did not think any of our Nigerian chiefs would have been that stoically accommodating.

After learning about the chief, we were treated to music and to a dance by six or seven Indian men. Their dance completed, the music changed rhythm, and several women were the dancers. One by one, they came to members of our group and invited us into the dance. I was only slightly startled when a bare-breasted grandmother came and took my hand. For the next five minutes, she held fast, guiding me into the paces of the dance. Oh, for a video to demonstrate my dancing skills.

We moved out from the round house into the market place. Persons had a variety of their crafts for sale. Because I was not purchasing anything, I sat and watched. A small boy, perhaps seven or eight years old, came up to me. He pointed to my pen, then to himself. I pointed to myself. He pointed to my notebook, then to himself. I pointed to myself. He pointed to my watch and then to himself. Shaking my head (dangerous; who knew but that a headshake was agreement?), I pointed to myself. He pointed to my good walking stick. I pointed to myself. He pointed to my hearing aid. I pointed to myself. Even though he had no success, he gave me a big smile as he moved on.

Back at our lodge, most of the group went to their quarters to freshen up for supper. Not me. This was Amazon country. I joined some others in the boat which took us to the broad expanse of the river. Even though we were in its far upper reaches, the river was more than a half mile wide. We were in an ideal spot—no obstructions whatsoever—to watch a beautiful setting of the sun. After supper and into a late hour, I joined another boat ride, this time propelled by oars, into a remote section of the swampy forest. We stopped. Jaco asked for complete silence for the next twenty minutes, and we listened. Without being able to identify sounds, we heard)—among other things—a repetitive frog, birds, the soft murmur of the wind, an occasional splash in the water, and even some distant human voices. Fantastic "silence!" Next morning, back to Lima—and then back to the United States.

Chapter Fifty-One

BENEDICTIONS

And back to work. To help define the program relationship with the church in Nigeria, the District Witness Commission appointed a task force, the ANE/EYN Ministry Team. Our assignment was to seek and recommend programs which would be mutually beneficial and or involve material aid rather than funds. One of the programs was clear—work camps—and likely tour groups. The next one we decided to pick up was the collection of books, primarily for the Theological College and Kulp Bible College, but also for new Bible Schools which EYN kept opening. Later, perhaps, we would consider secondary school textbooks.

We decided to seek 5,000 books the first year, planning to send out the first thousand with the summer work campers. How to send the rest—well, a way would turn up. It was necessary to have a sizable area for accumulation, packing, and storing the books. We were able to secure a small portion of one of Brethren Village's warehouses. It was essential to have strong packing boxes, tape for closures, and rope for extra strength and for convenience in moving. We launched a small fund drive which quickly surpassed a thousand dollars.

My responsibilities for the book drive turned out to be trifold. I would see that the bills were paid. I would disseminate the kind of information which could attract donors of books or money. And I would see to the sorting and packing of the books. Sorting was mentally strenuous; packing was bodily strenuous. Occasionally there were helpers with the packing.

The summer was also made special by two weddings. Grandson Troy and his fiancee, Katie Graves, asked me to have their wedding at the chapel of the famous Riverside Church in New York. It was a pretty and a simple wedding though with some difficulty between the youth minister at Riverside and me. It was also the first wedding I performed without doing the rehearsal; a Riverside staff member was the wedding coordinator. A month later, our granddaughter Diana wedded Tom Locke in a

Quaker ceremony in the beautiful out-of-doors of Rockford Plantation in Southern Lancaster Park. We felt blessed to welcome these two young people into our family.

My brother George had for about eighteen years been providing spiritual healing for literally hundreds of persons. (It was hard to know how to write that sentence. He didn't provide the healing. God did. Still, it felt strange to write, "channeling spiritual healing.")

Alas, he had been overtaken by emphysema, and his life expectancy was drastically reduced. I was delighted that he and his good wife, Monte, had decided to publish his theology of healing. He wrote and published a book, *Miracles in the Making*, thoroughly expounding it, and including some of his sermons. I was always proud of my brother for his bold—sometimes brash, to me—assertiveness, and of my sister, Mae, for tremendous powers of endurance. Both of those strengths came to the forefront in summer 2001; hence it became important to mention them. For George, it was the bold confidence in his understanding of the healing ministry. For Mae it was the uncomplaining way in which she endured more than a year of the burning pains of widely spread shingles on her body.

By September 2001, our family was well scattered. Larry and Nancy were still close by, in Lancaster, but Diana and Tom were in Alamosa, Colorado, and Alisa and Sam in Seattle, Washington. Dale was in Durham, North Carolina, on the staff of the medical college of NCU, with Carla in the third year of residency. Ben managed to be nearby—Fredericksburg—and Kirsten and Darrel were enjoying their service of Christ and the church in Harrisburg. Bonnie and Dan were in the process of buying a home in western Wisconsin into which they would shortly move. Marla and Jim served two different congregations in Akron, Ohio. Troy was in graduate study at Princeton and Katie continuing at Barnard, their Elizabeth, New Jersey, apartment a half-way point. Joel was enjoying life at Juniata. Even the Miller family split up. Doreen and Myron were still working in medicine and church at Jonestown, but Amaris went off to Gordon College near Boston and Rebekah to Asbury College in Kentucky, leaving Charis in high school and Dara in middle school. Wow! Five grandchildren in university and one other considering graduate study. I must really be getting old. If so, it is time to bring this thesis to a close.

Well, first, let's take that Canada trip. One of my longtime quiet yearnings had been to visit the maritime provinces of Canada. When the opportunity opened, Mary Beth and I joined a tour organized by Mennonite Your Way, which took us to Maine then into four of the provinces of "Atlantic Canada." There were fifty-five of us on the coach, a friendly, happy, family committed partly to observing beauties of God's world and partly—at least by some—to buying the souvenirs essential to proof of the visit.

After a night in Portsmouth, New Hampshire, we were in Maine, seeing the lonesome beauty of the Portland Head Light House, stopping at the famous L.L. Bean (sorry, not really interested any more), and enjoying a crab chowder for lunch. Next morning, we struck Canada for the first time. First stop was Campobello Island, where the Franklin D. Roosevelt family had a summer residence. So what! A house is a house is a house; antiques are antiques; it doesn't matter who owned them. And I really could not feel sad that there were only twenty or so rooms in the house! Much more interesting were the Reversing Falls, which we viewed from our dinner restaurant. It seems that the Bay of Fundy has tremendously high tides. Twice a day they are so high that they literally push up past the downflowing river, making a series of small falls going the wrong way. We were also treated to an artificial phenomenon, the "Magnetic Hill." Riders in the coach were deluded by the way the terrain had been arranged, into believing we were being pulled up hill by the force of powerful natural magnets. Try it!

From New Brunswick we crossed the long Confederation Bridge to Prince Edward Island, where Mary Beth and I met "Anne of Green Gables" for the first time. Lucy Maud Montgomery's story of the redhaired, unbelievably energetic, openly emotional, large vocabularied orphan girl is almost alive in the green pastures and rustic villages of Prince Edward. Mary Beth and I had been sadly neglected; in neither of our schools had Anne's story been read; but our co-travelling Mennonites all seemed familiar with it. To try an Anne-style sentence: We were left in the depths of despair by our deprivation. Our introduction was via a musical presentation of the story, which was both hilariously funny and quietly moving.

We left Prince Edward Island, Canada's "Million Acre Farm," where more than forty percent of the land is under cultivation, and went by Woods Island Ferry to Nova Scotia. I made two important discoveries there. The first was that I was aging. We were offered the choice of a two-mile woodland walk or a three-mile coach ride. A long strider who liked going up stairs two steps at a time, I chose the walk and started striding. Alas, it didn't take long for my strides to shorten, and I was so weary that the last quarter mile found me struggling to place one foot in front of the other, at the rear of all the other walkers.

The second discovery was really a series of learnings about Alexander Graham Bell. To my meager awareness that he was of Scots ancestry and had invented the telephone were added the facts that he was Canadian, that his mother was deaf, which was likely responsible for much of his interest in hearing; that he had numerous inventions which were brought to the public eye and production through the enterprise of his wife, Maud; and that he had contributed much to the development of aviation, of boats lifted and empowered by air pressure, and of other ingenious devices.

In Nova Scotia we were also delighted to visit with the Walter Penner family and worship with them briefly in their church before they furnished lunch for us. Shuffled from Russia and the Netherlands, a group of Mennonites (to us, the Penners most prominent) had found land available in Nova Scotia, and had established a communal society almost completely self-supporting. Their community includes a variety of occupations, all contributing to the welfare of the whole. We thoroughly enjoyed a visit to their home, their farm, their greenhouse, and the delicious aroma of their bakery.

It was the evening of our visit on the farm that startling news reached us. It had been a good day; another passenger and I celebrated our birthday, September 11, 2001. When we stopped at the Citadel Hotel in Halifax, the hostess boarded the coach. "I must be the bearer of bad news," she began. "Terrorists bombed the World Trade Center and the Pentagon this morning. There was terrible destruction and thousands of lives lost. We want to offer you our very sincere sympathy. You will want to turn your television sets on to get the latest reports."

"Hotels are crowded," she went on. "There are about 8,000 overseas travelers who were not permitted to land in the United States for the time being." We did, indeed, turn the TV on and saw those terrible and terrifying pictures of destruction which were to be repeated so often over the next several days.

We hardly knew how to react. I am quite sure that, despite my strong pacifist leanings, my first reaction was less one of fear than one of revenge.

"We have to get them!" In later, more reflective moments, I developed strong reactions against the possibility of mass killings which would certainly have to be a factor in revenge. More killing would not restore the victims. My mind went rather to questioning.

"What made them hate the United States so much?"

To combat terrorism, it seemed clear to me we must get to its roots, the strong antipathy to United States that made terrorists and motivated them even to self-destruction.

A second question came: "How much are those 'on our side' motivated by a real sense of kinship, and how much by self advantages?"

I was deeply moved, a day or so later, when TV brought the image of a day of prayer service in Ottawa, which concluded with that huge crowd of Canadians singing "The Star Spangled Banner."

Our tour continued. As we traveled, we shared Bible verses of comfort and encouragement, and we joined in prayer both for the victims and for the perpetrators. We viewed the natural beauty of Cape Breton Island, part of Nova Scotia. Mary Beth, well bibbed and fully instructed, dared and enjoyed her first lobster, a female generously embellished with hundreds of tiny eggs. We visited Grand Pre' Park and were reminded of the sad story of Longfellow's *Evangeline*, the forcing from their homes of hundreds, many of whom would settle in Louisiana.

We boarded the ferry from Yarmouth to Bar Harbor (Bah Hahbah to the initiate) with some trepidation. One report said that a terrorist entry into the United States was the same route we were taking. Canadian security people did, indeed, randomly search through our lighter luggage. The ferry trip was three hours long, smooth and in reasonable comfort. Arrived in Bar Harbor, we boarded the coach and proceeded to customs. Passports in hand, we watched the official come aboard. He had received a list of the passengers. Observing the prayer coverings of some of the ladies, he commented, "Oh, Amish travelers."

Two ladies were from Punxutawny; he observed, "Ah, yes, the groundhog city." He passed us through without incident.

I was not particularly impressed by Bar Harbor, but I was glad to be there. I recalled that Kenneth Crummer, our director of instruction when I was in nurse training, had spoken of it often. While we strolled through the town, we heard a radio broadcast of the national prayer service in Washington, with Billy Graham speaking. A day later, we on our way home. On the way north, Leon Stauffer had carefully pointed out the New York skyline, marked by the twin towers of the World Trade Center. Going south, our route was altered to let us see it again, in stark emptiness with billows of smoke and dust still rising from its vicinity.

Though marred by the disaster near its close, it had been a good trip. We thoroughly enjoyed and appreciated the beauty of Atlantic Canada, the friendliness of its people, the comfortable companionship of our travel mates, the beyond-the-call-of-duty caring of Leon and Nancy Stauffer, and the natural and historical learnings. Some descriptive titles would stick in our minds, without becoming part of our daily vocabulary: Green Gables; Avonlea; Antigonish; Reversing Falls; Magnetic Hill; Peggy's Cove; Grand Preí; Cahbern (Cape Breton) Rusty Anchor; Westfield Settlement.

The story goes on, but I had determined to close this saga with the Canada trip. To rack my memory over seventy-nine years (my earliest memory is of a dream at age three) has been both hard work and fun. My computer and I are on better terms than a couple of years ago, but still not fully compatible. Remembering and reviewing forces reevaluation. It has been a good life, blessed by many, many persons who have contributed to it, rubbed off rough edges, made corrections. I have been as honest as my memory would allow, except that it did not seem appropriate or necessary to include a full inventory of my faults, sins, or shortcomings; the story would be infinitely longer!

There were probably some paths I would have chosen differently, but I would still choose to be Brethren; to have attended Juniata College, Pennsylvania Hospital Nursing, and Bethany Seminary; to have served in Nigeria; and to have served as a pastor and district minister. Mary Beth. whom I love even more after sixty-plus years, has been the perfect wife for me, and I am deeply grateful to God for bringing us together. As I have said earlier, I am very proud of our family and find my greatest contentment when we are together. As Tim Cratchet said, "God bless us all."

Life goes on, but it is obviously impossible to make an autobiography complete. How can I end it? Well, I have decided that I would just . . .